PRINCETON-CAMBRIDGE STUDIES IN
CHINESE LINGUISTICS

IV

Injustice to Tou O
(Tou O Yüan)

INJUSTICE TO TOU O

(TOU O YÜAN)

A STUDY AND TRANSLATION
BY
CHUNG-WEN SHIH

Professor of Chinese, George Washington University

CAMBRIDGE

AT THE UNIVERSITY PRESS

1972

Published by the Syndics of the Cambridge University Press
Bentley House, 200 Euston Road, London NW1 2DB
American Branch: 32 East 57th Street, New York, N.Y. 10022

Library of Congress Catalogue Card Number: 74–155585

ISBN: 0 521 08228 5

Printed in Hongkong by Dai Nippon Printing Co., (International) Ltd.

CONTENTS

CONTENTS

ILLUSTRATIONS

FOREWORD

A striking phenomenon in Chinese cultural history is the development of drama under the foreign Mongolian rule and the creation within a century of the greatest dramatic works in the entire Chinese history. A half-dozen dramatists, representing the leadership of this new field in the late thirteenth and early fourteenth centuries, took part both in creating the form and in carrying it to its highest perfection. The most renowned of these literary and dramatic geniuses is Kuan Han-ch'ing, whose *Tou O Yüan (Injustice to Tou O)* Dr Chung-wen Shih so ably translates and interprets here.

Yüan drama is a subject of great difficulty. In the first place, serious study of the dramatic texts has begun only in this century in China and Japan; despite remarkable achievements, it can be said to be still in the pioneer stage. The language of the Yüan *tsa-chü* drama, covering a wide range of styles, from classical to colloquial, offers innumerable difficulties for the modern reader. The music of the plays, of underlying significance for the prosody of the songs and dramatic performance, is largely lost and little studied. The forms of the theater and the style of stage production are difficult to reconstruct. The nature of the audience, the sponsorship, and the social background of the authors are issues that remain unsolved. At the same time, the intrinsic value of this drama and its historical significance are extraordinarily high; so the rewards are as great as the difficulties.

Dr Shih makes a genuine contribution to literary scholarship in her translation of *Tou O Yüan* and in illuminating the context in which the play is to be studied and understood. In concise and lucid language, she explains how Yüan drama, like many other great literary achievements, was brought about by the fortunate coincidence of men and the time. Some traditionally trained scholars, deprived of access to officialdom under the alien rule, turned to play writing as an outlet for their creative energies, giving rise to rapid development of a dramatic literature. Of particular significance is Dr Shih's material relating the development of this new genre to the ongoing tradition of oral narrative, for it is the adoption of various devices and conventions from the oral tradition that gives both Yüan and later drama many of its unique characteristics. Her analytical comparison of the

ix

speech of Yüan drama (Old Mandarin) with modern Mandarin is of interest to both linguists and students of literature. With illustrations of the use of grammatical particles, a salient feature of colloquial Chinese, Dr Shih demonstrates 'that the Yüan dramatists made good use of the language as they found it and took few, if any, liberties with the spoken language' (p. 21). Her study of the imagery in *Injustice to Tou O* and her demonstration of how, through the use of imagery, the dramatist significantly enlarges the scope of the play, illustrate Dr Shih's skillful application of her training in Western literature to the study of Chinese traditional works. Her analysis and explanation of the *ch'ü* form, though technical, is clear and easily comprehensible. Lastly, her discussion of the play's theatricality dispels a popular concept that Yüan drama, because it is essentially poetry, is not good theater. Dr Shih's approach, thoughtful and luminous, makes her study a delightful piece of scholarly work.

In translating the play, Dr Shih has drawn upon her skills as a specialist in Chinese and comparative literature. She has translated with grace and fidelity so that the play can be read in English with pleasure and interest. She has annotated in ways that explicate cultural life and social history as well as the intricacies of linguistics. Her notes correlating the two most important texts of *Tou O Yüan* provide scholars with added insight into the textual difficulties inherent in the study of a thirteenth-century work, and lead to a better understanding of the play itself. She has romanized the entire text so that students can the more conveniently read it aloud and gain access to its language both by ear and by eye. Finally, she has provided the serious student with a substantial bibliography on the language of the Yüan drama, citing works in Chinese, Japanese and English. Quite apart from its value as a contribution to the study of Chinese literature, this volume is important as a text in thirteenth-century language.

In fact, I believe that this volume will stand as a model of the kind of teaching materials demanded by the present level of development in Chinese studies. In 1967, Dr Shih was one of a group of linguists and language teachers participating in the Second Conference on Chinese Linguistics sponsored by the Chinese Linguistics Project at Princeton University. As she has noted in her Preface, a major focus of that conference was how best to teach Chinese on all levels in Western colleges and how to provide textbooks for direct reading of literary, especially classical, Chinese. A plea was made for specialists in language and literature to prepare texts which would provide romanization, interlinear translation, and notes, to enable students to make an easy transition from reliance on textbooks to a direct reading of difficult Chinese texts. A second plea was made for scholars to prepare well-annotated texts to make classical Chinese writings more easily accessible. This conference served as an impetus for Dr Shih to divert her attention from her study of Yüan drama to produce this present volume, the study of a specific Yüan play.

Dr Shih's contributions are to both practical and historical linguistics, to literary history, to comparative literature, and to the study of Chinese literature and civilization during the Yüan period. Students of all these fields, but especially students of the Chinese language who want to take on the challenge of a fine thirteenth-century literary text, will be grateful to her for the uncommon assistance she provides them.

FREDERICK W. MOTE
Princeton University

PREFACE

This work consists of two parts. Part One is a study of *Tou O Yüan*, a play by Kuan Han-ch'ing, the leading dramatist of Yüan times. A careful analysis of this play, with reference to the times, its narrative tradition, conventions, language, prose style, and poetic qualities, should contribute to the understanding of not only the genre itself, but also of Chinese drama as a whole, and of other vernacular forms derived from this tradition. Part Two is the outcome of a discussion on Chinese language and literature teaching at the Chinese Linguistic Conference at Princeton University in October 1967. The consensus was that there was an urgent need for material including the original text, transliteration, a word-by-word translation, a readable English version, and notes. This present work is a modest attempt to help fill that need.

In the transliteration of the text, modern Mandarin pronunciation is followed in order to make the text conveniently readable for students. While a final reconstructed reading of Old Mandarin is yet to be agreed upon among linguists, they have determined that Old Mandarin pronunciation is closely cognate to modern Mandarin pronunciation.[1] When rhyme obviously calls for a reading different from modern pronunciation, such a reading is given in the notes. Those wishing to experiment with a reconstructed reading in Old Mandarin pronunciation may profitably refer to the works by modern linguists mentioned below in this study.[2] For those desiring more information on the language of *Tou O Yüan*, a selected bibliography on the subject is included at the end of this work.[3]

I have used the *Pin-yin* romanization for the transliteration of the text, and the Wade-Giles system for the translation and the bibliography. In the notes, *Pin-yin* is used except for source reference – authors and titles of works – and for the spelling of dynasties. *Pin-yin* is adopted because it is the simplest form of spelling among the currently used systems, and the Wade-Giles is retained in the translation and

---

[1] See pp. 7–10 below.
[2] *Ibid.*
[3] A bibliography on Yüan drama will be given in my forthcoming work on the genre.

bibliography because of its familiarity to most readers.[1] I have followed the convention of using tonal marks with *Pin-yin* and not using tonal marks with the Wade-Giles system.

In the interlinear translation, words are added when they become necessary to make the meaning clear; objects for transitive verbs, for instance, are supplied, since the English verb will not function as it must unless it has the implied object. Hyphens are used where characters are glossed as a compound or a group, or when it is necessary to rearrange the word order in the English to provide a more natural equivalent (see l. 196). Particles, pretransitives, measure words, localizers, and directional complements are marked with symbols. The use of these symbols is in making the interlinear translation correspond more closely to the original; it does not represent a grammatical analysis. (On the usage of localizers, directional complements, etc., I have consulted mainly Y.R. Chao, *A Grammar of Spoken Chinese*, Berkeley, 1968.)

The Chinese text, though set in horizontal lines for practical reasons, is conventional in format in that it uses a smaller type for prose than for songs. The Chinese convention is not to typeset an individual line of verse as a separate metrical unit. Instead, the verse is typeset in lines of equal length, which disregard the meter.

There are two important texts of *Tou O Yüan*, both from the Ming period. The *Ku ming-chia pen* 古名家本 of 1588, known also as the Hsü text, is preferred by certain modern scholars in the belief that it is closer to the original.[2] The *Yüan ch'ü hsüan* 元曲選 text of 1616, edited by Tsang Chin-shu 臧晉叔, has traditionally been the choice of scholars, as it is a fuller and more readable one.[3] Here I use the *Yüan ch'ü hsüan* as the basic text, supplemented by critical notes on the differences between this and the *Ku ming-chia pen* text in the hope that this approach will offer the maximum of useful information to scholars. In citing the variants, I include everything above the level of wording,

---

1 A comparable method is adopted in David Hawkes' *A Little Primer of Tu Fu*. Hawkes says in his preface that the use of more than one system may strike some people as confusing, but it is 'less confusing than any alternative would have been' (Oxford University Press, 1967, p. x.).

2 A Mr Hsü 徐 of Lung-feng 龍峯 is thought to be the wood engraver, and Ch'en Yü-chiao 陳與郊 the editor of this edition (*Kuan Han-ch'ing hsi-ch'ü chi*, 關漢卿 戲曲集, ed. Wu Hsiao-ling 吳曉鈴 *et al.*, (Peking, 1958), pp. 1056-7; see also § 2, p. 37 below).

3 Professor Yoshikawa Kōjirō 吉川幸次郎 and his colleagues, for instance, used the Tsang text in their annotated edition of six Yüan plays (*Genkyokusen Shaku* 元 曲選釋, Kyoto: Kyoto University, 1952).

synonym variations, and what I consider to be minor details.[1]

In the preparation of the manuscript, I received much help from my students and colleagues. I owe special thanks to Professor Lien-sheng Yang for reading the interlinear translation and for his comments, to Professor Paul Fu-mien Yang for checking the phonetic transcription and for his suggestions, to Professor E. Bruce Brooks for reading the entire manuscript and for his suggestions and criticisms, and to Professors Fritz Mote, Yu-kung Kao, Mantaro Hashimoto, Frank Kierman, and Chi-yu Wu for their interest and assistance. The Research Committee and the Sino-Soviet Institute of The George Washington University provided part of the materials and secretarial service, and they are gratefully acknowledged. The mistakes and inconsistencies are mine, and I shall appreciate corrections from the reader.

[1] For additional notes on the differences between these two texts, one may refer to *Kuan Han-ch'ing hsi-chü chi*, in which *Ku ming-chia pen* is used as the basic text.

PART ONE

A STUDY OF *TOU O YÜAN*

The play, *Injustice to Tou O* (*Tou O Yüan* 竇娥冤) by Kuan Han-ch'ing 關漢卿, written in the thirteenth century, has remained a popular favorite in its many different versions through the ages. It is still presented in the Peking opera theatres under the title *Snow in Midsummer* (*Liu-yüeh hsüeh* 六月雪). Several editions of the original Yüan play have come from The People's Republic of China in recent years. Thus, despite turbulent political and social changes, the play continues to be appealing, because it represents ideas strong and persistent among the Chinese.

Yüan drama is a well-defined genre, derived from a long tradition of stylization, with a consistent structure and a formal pattern carefully observed by the playwrights. The Chinese stage has inherited from Yüan drama many of its techniques, conventions, plots, and themes. A clear understanding of one Yüan play can thus add considerably to our knowledge of the genre and its relation to later Chinese drama.

Kuan Han-ch'ing and his time

Yüan drama, like many other great literary achievements, profited, no doubt, by the coincidence of men and the moment. The sudden blossoming of the drama during the Yüan dynasty was largely due to the political climate which, though adverse to the Chinese people, was favorable for the development of this new literary genre. Civil service examinations for the selection of officials were suspended in the north in 1237, soon after the conquest of the Chin 金 by the Mongols, and in the south in 1274 just before the fall of the Sung; and they were not to be reinstated until 1315. The seventy-eight year suspension of this institution in China deprived scholars of the traditional road to government service and frustrated their hopes for success and glory. Barred from officialdom, the *literati* experienced financial difficulties and a drastic change of social position. The practical need to make a living and the psychological need to win prestige and fame thus attracted some of them to play writing.

1

Their attempts in the theatre found support among both the rulers and the Chinese people. The Mongols, generally unappreciative of classical Chinese writing, easily found enjoyment in the acted stories with their singing and dancing. The Chinese audience found further reward in a theatre which provided an outlet for their frustrations and an easy flight into fantasy. Two overlapping lists of Yüan plays, one by a contemporary author, containing 452 titles,[1] and one by an early Ming writer, of 535 titles,[2] indicate the popularity of Yüan drama. While the collective energy of the *literati* helped to gain this popularity for drama during the Yüan dynasty, the creative genius of a few poets like Kuan Han-ch'ing, Ma Chih-yüan 馬致遠, Cheng Kuang-tsu 鄭光祖, Po P'u 白樸, and Wang Shih-fu 王實甫 also established the genre as a brilliant and unique achievement in Chinese literary history.

Kuan Han-ch'ing is listed first among the playwrights in *A Register of Ghosts*, a contemporary record of Yüan poets and dramatists, published in 1330. There he is said to be 'a native of Ta-tu' (大都, present-day Peking); he is styled as 'old man of the Yi Study' (*Yi-chai sou* 已齋叟), and a member of the Academy of Imperial Medical Affairs (*T'ai-yi yüan yin* 太醫院尹).[3] The dates of his birth and death are a matter of controversy. He is mentioned in *A Register* as a contemporary of Po P'u, who lived from 1226 to 1285 and whose birthdate is the only one of the Yüan dramatists to be known with certainty. Kuan Han-ch'ing was probably born just a few years before Po P'u, and he must have died before 1330, as he was listed among the deceased in *A Register of Ghosts*.[4]

The range of Kuan Han-ch'ing's subjects is wide. He wrote sixty-

---

1 *A Register of Ghosts* (*Lu-kuei pu* 錄鬼簿), by Chung Ssu-ch'eng 鍾嗣成, 1330. A critical edition in *Chung-kuo ku-tien hsi-ch'ü lun-chu chi-ch'eng* 中國古典戲曲論著集成, (Peking, 1959), vol. II, pp. 105–37.

2 *A Register of the Sounds of Universal Harmony* (*T'ai-ho cheng-yin p'u* 太和正音譜) by Prince Chu Ch'üan 朱權 of the early fifteenth century, lists about 500 titles (allegedly 535 titles, but only 418 in extant editions). In *Chung-kuo ku-tien hsi-ch'ü lun-chu chi-ch'eng*, (Peking, 1959), vol. III, pp. 26–43.

3 *A Register of Ghosts*, p. 104.

4 For information on Kuan Han-ch'ing's life, see T'an Cheng-pi 譚正璧, *Short Biographies of Six Yüan Master Playwrights* (*Yüan ch'ü liu ta-chia lüeh chuan* 元曲六大家畧傳), (Shanghai, 1955), pp. 4–118; *A Collection of Essays on Kuan Han-ch'ing* (*Kuan Han-ch'ing yen-chiu lun-wen chi* 關漢卿研究論文集) ed. Ku-tien wen hsüeh ch'u-pan-she, 1958, pp. 11–46; and J. P. Seaton, Jr., 'A Critical Study of Kuan Han-ch'ing: The Man and His Works', an unpublished Ph. D. dissertation, (Indiana University, 1969), pp. 227-32.

three plays, of which eighteen are extant.[1] Eight of these have recently been translated into English: *Injustice to Tou O*, *The Butterfly Dream* (*Hu-tieh meng* 蝴蝶夢), and *The Wife-snatcher* (*Lu chai lang* 魯齋郎) deal with trials and justice; *Rescued by a Coquette* (*Chiu feng-ch'en* 救風塵), *The Jade Mirror-stand* (*Yü ching-t'ai* 玉鏡臺) and *The Riverside Pavilion* (*Wang-chiang t'ing* 望江亭) are comedies dealing with courtship and marriage; *Lord Kuan Goes to the Feast* (*Tan tao hui* 單刀會) and *Death of the Winged-tiger General* (*K'u Ts'un-hsiao* 哭存孝) celebrate historical incidents.[2] He shows in these plays that he was adept at writing tragedy as well as comedy and satire.

He is known to have 'appeared on the stage himself, with his face painted black and white, considering this his profession, and having no objection to the company of actors'.[3] His experience as an actor, living on intimate terms with other actors, and his attention to the requirements of the actors, the stage, and the audience, must have contributed to his understanding of the theatre and to his progress in dramatic technique. Chia Chung-ming 賈仲明, an early Ming dynasty writer, calls Kuan Han-ch'ing in an elegy 'the leader of the theatre, the master of the *tsa-chü* performing team' (*li-yüan ling-hsiu*, . . . *tsa-chü pan t'ou* 梨園領袖 . . . 雜劇班頭).[4]

The narrative tradition and the play's source

Yüan Northern drama, usually called the *tsa-chü* ('variety play'), acquired this generic name from earlier plays of quite a different nature. It consists of acting, dialogue, singing, dancing, and music. Whereas earlier theatricals enriched the format of the Yüan stage, the *pien-wen* 變文 (originally popularized versions of Buddhist scriptures) and the *ch'uan-ch'i* 傳奇 ('tales of the marvelous') of the T'ang 唐, and the oral story-telling of the Sung 宋 times, had the greatest bearing on the emergence of the Yüan dramatic literature. The *pien-wen*, with its earthy and colloquial language, ushered in the possibility of telling a long, continuous story through songs and prose dialogue. The *ch'uan-ch'i*, with amazing skill in narrative art and insight into human

1 See 'A Complete List of Kuan Han-ch'ing's Plays' ('Kuan Han-ch'ing tsa-chü ch'üan-mu' 關漢卿雜劇全目) and postscript in *A Collection of Kuan Han-ch'ing's Plays (Kuan Han-ch'ing hsi-ch'ü chi* 關漢卿戲曲集), pp. 1003–52 and 1053–70.
2 Hsien-yi Yang and Gladys Yang, trans., *Selected Plays of Kuan Han-ch'ing*, (Peking, 1958).
3 Tsang Chin-shu 臧晉叔, 'Preface', *Selected Yüan Plays (Yüan-ch'ü hsüan* 元曲選), 1616, vol. I, pp. 1a–b.
4 *A Register of Ghosts*, note 130, p. 151.

psychology, aroused great interest in stories about people, rather than spirits, which dominate the pre-T'ang tales. In addition to these, the 'medley' (*chu-kung tiao* 諸宮調) type of oral narrative, current in the Sung and Chin period, was a major shaping force for the Yüan plays.

The urgent needs of the theatre encouraged the playwrights to turn to a variety of source materials – oral narratives, literary tales, or histories. By the time the story was appropriated by the Yüan dramatist, the original tale had often gone through several versions and had proven its value as popular entertainment. An example of this course of development is the famous story of Ying-ying 鶯鶯, which originated in T'ang *ch'uan-ch'i*, developed through several versions of Sung and Chin oral narratives, and was finally celebrated in the outstanding Yüan play, *The Romance of the Western Chamber* (*Hsi hsiang chi* 西廂記).[1]

The basic story in *Injustice to Tou O*, of a filial woman of Tung-hai 東海, is from the *History of Han* (*Han-shu* 漢書) and from an expanded version of the story in the *Records of Spirits* (*Sou shen chi* 搜神記) of the fourth century. The biography of Yü Ting-kuo 于定國 in the *History* reads as follows:

> In Tung-hai there was a filial woman who became a widow at a young age and then also lost her son. She diligently served her mother-in-law, who wanted her to remarry, but she refused. Her mother-in-law told the neighbors, 'My daughter-in-law serves me diligently. I pity her for losing her son in her widowhood. I am old and am such a burden to a young person. What shall I do?' Later the mother-in-law strangled herself. Her daughter went to the officials, saying, 'The woman killed my mother!' The magistrate arrested the filial woman, but she denied the charge of murdering her mother-in-law. The magistrate cross-examined her, and she confessed under severe pressure. Lord Yü [the father of Yü Ting-kuo, and at the time an officer in charge of prisons] believed that this woman, who in serving her mother-in-law for more than ten years was known for her filial piety, could not have been a murderer. The prefect refused to listen. Failing to win his case, Lord Yü, holding the case

1 The T'ang story entitled 'An Account of Meeting an Immortal' (*Hui chen chi* 會眞記), also known as 'The Story of Ying-ying' (*Ying-ying chuan* 鶯鶯傳), is by Yüan Chen 元稹 (779–831). Three versions of the Sung oral narratives have survived: 'The Flirtation Song Turns' (*T'iao-hsiao ling chuan-t'a* 調笑令轉踏) by Ch'in Kuan 秦觀 (1049–1101); 'A Drum Song of an Account of Meeting an Immortal' (*Hui chen chi ku-tzu tz'u* 會眞記鼓子詞) by Chao Ling-chih 趙令畤 (ca. 1110); a prose-song version known as 'Shang mode: The Butterfly in Love with Flowers' (*Shang tiao Tieh lien hua* 商調蝶戀花). Tung Chieh-yüan's 董解元 *The Western Chamber Medley* (*Hsi hsiang chi chu-kung-tiao* 西廂記諸宮調), a narrative consisting of prose and verse, is the most significant shaping force of the Yüan play and its immediate source.

records in his hands, wept at the hall of the prefecture and finally resigned on the excuse of sickness. The prefect, after all, executed the filial woman. A severe drought lasted for three years in the prefecture. Later when a new prefect arrived, he tried to find the reason by divination for this disaster. Lord Yü said: 'The former prefect dealt the sentence; could this be the cause of the disaster?' Then the prefect slaughtered an ox, personally offered sacrifice at the filial woman's home, and offered praise in front of the grave. Immediately there was a great rainfall, followed by a good yield in the harvest.[1]

The version in *Records of Spirits* is the same as in the *History* except for the following appended statement:

It is stated in the biography of the elderly man: 'The filial woman's name was Chou Ch'ing 周 青. When Ch'ing was about to die, she had carried in a carriage a one hundred-foot long bamboo pole from which to hang five streamers, and she made a vow in front of the people: "If I am guilty, and deserve to be executed, my blood should flow down; if I die unjustly, my blood shall flow in the opposite direction." After she was executed, her blood, of a dark yellow color, poured upward along the bamboo pole, reaching the streamers, and then flowed down again.'[2]

The incident of a snowfall in midsummer is derived from a story in *Huai-nan tzu* 淮 南 子, a collection of Taoist writings compiled under the patronage of Liu An 劉 安, the talented prince of Huai-nan, of the second century B.C.: 'Tsou Yen 鄒 衍, in the service of King Hui 惠 of the state of Yen 燕, was extremely loyal. However, the people around the king slandered him, and he was imprisoned. Looking up to Heaven, he cried bitterly. It was the summer season in the fifth month, yet Heaven sent down frost for his sake.'[3]

Conventions of Yüan drama

Whereas the borrowing of actual stories and thematic material from the oral narratives is obvious, the survival in drama of structural devices and conventions of the oral tradition is also significant. By Yüan times, oral story telling was an established institution with proven value as popular entertainment; it is only natural that the dramatists exploited the possibilities inherent in the conventions of the oral performance. The opening verse, self-identification, direct and lyrical expression, recapitulation, alternate use of verse and prose,

1 *History of Han* (*Han-shu* 漢 書, *Po-na ed.*), *chüan* 71, p.p. 5b–6a.
2 Kan Pao 干 寶, *Records of Spirits* (*Sou shen chi* 搜 神 記), (Shih-chien Book Co., 1959), *chüan* 11, p. 84.
3 Quoted in *The Imperial Encyclopedia* (*T'ai-p'ing yü lan* 太 平 御 覽, *SPTK san-pien*), *chüan* 14, p. 2b.

restriction to one singing role, and the sequential presentation of stories, are apparently all formal legacies from oral story telling. The Yüan dramatists adopted these features partly because of tradition, and partly because of their inherent theatrical value.

Yüan drama, as a well-defined genre, was heir to a complex artistic tradition composed of many strands: fascination with story telling, delight in poetry, concern for music, and interest in acting and acrobatics. A convention in Yüan drama which seems to have come from the four-part 'variety play' (*tsa-chü*) of the Sung dynasty is the four-act (*che* 折) division. However, there is often placed in the beginning of a play or between two acts a *hsieh-tzu* 楔子, commonly translated as the 'wedge' (see p. 37, n. 3 below); this mobile unit, in some ways comparable to a prologue or an interlude in Western plays, adds great variety to the otherwise rigid four-act structure.

Another interesting convention of Yüan drama is the role system, which is reminiscent of the now almost extinct 'stock company' that prevailed in many eastern American towns and cities in the early nineteenth century. Professional actors and actresses, belonging to a resident dramatic group, were designated by the type of roles they habitually played, such as 'the leading woman', 'the leading man', 'old gentleman', 'ingenue', 'comedian', or 'juvenile'. In the Yüan plays, although no description of the *dramatis personae* is given, mention is always made of the proper role of each character. In the Prologue in *Injustice to Tou O*, for instance, upon the entrance of Tou O and her father, it is stated: 'the supporting actor impersonating Tou T'ien-chang, guiding the female lead impersonating Tuan-yün, enters' (ll. 24–6).

In each play, there is one leading male or female role, who does all the singing in the four acts, whereas singing in the 'wedge' (*hsieh-tzu*) may be performed by other roles. Among the male roles are *cheng mo* 正末, the principal male-role; *fu mo* 副末, or *ch'ung mo* 冲末, a supporting male role; *po-lao* 孛老, an old man (here as the part of Donkey Chang's father); and *hsiao mo* 小末, a youth. Among the female roles are *cheng tan* 正旦, the principal female role (here as the part of Tou O); *pu-er* 卜兒, an old woman (here as the part of Mistress Ts'ai); *hun-tan* 魂旦, a female ghost (here as the part of Tou O's ghost). Other roles are *ching* 净, usually a villainous person (here as the part of Dr Lu and also as the prefect T'ao Wu); *fu-ching* 副净, a secondary villainous person (here as the part of Donkey Chang); *wai* 外, usually a serious person (here as the part of the execution officer and also of the prefect who succeeded T'ao Wu); *ch'ou* 丑, a clownish person (here as the part of the servant Chang Ch'ien and the guard). Although one actor in a certain role generally plays the part of one character in a play, he can play the parts of two or more, as the *wai* and *ching* roles in this play demonstrate. Although the two *ching* roles here could be played by two different actors, it is probable, since they never meet on stage, that the two characters Dr Lu and Prefect T'ao are played by one *ching* actor. The role system seems to make the minor characters, such as servants and officials, types instead of individuals; however, in the hands of master playwrights like Kuan Han-ch'ing, the protagonists are remarkably alive and interesting.

The role system has persisted in the Chinese classical theatre, where an evening's program often consists of a number of different episodes from a variety of plays, providing an opportunity for the individual actors and actresses to demonstrate the roles in which they excel.

Yüan Northern dialect

Colloquial speech in the Yüan plays is identified with the Northern, rather than the Southern dialect. Since in the beginning the performances centered around Ta-tu, and the playwrights were predominantly from the northern region, it is natural to assume that the speech and its delivery on stage were current with that of the capital and its adjacent area.

Chou Te-ch'ing 周德清, the authoritative Yüan scholar on *ch'ü* 曲, asserts that in writing *ch'ü*, 'one must use the correct language; and in the choice of correct language, one must follow the sounds of the Central Plains', and he adds that the perfection of *ch'ü* 'comes with the new creations of Kuan, Cheng, Po, and Ma, whose rhymes all preserve the natural sounds and whose words are those of the universal language'.[1] Of these four master *ch'ü* writers, Kuan Han-ch'ing and Ma Chih-yüan were from Ta-tu, Cheng Kuang-tsu was from P'ing-yang 平陽, Shansi 山西, and Po P'u from Chen-ting 眞定, Hopei 河北, all in North China. Chou Te-ch'ing's statements make it clear that the work of these poets was written in the spoken language of the Yüan period in North China, a language easily understood by a large number of people in China. Historical linguistic evidence also supports the belief that the sound and rhyme system used in the Yüan plays is that of a Mandarin dialect.[2] The third and clearest piece of evidence

1 Chou Te-ch'ing 周德清, *Chung-yüan yin-yün* 中原音韻, 1324. In *Chung-kuo ku-tien hsi-ch'ü lun-chu chi-ch'eng*, (Peking, 1959), vol. I, p. 175.
2 Hugh M. Stimson, 'Phonology of the *Chung-yüan yin yün*', *Tsing Hua Journal of Chinese Studies*, New Series, III (1962), 147.

7

showing the affinity of Yüan dramatic prose to the Northern dialect lies in the texts of the plays themselves. Except for some occasional expressions, the prose speech is very similar to the Northern speech of today.

On the phonetics of Yüan Northern dialect, known as Old Mandarin or Ancient Mandarin, there exists today, fortunately, Chou Te-ch'ing's *Sound and Rhymes in the Central Plains* (*Chung-yüan yin yün*, hereafter referred to as *CYYY*). With a preface dated 1324 and published at the height of the popularity of Yüan drama, this is essentially a handbook on versification for writers of the *ch'ü*. It consists of two sections: part one is primarily a listing of the rhymes and their homonyms; part two, entitled 'Beginner's models in the composition of *tz'u* according to the standard pronunciation of the CYYY' (*CYYY cheng-yü tso-tz'u ch'i-li* 中原音韻正語作詞起例), contains many statements about the sounds and rhymes of the language of the Yüan drama.

1. *The initials.* An analysis of the *CYYY* by Chao Yin-t'ang 趙蔭棠 yields twenty-one initials;[1] Tung T'ung-ho 董同龢, however, questions the existence of the inital 'η' and believes that there might have been only twenty initials. The following chart by Tung of Old Mandarin initials with inclusion of Chinese characters makes easily discernible the difference in pronunciation of the initials of certain characters in Old Mandarin and modern Mandarin:[2]

p	p'	m	f	v
(班 辦)	(盤 判)	(慢)	(反 飯)	(晚)
t	t'	n		l
(丹 但)	(壇 歎)	(難)		(闌)
ts	ts'		s	
(贊 尖)	(殘 餐 錢)		(珊 先)	
tʃ	tʃ'		ʃ	ʒ
(展 棧)	(廛)		(山)	(然)
k	k'	(η)	x	
(干 堅)	(看 牽)		(漢 現)	
O [zero]				
(安 顏 顙 元)				

[1] Chao Yin-t'ang, *Chung-yüan yin yün yen-chiu* 中原音韻研究, (Shanghai, 1936), pp. 62–3.
[2] Tung T'ung-ho, *Chung-kuo yü-yin shih* 中國語音史, (Taipei, 1954), p. 24.

The most obvious difference is that Old Mandarin initials 'ts', 'ts''
and 's', and 'k', 'k'' and 'x' before the vowel 'i' are, with few exceptions, palatalized in modern Mandarin, as illustrated in the following characters:

Old Mandarin (transcription according to Tung's system)	*Modern Mandarin* (transcription according to Wade-Giles system)
尖 tsiem	chien
錢 ts'ien	ch'ien
先 sien	hsien
堅 kien	chien
牽 k'ien	ch'ien
現 xien	hsien
居 kiu	chü
去 k'iu	ch'ü
虛 xiu	hsü

No such palatalization occurs before other vowels; thus the initials
before the vowel 'a' in *tsan* 贊, *ts'an* 殘, *san* 珊, and *kan* 干, *k'an* 看,
han 漢, for example, are the same in Old Mandarin and modern
Mandarin.

2. *The finals.* In the *CYYY*, the syllables, classified according to the
finals in the Northern dialect, fall into nineteen rhyme groups. They
appear in the original order as follows; the pronunciation is Tung
T'ung-ho's reconstruction:[1]

(1) 東鍾 uŋ, iuŋ
(2) 江陽 aŋ, iaŋ, uaŋ
(3) 支思 ï
(4) 齊微 i, iei, uei
(5) 魚模 u, iu
(6) 皆來 ai, iai, uai
(7) 眞文 ən, iən, uən, yən
(8) 寒山 an, ian, uan
(9) 桓歡 on
(10) 先天 ien, yen
(11) 蕭豪 au, au, iau, (uau)
(12) 歌戈 o, io, uo
(13) 家麻 a, (ia), ua
(14) 車遮 ie, ye
(15) 庚青 əŋ, iəŋ, uəŋ, yəŋ,
(16) 尤候 ou, iou
(17) 侵尋 əm, iəm
(18) 監咸 am, iam
(19) 廉纖 iem

Some of the striking differences of finals between Old Mandarin
and modern Mandarin may be summarized as follows:[2]

Old Mandarin (Tung's system)	Modern Mandarin (Wade-Giles)	*Conditions*	*Examples*
–uŋ	–eng	after p–, p'–, m–, f–	崩烹夢風

[1] Tung T'ung-ho, *Chung-kuo yü-yin shih*, pp. 27–34.
[2] See *ibid.*, pp. 27–34 for details.

–iuŋ	–ung	after n–, l–; ts–, ts', s–	膿籠 宗叢鬆
–uei	–ei	after n–, l–	內淚
–iən	–en	after tʃ–, tʃ'–, ʃ–, ʒ–	眞陳神人
–on	–an	after p–, p', m–	搬判滿
–on	–uan	after t–, t'–, n–, l–; ts–, ts'–, s–; k–, k'–, x–; o–	端團煖亂 鑽攢酸 官寬歡 玩
-ien	–an	after tʃ–, tʃ'–, ʃ–,ʒ–	展塵扇然
–iəŋ	–eng	after tʃ–, tʃ'–, ʃ–,ʒ–	正稱聲仍
–iou	–ou	after tʃ–, tʃ'–, ʃ–,ʒ–	晝丑受肉
–m	–n	in all cases	

3. *The tones.* In Ancient Chinese, there are four tones: *p'ing* 平 or 'level', *shang* 上 or 'rising', *ch'ü* 去 or 'falling', and *ju* 入 or 'entering'. Chou Te-ch'ing further distinguishes the *p'ing* tone into two groups: the *yin-p'ing* 陰平 and *yang-p'ing* 陽平. The *ju* tone does not exist in *ch'ü* prosody. In the rhyme book section in *CYYY* the erstwhile *ju*-tone graphs are re-distributed into the other tone groups, but set apart in separate listings. In all, there are three main tone groups with the possible subdivision as follows:

> *p'ing*: *yin-p'ing*
> *yang-p'ing*
> *ju* tone as *p'ing* tone
> *ch'ü* tone as *p'ing* tone
> *shang*: *shang*
> *ju* tone as *shang* tone
> *ch'ü*: *ch'ü*
> *ju* tone as *ch'ü* tone

Whether *ju* tone existed in the *CYYY* dialect in the Yüan period has remained a controversial question. Chou Te-ch'ing states in the very beginning of his discourse on the composition of *ch'ü* that '*ju* tone has been assigned to the three tones, *p'ing*, *shang*, and *ch'ü*, merely for the convenience of rhyming when composing *tz'u* 詞. In actual speech, however, the distinction of the *ju* tone still exists.'[1]

1 Chou Te-ch'ing, *Chung-yüan yin-yün*, p. 211.

Later scholars fail to agree on this point. Some, such as Lu Chih-wei 陸志韋, are inclined to take Chou Te-ch'ing's statement literally in the belief that the *ju* tone indeed existed in the Northern dialect of the Yüan period.[1] Others, notably Yoshikawa and Chao Yin-t'ang, believe in the absence of the *ju* tone in the dialect.[2] Chao Yin-t'ang disposes of Chou's statement simply as an attempt to forestall attacks; for although Chou's classification of tones on the basis of current speech was a remarkable achievement, he was too shy to admit to having formalized a new sound system. Chao Yin-t'ang finds support for his argument in another Yüan author, T'ao Tsung-yi 陶宗儀, who states in his *Notes Made While Resting from Farming* (*Cho keng lu* 輟耕錄) that 'in today's Central Plain rhymes, *ju* tone sounds like *p'ing* tone, and it can also be used as *ch'ü* tone'.[3] Chou Te-ch'ing was a southerner; thus it was possible that he mistakenly thought *ju* was pronounced by northerners.

A romanized version of *Chung-yüan yin-yün* according to Tung T'ung-ho's reconstruction of its phonetic system was made available in 1962.[4] Hugh Stimson in 1966 published his *The Jongyuan in yunn*, essentially a list of the total 5865 graphs in the Old Mandarin rhyme book. He rearranged the graphs to conform to an order based on phonological principles. Middle Chinese and Modern Peking readings as well as Old Mandarin readings are included. Only a few graphs, such as *ai* 哎 (l. 744), *can* 㳠 (l. 193), and *zhan* 佔 (l. 793), which are in *Tou O Yüan* are not included in the *CYYY*; thus one may refer to Tung's or Stimson's work if interested in working out a reconstructed reading in Old Mandarin pronunciation of this play.

Besides the reconstruction of the Old Mandarin phonetics on the basis of *CYYY*, other investigations have been made using different sources. Dragunov's study of Old Mandarin is based on *h*Phags-pa material. *h*Phags-pa is a script devised by *h*Phags-pa, a Tibetan lama in the beginning of the Yüan dynasty, for transcription of different languages in the Yüan empire. A number of writings of Chinese in this script from the Yüan dynasty have been preserved. Dragunov's source materials consist of transliterations in *h*Phags-pa script of

---

1 See Lu Chih-wei, 'Shih *Chung-yüan yin-yün*' 釋中原音韻, *Yenching hsüeh-pao*, XXXI (1946), 36.
2 Yoshikawa Kōjirō, *Gen zatsugeki kenkyū* 元雜劇研究, translated from the Japanese by Cheng Ch'ing-mao, (Taipei, 1960), p. 287; Chao Yin-t'ang, *Chung-yüan yin yün yen-chiu*, p. 13.
3 Quoted in Chao Yin-t'ang, *ibid.* pp. 13-14.
4 Liu Te-chih 劉德智, *Yin chu Chung-yüan yin yün* 音注中原音韻 (Taipei, 1962), pp. 1-55.

Chinese documents, and Chinese words found in Mongolian documents. They amount to 703 Chinese graphs occuring a total of 1820 times.[1] Dragunov's source materials seem to represent a slightly earlier stage of Old Mandarin than that of *CYYY*, with the entering-tone as a phonologically distinct entity.[2]

Paul Denlinger attempted a reconstruction of Old Mandarin phonetics on the basis of *Lao Ch'i-ta* 老乞大. This and *P'u t'ung-shih* 朴通事 are two textbooks believed to have been used in Korea during the Yüan dynasty for teaching Koreans conversational Chinese. The sound glosses in these two works are in the Korean alphabet. Denlinger is of the opinion that the phonetic system reconstructed from the Korean text *Lao Ch'i-ta* is very similar to the reconstructed pronunciation of the *CYYY* except that 'the *CYYY* material seems slightly earlier in point of time in that it still contains "m" finals whereas those have completely disappeared in *LCT* [*Lao Ch'i-ta*]'.[3]

Vernacular speech

The vernacular prose speech in Yüan drama draws its greatest vigor and pliancy from the fact that it was written to sound like the spoken language of the time. A comparison of the prose speech with contemporary non-dramatic vernacular works indicates that the Yüan dramatists made good use of the language as they found it. The prose passages, called *pai* 白 (plain speech), or *pin* 賓 (secondary; guest), or *pin-pai*, appear as both monologues and dialogues. Where the songs in a play are performed by only one actor or actress, the prose speech is used by all the characters, and forms an essential part of the plays.

The feat of developing Chinese vernacular prose writing must have been a difficult task. In a logographic script like Chinese, the process of writing down oral expression must have been infinitely harder than a comparable process in a phonetic and alphabetic script; the numerous grammatical particles and colloquial expressions which had never before appeared in writing called for the invention of new characters,

1 See A.A. Dragunov, 'The *h*Phags-pa script and Ancient Mandarin', *Izvestiya Akademii Nauk SSSR, 7th Series, Otdelenie Gumanitarnyx Nauk,* IX (1930), 627–47; X (1930), 775–97. Translated by T'ang Yü.
2 The difference between the Old Mandarin represented by Dragunov's source material and that of *CYYY* is further seen in the former's three-way distinction of initial stops and affricatives; and voiceless-voiced distinction of fricatives. (See Hashimoto, 'Phonology of Ancient Chinese', unpublished dissertation [Ohio: Ohio State University, 1965], vol. II.)
3 Denlinger, 'Studies in Middle Chinese', unpublished Ph.D. dissertation (Seattle: Univ. of Washington, 1962), p. 4.

or ingenious borrowings. Sometimes a final form would not be resolved for a long time. For instance, for the expression 'what' (shem-me 甚麼), there exists in the Yüan plays several variant written forms. In *Injustice to Tou O*, variants such as the following indicate the fluid state of vernacular writings at the time:

chiao 敎 for chiao 叫 (l. 231)
hui 侮 for hui 晦 (l. 422)
cheng-hou 證候 for cheng-hou 症候 (l. 539)
hu-t'u 糊突 for hu-t'u 糊塗 (l. 736)
wu-fu 於伏 for wu-fu 誣服 (l. 1356)

It would have been preferable to base such an analysis of the language on a contemporary edition, but the only extant Yüan edition, the *Yüan k'an tsa-chü san-shih chung* 元刊雜劇三十種 (*A Yüan printed edition of Thirty Plays*), contains too little prose dialogue to be of use. The adoption of a later collection presents a disadvantage: that the plays were collected and published as one work gives rise to the danger that they have been made more readable and that the language has been modified by the usage of a later date. The many editions from the Ming dynasty nevertheless serve as a rich source for study.

Vernacular and semi-vernacular writings of the Yüan, as well as of the preceding Sung and the succeeding Ming dynasties, offer valuable insight into the vocabulary and grammar of the spoken language of the Yüan period. Works such as the following from the three periods, and other letters, dispatches, and recorded sayings of eminent Buddhists, statesmen, and scholars, make it possible to ascertain the nature of Yüan prose speech. Knowledge of contemporary colloquial writings is indispensable to our understanding of Yüan dramatic prose.

Among works from the Sung Dynasty, *The Recorded Sayings of Chu Tzu* 朱子 (*Chu-tzu yü-lei* 朱子語類) is one of the earliest sources important in the study of colloquial prose. Containing observations of the great Sung philosopher, the work demonstrates how successfully colloquial sayings could be committed to paper. There are several other interesting narratives in the vernacular language from the Sung-Yüan period, notably *The Shih-hua Version of Tripitaka's Quest for Scriptures* (*Ta-T'ang San-tsang ch'ü-ching shih-hua* 大唐三藏取經詩話), and *Events of the Hsüan-ho Period of the Great Sung* (*Ta Sung Hsüan-ho yi-shih* 大宋宣和遺事).

Most significant among the works contemporary with the Yüan plays are five historical narratives in the colloquial language, collected under the title *Five Fully Illustrated P'ing-hua* (*Ch'üan-hsiang p'ing-hua wu-chung* 全相平話五種). They were discovered in the twentieth century

13

in the Cabinet Library, Japan, and are rare, datable vernacular works from the Yüan period. The works record the time of the publication: [Yüan] Chih-chih 至 治 (1321–4); the place of publication: Chien-an 建 安; and the name of the publisher: *Yü-shih* 虞 氏. Of great value also are several official documents, such as *The Imperial Edicts* (*Sheng chih pei* 聖 旨 碑) and the *Yüan Code* (*Yüan tien-chang* 元 典 章). Although official documents were traditionally written in classical Chinese, during the Mongol rule they were written in semi- or quasi-vernacular prose. Rendered in a comparable medium are some Confucian classics, such as *The Essentials of Great Learning* (*Ta-hsüeh yao lüeh* 大 學 要 略), *Interpretations of the Golden Mean* (*Chung-yung chih-chieh* 中 庸 直 解), and *Interpretations of the Classic of Filial Piety* (*Hsiao-ching chih-chieh* 孝 經 直 解). Of unusual interest among works of this period are the two Korean textbooks in spoken Chinese mentioned earlier. The title *Lao Ch'i-ta* probably came from the term 'Lao Ch'i-tan' (老 契 丹), a reference to China because of the association with Khitan[1], and the title *P'u t'ung-shih* indicates that the book was most likely written by a Mr P'u who held the official title of *t'ung-shih* (Interpreter).

In the following Ming dynasty, there emerged several collections of short stories in the vernacular: the *Story Books of Ch'ing-p'ing-shan-t'ang* (*Ch'ing-p'ing-shan-t'ang hua-pen* 清 平 山 堂 話 本) and Feng Meng-lung's 馮 夢 龍 three anthologies, namely, *Yü-shih ming-yen* 喩 世 明 言, *Ching-shih t'ung-yen* 警 世 通 言 and *Hsing-shih heng-yen* 醒 世 恆 言 (*Stories to Enlighten the World, Stories to Admonish the World*, and *Stories to Awaken the World*). In addition to the short stories, there were a number of novels, *Romance of The Three Kingdoms* (*San kuo yen-yi* 三 國 演 義), *Water Margin* (*Shui-hu chuan* 水 滸 傳), and *Monkey* (*Hsi yu chi* 西 遊 記), which demonstrate considerable development in the use of colloquial prose.

In the annotation of the text of *Tou O Yüan*, citations from writings around the Yüan period help make intelligible a number of obscure expressions. Here I have singled out one salient feature of colloquial Chinese, namely, the use of grammatical particles, to illustrate the differences and similarities between Old Mandarin and modern Mandarin grammar. Because the dialogue was made to imitate actual speech, the particles occur with great frequency with a number of functions. Many of them, appearing in both the Yüan plays and modern Mandarin, are found to have identical functions. On the other

1 Yang Lien-sheng 楊 聯 陞 '*Lao Ch'i-ta, P'u T'ung-shih* li te yü-fa yü-hui' [老 乞 大] [朴 通 事] 裏 的 語 法 語 彙, *Bulletin of the Institute of History and Philology* (*Academia Sinica*), XXIX (1957), 197.

hand, some of the particles in the Yüan plays are no longer used today, but these obsolete usages are found in other Yüan writings. The fact that the now unfamiliar expressions in Yüan drama have counterparts in other contemporary writings points to their currency during the Yüan period. The following examples are drawn, with few exceptions, from *Tou O Yüan*; for the non-dramatic passages I have used chiefly *P'u T'ung-shih* and *Lao Ch'i-ta*, the two textbooks on conversational Chinese cited above.

1. The final particles *le* 了 and *yeh* (*ye*) 也:

a. *Le, yeh* as indications of a new situation. In modern Mandarin, word-suffix *le* indicates completed action, and final particle *le* (also called sentence *le* or inchoative *le*) indicates a situation which is new or new to the speaker. As Y. R. Chao observes, '*le* expresses completed action or a new situation, the two often forming two sides of the same thing'.[1] In *Injustice to Tou O*, the final particle *le* is used in the same way as in modern Mandarin to indicate a new situation, as the following lines illustrate:

> 這等你是我親家了　　　65
> 我如今打嘔不要這湯吃了　508-9
> (See also l. 186.)

Similarly, *yeh* is used as a final particle in Yüan drama:

> 我今二十歲也　182
> 過門去也　　318
> (See also ll. 128, 573, and 790.)

Sometimes the final particle *yeh* appears with the word-suffix *le*:

> 悮了時辰也　746-7
> 時辰到了也　824
> (See also ll. 533, 882, 995, and 1035.)

b. *Yeh* as a vocative. As a vocative, *yeh* parallels the modern article *a* 啊, which, according to Y. R. Chao, gives a more airy and less blunt effect to a direct address.[2] R. Miller feels that as a vocative, *yeh* tends to emphasize the element or elements to which it is bound.[3] In *Injustice to Tou O*, there are abundant examples of *yeh* as a vocative:

> 竇娥也你這命好苦也呵　186-7
> 孩兒也你教我怎生說波　231-2
> (See also ll. 294, 326, 441, 742 and 743.)

[1] Y.R. Chao, *Mandarin Primer* (Cambridge, Mass., 1948), p. 193, n. 48.
[2] Y.R. Chao, *A Grammar of Spoken Chinese* (Berkeley and Los Angeles, 1968), p. 804.
[3] Robert P. Miller, 'The Particles in the Dialogues of Yüan Drama. A Descriptive Analysis', unpublished Ph.D. dissertation (Yale University, 1952), p. 52. Mr Miller analyzes twelve particles in the play, *Lao sheng er*, and our conclusions differ considerably.

c. *Yeh* as an intonational particle. Comparable to *a* 啊 in modern usage, *yeh* is used for intonational effect. When linked to a preceding consonant, *a* sometimes becomes *ya*, 呀, *na* 哪, or *wa* 哇.

這廝好大膽也　410
這事怎了也　561
(See also l. 682.)

This usage of *yeh*, as L. S. Yang observes, is commonly seen in recorded Buddhist sayings in the T'ang and Sung periods.[1] The usage of *yeh* or *le-yeh* as a final particle to indicate a new situation is also found in non-dramatic writings of the Yüan times, as in the following (romanization is given below for examples other than those from *Tou O Yüan*):

遭是你來也　　　　　　　(*P'u t'ung-shih*, p. 156)
Tsao shih ni lai yeh.
Just right that you have come.

卻早年節下也　　　　　　(*P'u t'ung-shih*, p. 244)
Ch'üeh tsao nien chieh hsia yeh.
Already the new year's season has come.
(See also pp. 59, 68, 103, in the same text.)

Ōta Tatsuo observes:[2]

In the T'ang dynasty, only *le* is used:
　i. verb + *le*.
　ii. verb + object + *le*.
In the Sung dynasty, the following structure appears:
　iii. verb + *le* + object.
In the Yüan period, the final particle *yeh* is used:
　iv. verb + *le* + object + *yeh*.
Since the Ming period, a final *le* at times replaces *yeh*:
　v. verb + *le* + object + *le*.

2. Imperative particles. Particles which make up the imperatives in Yüan colloquial language are greater in number than such particles in modern Mandarin and function in a wider range.

a. *Tsa* (*za*) 咱. Besides its usage as 'I', as in certain modern dialects, *tsa* as a final particle in Yüan drama functions as an optative or advisative:

待我慢慢地尋思咱　　169-70
我將這文卷看幾宗咱　　946
你再尋思咱　　　　　251
看小生薄面看覷女孩兒咱　74-5
(See also ll. 648, 954, 958, 971, 993, 1004 and 1070.)

1 Yang Lien-sheng, '*Lao Ch'i-ta, P'u T'ung shi* li te yü-fa yü-hui', p. 200.
2 See Ōta Tatsuo 太田辰夫, '*Rōkitsudai* no gengo ni tsuite 老乞大の言語につ いて,' *Chūgoku gogaku kenkyūkai ronshū*, 中國語學研究會論集 I (1953), 7-8.

A compound particle *tse-ke* (*ze-ge*) 則個 is at times used as a variant for *tsa*, as is seen in a comparison of the following sentence and the one immediately above:

女孩兒在此只望婆婆看覷則個   63-4

b. *Po* (*bo*) 波. *Po* is sometimes used interchangeably with *tsa*. The final particle *tsa* in l. 946 quoted above, for instance, is not distinguishable from the final particle in the following line:

待老夫燈下看幾宗波   940
(See also ll. 442 and 492.)

c. *Pa* (*ba*) 罷. Similar to *tsa* and *po* as mild imperatives is the final particle *pa*. Its function in Yüan colloquial language is the same as its function in modern Mandarin, as is seen in the following lines:

仍舊勒死了你罷   168
你老人家吃罷   509-10
(See also ll. 133, 312, 333, 420, 690, 904, 943 and 953.)

d. *Lai* 來. When used with *ch'ü* 去, the particle *lai* can function as a mild imperative:

跟老身前後執料去來   101-2
你爺兒兩個隨我到家中去來   173-5

Lai, as a final particle, is also used in the sense of *lai-che* 來着 in modern Mandarin, which, as Y. R. Chao observes, usually is applied to events of the recent past and gives a slightly lively effect.[1] It is used frequently in Yüan drama:

都不是敢是我下的毒藥來   624-5
可真個是爲你來   1153
(See also ll. 415, 687, 690, 1154 and 1185.)

e. *Che* (*zhe*) 着 and *che* (*zhe*) 者. These two particles are used to form far stronger imperatives than the particles just discussed. Their function and range are indicated in the following stern commands given by the magistrates in the court scenes:

與我選大桿子打着   664-5
你老人家放精神着   530-1
毋得違誤片刻者   1205-6
張千喝攛厢者   1170

As imperatives, or optatives, *tsa*, *po*, and *pa* are found frequently in non-dramatic colloquial writings of the Yüan-Ming period. *Che* 着 as an imperative particle appeared in T'ang writings, and also in Yüan works, as in the following:

1 Y.R. Chao, *Grammar*, p. 810.

17

吹笛兒着   (*P'u t'ung-shih*, p. 18)
Ch'ui ti-er che.
Play the flute.

咱賭一個羊着   (*P'u t'ung-shih*, p. 47)
Tsa tu i-ke yang che.
Let me bet a sheep.

Whereas *che* 者, as an imperative, is now extinct in spoken Chinese, *che* 着 is still used, though infrequently, as in the following instances:

聽着聽我說
T'ing che! T'ing wo shuo.
Listen! Listen to me.

你等着我就回來
Ni teng-che; wo chiu hui-lai.
You wait; I'll be right back.

The use of *lai* as an optative particle is found in *P'u t'ung-shih*:

罷罷去來
Pa, pa. Ch'ü lai.
All right, all right. Let's go (p. 28).

午門外前看操馬去來
Wu men wai ch'ien k'an ts'ao ma ch'ü lai.
Let's go to the palace's main gate to see the horse drill (p. 52).

Professor L. S. Yang observes that this usage of *lai* existed before the Yüan period. In T'ao Ch'ien's 陶潛 (365-427) 'Song of the Returning to the Homestead' (*Kuei ch'ü lai tz'u* 歸去來辭), his repeated phrase *kuei ch'ü lai* is comparable to the present *hui ch'ü pa* ('let's return'). When Feng Hsüan 馮諼 of the Warring States period (403-221 B.C.) sang his famous line, 'Long sword! Let us go home', (*ch'ang chia kuei lai* 長鋏歸來), the particle *lai* functions as an optative particle rather than a directional complement, because this song was composed when Feng was still a guest at Meng Ch'ang-chün's 孟嘗君 household; he would have to say *kuei ch'ü* ('go back') instead of *kuei lai* ('come back') if a directional complement were used.[1]

3. *Na* 那 as an interrogative particle.

    a. Comparable to *a* 啊 in modern Mandarin, *na* is used for a rhetorical question. For instance, when Mistress Ts'ai informs Tou O that she intends to marry Old Chang, Tou O says to her,

六十以外的人怎生又招丈夫那   255-6
You are over sixty years old; how can you take another husband?

[1] Yang Lien-sheng, '*Lao ch'i-ta, P'u T'ung shi* li te yü-fa yü-hui', p. 201.

18

meaning, of course, that she should not marry again. Later, at the execution ground, the officer, sensing that Tou O has something to tell, says to her:

此 時 不 對 監 斬 大 人 說 幾 時 說 那   849–50
If you don't tell his honor now, when are you going to tell?

He thus suggests that she should say it now. Similar use of *na* is found in Yüan text books, as pointed out by L. S. Yang:[1]

我 不 打 火 喝 風 那   (*Lao Ch'i-ta*, p. 35)
Wo pu ta huo, he feng na?
If I don't eat, do I feed on wind?

這 般 收 拾 的 整 齊 時 不 好 那   (*P'u t'ung-shih*, p. 227)
Che pan shou-shih te cheng-ch'i shih, pu hao na?
Isn't it good that I tidied up like this?

   b. As an interrogative particle for regular questions, *na* is comparable in function to *ne* 呢, *ne* 吶, *ne* 哪, in modern Mandarin:

你 為 甚 麼 煩 惱 啼 哭 那   243–4
直 恁 的 好 睡 那   1164–5

4. *Li* 哩 as a durative particle. In its use to express a continuing state or action, *li* occurs in *Injustice to Tou O* as follows:

誰 喚 你 哩   140
就 說 女 婿 在 門 首 哩   228

Whereas in its function as a durative, *li* is replaced by *ne* 呢 or *ne* 吶 in modern Mandarin, this particle still exists in certain dialects. As Y. R. Chao observes, 'The character *li* is found in old novels, and the pronunciation *li* which it naturally suggests is actually used in dialects in which 呢 is pronounced *ni* or *nyi*'.[2]

5. *Te* (*de*) 的 (or 得, a variant in certain usages) as a subordinate particle. Besides its use as a potential or perfective complement, *te* performs several functions as a subordinate particle in the language of Yüan drama as follows:

   a. a subordinate particle translatable as '...'s' or 'of...' to indicate possessive case:

他 的 恩 德   632–3
竇 娥 的 血   896

1 *Ibid.* p. 199.
2 Y.R. Chao, *Grammar*, p. 802.

b. a subordinate particle translatable as '-*ly*' to form an adverb:

你 只 管 放 心 的 去 　 78
委 實 的 寃 情 不 淺 　 839–40

c. a subordinate particle translatable by an adjective or an adjectival phrase, or clause:

糊 突 的 官 　 1188
六 十 以 外 的 人 　 255
衝 天 的 怨 氣 　 855

d. a subordinate particle as a nominalizer:

我 隨 身 帶 的 有 繩 子 　 138–9
這 的

These usages are all retained in modern Mandarin except the last one. *Che-te* 這 的 in the sense of 'this' (or 'these') is replaced in modern Mandarin by *che* or *che-ke* 這 個. Though not found in *Injustice to Tou O*, this usage appears in several other Yüan plays:

這 的 是 隨 州 城 新 置 倉 　 (*Mo-ho-lo* 魔 合 羅, Act III, Song
Che-te shih Sui-chou ch'eng hsin chih ts'ang. 　 No. 7, 'Ts'u hu-lu' 醋 葫 蘆)
This is the newly built granary of the
city of Sui-chou.

這 的 是 東 林 寺 　 (*Tung-p'o meng* 東 坡 夢, Act IV,
Che-te shih Tung-lin szu. 　 prose interpolation in Song 2,
This is East-forest Temple. 　 'Shui hsien-tzu' 水 仙 子)

這 的 是 喒 父 親 母 親 　 (*Lao sheng erh* 老 生 兒, Act III, prose
Che-te shih tsan fu-ch'in mu-ch'in. 　 speech following Song No. 2, 'Tzu
These are my father and mother. 　 hua-er hsü' 紫 花 兒 序)

In Yüan non-dramatic literature, *che-te* and a comparable expression *na-te* are found in the following instances:

這 的 是 傘 　 (*P'u t'ung-shih*, p. 76)
Che-te shih san.
This is an umbrella.

這 的 你 不 須 說 　 (*P'u t'ung-shih*, p. 35)
Che-te ni pu hsü shuo.
This you need not say.

那 的 最 容 易 打 甚 麼 不 緊 　 (*P'u t'ung-shih*, p. 91)

Na-te tsui yung-i, ta shem-me pu chin.
That is the easiest – nothing of importance.

The study of particles, a prominent grammatical feature of Chinese colloquial language, in *Injustice to Tou O* makes clear that many usages now obsolete are found in contemporary non-dramatic writings. Some acquaintance with these and other established facts concerning contemporary speech habits indicate that the Yüan dramatists took few, if any, liberties with the spoken language; the present unfamiliarity of some of the expressions in Yüan drama came about because of the barrier created by the normal process of historical change in language between the thirteenth century and the present. On the whole, the language barrier thus created is surprisingly small.

In Chinese literary history the vernacular prose in Yüan drama occupies a significant position, because here for the first time vernacular prose was produced by a great number of professional writers. With only scanty and simple examples to follow, the Yüan dramatists developed vernacular prose into an expressive medium.

The poetry

Injustice to Tou O, a play about the tragic fate of a young woman, acquires a universality which raises it from the level of popular entertainment to that of important literature through the dramatist's skillful treatment of the subject, as well as his imagery and poetry. In the depiction of character, Chinese poetry can be effective because of its concision and connotative power. In the character portrayal in Yüan drama the theatrical conventions of the role system, the ethical emphasis on propriety, and the traditional literary models all tend to stress the typical or emblematic in character. Leading Yüan dramatists like Kuan Han-ch'ing, however, exhibit an expressive vitality in characterization that often transcends these limitations, creating a number of dramatic figures which are compelling and lively. A variety of factors combine in these plays to produce characters which spring to life, but perhaps most important among these are the liveliness of the prose dialogue, discussed above, and the vigor of the verse. A few passages from *Injustice to Tou O* should illustrate the poetic vigor which gives animation to characterization.

In Tou O's opening lines, as she recalls her mother's early death, her father's leaving her and 'selling' her to Mistress Ts'ai, and her own tragic widowhood at eighteen, she sings her suffering in the following lyric:

Of my heart full of sorrow,
Of my years of suffering,

21

Is Heaven aware?
If Heaven only knew my situation,
Would it not also grow thin?
(ll. 188-91)

Throughout the play, poetic imagery of this type recurs in the songs sung by Tou O, intensifying the individual grief by the introduction of cosmic images which lead the imagination to another world, into which the immediate human domain seems limitlessly extended.

When Tou O's mother-in-law seems all too ready to violate traditional precepts concerning chastity, and assents to the demands of the two rogues that she and Tou O give up their widowhood and marry them, Tou O's moral indignation bursts forth in these lines:

Swallows and orioles in pairs!
Mother-in-law, don't you feel shame?
My father-in-law worked in different prefectures and states;
He amassed a solid fortune, lacking in nothing.
How can you let the wealth he secured be enjoyed now by Donkey Chang?
(ll. 334-40)

All that she has and feels is thrown into conflict – her Confucian background, her devotion to her family, her anger that two complete strangers should presume to enter into her household, her physical revulsion to Donkey Chang, and her loyalty to her deceased husband and to her idea of chastity.

After Old Chang has accidentally drunk the poisoned soup intended by Donkey Chang for Mistress Ts'ai, Donkey Chang accuses Tou O of the murder and drags her to court. She submits to beating by the corrupt and muddle-headed magistrate, but when he threatens to beat her mother-in-law too, the filial Tou O makes a false confession and is condemned to death. Again, the lines sung by Tou O link the cosmic and human spheres, as in utter despair she accuses Heaven and Earth of having failed in their duty to maintain justice:

Even Heaven and Earth have come to fear the strong and oppress the weak.
They, after all, only push the boats following the current.
Oh Earth, as you fail to discriminate between good and evil,
    How can you function as Earth?
Oh Heaven, in mistaking the sage and the fool,
    You are called Heaven in vain!
(ll. 739-44)

Effective use of images such as these give the action greater significance and provide the channel through which cosmic forces begin to take part in the play as active agents.

When the laws of the human world break down, when lust and greed disrupt the human order, when corruption and stupidity rule the court and the whole human world falls to pieces, then cosmic powers take over. On the day of Tou O's execution, her final appeal to Heaven to prove her innocence takes the form of three wishes. First, that her blood fly upward to stain a white silk pennant, flying high above the execution ground; secondly, though it is midsummer, that three feet of snow fall to cover her corpse; and thirdly, that a three-year long drought visit the district.

Even as Tou O is singing,

The wandering clouds darken for my sake,
The mournful wind whirls on my behalf,

(ll. 885–6),

she is executed. To the amazement of all, snow starts to fall, and the blood of the innocent woman gushes upward, staining the white pennant. In the course of time the third wish is also fulfilled, and it is this last calamity which brings Tou O's father, now a high official, to the district. Upon re-examining the case, he brings justice to all, punishing the guilty and clearing the young widow's name.

In these and other verses, we have a portrait of Tou O – filial, chaste, and loyal to the Ts'ai family. Because the Yüan stage conventions require that singing in a play be rendered by only one performer, Tou O, as the center of the action, is seen going through the whole gamut of human emotions: grief, impatience, contempt, hatred, weariness, loneliness, determination, indignation, despair, hope, and relief. All these emotions are created by the playwright's greatly moving poetry. Much of what she says through poetry conveys her feelings to the hearts of the readers or spectators. The intensity of her feelings often radiates into images which are beyond what impassioned prose can sustain. Thus the authority and the force of fine poetry do much to create a really moving human being.

Injustice to Tou O also illustrates how the use of poetic imagery can significantly enlarge the scope of the play. Tou O's suffering, although seen on stage as an individual experience, points beyond the limit of her personal fate. The magnitude of the action is made clear through effective use of the cosmic images of Heaven and Earth, the snow, the long drought, and other supernatural forces. Here the events of one poor woman's life relate to the lives of all her fellow men. Behind the personal sufferings of Tou O stand the sufferings of countless defenseless common people. No longer is the maid merely fighting for her life; the conflict is not so much between her and her enemies, as between the powers of good and evil in this world. By means of these images, a helpless woman's affairs are transformed into powerful events and the play gains a remarkable universality.

The *ch'ü*, the verse form used in Yüan drama, has long been recognized for its lyrical beauty. *Ch'ü* were originally popular songs composed to musical tunes current in the Yüan period. Popular songs have traditionally provided the impetus for the development of important new poetic genres in Chinese literary history. For example, many of the poems in the *Book of Poetry* originated in folk songs from the early Chou period, while much of the great early lyric poetry from the Han and the following period of disunion reflects the themes, figures, and techniques of the popular ballad tradition. During the T'ang period, great poets looked to the tunes sung by singing girls, probably influenced by musical modes from Central Asia, for models offering more varied prosody and fresher expression, and this led to the development of *tz'u* 詞. As the Sung *tz'u* became more self-consciously 'literary', the desire to transcend the formal and stereotyped led to the rise of another genre. Under the occupation of Northern China by the Liao 遼 and Chin, and the eventual conquest by the Mongols, a great number of new tunes were introduced. Poets making use of this contemporary music composed lyrics which resulted in yet another form, the *ch'ü*.

In Chinese prosody, the tones of the syllables play an important role in meter and rhyme. In the make-up of the metrical patterns, in the *shih* and *tz'u*, generally a distinction is made only between the level (*p'ing*) tone and the other three (*shang, ch'ü, ju*) tones grouped together as the deflected tone. In the *ch'ü* verse form however, *p'ing, shang*, and *ch'ü* tones are conventionally distinguished in the make-up of metrical patterns.

The six possibilities in the choice of tones in a *ch'ü* song are as follows:

1. *p'ing* only: P
2. *shang* only: S
3. *ch'ü* only: C
4. *tse* (*shang* or *ch'ü*): T
5. *p'ing* or *shang*: P/S
6. *p'ing* or *tse* (any of the four tones): P/T

The meter and rhyme scheme of the songs written to the tune of 'Joy Under Heaven' (*T'ien-hsia le*) in the *Hsien-lü* mode, for example,

24

is as follows (see ll. 217-22 for lyrics).[1]

Tones of characters							Rhyme	Line
T/P	T	P	P	T	T	P	R	1
P/T	P	P	T	P			R	2
T	T	P/T	P	P	T	P	R	3
T	T	P					(R)	4
P	T	P/S					R	5
P	P	P	C	S			R	6

In this song there are thirty prescribed syllables in six lines of unequal lengths: 7, 5, 7, 3, 3, and 5 characters respectively. Rhyme in line 4 is optional, but in the remaining five lines rhyming is required.

Meter in *ch'ü* songs, as in T'ang and Sung poetry, is based on the tones of individual syllables, and the choice of tones in a *ch'ü* is influenced by the melody it adopts. The use of different tunes from a large number of music modes allows *ch'ü* songs an almost infinite variety of tonal arrangements, and over 500 meters have been preserved.

Prince Chu Ch'üan 朱權 of the early Ming dynasty collected in his *A Register of the Sounds of Universal Harmony* 335 songs with accompanying metrical patterns; this collection contains the earliest extant models. Later, several song registers of this nature appeared, of which the most comprehensive and well-known are *Pei tz'u kuang cheng p'u* 北詞廣正譜, *ca.* 1644, by Li Hsüan-yü 李玄玉, containing 445 songs and patterns; and *Ch'in ting ch'ü p'u* 欽定曲譜, 1715, by Wang

---

[1] The scansion is based on the meter analysis in Wang Li's *Chinese Poetics (Han-yü shih-lü hsüeh)*, p. 8o6. In Wang's symbols, the meter is as follows: 7B/ 5Y/ 7Y/ 3B3b/5H//. Wang Yü-chang 王玉章, in his study of base words in the *ch'ü* songs, regards line 2 here as of two lines of two- and three-character length (*Yüan t'zu chiao lü* 元詞斠律, [Shanghai, 1936], vol. **4**, pp. 72-3).

I-ch'ing 王奕清 and others.[1] These books of tonal patterns include individual songs (*hsiao ling* 小令), and songs from song-sequences (*t'ao-shu* 套數) and from plays. The meters are identified by the tune titles, which are unfailingly noted at the head of each piece. Metrical dexterity, effected by the myriad melodies of the Yüan times, remains an outstanding quality of the *ch'ü*.

Additional vivacity and freedom in the *ch'ü* genre come from the use of *ch'en-tzu* 襯字 – words inserted in addition to the prescribed syllables. *Ch'en-tzu*, a unique prosodic element of the *ch'ü*, is translatable as 'non-metric', 'extra-metric', 'padding', 'additional', or 'foil' words, although none of these meanings is quite equivalent to the original. With the insertion of 'extra-metric' words, the irregularity of the line length is further amplified. The following is the fourth lyric from Act I (ll. 217–22), written to the tune of 'Joy Under Heaven'. Besides the thirty prescribed characters, a number of 'extra-metric' words appeared, as italicized below:

Mò bú shì qián shì-*li* shāo-xiāng bú dào tóu,	1
Jīn *ye-bo* shēng zhāo huò-yóu?	2
Quàn jīn rén zǎo jiāng lái-shì xiū.	3
Wǒ jiāng zhè pó shì-yǎng.	4
Wǒ jiāng zhè fú-xiào shǒu,	5
Wǒ yán-cí xū yìng kǒu.[2]	6

These non-metric words, as is evident here, are predominantly colloquial expressions. The close interdependence of the words in a verse is such that the classical expressions are quick to take color from their colloquial companions and gain an immediate touch of spontaneity. The interpolation of 'extra-metric' words sometimes run as high as twenty syllables. The consequent transformation of the original lines is often striking. The Northern *ch'ü*, helped by the use of these extra-metric words, ranks above all other forms of Chinese poetry, except

1 Both books are from the Ch'ing dynasty. Of recent works, Wang Li's 王力 *Han-yü shih-lü hsüeh* 漢語詩律學 (Shanghai, 1962) is most thorough, containing 151 formulas for *ch'ü* tonal patterns and rhyme schemes. Lo K'ang-lieh's 羅康烈 *Pei hsiao-ling wen-tzu p'u* 北小令文字譜 (Hong Kong, 1962), and Lo Chin-t'ang's 羅錦堂 *Pei ch'ü hsiao-ling p'u* 北曲小令譜 (Hong Kong, 1964), both give descriptions of individual song forms with notations of the number of characters and lines, the rhyme scheme, tonal patterns, comments, and illustrations.
2 Tones of five characters do not agree with Wang Li's meter (*bú* in line 1, *jīn rén* in line 3, and *pó* and *yǎng* in line 4). The variation could be because of the freedom the Yüan poets frequently asserted in the handling of poetic components within a framework of carefully defined form. Dale Johnson explains the many variations that occur within the structure of the lines in a *ch'ü* as a development of a system of mutation. ('The Prosody of Yüan Drama', *T'oung Pao*, vol. LVI, [1970], 96-146.)

modern vernacular verse, in irregularity in the length of lines and rhythm, and in its consequent approximation to living speech.

Rhymes in *ch'ü* occur far more frequently than in T'ang and Sung poetry. In the T'ang *shih*, usually only the even lines use rhymes, and in the Sung *tz'u*, rhymes occur at irregular intervals. In the *ch'ü*, however, almost every line ends in a rhyme. The use of a single rhyme throughout a poem has long been a favorite with Chinese poets, but the use of one rhyme within an act of a play, engaging sometimes up to two hundred words of the same rhyme, is unique with the *ch'ü*. In the song, 'Joy Under Heaven', quoted above, five words of the same rhyme (*tóu, yóu, xiū, shǒu, kǒu*) are used in a total of six lines. In the first song in Act I, written to the tune of 'Painting Lips Red', for example, all five lines end in rhyme words: *chóu, shóu, fǒu, yóu, shòu*. These rhyme words belong to group sixteen, called the '*yu-hou*' (尤侯) rhyme group, in the *CYYY*. Since its appearance, the *CYYY* has been the orthodox guide book for technique in the Northern *ch'ü* rhymes.

The vitality of *ch'ü* poetry is easily seen in its use of arresting poetical images; the new way it found of using the Chinese language, with its large number of fresh colloquial expressions; and the hitherto unrecorded combination of sound and sense introduced by the novel music of the time.

The music

Yüan drama is inseparably associated with music. Not only do songs written to current tunes appear in every act, but music also provides a Yüan play with an overall structure. To make a combination of various arts – songs, prose-speech, storytelling, acting, singing, dancing, and acrobatic feats – into a workable and artistic product, a framework must be provided to give the diverse arts free play, allowing exploitation of the aesthetic power and effect of each. In a Yüan play, such a framework is largely supplied by its music.

The lack of surviving music scores of the Yüan plays is a serious problem in the study of their music.[1] However, much can still be learned from a careful assessment of available evidence. The names of music modes used in the plays, titles of tunes composed in these modes, and surviving printed texts of the lyrics are invaluable material.

[1] The earliest extant collections of music notation, published in the Ch'ing dynasty, are notably the following: *Chiu kung ta ch'eng nan pei tz'u kung p'u* 九宮大成南北詞 宮譜, first published in 1746, the largest repository of what purports to be Sung *tz'u, chu-kung tiao, san ch'ü* and *tsa-chü* music; *Na-shu-ying ch'ü p'u* 納書楹曲譜, published in 1784 and 1795.

Stage directions and dialogue also give indications of the habits and conventions governing the use of vocal and instrumental music. Even brief notations, such as 'so-and-so sings', are informative, because they indicate the unique practice of limiting the singing to one actor or actress in a single play. Besides the internal evidence in the plays themselves, accounts and treatises around the Yüan period also serve as sources of information.[1]

The music modes used in extant Yüan plays total ten, and are known by their traditional popular names:

Cheng-kung	正宮
Chung-lü	中呂
Hsien-lü kung	仙呂宮
Huang-chung kung	黃鐘宮
Nan-lü	南呂
Shang-tiao	商調
Shuang-tiao	雙調
Ta-shih tiao	大石調
Yüeh tiao	越調
Pan-she tiao[2]	般涉調

Chou Te-ch'ing, in his *CYYY*, names an additional two modes as follows:

Hsiao-shih tiao	小石調
Shang-chüeh tiao	商角調

Here in *Injustice to Tou O*, four musical modes are used. The *Hsien-lü* mode is used in both the prologue and first act, which contain one and nine songs respectively. *Nan-lü*, *Cheng-kung*, and *Shuang-tiao* modes are used in the following three acts, which contain respectively, eleven, ten, and ten songs with their tune titles as follows:

Prelude: *Hsien-lü* Mode 仙呂
      'Enjoying Flowers Season' 賞花時
Act I   *Hsien-lü* Mode: 仙呂
      'Painting Lips Red' 點絳唇
      'Roiling River Dragon' 混江龍
      'Oil Gourd' 油葫蘆
      'Joy Under Heaven' 天下樂
      'One Half' 一半兒
      'Backyard Flowers' 後庭花
      'Green Parrot' 青哥兒
      'Parasite Grass' 寄生草
      'Coda' 賺煞

1 See Fu Hsi-hua 傅希華, *Ku-tien hsi-ch'ü sheng yüeh lun-chu ts'ung-pien* 古典戲曲聲樂論著叢編, (Peking, 1957).
2 This mode is used rarely in Yüan drama.

Act II	*Nan-lü* Mode: 南呂
	'One Twig of Blossoms' 一枝花
	'Liang-chou No. Seven' 梁州第七
	'Separate Tail' 隔尾
	'Congratulating the Bridegroom' 賀新郎
	'Fighting Frogs' 鬥蝦蟆
	'Separate Tail' 隔尾
	'Pasturing-Sheep Pass' 牧羊關
	'Scold Jade-man' 罵玉郎
	'Thanking Imperial Favor' 感皇恩
	'Picking Tea Song' 採茶歌
	'Yellow-bell Coda' 黃鍾尾
Act III	*Cheng-kung* Mode 正宮
	'Proper and Good' 端正好
	'Rolling An Embroidered Ball' 滾繡球
	'Surprised Scholar' 倘秀才
	'Chattering Song' 叨叨令
	'Happy Three' 快活三
	'Old Man Pao' 鮑老兒
	'Playing Dolls' 耍孩兒
	'Secondary Coda' 二煞
	'Penultimate Coda' 一煞
	'Coda' 煞尾
Act IV	*Shuang-tiao* Mode 雙調
	'New Water Song' 新水令
	'Intoxicated in the East Wind' 沉醉東風
	'Lofty Sign' 喬牌兒
	'A Wild Goose Descends' 鴈兒落
	'Victory Song' 得勝令
	'Stream Stirs Oar' 川撥棹
	'Seven Brothers' 七弟兄
	'Plum Blossom Wine' 梅花酒
	'Recovering The South of The River' 收江南
	'Mandarin-Ducks Coda' 鴛鴦煞尾

The emotional quality of the modes was expounded by Yen-nan Chih An 燕南芝菴 of the early Yüan period, in his 'Discourse on Singing' (*Ch'ang lun* 唱論). In succinct, four-character phrases, he comments on the modes as follows:[1]

Cheng kung: sorrowful and powerful (*ch'ou-chang hsiung-chuang* 惆悵雄壯)
Chung-lü: abrupt and elusive (*kao-hsia shan-chuan* 高下閃賺)
Hsien-lü kung: refreshing and soft (*ch'ing-hsin mien-miao* 清新綿邈)
Huang-chung: rich and luxurious (*fu-kuei ch'an mien* 富貴纏綿)
Nan-lü: wistful and sad (*kan t'an shang-pei* 感嘆傷悲)
Shang tiao: sorrowful and longing (*ch'i-ch'ang yüan-mu* 悽愴怨慕)
Shuang tiao: energetic and brisk (*chien-chieh chi-niao* 健捷激裊)
Ta-shih tiao: romantic and suggestive (*feng-liu wen-chi* 風流醞藉)

[1] In *Chung-kuo ku-tien hsi-ch'ü lun-chu chi-cheng* series, (Peking, 1959), vol I, pp. 160-1.

Yüeh tiao: sarcastic and cynical (*t'ao-hsieh leng-hsiao* 陶 寫 冷 笑)
Hsiao-shih tiao: lovely and flirtatious (*i-ni fu-mei* 旖 旎 嫵 媚)
Pan-she tiao: sharp and staccato (*shih-to k'eng-ch'ien* 拾 掇 坑 塹)
Shang-chüeh tiao: grievous and melodious (*pei-shang wan-chuan* 悲 傷 宛 轉)

Music with such emotional significance and appeal would naturally be used to heighten dramatic effects; to intensify the impact of the language; to create an atmosphere for an occasion, be it serious or relaxed; to delineate a setting, be it romantic or solemn; to portray a character, be he comic or dignified; or to forward an action, be it slow or swift. Because in a Yüan play only one musical mode is used in an entire act, an inconsistency between the music and words in certain scenes is sometimes unavoidable, but the overall effect created by a certain music mode in one act can still be significant.

An examination of the extant plays reveals a tendency to use certain musical modes in certain acts. The *Hsien-lü* mode is used in the first act in 168 out of the total of 171 plays. The *Shuang-tiao* mode appears in the last act of 121 plays. In the middle acts, *Chung-lü* and *Cheng-kung* are the most popular. While *Cheng-kung* appears 44 times in the second act and 34 times in the third, and totals 94 times in all four acts, *Chung-lü* appears 31 times in the second act and 53 times in the third, and totals 103 times in the four acts.[1] A preference for a certain musical mode for each of the four acts is thus quite evident. The almost exclusive use of *Hsien-lü*, with its 'refreshing and soft' nature, in the initial act, when people and events are generally introduced, and the predominant use of *Shuang-tiao* with its 'energetic and brisk' nature, in the last act, when events are reaching their climax, indicate a relevancy of music to dramatic effects. In *Injustice to Tou O*, the use of *Nan-lü* mode of a 'wistful and sad' nature in Act II, and of *Cheng-kung* mode of a 'sorrowful and powerful' nature in Act III, further points to this relevancy.

The division of acts in a Yüan play is based on its music, as well as on its action. In each act, songs are written to the music of one mode. The plot of a Yüan play, because of its sequential approach, tends to be episodic. The four-act pattern, with each act built on the music of a single mode, gives the play an added sense of structural unity.[2]

1 See Ts'ai Ying 蔡 瑩, *Yüan chü lien-t'ao shu-li* (元 劇 聯 套 述 例 *On the Sequence of the Arias in Yüan drama*), (Shanghai, 1933); Hugh Stimson, 'Song Arrangements in Shianleu Acts of Yuan Tzarjiuh', *Tsing Hua Journal of Chinese Studies*, New Series v, no. 1 (July 1965), 86-106.
2 The *ta-ch'ü* (大 曲 'Big songs') in the T'ang dynasty, and the 'Medley' in the Chin-Yüan period also use only one music mode in one song-sequence.

The popularity of *Injustice to Tou O* is easy to understand; it is a marvelous variety show. To begin with, there is the heart-rending separation of a poor scholar and his orphaned daughter. Then in rapid succession come the attempted strangling of an old woman money-lender, the appearance of two rascals boisterously demanding the widows' hands, the murder of a father, the trial and torture in court, the execution of an innocent woman, and the spectacular intervention of supernatural forces, as the blood of a wronged woman unnaturally flows upward, snow falls in midsummer, and a long drought strikes the land. The play ends with the eventual reappearance of the erstwhile poor scholar, now turned powerful Imperial Commissioner, the visit of his daughter's woeful ghost, and another court trial leading to final justice for all. These scenes, some appealing, some interesting, and some startling, offer a feast of excitement strong enough to satisfy the run-of-the-mill theatre-goers of any age, while the eloquent poetry further provides an added treat for the sophisticated.

PART TWO

TOU O YÜAN

SYMBOLS AND ABBREVIATIONS

( ) To enclose symbols in the interlinear translation, and stage direction and names of aria-tunes in the Chinese text.

(–) To indicate untranslated character.

[ ] For added words.

/ To indicate parallel or co-ordinate elements.

§ For notes on textual differences between *Yüan ch'ü hsüan* and *Ku ming-chia pen*. See p. xiv and §2, p. 37.

* Symbols in the Glossary indicating more detailed notes in the main text.

† Symbols indicating cited works in the Bibliography which are not specifically related to the subject of Old Mandarin.

C	Directional complement
CKKTHCLCCC	*Chung-kuo ku-tien hsi-ch'ü lun-chu chi-ch'eng* 中國古典戲曲論著集成
CYYY	*Chung-yüan yin yün* 中原音韻
HJAS	*Harvard Journal of Asiatic Studies*
KMCP	*Ku ming-chia pen* 古名家本
KPHCTK	*Ku pen hsi-ch'ü ts'ung-k'an* 古本戲曲叢刊
l.	line
L	locative
M	measure word
n.	note
P	particle
Pl	plural suffix
Pr	pretransitive
SPPY	*Ssu-pu pei-yao* 四部備要
SPTK	*Ssu-pu ts'ung-k'an* 四部叢刊 (in the case of standard histories, references are to *SPTK Po-na* 百衲 edition)
YCH	*Yüan ch'ü hsüan* 元曲選

Caption in the upper righthand corner: 'Arousing Heaven and Stirring Earth is Tou O's Injustice' (which is both the title of the play and the concluding line of the text). From *Yüan ch'ü hsüan*, 1616; courtesy of the Syndics of the Cambridge University Library.

DRAMATIS PERSONAE[1]

(listed in the order of their appearance)

蔡婆婆 MISTRESS TS'AI, a widow

竇天章 TOU T'IEN-CHANG, a poor scholar, later a surveillance commissioner

竇娥 (端雲) TOU O (Tuan-yün) Tou T'ien-chang's daughter.

賽盧醫 DOCTOR LU

孛老 OLD CHANG

張驢兒 DONKEY CHANG, Old Chang's son

桃杌 PREFECT T'AO WU

祗候 ATTENDANT to a magistrate

監斬官 THE OFFICER in charge of executions

公人 YAMEN RUNNERS

劊子 EXECUTIONER

張千 CHANG CH'IEN, attendant to Tou T'ien-chang

州官 MAGISTRATE succeeding T'ao Wu

解子 THE GUARD escorting prisoners

---

1 The *Dramatis Personae*, as is the convention of traditional Chinese drama, is absent in the Chinese text.

感天動地竇娥冤雜劇

1
Gǎn tiān dòng dì Dòu É yuān zá-jù
'Arousing Heaven Stirring Earth
[Is] Tou O's Injustice' Play

元大都關漢卿撰

2
Yuán Dà-dū Guān Hàn-qing zhuàn
Yüan Ta-tu Kuan Han-ch'ing Composed

楔子
3
Xiē-zi
Wedge

（卜兒蔡婆上詩云）花有重
4
(Bǔ-er Cài Pó shàng. Shī yún:) Huā yǒu chóng-
(Old-woman Ts'ai dame enters. [In] verse says:) 'Flowers have
re-

開日人無再少年不須長
5
kāi rì, rén wú zài shào nián. Bù xū cháng
opening day; people have-not again young years. No need-to
always

AROUSING HEAVEN STIRRING EARTH IS TOU O'S INJUSTICE

Kuan Han-ch'ing of Ta-tu in the Yüan Dynasty

PROLOGUE

(Enter the old woman Mistress Ts'ai.)

TS'AI (recites):

Flowers will bloom again,
But men may never regain their youth.
One need not always be rich and noble;

1] *Găn tiān dòng dì Dòu É yuān* is also the first line of the couplet at the end of the play. A Yüan play conventionally concludes with two or four seven-character lines, generally summing up the story of the play. One of the lines usually appears also as the full title of the play.

    zá-jù: the Yüan plays presumably borrowed the name from the Sung dynasty four-act 'Variety Play' (*zá-jù*), a term no longer fitting for a play based on a plot.

2] In the *Yüan ch'ü hsüan* text, the editor's name and identity are given after the playwright's, as follows: *Ming Wu-hsing Tsang Chin-shu chiao* 明吳興臧晉叔校

3] *Xiē-zi*: this term, borrowed from carpentry, is used in the Yüan drama as a prologue or interlude. It has only one or two songs in it, unlike a regular act, which has a *tào-shù* (套數 song-sequence) See Sun K'ai-ti 孫楷第, *Ts'ang-chou chi* 滄州集, pp. 321-4.

4] *Bŭ-er*: in Yüan drama, *bŭ-er* denotes 'the old woman'. The origin of this term is not clear. In Sung-Yüan times, the abbreviated form for *niáng* 娘, 'woman', is 奵 or 卜 (Ku Chao-ts'ang 顧肇倉, *Yüan jen tsa-chü hsüan* 元人雜劇選, p. 6, note 3). Wang Kuo-wei 王國維 asserts that *bŭ-er*, like *bó-lăo* 孛老, 'the old man' role, and *bāng-lăo* 邦老, 'the role for playing robbers and thieves', is a derivative from the term *bāo lăo* 鮑老, ('*Ku chü chiao-se k'ao*' 古劇脚色考 in *Hai-ning Wang Ching-an hsien-sheng i shu* 海寧王靜安先生遺書, Ch'ang-sha, 1940, vol. 45, p. 8*b*); he also points out that *bŭ-er* may be a variant of *băo* 鴇, which is listed as a role type in *T'ai-ho cheng-yin p'u* 太和正音譜 (*ibid.*). Since no interpretation is conclusive, I here follow the modern reading of the character *bŭ*.

§2] *Dà-dū*: not in *Ku ming-chia pen* 古名家本 (hereafter referred to as *KMCP*). The *KMCP* used here is a photo-reprint of the copy in the *Mo-wang kuan ch'ao-chiao pen ku chin tsa-chü* 脉望館鈔校本古今雜劇 collection, included in the *Ku pen hsi-ch'ü ts'ung-k'an ssu chi* 古本戲曲叢刊四集 (*KPHCTK*), Shanghai, 1958, vol. 16.

§3] *Xiē-zi*: *Dì-yī chū* 第一齣 in *KMCP*, .p. 1*a*.

§4] *Bŭ-er...shàng*: *chōng-mò bàn bŭ-er shàng* 冲末扮卜兒上 in *KMCP*, p. 1*a*. Here is evidence of a man playing the role of an old woman in the Yüan period, a practice which persists in the Chinese classical theatre today.

    Shī yún: not in *KMCP* (same omission in ll. 26, 367, etc.)

§5–6] *Bù xū...shén-xian*: not in *KMCP*.

富貴安樂是神仙老身蔡

6 *fù guì, ān lè shì shén-xian. Lǎo-shēn Cài*
be-rich/noble; to-be-peaceful/happy is-to-be immortals. Old-self Ts'ai

婆婆是也楚州人氏嫡親

7 *Pó-po shì yě. Chū-zhōu rén-shì. Dí-qīn*
P'o-p'o is (P). Ch'u-chou native. Directly-related [are]

三口兒家屬不幸夫主亡

8 *sān kǒu-er jiā-shǔ. Bú-xìng fū-zhǔ wáng-*
three (M) family-members. Unfortunately husband passed-

逝已過止有一箇孩兒年

9 *shì yǐ-guò, zhǐ yǒu yí ge hái-er, nián*
away already. Only have one (M) child, age

長八歲俺娘兒兩箇過其

10 *zhǎng bá suì. Ǎn niáng ér liǎng gè guò qí*
has-grown-to-be eight years. We mother/child two (M) pass the

日月家中頗有些錢財這

11 *rì yuè. Jiā zhōng pō yǒu xiē qián-cái. Zhè-*
days/months. Family (L) fairly has some money. Hereabout

裏一箇竇秀才從去年間

12 *li yí ge Dòu xiù-cai, cóng qù-nián wèn*
(L) one (M) Tou scholar since last-year from

我借了二十兩銀子如今

13 *wǒ jiè-le èr-shí liǎng yín-zi. Rú-jīn*
me borrowed (P) twenty taels silver. As-of-now

本利該銀四十兩我數次

14 *běn-lì gāi yín sì-shí liǎng. Wǒ shù cì*
[in] capital/interest owes silver forty taels. I several times

To have peace and happiness is to be like the immortals.

I am Mistress Ts'ai, a native of Ch'u-chou. There were three of us in the family. Unfortunately my husband passed away some time ago, and I have only this one child, who is now eight years old. We two, mother and son, live together and are fairly well off. Hereabouts is a Scholar Tou, who last year borrowed twenty taels of silver from me, and now owes forty taels in capital and interest. I have asked several times for the money. But Scholar Tou only claimed that he was

6] *Lǎo-shēn*: a humble way for an old woman to refer to herself. *Shēn* is used in the sense of 'self'; cf. *Shēn shì Zhāng Yì-dé yě, kě lái gòng jué sǐ* 身是張益德也，可來 共決死 (Biography of Chang Fei in *San-kuo chih* 三國志, *History of The Three Kingdoms*, Po-na 百衲 ed., *chüan* 36, p. 4*b*).

7] *Pó-po*: literally 'mother-in-law'; generally used as a courteous address to an old woman.

　　yě: a particle (see pp. 15–16).

　　rén-shì: a native of, a resident of (cf. l. 146).

8] *kǒu-er*: *kǒu*, literally 'mouth', is here used as a measure word.

12] *xiù-cai*: in the T'ang dynasty, *xiù-cai* was a degree for one who passed a state examination. The term became generalized in Sung-Yüan times, when it referred to a scholar, or a candidate for a state examination (Morohashi, *Dai Kanwa Jiten*, VIII: 24911 : 44).

13] *liǎng*: a Chinese unit of weight, which is slightly more than an English ounce.

§11–12] *Zhè-li: Zhè Shān-yáng jùn* 這 山陽郡 in *KMCP*, p. 1*a*.

§13] *èr-shí liǎng: wǔ liǎng* 五兩 in *KMCP*, p. 1*a*. (same difference in l. 39).

§14] *sì-shí liǎng: shí liǎng* 十兩 in *KMCP*, p. 1*a* (same difference in ll. 19–20, 41, 66)

索取那竇秀才只說貧難

15 *suǒ-qǔ. Nà Dòu xiù-cai zhǐ shuō pín-nàn,*
demanded [it]. That Tou scholar just said poor, in-difficulty,

沒得還我他有一箇女兒

16 *méi-de huán wǒ. Tā yǒu yí ge nǚ-er*
had-nothing to-repay me. He has a (M) daughter,

今年七歲生得可喜長得

17 *jīn nián qí suì. Shēng-de kě-xǐ, zhǎng-de*
this year seven years-old. Was-born (P) likeable; grew (P)

可愛我有心看上他與我

18 *kě-ài. Wǒ yǒu xīn kàn-shang tā, yǔ wǒ*
lovable. I have mind to-approve her for my

家做箇媳婦就准了這四

19 *jiā zuò ge xí-fu. Jiù zhǔn-le zhè sì-*
family to-be [a] (M) daughter-in-law. Then let-go (P) this forty

十兩銀子豈不兩得其便

20 *shí liǎng yín-zi. Qǐ-bù liǎng dé qí biàn?*
taels silver. Isn't-it 'both-sides obtaining the benefits'?

他說今日好日辰親送女

21 *Tā shuō jīn-rì hǎo rì-chén. Qīn sòng nǚ-*
He said today good day/time. Personally send daughter

兒到我家來老身且不索

22 *er dào wǒ jiā lái. Lǎo-shēn qiě bù suǒ*
to my house (C). Old-self meanwhile not to-collect

錢·去專在家中等候這早

23 *qián qù, zhuān zài jiā zhōng děng-hòu. Zhè zǎo-*
money go; specifically at home (L) wait. This time

晚竇秀才敢待來也（冲末 ·

24 *wǎn Dòu xiù-cai gǎn-dài lái yě. (Chōng-mò*
Tou scholar most-likely will-be-coming (P).' (Supporting male-
role

40

poor and unable to pay. He has a daughter, who is seven this year. She was born cute and has grown to be lovely. I have a mind to make her my daughter-in-law. Then I would cancel the forty taels of silver. Isn't it a case of 'both sides getting some benefit out of it'? He has said that today is an auspicious day and he would bring his daughter to me in person. I shall not, for the time being, go out to collect from my debtors, but wait for them at home. Now Scholar Tou must soon arrive.

(The supporting actor impersonating Tou T'ien-chang, guiding the

17] *Shĕng-de*: *de* is a particle, which with a resultative complement forms a descriptive complement (Y.R. Chao & L.S. Yang, *Concise Dictionary of Spoken Chinese*, Cambridge, Mass., 1947, p. 78).

19] *zhŭn*: to grant; to compound for a money payment by an equivalent.

20] *Qĭ-bù*: 'isn't it. . .?'; a rhetorical question in negative form expecting a positive answer.

23-4] *zăo-wăn*: literally 'early/late', an idiom for 'time' or 'soon'. (See Chang Hsiang 張相, *Shih tz'u ch'ü yü tz'u-tien* 詩詞曲語辭典 Taipei edition, 1957, p. 176; Chu Chü-i 朱居易, *Yüan chü su-yü fang-yen li-shih* 元劇俗語方言例釋, Shanghai, 1956, p. 114; Lu Tan-an 陸澹安, *Hsiao-shuo tz'u-yü hui-shih* 小說詞語滙釋, Peking, 1964, pp. 208-9. These books and Hsü Chia-jui's 徐嘉瑞 *Chin Yüan hsi-ch'ü fang-yen k'ao* 金元戲曲方言考, Shanghai, 1956, are very useful in their many citations of comparable unfamiliar usages from Yüan drama and other poetic works.)

24] *găn-dài*: most likely.

Chŏng mò: a supporting male role (see p. 6 above).

§15-16] *Nà Dòu xiù-cai. . . huán wŏ: Tā duì-fù bù-qĭ* 他兌付不起 in *KMCP*, p. 1a.

§17-18] *jĭn nián. . . kĕ-ài*: not in *KMCP*.

§20] *Qĭ-bù. . . biàn*: not in *KMCP*.

§24] *Dòu xiù-cai*: *Dòu xiăn-sheng* 竇先生, in *KMCP*, p. 1b.

§24-5] *Chŏng-mò bàn*: not in *KMCP*.

41

扮竇天章引正旦扮端雲

25 bàn Dòu Tiān-zhāng yǐn zhèng dàn bàn Duān-yún
impersonating Tou T'ien-chang leading principal female-role
impersonating Tuan-yün

上詩云）讀盡縹緗萬卷書

26 shàng. Shi yún:) Dú jìn piǎo xiāng wàn juàn shū,
enters. [In] verse says:) 'Having-read through blue-silk/light-
yellow-silk ten-thousand volumes (M) [of] books,

可憐貧殺馬相如漢庭一

27 kě-lián pín shā Mǎ Xiàng-rú. Hàn tíng yí
pitiable [is] poor extremely Ma Hsiang-ju. [To the] Han court
one

日承恩召不說當罏說子

28 rì chéng ēn zhāo, bù shuō dāng lú shuō Zǐ
day [he] received gracious summons, no-more spoke-of being-
in-the-presence-of wine-jars, [but] spoke-of "Master

虛小生姓竇名天章祖貫

29 Xū. Xiǎo shēng xìng Dòu, míng Tiān-zhāng. Zǔ-guàn
Fantasy." Insignificant person's surname [is] Tou, given-name,
T'ien-chang. Ancestral-domicile [being at]

長安京兆人也幼習儒業

30 Cháng-ān Jing-zhào rén yě. Yòu xí rú yè,
Ch'ang-an Ching-chao person (P). In-childhood learned Confucian studies,

飽有文章爭奈時運不通

31 bǎo yǒu wén-zhāng. Zhēng-nài shí-yùn bù tōng,
fully possesses literary-learning. What-to-do: time/fate not
propitious,

功名未遂不幸渾家亡化

32 gōng míng wèi suí. Bú-xìng hún-jiā wáng-huà
achievement/fame have-not attained. Unfortunately, wife
passed-away

已過撇下這個女孩兒小

33 yǐ-guò, piē-xià zhè-ge nǚ-hái-er, xiǎo
already; left-behind (C) this (M) girl, humble

female lead impersonating Tuan-yün, enters.)

TOU (recites):

Having read ten thousand books of great profundity,
Ssu-ma Hsiang-ju still remained as poor as he could be.
When the Emperor summoned him to the court of Han one day,
He spoke no more of wine but of his 'Master Fantasy'.

My family name is Tou, and my given name is T'ien-chang.
My ancestral home is in the Ching-chao District of Ch'ang-an.
I have studied the classics since childhood and have learned
a great deal. However, the times have not been favorable,
and fame has not yet come to me. Unfortunately too, my
wife has died, leaving me this daughter, whose name is Tuan-yün.

25] *bàn*: in the make-up of; 'impersonating'.
   zhèng dàn: female lead (see p. 6).
26] *piǎo xiāng*: *piǎo* is a blue silk and *xiāng* is light yellow silk. *Piǎo-xiāng* is used to
   denote 'valuable books', because formerly bright silk was used to wrap books or
   scrolls.
26–9] This poem shows Tou's hope to rise in a similar way from obscurity to literary
   eminence.
27] *shā*: same as *shà* 煞, 'exceedingly'.
   Mǎ Xiàng-rú: an abridged form of '*Sī-mǎ Xiàng-rú*'.
28] *lú*: *lú* is a place where wine is stored and sold; it is built in the shape of a forge with
   mud walls on the sides (annotation by Wei Chao 韋昭, *Shih chi* [史記 *Historical
   Records*, *Po-na* ed.], *chüan* 117, p. 2*b*).
28–9] '*Zǐ Xū*': abbreviated title of '*Zǐ Xū fù*' ('Master Fantasy'), a *fù* (賦 prose-
   poem) by Sī-mǎ Xiàng-rú (179–117 B.C.), a native of Chéng-dū 成都.
   While playing lute at the house of the rich and powerful Zhuó Wáng-sūn 卓
   王孫, of Lín-qióng 臨邛, he aroused the interest of Zhuó's daughter, widowed
   Wén-jūn 文君. She eloped with him to Chéng-dū, only to find that his home
   consisted of 'four bare walls'. Because of need, they operated a small tavern,
   where Wén-jūn sold wine while Sī-mǎ did the cleaning and other menial
   work. When Emperor Wǔ of Han read Sī-mǎ Xiàng-rú's '*Zǐ Xū fù*', he was
   impressed by the writer's talent and later summoned him to court and bestowed
   upon him great honor.
29] *Xiǎo-shēng*: a traditional humble way for a young man to refer to himself.
   Zǔ-guàn: 'ancestral domicile'; 'one's original domicile'.
30] *Cháng-ān*: several times the capital in ancient China.
   Jīng-zhào: a district of Cháng-ān.
32] *hún-jiā*: originally meaning 'whole family', this term later is used also in the sense
   of 'wife'; cf. l. 162 (see Sun K'ai-ti, *Ts'ang-chou chi*, p. 613).

§25–6] *zhèng dàn bàn Duān-yún*: *bǎo-er* 保兒 in *KMCP*, p. 1*b*.
§26–9] *Dú jìn*... *Zǐ Xū*: *Fù zhōng xiǎo jìn shì-jiān shì, mìng lǐ bù-rú tiān-xià rén* 腹中
   曉盡世間事,命裡不如天下人 in *KMCP*, p. 1*b*.
§31–2] *bǎo yǒu*... *wèi suī*: *Pō kàn shī shū. Xiǎo-shēng wèi céng jìn-qǔ gōng-míng* 頗看詩書
   小生未曾進取功名 in *KMCP*, p. 1*b*.

字 端 雲 從 三 歲 上 亡 了 他

34   *zì Duān-yún. Cóng sān-suì-shàng wáng-le tā*

name [is] Tuan-yün. Since three years-old (L) lost (P) her

母 親 如 今 孩 兒 七 歲 了 也

35   *mǔ-qin, rú-jin hái-er qí suì le yě.*

mother; now child seven years-old (P) (P).

小 生 一 貧 如 洗 流 落 在 這

36   *Xiǎo shēng yì pín rú xǐ, liú-luò zài zhè*

Insignificant person completely poor as-if scoured, drifted to this

楚 州 居 住 此 間 一 箇 蔡 婆

37   *Chǔ-zhōu jū-zhù. Cǐ-jiān yí ge Cài Pó-*

Ch'u-chou to-live. Hereabout (L) a (M) Ts'ai *p'o-*

婆 他 家 廣 有 錢 物 小 生 因

38   *po, tā jiā guǎng yǒu qián-wù. Xiǎo shēng yīn*

p'o, her family much has money/things. Insignificant person because

無 盤 纏 曾 借 了 他 二 十 兩

39   *wú pán-chan, céng jiè-le tā èr-shí liǎng*

had-no traveling-expense, once borrowed (P) [from] her twenty taels

銀 子 到 今 本 利 該 對 還 他

40   *yín-zi. Dào jīn běn-lì gāi duì-huán tā*

silver. Up-to now capital/interest should in-double-amount-repay her

四 十 兩 他 數 次 問 小 生 索

41   *sì-shí liǎng. Tā shù cì wèn xiǎo shēng suǒ-*

forty taels. She several times from insignificant person demanded [it].

取 教 我 把 甚 麽 還 他 誰 想

42   *qǔ. Jiào wǒ bǎ shém-me huán tā? Shéi xiǎng*

Ask me take what to-repay her? Who expected

蔡 婆 婆 常 常 着 人 來 說 要

43   *Cài Pó-po cháng-cháng zháo rén lái shuō yào*

Ts'ai P'o-p'o often had people come to-say wanting

She lost her mother when she was three and now she is seven. I am as poor as if I had been scoured; now I have drifted aimlessly here to Ch'u-chou to live. Around here is a Mistress Ts'ai, who is quite well off. Lacking traveling money, I once borrowed from her twenty taels of silver. Now I should repay her forty taels including interest. She has asked for the money several times, but with what am I supposed to pay her back? Who would have thought that she would often send people over to say that she wants my daughter to

36] *yì pín rú xǐ:* 'as completely poor as if washed' – poor as though everything was washed away; cf. English expression, 'cleaned out'.
40] *duì-huán: duì běn duì lì de huán* 對 本 對 利 的 還, pay double the amount, with the interest same as the principal.
43] *zháo:* 'zháo' is used in many ways in Old Mandarin; here it means 'to order', 'to send'. For other uses, see Glossary.

§36–7] *liú-luò. . . jū-zhù: jīn zài zhè Chǔ-zhōu Shān-yáng jùn zhù-zuò* 今 在 這 楚 州 山 陽 郡 住 坐 in *KMCP*, p. 1*b*.
§38] *tā jiā. . . qián-wù: Zǐ mǔ èr rén guò-rì, zhè pó-po yǒu xiē qián-wù* 子 母 二 人 過 日 這 婆 婆 有 些 錢 物 in *KMCP*, p. 1*b*.

小生女孩兒做他兒媳婦

44 *xiǎo shēng nǔ-hái-er zuò tā ér xí-fu?*

insignificant person's daughter to-be her son's wife?

況如今春榜動選場開正

45 *Kuàng rú-jīn chūn bǎng dòng; xuǎn chǎng kāi. Zhèng*

Moreover, now spring list begins; examination ground opens. Just

待上朝取應又苦盤纏缺

46 *dài shàng cháo qǔ-yìng. Yòu kǔ pán-chan quē-*

about to-go-up to-court to-take-examination. Again suffer-from traveling-expense insufficiency.

少小生出於無奈只得將

47 *shǎo. Xiǎo shēng chū-yú wú-nài, zhǐ dé jiāng*

Insignificant person out-of no-other-way, only can (Pr)

女孩兒端雲送與蔡婆婆

48 *nǔ-hái-er Duān-yún sòng yǔ Cài Pó-po*

daughter Tuan-yün send to Ts'ai *P'o-p'o*

做兒媳婦去（做歎科云）嗨

49 *zuò ér-xí-fu qù. (Zuò tàn kē yún:) Hài!*

to-be daughter-in-law (C).' (Performs sighing gesture, says:) 'Hai!

這箇那裏是做媳婦分明

50 *Zhè-ge nǎ-lǐ shì zuò xí-fu? Fēn-míng*

This (M) how is to-be daughter-in-law? Clearly

是賣與他一般就准了他

51 *shì mài yǔ tā yì-bān. Jiù zhǔn-le tā*

is selling to her like. Just to-settle (P) she

那先借的四十兩銀子分

52 *nà xiān jiè-de sì-shí liǎng yín-zi; fèn-*

that formerly lent (P) forty taels silver; in-addition,

外但得些少東西勾小生

53 *wài dàn dé xiē-shǎo dōng-xi, gòu xiǎo shēng*

only receive some-few things, enough-for insignificant person's be her daughter-in-law? Since the spring examinations will soon start, I should be going to the capital. However, I have no traveling money. I have no other choice; I just have to send my daughter Tuan-yün to Mistress Ts'ai to be her future daughter-in-law. (He sighs.) Hai! How can one say that this is marrying her off to be a daughter-in-law? It is clearly the same as selling the child to her. If Mistress Ts'ai would cancel the forty taels she has lent me, and if I can get a little something extra for my expenses while taking the examination,

44] *ér-xí-fu:* in the old Chinese society, it was customary for a family to take in a girl, usually from a poor family, to be a future daughter-in-law. Before marriage, she was generally referred to as *túng yǎng xí* 童養媳, 'child-daughter-in-law', but here Tou O is referred to simply as 'daughter-in-law'.
45] *bǎng:* name list, a list of successful candidates in the examinations.
   chūn. . . kāi: the examinations are about to take place in the spring. Formerly, the examination for *jìn-shì* 進士 a third-degree graduate, and the announcement of the list of successful graduates took place in the spring.
46] *shàng cháo qǔ-yìng:* to go to the capital to take the examination.
47] *chū-yú wú-nài:* because there is no other way out.
   jiāng: a pretransitive, comparable to *bǎ* 把. For other uses of *jiāng*, see Glossary.
49] *kē:* a technical term in Yüan drama denoting gesture or action on stage.
51-2] *tā. . . sì-shí liǎng:* 'the forty taels that she formerly lent [me]' should have been 'the forty taels that I owe her' or 'the twenty taels that she formerly lent me' (see l. 41).
53] *gòu:* same as 夠.

§49-50] *Zuò tàn. . . Zhè-ge:* not in *KMCP*.
§53] *dé: jiè* 借 in *KMCP*, p. 2a.

47

應 舉 之 費 便 也 過 望 了 說
54 yìng-jǔ zhī fèi, biàn yě guò wàng le. Shuō-
examination (P) expenses, then also would-exceed expectations
(P). Talking's

話 之 間 早 來 到 他 家 門 首
55 huà-zhī-jiān, zǎo lái dào tā jiā mén-shǒu.
(P) midst (L), already come to her family gate.

婆 婆 在 家 麼 （ 卜 兒 上 云 ） 秀
56 Pó-po zài jiā ma? (Bǔ-er shàng, yún:) Xiù-
P'o-p'o is-at home (P)?' (Old-woman enters, says:) 'Scholar,

才 請 家 裏 坐 老 身 等 候 多
57 cai, qǐng jiā-li zuò. Lǎo-shēn děng-hòu duō
please house's-inside (L) sit. Old-self has-waited long

時 也 （ 做 相 見 科 竇 天 章 云 ）
58 shí yě. (Zuò xiāng-jiàn kē. Dòu Tiān-zhāng yún:)
time (P).' (Perform seeing-each-other gesture. Tou T'ien-chang
says:)

小 生 今 日 一 徑 的 將 女 孩
59 Xiǎo shēng jīn-rì yí-jìng-de jiāng nǚ-hái-
'Insignificant person today straight-way (P) (Pr) daughter

兒 送 來 與 婆 婆 怎 敢 說 做
60 er sòng lái yǔ pó-po. Zěn gǎn shuō zuò
send here (C) to p'o-p'o. How dare say to-be

媳 婦 只 與 婆 婆 早 晚 使 用
61 xí-fu; zhǐ yǔ P'ó-po zǎo-wǎn shǐ-yòng.
daughter-in-law; only for p'o-p'o morning/evening to-make-use-
of.

小 生 目 下 就 要 上 朝 進 取
62 Xiǎo shēng mù-xià jiù yào shàng cháo jìn-qǔ
Insignificant person now immediately will to court to-seek

功 名 去 留 下 女 孩 兒 在 此
63 gōng-míng qù. Liú-xià nǚ-hái-er zài cǐ,
achievement/fame leave. Leaving daughter in here,

it would be more than I can hope for. While talking, I have come to her gate already. Is Mistress Ts'ai at home?

(Enter Mistress Ts'ai.)

TS'AI: Will the scholar please come in. I have been waiting for you for a long time.

(They see each other.)

TOU: I have brought you my daughter, madam. How dare I presume to present her to be your future daughter-in-law; I am giving her to you only to serve you day and night. Presently I have to go to the capital to take the examination. Leaving my daughter here,

54] *yìng-jǔ*: to take a state examination. It is an abridged form of *yìng xuǎn jǔ zhi shì* 應選舉之事.

59] *yí-jìng-de*: 'straight'; 'do nothing but'.

62] *mù-xià*: 'under the eyes'; 'at the moment'; 'now'.

62–3] *shàng... míng*: 'to go to the capital to seek a higher degree'.

§54] *biàn yě guò wàng le*: *zú kě gōu le yě* 足可勾了也 in *KMCP*, p. 2a.
    After *wàng le*: *Duān-yún hái-er yě shì nǐ fù-qin chū yú wú-nài* 端雲孩兒也是你父親出于無奈 in *KMCP*, p. 2a.

§55] *zhī-jiān*: *zhōng jian* 中間 in *KMCP*, p. 2a.
    tā jiā mén-shǒu: not in *KMCP*.

§56] *Bǔ-er shàng, yún*: merely *Bǔ* in *KMCP*, p. 2a (hereafter *bǔ-er yún*, *bǔ-er shàng*, or *bǔ-er* in *YCH* appear as *bǔ shang* or *bǔ* in *KMCP*).

§58] *Dòu Tiān-zhāng yún*: merely *Dòu* in *KMCP*, p. 2a (hereafter *Dòu Tiān-zhāng yún* or *Dòu Tiān-zhāng* in *YCH* appear as *Dòu* in Act I, and *Tiān-zhāng* in Act IV in *KMCP*).

§62] *jiù yào shàng cháo*: not in *KMCP*.

§63–4] *Liú-xià... zhǐ wàng*: not in *KMCP*.

只 望 婆 婆 看 覷 則 箇 （ 卜 兒
64 zhǐ wàng pó-po kàn-qù zé-ge. (Bǔ-er
only hope p'o-p'o look-after [her] (P).' (Old woman

云 ） 這 等 你 是 我 親 家 了 你
65 yún:) Zhè děng, nǐ shì wǒ qìn-jia le. Nǐ
says:) 'This way, you are my in-law (P). You

本 利 少 我 四 十 兩 銀 子 兀
66 běn-lì shǎo wǒ sì-shí liǎng yín-zi. Wǔ-
capital/interest owe me forty taels silver. This

的 是 借 錢 的 文 書 還 了 你
67 de shì jiè qián de wén-shū, huán-le nǐ.
is borrowing money (P) document; return (P) [to] you.

再 送 與 你 十 兩 銀 子 做 盤
68 Zài sòng yǔ nǐ shí liǎng yín-zi zuò pán-
Moreover, present to you ten taels silver, to-be traveling

纏 親 家 你 休 嫌 輕 少 （ 竇 天
69 chan. Qìn-jia, nǐ xiū xián qīng-shǎo. (Dòu Tiān-
money. In-law, you don't mind slight/little.' (Tou T'ien-

章 做 謝 科 云 ） 多 謝 了 婆 婆
70 zhāng zuò xiè kē, yún:) Dūo xiè-le Pó-po.
chang performs thanking gesture, says:) 'Greatly thank (P)
P'o-p'o.

先 少 你 許 多 銀 子 都 不 要
71 Xiān shǎo nǐ xǔ-dūo yín-zi; dōu bú yào
Formerly owed you much silver; all not want

我 還 了 今 又 送 我 盤 纏 此
72 wǒ huán-le; jīn yòu sòng wǒ pán-chan. Cǐ
me to-return (P); now again give me traveling money. This

恩 異 日 必 當 重 報 婆 婆 女
73 ēn yì rì bì-dāng zhòng bào. Pó-po, nǚ-
kindness another day must heavily requite. P'o-p'o, daughter

50

I only hope that you will look after her.

TS'AI: Now you are my in-law. As to the forty taels you owe me, including interest, here is your promissory note, which I am returning to you. In addition, I am presenting you with ten taels of silver for your traveling expenses. In-law, I hope that you do not find this too little.

(Tou T'ien-chang thanks her.)

TOU: Many thanks, madam. Not only have you cancelled the amount I owe you, but you have also presented me with traveling money. Someday I shall greatly repay you for your kindness. Madam, when

64] *zé-ge*: a final particle, same as *zhe* 着 or *zhe* 者; cf. *dài nú-jiā zháo xiē dào-lǐ quàn jiě zé-ge* 待奴家着些道理勸解則個, 'Let me use some reasoning to counsel and make peace.' (The speech following the first song in Act x of Kao Ming 高明, *P'i-pa chi* [琵琶記 *Lute Song*], Shanghai, 1960, p. 69.) See also p. 17.

65] *qìn-jia*: an abbreviated form of *qìn-jia-wēng* 翁 or *qìn-jia-mǔ* 母, titles of address used between parents of the married couple to each other.

66–7] *Wǔ-di* (or *Wǔ-de*): used frequently in Yüan drama, *wǔ-di* is the demonstrative pronoun 'this' in Yüan Northern dialect.

Yáng Yù 楊瑀 of the Yüan dynasty mentioned that *wǔ-di* 阿底 existed in the Northern dialect of his time; and he believes that *wǔ-di* and *wǔ-di* were variants of *wǔ-du* 阿堵, an earlier expression for 'this' found in the biography of Wáng Yǎn 王衍 in the *History of the Chin* 晉 *Dynasty* (*Shan chü hsin hua* 山居新話 in *Chih-pu-tsu-chai ts'ung-shu* 知不足齋叢書, vol. 12, p. 47*b*. For further information, see Sun K'ai-ti, *Ts'ang-chou chi*, pp. 589–97.)

§65] *Zhè děng... qìn-jia le*: *xiù-cai* 秀才 in *KMCP*, p. 2*b*.
§68] *sòng... shí liǎng*: *jiè yǔ nǐ èr liǎng* 借與你二兩 in *KMCP*, p. 2*b*.
§69] *qìn-jia, nǐ*: *Xiù-cái* 秀才 in *KMCP*, p. 2*b*.

孩兒早晚呆癡看小生薄

74　hái-er zǎo-wǎn dāi-chí, kàn xiǎo shēng bó

morning/evening dumb-silly; look-upon insignificant person's
unworthy

面看覷女孩兒咱（卜兒云）

75　miàn, kàn-qù nǚ-hái-er zɑ. (Bǔ-er yún:)

face, look-after daughter (P).' (Old woman says:)

親家這不消你囑付令愛

76　Qìn-jia, zhè bù xiāo nǐ zhǔ-fu, Lìng-ài

'In-law, this not need you enjoin. Your-beloved-daughter

到我家就做親女兒一般

77　dào wǒ jiā, jiù zuò qīn nǚ-er yì-bān

comes-to my home, [I] then as own daughter same-way

看承他你只管放心的去

78　kàn-chéng tā; nǐ zhǐ-guǎn fàng-xīn-de qù.

look-after her; you just with-relaxed-mind (P) leave.'

（竇天章云）婆婆端雲孩兒

79　(Dòu Tian-zhāng yún:) Pó-po, Duān-yún hái-er

(Tou T'ien-chang says:) 'P'o-p'o, Tuan-yün child

該打呵看小生面則罵幾

80　gāi dǎ he, kàn xiǎo shēng miàn, zé mà jǐ

deserves beating (P), look-upon insignificant person's face, only
scold [her] a-few

句當罵呵則處分幾句孩

81　jù; dāng mà he, zé chǔ-fèn jǐ jù. Hái-

(M) [words]; deserves scolding (P), only lightly-rebuke [her]
(M) [words]. Child,

兒你也不比在我跟前我

82　er, nǐ yě bù bǐ zài wǒ gēn-qián. Wǒ

you indeed are-not like being-in my presence (L). I

是你親爺將就的你你如

83　shì nǐ qīn yé, jiāng-jiù-de nǐ. Nǐ rú-

am your own father, can-be-tolerant-of you. You as-of-

52

my little girl acts silly, for my sake, please look after her.

TS'AI: In-law, you need not worry. Now that your worthy beloved daughter has come to my family, I shall look after her just as though she were my own daughter. You may leave with your mind at ease.

TOU: Madam, when Tuan-yün deserves a beating, please, for my sake, just scold her. When she deserves to be scolded, please just speak to her. My child, now it won't be like staying with me anymore; I, as your father, can be tolerant of you. Now if you are naughty here,

75] *za*: an optative particle, or advisative particle, as *ba* 罷 or *po* 波. See pp. 16–17.
76] *Ling-ài*: 'worthy beloved one', an idiomatic courteous way of saying 'your daughter'.
78] *de* (or *di*): a subordinate particle translatable as '-ly' to form an adverb (see p. 20 above). Kao Ming-k'ai asserts that by the end of the Sung dynasty, 底 had been superseded by 的 in vernacular writings; he cites, among others, six examples from *Tou O Yüan* for his argument. ('Han-yü kuei-ting tz'u "ti", 漢語規定詞 [的], *Han hiue* 漢學 I, [1944], 54–5.)
80] *zé*: comparable to *zhǐ* 只, 'only'.
81] *chù-fèn*: 'to settle or adjust'; 'to rebuke'. Here it means 'to rebuke lightly'.
82] *gēn-qián*: 'front' – 'presence' (Chao, *Grammar*, p. 623).
83] *jiāng-jiù*: as *qiān jiù* 遷就 'to make a compromise', 'to give in'.
  de: a potential complement: 'can'

§75] *kàn-qù*: *kàn-qǔ* 看取 in *KMCP*, p. 2b.
§76–7] *Qìn-jia*. . . *wǒ jiā*: not in *KMCP*.
§79] *Dòu Tian-zhāng*: *Dòu gui-xià* 竇跪下 in *KMCP*, p. 2b.

今 在 這 裏 早 晚 若 頑 劣 呵

84   *jīn zài zhè-li, zǎo-wǎn rùo wán-lüè he,.*
    now are-in here (L); morning/evening if naughty (P),

你 只 討 那 打 罵 喫 兒 嚇 我

85   *nǐ zhǐ tǎo nà dǎ mà chī. Ér luo! Wǒ*
    you only ask-for that beating/scolding to-take. Child (P), I

也 是 出 於 無 奈 （ 做 悲 科 唱 ）

86   *yě shì chū-yú wú-nài. (Zuò bēi kē; chàng:)*
    also am out-of no-alternative.' (Performs grieving gesture,
    sings:)

（ 仙 呂 賞 花 時 ） 我 也 只

87   *(Xiān-lǚ: Shǎng huā shí) Wǒ yě zhǐ*
    (*Hsien-lü* [mode]: 'Enjoying Flowers Season') 'I (–) only

爲 無 計 營 生 四 壁 貧

88   *wèi wú jì yíng-shēng sì bì pín.*
    because-of having-no scheme to-make-living, four walls
    poor.

因 此 上 割 捨 得 親 兒

89   *Yīn-cǐ-shàng gē-shě-de qīn ér*
    Because-of-this, give-up own child –

在 兩 處 分 從 今 日 遠

90   *zài liǎng chù fēn. Cóng jīn-rì yuǎn*
    to-be-at two places separated. From today, far-away

踐 洛 陽 塵 又 不 知 歸

91   *jiàn Luò-yáng chén. Yòu bù zhī guī*
    step-on Lo-yang dust. Furthermore, not know [when my]
    return

期 定 准 則 落 的 無 語

92   *qī dìng-zhǔn, zé luò de wú yǔ*
    date is-fixed, only am-reduced to, without words,

闇 消 魂 （ 下 ）

93   *àn xiāo-hún. (xià)*
    becoming-pale, losing-spirit.' (Exit.)

54

you will be asking for a scolding and a beating. My child, I do what I do because there is no other way. (He becomes sad. Sings lyric):

Having no way to make a living,
I am surrounded by four bare walls;
Therefore I must make a sacrifice and be separated from my child.
Today I shall travel afar to the dust of Lo-yang.
Not knowing the date of my return,
I become speechless, pale, and listless. (Exit.)

87] yě: the sense of 'also' is slight; yě is mostly taking up space for rhythmic purpose.
88] sì bì pín: 'poor with only four bare walls'.
89] Yīn-cǐ-shàng: comparable to the present yīn-cǐ, 'because of this'.
　　gē-shě-de: 'to sacrifice' or 'to give up' (cf. ll. 363-4; 549).
91] Luò-yáng: several times capital of ancient China.
92] de: 'to' as applied to extent or degree: 'so... that','so... as', 'as', 'till' (Chao, Grammar, pp. 354-5).
93] xiāo-hún: 'to be heartbroken', 'to lose one's spirit'. Jiāng Yān 江淹 (444-505) made this expression famous in his Pieh fu (別賦, 'Parting Prose-poem'): Ăn rán xiāo hún zhe, wéi bié ér yǐ yi, 黯然銷魂者惟別而已矣, 'What makes one pale and lose his spirit is no more than parting' (Wen hsüan 文選 [SPTK] chüan 16, pp. 35a-b].

§84] wán-lüè he: wán-kě 頑可 in KMCP, p. 2b.
§85] chī: lǐ 裡 in KMCP, p. 2b.
　　luo: hē 呵 in KMCP, p. 2b.
§85-6] Wǒ... wú-nài: Wǒ zhè yí qù le he, jǐ-shí zài de xiāng-jiàn yě 我這一去了呵幾時再得相見也 in KMCP, p. 2b.
§87-93] Xiān-lü... xiāo hún: Tán jiàn zì shāng bēi, wén-zhāng xí Zhòng-ní, bú-xìng qī xiān sàng, fù zǐ liǎng fēn-lí 彈鈙自傷悲文章習仲尼不幸妻先喪父子兩分離 in KMCP, pp. 2b-3a.

55

（卜兒云）竇秀才留下他這

94 *(Bǔ-er yún:) Dòu Xiu-cai liú-xià tā zhè*
(Old-woman says:) 'Tou Scholar has-left his this

女孩兒與我做媳婦兒他

95 *nǚ-hái-er yǔ wǒ zuò xí-fu-er. Tā*
daughter to me to-be daughter-in-law. He

一徑上朝應舉去了（正旦

96 *yí-jìng shàng cháo yìng-jǔ qù le. (Zhèng dàn*
straight-way to court to-take-examination has-left (P).' (Principal female-role

做悲科云）爹爹你直下的

97 *zuò bēi kē, yún:) Diē-die, nǐ zhí xià-de*
performs grieving gesture, says:) 'Father, you really bear

撇了我孩兒去也（卜兒云）

98 *piē-le wǒ hái-er qù yě! (Bǔ-er yún:)*
discarding (P) me [your] child to-go-away (P)!' (Old-woman
says:)

媳婦兒你在我家我是親

99 *Xí-fù-er, nǐ zài wǒ jiā, wǒ shì qin*
'Daughter-in-law, you are-at my home, I am [your] own

婆你是親媳婦只當自家

100 *pó; nǐ shì qin xí-fu, zhǐ dàng zì-jiā*
mother-in-law; you are own daughter-in-law, just regarded-as
own

骨肉一般你不要啼哭跟

101 *gǔ ròu yì-bān. Nǐ bú-yào tí-kū. Gēn-*
bones/flesh like. You do-not cry. With

老身前後執料去來（同

102 *lǎo-shēn qián-hòu zhí-liào qù-lái. (Tóng*
old-self [to] front/back to-attend-to-things go (P).' (Together

下）

103 *xià.)*
exeunt.)

56

TS'AI: Scholar Tou has left his daughter to be my daughter-in-law. He has gone straightway to the capital to take the examination. (Tou Tuan-yün is grieved.)

TOU TUAN-YÜN: Father, you really can bear to leave me, your child, behind!

TS'AI: Daughter-in-law, you are now in my house. I am your mother-in-law. You are my daughter-in-law and will be treated as my own flesh and blood. Don't cry. Follow me and we will go to the front and to the back of the house to attend to things. (Exeunt.)

97] *zhí*: comparable to *zěm-me* 怎麼, 'how'; *zhēn* 眞, 'really'; or *jìng rán* 竟然, 'after all'.

   xià-de: probably from the expression *xià-de shǒu* 下的手, 'to lay hands on', 'to act' (cf. *xià shǒu*, l. 138). The same as *rěn xīn* 忍心, 'to be hard-hearted'. For example, in 'Jen Feng-tzu 任風子,' when the butcher divorces his wife, she says to him, *Nǐ hǎo xià-de ye*, 你好下的也, 'How hard-hearted you are!' (Act III, following Song 9, 'P'u t'ien le' 普天樂).

   Xià-de may also be a variant of *shě-de* 捨得 (see Chang Hsiang, pp. 31–2).
102] *qù-lái*: comparable to *qù-ba* 去罷 (see pp. 17–18).

§96–101] *Zhèng dàn. . . tí-kū. Gēn*: not in *KMCP*.
§102] *qù-lái*: *qù-ye* 去也 in *KMCP*, p. 3a.

第一折

Dì-yī Zhé.
    Number-one Act

（ 淨 扮 賽 盧 醫 上 詩 云 ） 行 醫

105   *(Jìng bàn Sài Lú-yī shàng; shī yún:) Xíng yī*
    (Ching-role in-make-up-of 'Rival Lu-Doctor' enters; [in] verse
    says:) 'Practice medicine

有 斟 酌 下 藥 依 本 草 死 的

106   *yǒu zhēn-zhuó, xià yào yī Běn cǎo. Sǐ-de*
    with care, prescribe drugs according-to *Basic Herbs.* Dead-ones

醫 不 活 活 的 醫 死 了 自 家

107   *yī bu huó, huó-de yī sǐ liǎo. Zì-jiā*
    are-treated not to-come-alive; [the] living-ones are-treated
    [so that they] die (P). Myself

姓 盧 人 道 我 一 手 好 醫 都

108   *xìng Lú, rén dào wǒ yì shǒu hǎo yī; dōu*
    is-surnamed Lu. People say I [have] a hand good in-doctoring.
    All

叫 做 賽 盧 醫 在 這 山 陽 縣

109   *jiào-zuò Sài Lú-yī. Zài zhè Shān-yáng xiàn*
    call [me] 'Rival Lu-Doctor'. At this Shan-yang District

南 門 開 着 生 藥 局 在 城 有

110   *Nán mén kāi zhe shēng yào jú. Zài chéng yǒu*
    South Gate [I] open (P) raw drugs shop. In city there-is

箇 蔡 婆 婆 我 問 他 借 了 十

111   *ge Cài Pó-Po. Wǒ wèn tā jiè-le shí*
    [a] (M) Ts'ai *P'o-p'o.* I from her borrowed (P) ten

兩 銀 子 本 利 該 還 他 二 十

112   *liǎng yín-zi, běn-lì gāi huán tā èr-shí*
    taels silver; capital/interest should pay-back her twenty

兩 數 次 來 討 這 銀 子 我 又

113   *liǎng. Shù cì lái tǎo zhè yín-zi. Wǒ yòu*
    taels. Several times [she has] come to-ask-for this silver. I again

ACT ONE

[Thirteen years later]

(Enter Doctor Lu.)

LU:

> *I diagnose disease with care,*
> *And prescribe according to the medicine book.*
> *I cannot bring dead men back to life,*
> *But the live ones by my doctoring often die.*

My name is Lu. People say that I am good at doctoring, and call me 'Sai Lu-yi'. I keep an apothecary shop at the South Gate of Shan-yang District. In town there is a Mistress Ts'ai from whom I borrowed ten taels of silver. With interest I now owe her twenty taels. She has come several times for the money, but I have none to repay her.

104] *Zhé*: a technical term in Yüan plays to indicate division, comparable to an act. In Ming editions, Yüan plays are usually in four *zhé*, with one song-sequence in each. Although in the only extant Yüan edition, the plays are not so divided or labeled, it is certain that the term *zhé* was used in Yüan to indicate divisions, because in reference to the authorship of the play *Huang-liang meng* (黃粱夢 *Yellow Millet Dream*), a Yüan author notes: 'the first *zhé* is by Mǎ Zhì-yuǎn 馬致遠, second *zhé* by Lǐ Shí-zhōng 李時中, third *zhé* by Huā Lǐ-láng 花李郎, fourth *zhé* by Hóng-zì Lǐ-èr 紅字李二'; he also notes that some plays are of six *zhé* (Chung Ssu-ch'eng 鍾嗣成, *A Register of Ghosts*, in *Chung-kuo ku-tien hsi-ch'ü lun-chu chi-ch'eng*, vol. II, Peking, 1959, p. 117.)

105] *Jìng*-role: see p. 6–7.
　　Sài Lú-yī: Lú-yī refers to the famous doctor Biǎn Què 扁鵲 of the District Lu in the Warring States period (*Shih chi* 史記, *chüan* 105, p.1a). *Sài* means 'to rival'; in Yüan plays, the term *Sài Lú-yī* is often used ironically for incompetent doctors.

106] *Běn cǎo*: an early Chinese study in pharmaceutical material; *see* n. 502 below.
　　Sǐ-de: In the *de* construction, the word after *de* is understood; it is either omitted in the translation or translated by a substantive such as 'one,' 'that which', etc.; the nominalizing *de* is a morpheme (see Chao, *Grammar*, pp. 294–5).

108] *yì shǒu hǎo yī*: an idiomatic expression; cf. *yì shǒu hǎo zì* (words), 'a fine hand in calligraphy'; *yì shǒu hǎo zhēng* (needle) *xiàn* (thread), 'a fine hand in sewing'.

§104] *Dì-yī Zhé*: not in *KMCP*; cf. § 3.
§105] *Jìng bàn*... *shī yún: Sài lú-yī shàng* 賽盧醫上 in *KMCP*, p. 3a.
§107–9] *Zì-jiā xìng Lú*... *Sài Lú-yī: Zì-jiā Sài Lú-yī* 自家賽盧醫 in *KMCP*, p. 3a.
§109–10] *Shān-yáng xiàn Nán mén: Jìng-chōu* 荊州, *KMCP*, p. 3a.

114 無 的 還 他 若 不 來 便 罷 若
wú-de huán tā. Ruò bù lái biàn bà; ruò
had-nothing to-pay-back-to her. If [she] does-not come, then
no-more; if

115 來 呵 我 自 有 箇 主 意 我 且
lái he, wǒ zì yǒu ge zhú-yi. Wǒ qiě
[she] comes (P), I myself have an idea. I temporarily

116 在 這 藥 舖 中 坐 下 看 有 甚
zài zhè yào pù zhōng zuò xia. Kàn yǒu shém-
in this medicine shop (L) sit down (C); see there-will-be what

117 麼 人 來（卜 兒 上 云 ）老 身 蔡
me rén lái? (Bǔ-er shàng, yún:) Lǎo-shēn Cài
person (who) comes.' (Old-woman enters, says:) 'Old-self Ts'ai

118 婆 婆 我 一 向 搬 在 山 陽 縣
Pó-po. Wǒ yí-xiàng bān zài Shān-yáng xiàn
P'o-p'o. I for-quite-some-time-now have-moved to Shan-yang
District

119 居 住 儘 也 靜 辦 自 十 三 年
jū-zhù. Jǐn-yě jìng-ban. Zì shí-sān nián
to-live. Fully (P) quiet. Since thirteen years

120 前 竇 天 章 秀 才 留 下 端 雲
qián Dòu Tiān-zhāng xiù-cai liú-xia Duān-yún
ago Tou T'ien-chang Scholar left Tuan-yün

121 孩 兒 與 我 做 兒 媳 婦 改 了
hái-er yǔ wǒ zuò ér xí-fu, gǎi-le
child for me to-be son's wife; changed (P)

122 他 小 名 喚 做 竇 娥 自 成 親
tā xiǎo míng, huàn-zùo Dòu É. Zì chéng-qin
her humble name; call [her] Tou O. Since [the] wedding

123 之 後 不 上 二 年 不 想 我 這
zhi hòu, bú shàng èr nián, bù-xiǎng wǒ zhè
(P) (L), not up-to two years, unexpectedly my this

60

If she doesn't come again, then there's an end to it. If she comes, I
have an idea. Now I'll just sit down in the apothecary shop here
and see who will come.

(Enter Mistress Ts'ai.)

TS'AI: I am Mistress Ts'ai. Sometime ago, I moved to Shan-yang to
live. It is pretty quiet here. Since that time thirteen years ago when
Scholar Tou T'ien-chang left his daughter Tuan-yün behind to
be my daughter-in-law, I have changed her name to Tou O. Not
quite two years after the marriage, my son unexpectedly died of

---

114] *bà*: 'no more'; 'the end'.

118] *yî-xiàng*: for a short while; for a long while; up to now (see Chang Hsiang, pp. 1–4).

118–9] *bān. . . jū-zhù*: 'moved to live at a place' versus 'to remain at one's ancestral domicile'.

119] *jìng-ban*: 'quiet'; see Lu Tan-an, *Hsiao-shuo tz'u-yü hui-shih*, p. 790.

§115] *zì yŏu: bié yŏu* 别有 in *KMCP*, p. 3a.

§116] *zuò xia: zuò-de* 坐的, *KMCP*, p. 3a.

§118–19] *Wŏ yî-xiàng. . .jìng-ban*: not in *KMCP*.

§123] *bú shàng èr nián*: not in *KMCP*.

孩兒害弱症死了媳婦兒

124 hái-er hài ruò-zhèng sǐ-le. Xí-fù-er

child was-sick-of consumption, died (P). Daughter-in-law

守寡又早三箇年頭服孝

125 shǒu guǎ, yòu zǎo sān ge nián-tóu. Fú-xiào

has-observed widowhood, again already three (M) years. Wearing-mourning

將除了也我和媳婦兒說

126 jiāng chú-le ye. Wǒ hé xí-fu-er shuō

is-about-to end (P) (P). I to daughter-in-law explain

知我往城外賽盧醫家索

127 zhī, wǒ wǎng chéng-wài Sài Lú-yi jiā suǒ

I go-to outside-the-city (L) "Rival Lu-Doctor's" home to-ask-for

錢去也（做行科云）驀過隅

128 qián qù ye. (Zuò xíng kē, yún:) Mò guò yú-

money (C) (P).' (Performs walking action, says:) 'Going past angles,

頭轉過屋角早來到他家

129 tóu, zhuǎn guò wū jiǎo. Zǎo lái dào tā jiā

turning around house corners. Already come to his house

門首賽盧醫在家麼（盧醫

130 mén-shǒu. Sài Lú-yi zài jiā ma? (Lú-yi

gate. "Rival Lu-Doctor" is-at home (P)?' ('Lu-Doctor'

云）婆婆家裏來（卜兒云）我

131 yún:) Pó-po, jiā-li lái. (Bǔ-er yún:) Wǒ

says:) 'P'o-p'o, inside-the-house (L) come.' (Old-woman says:) 'My

這兩箇銀子長遠了你還

132 zhè liǎng ge yín-zi cháng-yuǎn le, nǐ huán-

these two pieces (M) silver [have been a] long-time (P), you repay consumption. My daughter-in-law has already been a widow for three years, and will soon be out of mourning. I have just told her that I am going outside the city gate to collect a debt from Sai Lu-yi. (She performs walking gesture.) I stride along the walls and go around the corners of many houses. I have already come to the door of Sai Lu-yi's house. Is Sai Lu-yi at home?

LU: Come in, madam.

TS'AI: You have kept my few pieces of silver for a long time. How about paying them back to me?

126] *chú*: *chú fú* 服 is 'to go out of mourning'.

128] *Mò guò*: here as *mài guò* 邁, or *mò guò* 抹, 'to go around'. *Mò guò yú tóu, zhuǎn guò wū jiǎo* is comparable to the present expression 轉彎抹角 'turning around curves, going around corners'. *Mò* 驀 usually means 'to leap over' or 'to flash by'.

§124] *hài ruò-zhèng*: not in *KMCP*.
§125–6] *Fú-xiào jiāng chú-le ye*: not in *KMCP*.
§127] *chéng-wài*: *chéng-lǐ* 城裡 in *KMCP*, p. 3b.
§128–9] *Zuò xíng kē*... *wū jiǎo*: not in *KMCP*.
§130–1] *Lú-yǐ yún*: hereafter *Sài Lú-yǐ yún* or *Lú-yǐ yún* in *YCH* appear as *Lú* in *KMCP*, except for the first appearance in each Act, where the full name is cited.

了我罷（盧醫云）婆婆我家

133   *le wǒ ba. (Lú-yi yún:) Pó-po, wǒ jiā-*
  (P) me (P).' ('Rival Lu-Doctor' says:) '*P'o-p'o*, in-my-house

裏無銀子你跟我庄上去

134   *li wú yín-zi. Nǐ gēn wǒ zhuāng-shàng qù*
  (L) there-is-no silver. You with me [to] village (L) go

取銀子還你（卜兒云）我跟

135   *qǔ yín-zi huán nǐ. (Bǔ-er yún:) Wǒ gēn*
  to-fetch silver to-repay you.' (Old-woman says:) 'I with

你去（做行科盧醫云）來到

136   *nǐ qù. (Zùo xíng kē. Lú-yi yún:) Lái dào*
  you go.' (Performs walking gesture. 'Lu-Doctor' says:) 'Come to

此處東也無人西也無人

137   *cǐ chù, dōng yě wú rén, xi yě wú rén.*
  this place, east also no person, west also no person.

這裏不下手等甚麽我隨

138   *Zhè-li bú xià-shǒu děng shém-me? Wǒ-suí-*
  [If] here (L) not lay-hands [on her], am-waiting for what?
  That-I-along-with-

身帶的有繩子兀那婆婆

139   *shēn-dài-de yǒu shéng-zi. Wǔ-nà Pó-po,*
  self-carried, there-is rope. Hey-there, old-woman

誰喚你哩（卜兒云）在那裏

140   *shéi huàn nǐ li? (Bǔ-er yún:) Zài nǎ-li?*
  who is-calling you (P)?' (Old-woman says:) 'At what-place
  (L)?'

（做勒卜兒科孛老同副淨

141   *(Zùo lēi bǔ-er kē. Bó-lǎo tóng fù-jìng,*
  (Performs strangling old-woman gesture. Old-man and sup-
  porting-*ching*-role

張驢兒衝上賽盧醫慌走

142   *Zhāng Lǘ-er chōng shàng. Sài Lú-yi huāng zǒu*
  Chang Donkey rush on (C). 'Rival Lu-Doctor' hurriedly walks

LU: Madam, I have no money at home. Come with me to the village, and I shall get the money for you.

TS'AI: I shall go with you.

(They start walking.)

LU: Well, here we are – nobody to the east, nobody to the west. If I don't do the job here, what am I waiting for? I have some rope with me. Hey, Mistress, who is calling you?

TS'AI: Where?

(Doctor Lu tries to strangle her. Old Chang and Donkey Chang rush forward; Doctor Lu hurries away. Old Chang revives Mistress

133] *ba:* a final particle (see p. 17).

136–8] Here is an example of a mixture of humorous and villainous behavior, typical of a *jing* role.

139] *Wŭ-nà:* a demonstrative pronoun meaning 'that' (see Chang Hsiang, p. 27). It often is used in direct address and has the force of introductory words like 'hey there', 'you, over there', or the like – always informal and sometimes threatening (cf. ll. 145, 161).

140] *li:* comparable to *ne* 吶 or *na* 哪 in modern Mandarin to indicate progressive action (see p. 19).

141] *Bó-lǎo:* role of an old man in Yüan drama (see n. 4).
   fù-jìng: a supporting *jing* role (see p. 6).

§136–7] *Lái dào cǐ chù: chū-de chéng-lái* 出 的 城 來 in *KMCP*, p. 3b.

§142] *Zhāng Lǘ-er:* not in *KMCP*. Hereafter the role appears in *KMCP* as *fù-jìng* in pp. 3a–5b, and *jing* from p. 5b on.

下孛老救卜兒科張驢兒
143　xià. Bó-lǎo jiù bǔ-er kē. Zhāng Lǘ-er
out. Old-man rescue old-woman gesture. Chang Donkey

云）爹是箇婆婆爭些勒殺
144　yún:) Diē, shì ge pó-po, zhēng-xie lēi-shā-
says:) 'Father, is [an] (M) old-woman, nearly strangled-to-
death

了（孛老云）兀那婆婆你是
145　le. (Bó-lǎo yún:) Wǔ-nà Pó-po, nǐ shì
(P).' (Old-man says:) 'Hey-there, old-woman, you are

那裏人氏姓甚名誰因甚
146　nǎ-li rén-shì? Xìng shén míng shéi? Yin shén
what-place (L) native? Surnamed what, named what? For what

着這箇人將你勒死（卜兒
147　zháo zhè-ge rén jiāng nǐ lēi-sǐ? (Bǔ-er
[did you] have this (M) person (Pr) you strangle-to-death?'
(Old-woman

云）老身姓蔡在城人氏止
148　yún:) Lǎo-shēn xìng Cài; zài chéng rén-shì. Zhǐ
says:) 'Old-self is surnamed Ts'ai; residing-in city person. Only

有箇寡媳婦兒相守過日
149　yǒu ge guǎ xí-fù-er, xiāng shǒu guò rì.
have [a] (M) widowed daughter-in-law; together keep-com-
pany, pass days.

因爲賽盧醫少我二十兩
150　Yin-wèi Sài Lú-yi shǎo wǒ èr-shí liǎng
Because "Rival Lu-Doctor" owed me twenty taels

銀子今日與他取討誰想
151　yín-zi, jin-rì yǔ tā qǔ-tǎo. Shéi xiǎng
silver, today from him [I] demanded [it]. Who would-have-
expected

他賺我到無人去處要勒
152　tā zuàn wǒ dào wú rén qù-chù, yào lēi-
he would-lure me to no person place, wanting to-strangle-

Ts'ai.)

DONKEY CHANG: Father, it's an old woman nearly strangled to death.

OLD CHANG: Say, Mistress, where are you from, what is your name? Why did that man want to strangle you?

TS'AI: My name is Ts'ai. I live in town and I have only one widowed daughter-in-law, who lives with me. Because Sai Lu-yi owes me twenty taels of silver, I went to ask it back from him today. Who would have thought that he'd lure me to a deserted place in order

---

144] *zhēng-xie:* comparable to the modern expression *chà-dian* 差 點, 'almost'.

152] *qù-chù:* 'place'. Cf. '*Wǒ zhè-li chū-jiā, shì qīng jìng qù-chù* 我 這 裡 出 家 是 清 淨 去 處, 'Here my place of religious devotees is a pure and clean place.' (*Shui-hu ch'üan chuan* 水 滸 全 傳 *Water Margin*, Peking, 1954, chap. 4, p. 74.)

§144] *Diē: fù-qin* 父 親 in *KMCP*, p. 3*b*.
§145] *Bó-lǎo yún: Bó-lǎo* in *KMCP*, and same difference hereafter.
§148–9] *Zhǐ yǒu. . . guò rì: pó fù èr rén giùo-rì* 婆 婦 二 人 過 日 in *KMCP*, p. 3*b*.
§150] *Yīn-wèi: yǒu gè* 有 箇 in *KMCP*, pp. 3*b*–4*a*.
§151–3] *jīn-rì. . . yín-zi: Zuàn wǒ dào jiāo-wài lēi sǐ wǒ* 賺 我 到 郊 外 勒 死 我 in *KMCP*, p. 4*a*.

死　我　賴　這　銀　子　若　不　是　遇
153　sǐ wǒ, lài zhè yín-zi. Ruò bú-shì yù-
to-death me, to-deny this silver. If were-not [for] encountering

着　老　的　和　哥　哥　呵　那　得　老
154　zhe lǎo-de hé gē-ge he, nǎ dé lǎo-
(P) old-one and older-brother (P), how would-have-kept old-

身　性　命　來　（　張　驢　兒　云　）　爹　你
155　shēn xìng-mìng lai? (Zhāng Lǘ-er yún:) Diē, nǐ
self's life (P)?' (Chang Donkey says:) 'Father, you

聽　的　他　說　麼　他　家　還　有　箇
156　tīng-de tā shuō ma? Tā jiā hái yǒu ge
heard (P) her speaking (P)? Her home still has [a] (M)

媳　婦　哩　救　了　他　性　命　他　少
157　xí-fu li. Jiù-le tā xìng-mìng, tā shǎo-
daughter-in-law (P). [We] have-saved (P) her life, she cannot-

不　得　要　謝　我　不　若　你　要　這
158　bù-de yào xiè wǒ. Bú-ruò nǐ yào zhè
but want to-thank us. Nothing-like you take this

婆　子　我　要　他　媳　婦　兒　何　等
159　pó-zi, wǒ yào tā xí-fu-er. Hé-děng
woman, I take her daughter-in-law. How

兩　便　你　和　他　說　去　（　孛　老　云　）
160　liǎng biàn. Nǐ hé tā shuō qù. (Bó-lǎo yún:)
[for] both convenient. You with her speak go.' (Old-man speaks:)

兀　那　婆　婆　你　無　丈　夫　我　無
161　Wù-nà pó-po, nǐ wú zhàng-fu, wǒ wú
'Hey-there, p'o-p'o, you have-no husband, I have-no

渾　家　你　肯　與　我　做　箇　老　婆
162　hún-jiā. Nǐ kěn yǔ wǒ zuò ge lǎo-po,
wife, [how about] you be-willing to me be [a] (M) wife –

to strangle me to escape a debt? Had it not been for you and this young man, how could I have come out of it alive?

DONKEY CHANG: Father, did you hear what she said? She has a daughter-in-law at home. We have saved her life; she will have to reward us. The best thing would be for you to take this old woman, and I'll take her daughter-in-law. What a convenient deal for both sides! Go and talk to her.

OLD CHANG: Hey, old lady, you have no husband and I have no wife; how about you being my old woman? How does that strike you?

154] *gē-ge:* 'older brother', here used as a courteous address to a young man.
156] *tīng-de:* comparable Pekingese usage is *tīng-jiàn* 聽見.

§153–4] *yù-zhe:* not in *KMCP*.
§157–8] *Jiù-le... Bú-ruò:* not in *KMCP*.
§159–60] *Hé-děng liǎng biàn:* not in *KMCP*.
§162] *lǎo-po: pó-po* 婆婆 in *KMCP*, p. 4a.

意下如何（卜兒云）是何言
163　yì-xià rú-hé? (Bǔ-er yún:) Shì hé yán-
　　in-your-opinion, like-what?' (Old-woman says:) 'Is what-kind-
　　of talk!

語待我回家多備些錢鈔
164　yǔ! Dài wǒ huí jiā, duō bèi xie qián-chāo
　　Wait-till I return home, amply make-ready some money/cash-
　　notes

相謝（張驢兒云）你敢是不
165　xiāng-xiè. (Zhāng Lǘ-er yún:) Nǐ gǎn-shi bù
　　to-thank-you.' (Chang Donkey says:) 'You must-be not

肯故意將錢鈔哄我賽盧
166　kěn, gù-yì jiāng qián-chāo hǒng wǒ? Sài Lú-
　　willing, intentionally using money/cash-notes to-fool me. "Rival
　　Lu

醫的繩子還在我仍舊勒
167　yi de shéng-zi hái zài; wǒ réng-jiù lēi-
　　Doctor's" (P) rope still is-here; I still strangle-

死了你罷（做拿繩科卜兒
168　sǐ-le nǐ ba. (Zuò ná shéng kē. Bǔ-er
　　to-death (P) you (P).' (Performs picking-up rope gesture. Old-
　　woman

云）哥哥待我慢慢地尋思
169　yún:) Gē-ge, dài wǒ màn-màn-de xún-sī
　　says:) 'Older-brother, wait-till I slowly (P) think-over

咱（張驢兒云）你尋思些甚
170　za. (Zhāng Lǘ-er yún:) Nǐ xún-si-xie shém-
　　(P).' (Chang Donkey says:) 'You think-over some what?

麼你隨我老子我便要你
171　me? Nǐ suí wǒ lǎo-zi, wǒ biàn yào nǐ
　　You follow my old-man, I then take your

70

TS'AI : What talk is this? Wait till I get home; I shall get some money to reward you.

DONKEY CHANG : You must be unwilling and want to bamboozle me with money. Doctor Lu's rope is still here; perhaps I had better strangle you after all. (Takes up rope.)

TS'AI : Brother, how about waiting till I think it over slowly?

DONKEY CHANG : Think what over? You go with my old man, and I'll take your daughter-in-law.

§164] *Dài wǒ huí jiā:* not in *KMCP*.
§165–8] *Nǐ gǎn-shi. . . nǐ ba: Nǐ bù-kěn wǒ yě lēi sǐ nǐ* 你不肯我也勒死你 in *KMCP*,
    p. 4a.
§168] *Zuò ná shéng kē:* not in *KMCP*.
§170] *za:* not in *KMCP*.
§170–1] *xie shém-me:* not in *KMCP*.

媳婦兒（卜兒背云）我不依

172　*xí-fu-er. (Bǔ-er bèi yún:) Wǒ bù yī*
daughter-in-law.' (Old-woman with-back-turned says:) '[If]
I do-not go-along-with

他他又勒殺我罷罷罷你

173　*tā, tā yòu lēi-shā wǒ. Bà, bà, bà, nǐ*
him, he again will-strangle-to-death me. No-more, no-more,
no-more, you

爺兒兩箇隨我到家中去

174　*yé ér liǎng ge suí wǒ dào jiā-zhōng qù*
father son two (M) with me to home (L) go

來（同下正旦上云）妾身姓

175　*lai. (Tóng xià. Zhèng dàn shàng; yún:) Qiè-shēn xìng*
(P).' (Together exeunt. Principal female-role enters, speaks:)
'Handmaiden is-surnamed

竇小字端雲祖居楚州人

176　*Dòu, xiǎo zì Duān-yún; zǔ jū Chǔ-zhōu rén-*
Tou, humble name Tuan-yün; [in terms of] ancestors' residence, [a] Ch'u-chou

氏我三歲上亡了母親七

177　*shì. Wǒ sān-suì-shang wáng-le mǔ-qin, qí-*
person. I at-three-years-of-age (L) lost (P) mother; at-seven-

歲上離了父親俺父親將

178　*suì-shang lí-le fù-qin; ǎn fù-qin jiāng*
years-of-age (L), was-separated (P) [from] father. My father
(Pr)

我嫁與蔡婆婆爲兒媳婦

179　*wǒ jià yǔ Cài Pó-po wéi ér-xí-fu,*
me married to Ts'ai p'o-p'o to-be son's-wife.

改名竇娥至十七歲與夫

180　*gǎi míng Dòu É. Zhì shí-qi suì yǔ fū*
Changed name [to] Tou O. Reaching seventeen years-of-age, to
[my] husband

72

TS'AI (aside): If I don't go along with him, he will strangle me. All right, all right, all right, you two, father and son, come home with me. (Exeunt.)

(Enter the female lead.)

TOU O: My family name is Tou; my humble name is Tuan-yün. My ancestors came from Ch'u-chou. When I was three, I lost my mother; at seven I was separated from my father. He gave me away to Mistress Ts'ai to be her daughter-in-law, and she changed my name to Tou O. When I reached the age of seventeen, I was married.

172] *bèi yún:* 'to speak in an aside'.

173] *bà:* 'no more', 'finished', or 'that is enough'; *bà, bà, bà,* an expression of an unwilling decision or compromise to indicate resignation to a situation; cf. n. 114.

175] *Qiè-shēn:* a humble way for a young female to refer to herself; cf. n. 6.

§173] *Bà, bà, bà:* not in *KMCP.*
      Before *nǐ: yún* 云 in *KMCP,* p. 4*a.*

§175] Before *Tóng xìa: (Fù-jìng:) Zǎ qù-lái* (付 淨) 喳 去 來, *KMCP,* p. 4*a.*
      Zhèng dàn shàng; yún: Zhèng-dàn bàn Dòu É shàng 正旦扮竇娥上 in *KMCP,*
      p. 4*a.*

73

成親不幸丈夫亡化可早

181　*chéng-qīn. Bú-xìng zhàng-fu wáng-huà, kě zǎo*
become-wedded. Unfortunately husband died, indeed already

三年光景我今二十歲也

182　*sān nián guāng-jīng. Wǒ jīn èr-shí suì yě.*
three years time. I now twenty years-old (P).

這南門外有箇賽盧醫他

183　*Zhè Nán mén wài yǒu ge Sài Lú-yī. Tā*
This South Gate outside, there-is [a] (M) "Rival Lu-Doctor".
He

少俺婆婆銀子本利該二

184　*shǎo ǎn Pó-po yín-zi; běn-lì gāi èr-*
owes my mother-in-law silver; [in] principal/interest owes

十兩數次索取不還今日

185　*shí liǎng. Shù cì suǒ-qǔ bù huán. Jīn-rì*
twenty taels. Several times [she has] demanded [it]; [he has]
not repaid [it]. Today

俺婆婆親自索取去了竇

186　*ǎn Pó-po qīn-zì suǒ-qǔ qù le. Dòu-*
my mother-in-law personally to-demand [it] went (P). Tou

娥也你這命好苦也呵（唱）

187　*É ye, nǐ zhè mìng hǎo kǔ yě hē (Chàng:)*
O (P), your this life very bitter (P) (P)!' (Sings:)

（仙呂點絳唇）滿腹閒

188　*(Xiān-lǚ: Diǎn jiàng chún) Mǎn fù xián*
(Hsien-lü [mode]: 'Painting Red Lips') '[Of this] whole
belly idle

愁數年禁受天知否

189　*chóu, shù nián jìn-shòu, Tiān zhī fǒu?*
sorrow, several years suffering, [does] Heaven know, [or]
not?

Unfortunately my husband died, and it has already been three
years. Now I am twenty years old. Outside the South Gate there
is a Sai Lu-yi, who owes my mother-in-law twenty taels of silver in
principal and interest. Although he has been asked several times for
the money, he has not returned it. Today my mother-in-law has
gone to ask for it herself. Ah, Tou O, this life of yours, how miser-
able! (Sings first lyric):

> *Of my heart full of sorrow,*
> *Of my years of suffering,*
> *Is Heaven aware?*

181] *kě:* 'indeed, certainly'. Here, with the following phrase, 'already three years',
it indicates Tou O's surprise at the swiftness of time, which she shares with the
audience. (Cf. l. 912.)

181–2] Tou O was married when she was seventeen (l. 180); not quite two years later,
her husband died (ll. 123-4) and she has remained a widow for three
years already (ll. 181–2). In the Western way of reckoning, she should be
about twenty-two or at least twenty-one years old by this time, when she
claims, 'I am now twenty years of age.' In Chinese, *sān nián* may refer to
three different years; thus after three years of mourning, Tou O can still be
twenty, as seen below:
> Tou O's age
> 17 – married at seventeen
> 18 – husband died, not quite two years later
> 19
> 20 – Tou O at twenty, being widowed for three years already.

187] *yě:* a vocative (see p. 15).

188] *fù:* 'belly'. Instead of saying 'my heart is full of sorrow', and 'my heart is broken',
the Chinese often say 'my *belly* is full of sorrow', and 'my bowels are broken'.

§183] *Nán mén wài: zài chéng* 在 城 in *KMCP*, p. 4*b*.

§187] *nǐ zhè. . . yě hē: jǐ-shí shì ǎn mìng tōng shí-jié yě hē* 幾 時 是 俺 命 通 時 節 也 呵
in *KMCP*, p. 4*b*.

§189] *jìn-shòu: zuò-shòu* 坐 受 in *KMCP*, p. 4*b*.

§189-91] *Tiān zhī fǒu. . . hé tiān shòu: Cháng xiāng shǒu wú liǎo wú xiu; zhāo mù yī-rán
yǒu* 常 相 守 無 了 無 休 朝 暮 依 然 有 in *KMCP, p. 4b*.

75

190 天若是知我情由怕
Tiān ruò-shi zhī wǒ qíng-yóu, pà-
Heaven if knew my situation, perhaps

191 不待和天瘦
bú-dài hé tiān shòu.
even Heaven would-be-thin.'

192 （混江龍）則問那黃
(Hǔn jiāng lóng) Zé wèn nà huáng-
('Roiling River Dragon') '[I] just ask: that evening

193 昏白晝兩般兒忘湌
hūn bái-zhòu, liǎng-bān-er wàng cān,
daytime both forgetting to-eat [and]

194 廢寢幾時休大都來
fèi qǐn jǐ shí xiū? Dà-dōu-lái
losing sleep, what time will-end? Always

195 昨宵夢裏和着這今
zuó-xiāo mèng lǐ, hé-zhe zhè jin-
last-night's dream (L) lingers (P) [in] this today's

196 日心頭催人淚的是
rì xin-tóu. Cui-rén-lèi-de shì
heart. What-hastens-person's-tears is

197 錦爛熳花枝橫繡闥
jǐn làn-màn huā zhī héng xiù tā.
brocade shining, flower twigs lying-across embroidered
door-hanging.

198 斷人腸的是剔團圞
Duàn-rén-cháng-de shì ti-tuán-luán
What-breaks-person's-bowels is round

76

If Heaven only knew my situation,
Would it not also grow thin?

(Second lyric):

I just want to ask:
To go without eating or sleep both day and night –
When is this to end?
What appears in last night's dream often lingers in the mind today.
Embroidered flowers lying across the door call forth tears;
The full moon hanging above the lady's chamber breaks one's heart.

190–1] *pà-bú-dài*: same as the present expression *qǐ bú yào* 豈不要, 'will it not', meaning 'it will'.

191] *hé tiān shòu*: same as *lián tiān yě shòu le* 連天也瘦了, 'even Heaven will grow thinner (because of grief)'. This is comparable to the poet Li Ho's 李賀 (790–816) line: *Tiān ruò yǒu qíng, tiān yì lǎo* 天若有情天亦老, 'If Heaven has feelings, Heaven will also grow old.' (*Chin-t'ung hsien-ren tz'u Han ke* 金銅仙人辭漢歌, 'Song of the Golden-brass Immortal Bidding Farewell to the Han Rule' (*Li Ho ke shih pien* 李賀歌詩編 [*SPTK*] *chüan* 2, p. 1*a*).

194] *Dà-dōu-lái*: an expression in Yüan Northern dialect. *Dà-dōu* is the same as *dà-dǐ* 大抵, 'generally', and *lái* is a particle.

197] *tā*: 'door of an inner room'; 'a hanging above a door'.

198] *cháng*: see n. 188 on *fù*.

tī-tuán-luán: 'round', an expression often used in Yüan plays.

§192] *zé wèn nà*: not in *KMCP*.

§193–4] *liǎng-bān-er . . . jí shí xiū*: *wàng cān fèi qǐn liǎng-bān yōu* 忘餐廢寢兩般憂, in *KMCP*, p. 4*b*.

§194–5] *Dà-dōu-lái, . . . mèng lǐ*: *Yè lái mèng lǐ* 夜來夢裡 in *KMCP*, p. 4*b*.

§195] *hé-zhe zhè*: not in *KMCP*.

§196–202] *cuī-rén . . . jiàn zhòu*: *Dì jiǔ tiān cháng nán guò qiān; jiù chóu xīn hèn jǐ shí xiū. Zé zhè yè yǎn kǔ, chóu méi zhòu*, 地久天長難過遣舊愁新恨幾時休則這業眼苦愁眉皺 in *KMCP*, p. 4*b*–5*a*.

77

月色掛粧樓長則是

199   *yuè-sè guà zhuāng lóu. Cháng zé shì*
     moon hanging-by lady's-powder chamber. Long then
     [have I] been

急煎煎按不住意中

200   *jí-jiān-jiān àn bú-zhù yì-zhōng*
     burningly-anxious, suppress unable mind-within (L)

焦悶沉沉展不徹眉

201   *jiāo. Mèn-chén-chén, zhǎn-bú-chè méi*
     worries. Deeply-depressed, [I am] unable-to-relax brow

尖皴越覺的情懷冗

202   *jiān zhòu, yuè jué-de qíng-huái rǒng-*
     tip frowns; more feel heart heavy,

冗心緒悠悠

203   *rǒng, xin-xù yōu-yōu.*
     thought-threads anxious-and-long.'

（云）似這等憂愁不知幾時

204   *(Yún:) Sì zhè děng yōu-chóu, bù zhi jǐ-shí*
     (Says:) 'Like this kind sorrow, [I] do-not know what-time

是了也呵（唱）

205   *shì liǎo yě he! (Chàng:)*
     will end (P) (P)!' (Sings:)

（油葫蘆）莫不是八字

206   *(Yóu hú-lu) Mò bú shì bá-zì-*
     ('Oil Gourd') 'Could-it-not not be fate [which]

兒該載着一世憂誰

207   *er gāi zài-zhe yí shì yōu? Shéi*
     decreed (that I) carry (P) a life-of sorrow? Who

I have long been anxious and unable to suppress my worries;
Deeply depressed, I cannot relax my knitted brows.
More and more my heart grows heavy,
And my thoughts become anxious and long. (Speaks.)
There is no knowing when this sorrow will end!
(Sings third lyric):
  Is it my fate, to be unhappy all my life?
  Who else knows such endless grief as I?

200] *jí-jiān-jiān:* 'anxious'.
206] *Yŏu hú-lu:* a gourd-container for storing oil.
    Mò bú shì: mò, 'not', *bú,* 'not', *shì,* 'is': a double negative. It is used in a
    rhetorical question expecting a positive answer; cf. *qĭ-bù* (l. 20).
206–7] *bá-zi-er: bá-zi,* literally 'eight characters' – the telling of fate on the basis of
    the eight horoscopic characters pertaining to the year, month, day, and hour
    of one's birth (see Morohashi, ɪɪ: 1450: 225).

§202] *yuè jué-de:* not in *KMCP.*
§204] *Yún:* not in *KMCP* (same omission in ll. 223, 243, etc.).
§205] *Chàng:* not in *KMCP.*

208

似我無盡頭須知道

sì wǒ wú jìn-tóu! Xū zhī-dao

is-like me, having-no end? [One] must know-that

209

人心不似水長流我

rén xīn bú sì shuǐ cháng liú. Wǒ

human heart is-not like water always flowing. I

210

從三歲母親身亡後

cóng sān suì mǔ-chin shēn wáng hòu,

since three years-old, mother body died (L);

211

到七歲與父分離久

dào qī suì yǔ fù fēn-lí jiǔ,

reaching seven years, from father was-separated [for] long.

212

嫁的箇同住人他可

Jià-de ge tóng-zhù-rén, tā kě

Married (P) [a] (M) mate; he, however,

213

又拔着短籌撇的俺

yòu bá-zhe duǎn chóu, piē-de ǎn

furthermore drew (P) short lot, leaving (P) us

214

婆婦每都把空房守

pó fù měi dōu bǎ kōng fáng shǒu.

mother-in-law/daughter-in-law (Pl) all (Pr) empty chambers to-keep.

215

端的箇有誰問有誰

Duān-de ge yǒu shéi wèn, yǒu shéi

Really (-), there-is who to-inquire-after [us], there-is who

216

偢

qiù

to-look-after [us]?'

We all know that human feelings, unlike water, cannot flow endlessly.
When I was three years of age, my mother died;
At seven, I was separated from my father.
And then I married a man who died young,
Leaving my mother-in-law and me to keep to our lonely chambers.
Who is there to care for us, who is there to look after us?

213] *bá-zhe duǎn chóu:* 'to draw a short lot', which indicates a short length of life in fortune-telling.

214] *měi:* a plural suffix in Sung-Yüan dialects, comparable to the present *men* 們. This usage is found in *Yung-lo ta tien* 永樂大典 and *Yüan-ch'ao pi shih* 元朝秘史 (see Chao, *Grammar*, p. 244).

215] *Duān-de:* 'really'.

§208] *jìn-tóu: jìn-xiū* 盡休 in *KMCP*, p. 5*a*.
   Xū zhī-dao: bìàn zuò-dào 便做道 in *KMCP*, p. 5*a*.
§209] *bú sì: nán sì* 難似 in *KMCP*, p. 5*a*.
§211] *dào:* not in *KMCP*.

（ 天 下 樂 ） 莫 不 是 前

217 *(Tiān-xià lè) Mò bú shì qián*
('Heaven-below Joy') 'Could-it-not not be in-previous

世 裏 燒 香 不 到 頭 今

218 *shì-li shāo xiāng bú dào tóu, jin*
life (L) [in] burning incense [I] did-not reach end; [in] present

也 波 生 招 禍 尤 勸 今

219 *ye-bo shēng zhāo huò-yóu? ·Quàn jin*
(P) life call-down disaster/evil? [I] urge today's

人 早 將 來 世 修 我 將

220 *rén zǎo jiāng lái-shì xiū. Wǒ jiāng*
people early (Pr) next life to-cultivate. I (Pr)

這 婆 侍 養 我 將 這 服

221 *zhè pó shì-yǎng. Wǒ jiāng zhè fú-*
this mother-in-law serve/provide-for; I (Pr) this "wearing-

孝 守 我 言 詞 須 應 口

222 *xiào shǒu. Wǒ yán-cí xū yìng-kǒu.*
mourning" observe. My words must be-fulfilled.'

（ 云 ） 婆 婆 索 錢 去 了 怎 生 這

223 *(Yún:) Pó-po suǒ qián qù le. Zěn-shēng zhè*
(Speaks:) 'Mother-in-law to-demand money went (P). How this

早 晚 不 見 回 來 （ 卜 兒 同 孛

224 *zǎo-wǎn bú jiàn huí-lái? (Bǔ-er tóng bó-*
time [I have] not seen [her] return (C)?' (Old-woman and old-man,

老 張 驢 兒 上 卜 兒 云 ） 你 爺

225 *lǎo, Zhāng Lǘ-er shàng. Bǔ-er yún:) Nǐ yé*
Chang Donkey, enter. Old-woman speaks:) 'You father

兒 兩 箇 且 在 門 首 等 我 先

226 *ér liǎng ge qiě zài mén-shǒu děng, wǒ xiān*
son two (M) temporarily at gate wait; I first

(Fourth lyric):
> *Is it because I did not burn enough incense in my last life,*
> *That in this life I have to suffer?*
> *I urge people to do good deeds to cultivate a better next life.*
> *I serve my mother-in-law and mourn for my husband:*
> *My words must be fulfilled.*

Mother has gone to collect the debt. Why hasn't she come back by now?

(Enter Mistress Ts'ai with Old Chang and Donkey Chang.)

TS'AI: You two, father and son, stay here at the gate while I go in first.

217–8] *qián shì:* 'previous life' (in Buddhist belief).

218] *shāo xiāng bú dào tóu:* did not burn incense to the end, or did not burn enough incense (to warrant a better life in the following incarnation).

218–9] *jīn ye-bo shēng:* same as *jīn shēng*, 'this life'; *ye-bo* is a compound particle.

222] *yìng-kǒu:* 'to fulfill what has been said'; same as 應驗 *yìng yàn*.

223] *Zěn shēng:* 'why' or 'how'; comparable to modern usage *zěm-me* 怎麼.

§218–9] *jīn ye . . . huò-yóu: zhè qián-chéng shì yì-bǐ gōu* 這前程事一筆勾 in *KMCP*, p. 5a.

§219–20] *jīn rén: jīn shì* 今世 in *KMCP*, p. 5a.

§221] *Wǒ: Zài* 再 in *KMCP*, p. 5a.

227 進去（張驢兒云）妳妳你先
jìn-qu. *(Zhāng Lǘ-er yún:)* *Nǎi-nai, nǐ xiān*
go-in (C).' (Chang Donkey says:) 'Nai-nai, you first

228 進去就說女婿在門首哩
jìn-qu, jiù shuō nǚ-xu zài mén-shǒu li.
go-in (C); just say son-in-law is-at gate (P).'

229 （卜兒見正旦科正旦云）妳
(Bǔ-er jiàn zhèng dàn kē. Zhèng dàn yún:) *Nǎi-*
(Old-woman seeing principal female-role action. Principal
female-role says:) 'Nai-

230 妳回來了你喫飯麼（卜兒
nai huí lai le, nǐ chī fàn ma? (Bǔ-er
nai has-returned (C) (P). You have-eaten meal (P)?' (Old-
woman

231 做哭科云）孩兒也你教我
zuò kū kē, yún:) *Hái-er yě, nǐ jiào wǒ*
performs weeping gesture, says:) 'Child (P), you let me

232 怎生說波（正旦唱）
zěn-shēng shuō bo! (Zhèng dàn chàng)
how to-tell (P)?' (Principal female-role sings:)

233 （一半兒）爲甚麼泪漫
(Yí-bàn-er) *Wèi shém-me lèi màn-*
('One Half') 'For what tears overwhelmingly

234 漫不住點兒流莫不
màn bú zhù diǎn-er liú. Mò bú
not cease in-drops to-flow? Could-it-not not

235 是爲索債與人家惹
shì wèi suǒ zhài yǔ rén-jia rě
be because-of collecting debts with others provoked

236 爭鬭我這裏連忙迎
zhēng-dòu? Wǒ zhè-li lián-máng yíng-
fight? I here (L) quickly greet [her],

DONKEY CHANG: Mother, you go in first and say that your son-in-law is at the door.

(Mistress Ts'ai sees Tou O.)

TOU O: Mother, you're back. Have you eaten?

TS'AI (crying): Child, how can I tell you?

TOU O (Sings fifth lyric):

Why are tears flowing down unceasingly?
Is it because while collecting debts she provoked a quarrel with someone?
I hurry over to greet and inquire after her,

227] *Năi-nai:* same as *năi-nai* 奶 奶, a respectful address to a grown woman; may be used as a direct address to a mother-in-law.

231] *jiào* [*jiāo*]: Sometimes written as *jiāo* 交 in the Yüan printed edition.

232] *bo:* a final particle in Yüan Northern dialect, comparable to the modern Mandarin particle *ba* 吧 (see p. 17).

§228] *li: ba* 罷 , *KMCP*, p. 5b.

§233] *Wèi shém-me: Wŏ jiàn tā* 我 見 他 in *KMCP*, p. 5b.

§234–6] *Mò bú shì. . . zhĕng-dòu: Qíng mò-mò cháng huái yù mèn yōu* 情 脉 脉 常 懷 鬱 悶 憂 in *KMCP*, p. 5b.

237
接 慌 問 候 他 那 裏 要

jiē, huāng wèn-hòu, tā nà-li yào

hurry to-inquire-after [her]; she over-there (L) is-about

238
說 緣 由

shuō yuán-yóu.

to-tell reason.'

239
（ 卜 兒 云 ： ） 羞 人 答 答 的 教 我

(Bǔ-er yún:) Xiū rén dā-dā-de, jiào wǒ

(Old-woman says:) '[It] embarrasses person (P), allow me

240
怎 生 說 波 （ 正 旦 唱 ）

zěn-shēng shuō bo! (Zhèng dàn chàng:)

how to-say [it] (P)?' (Principal female-role sings:)

241
則 見 他 一 半 兒 徘 徊

Zé jiàn tā yí-bàn-er pái-huái

'Only see her half hesitating,

242
一 半 兒 醜

yí-bàn-er chǒu.

half ashamed.'

243
（ 云 ） 婆 婆 你 爲 甚 麼 煩 惱 啼

(Yún:) Pó-po, nǐ wèi shém-me fán-nǎo tí-

(Speaks:) 'Mother-in-law, you for what are-troubled [and] cry

244
哭 那 （ 卜 兒 云 ） 我 問 賽 盧 醫

kū na? (Bǔ-er yún:) Wǒ wèn Sài Lú-yi

(P)?' (Old-woman says:) 'I from "Rival Lu-Doctor"

245
討 銀 子 去 他 賺 我 到 無 人

tǎo yín-zi qù, tā zuàn wǒ dào wú rén

to-demand silver went; he lured me to no person

246
去 處 行 起 兇 來 要 勒 死 我

qù-chù, xíng-qǐ-xiōng-lai, yào lēi-sǐ wǒ

place, began-to-commit-violence; wanted to-strangle-to-death
me.

And she is about to give her reasons.

TS'AI: It's all so embarrassing; how can I ever say it?

TOU O:

She looks half hesitant and half embarrassed. (Speaks.)

Mother-in-law, why are you so upset and crying?

TS'AI: When I went to Sai Lu-yi to ask for my money, he lured me to a deserted place and tried to strangle me. Fortunately an old

237] *wèn-hòu:* 'to inquire after the health of another'; 'to send regards'.

239] *dā-dā-de:* an adverb which modifies 'to embarrass', connoting shyness.

239–240] The breaking up of the song text with prose dialogue is a convention in the Yüan drama and helps to reduce the distance between song and speech (cf. ll. 334, 342, etc.).

241] *pái-huái:* 'to walk back and forth'; 'to hesitate'.

242] *chǒu:* 'ugly'; here means 'embarrassed' or 'ashamed'.

244] *na:* a final particle, same as *na* 吶 or *na* 哪 in modern usage (see pp. 18–19). Listed in *CYYY* under *jiā-má* 家 麻 rhyme group.

246] *qǐ. . . lai:* 'begin to', a split aspect suffix (Chao, *Grammar*, p. 251). (In the case of a split expression such as this, hyphens are sometimes used to link the components of the expression.)

§239] *Xiū rén dā-dā-de:* not in *KMCP*.

§242] *chǒu: xiū* 羞 in *KMCP*, p. 5*b*.

§245–6] *wú rén qù-chù: jiāo-wài* 郊 外 in *KMCP*, p. 5*b*.

§246] *xíng-qǐ-xiōng-lai:* not in *KMCP*.

齁了一箇張老幷他兒子
247 Kui-le yí ge Zhāng lǎo bìng tā ér-zi
Fortunately (P), one (M) Chang elder and his son

張驢兒救得我性命那張
248 Zhāng Lǘ-er, jiù-de wǒ xìng-mìng. Nà Zhāng-
Chang Donkey saved (P) my life. That Chang

老就要我招他做丈夫因
249 lǎo jiù yào wǒ zhāo tā zuò zhàng-fu. Yīn
elder then wants me to-take him to-be husband. Therefore

這等煩惱（正旦云）婆婆這
250 zhè děng fán-nǎo. (Zhèng dàn yún:) Pó-po, zhè-
[I am] this way troubled.' (Principal female-role says:) 'Mother-
in-law, this

箇怕不中麼你再尋思咱
251 ge pà bù-zhōng ma. Nǐ zài xún-si za.
(P) [I] am-afraid would-not-do (P). You again think-over (P).

俺家裏又不是沒有飯吃
252 Ǎn jiā-li yòu bú-shì méi-yǒu fàn chi,
Our family (L) furthermore is-not having-no food to-eat,

沒有衣穿又不是少欠錢
253 méi-yǒu yi chuān, yòu bú-shì shǎo-qiàn qián
having-no clothing to-wear, again is-not owing money/

債被人催逼不過況你年
254 zhài, bèi rén cui-bi bú-guò. Kuàng nǐ nián-
debt, by people pressed inescapably. Moreover, your age

紀高大六十以外的人怎
255 jì gāo-dà. Liù-shí-yǐ-wài de rén, zěn-
is-advanced. Over-sixty [years old] (P) person, why

生又招丈夫那（卜兒云）孩
256 shēng yòu zhāo zhàng-fu na? (Bǔ-er yún:) Hái-
again take-in husband (P)?' (Old-woman says:) 'Child

man named Chang and his son, Donkey, saved me. Now Old Chang
wants me to take him as a husband. That's why I am so upset.

T O U O : Mother-in-law, I am afraid this won't work out. How about
thinking it over again? We are not starving, and we do not lack
clothing or owe money. We are not pressed by creditors. Besides,
you are advanced in years. You are over sixty years old; how can
you take another husband?

T S ' A I : Child, what you said is right. But I owe these two my life.

249] *zhāo...zhàng-fu:* 'to have a man marry into the wife's family'.
251] *za:* a particle for tentative statement: 'I suppose?'
255] *yǐ-wàì:* 'outside of', a localizer (Chao, *Grammar*, p. 620).

§247] *yí ge: zhè* 這 in *KMCP*, p. 5*b*.
§248–9] *Nà Zhāng-lǎo...zhàng-fu: Wǒ jiù zhāo Zhāng-lǎo zuò zhàng-fu* 我就招張
老做丈夫, in *KMCP*, p. 5*b*; an interesting difference between the two
texts.
§250–1] *zhè-ge pà:* not in *KMCP*.
§252–4] *Ān jiā-li...bú-guō: Jiā-li yòu bú qiàn shǎo qián-cái shǐ-yòng* 家裡又不欠少
錢財使用 in *KMCP*, p. 6*a*.
§255] *Liù-shí...rén:* not in *KMCP*.

兒 也 你 說 的 豈 不 是 但 是

257   *er yě, nǐ-shuō-de qǐ-bú-shì? Dàn-shì*

(P), what-you-said, is-it-not-so? But

我 的 性 命 全 虧 他 這 爺 兒

258   *wǒ-de xìng-mìng quán kuī tā zhè yé ér*

my (P) life entirely owes [to the fact that] they these father son

兩 箇 救 的 我 也 曾 說 道 待

259   *liǎng ge jiù-de. Wǒ yě céng shuō-dào, dài*

two (M) rescued (P) [it] I also have said, "Wait-till

我 到 家 多 將 些 錢 物 酬 謝

260   *wǒ dào jiā duō jiāng xiē qián-wù chóu-xiè*

I reach home, amply take some money/things to-reward

你 救 命 之 恩 不 知 他 怎 生

261   *nǐ jiù mìng zhī ēn. Bù zhi tā zěn-shēng*

you [for] rescuing life (P) favor."[I] don't know he how

知 道 我 家 裏 有 箇 媳 婦 兒

262   *zhi-dao wǒ-jiā-li yǒu ge xí-fu-er;*

knew in-my-family (L), there-was [a] (M) daughter-in-law;

道 我 婆 媳 婦 又 沒 老 公 他

263   *dào wǒ pó xí-fu yòu méi lǎo-gong, tā*

[they] said, we mother-in-law, daughter-in-law moreover had no "old-men", they

爺 兒 兩 箇 又 沒 老 婆 正 是

264   *yé ér liǎng ge yòu méi lǎo-po. Zhèng shì*

father son two (M) moreover had-no wives; [it] exactly was

天 緣 天 對 若 不 隨 順 他 依

265   *tiān-yuán tiān-duì. Ruò bù suí-shùn, tā yi-*

heaven-predestined, heaven-matched. If [I] did-not yield/obey, they still

舊 要 勒 死 我 那 時 節 我 就

266   *jiù yào lēi-sǐ wǒ. Nà shí-jié wǒ jiù*

wanted to-strangle-to-death me. That time I just

I also told them, 'Wait till I get home, I'll give you a lot of money to thank you for your kindness in saving my life.' I don't know how he found out I had a daughter-in-law at home. He argued that since we did not have husbands and they did not have wives, truly ours would be matches made in Heaven; and that if I did not agree with him, he still would strangle me to death. At the time I became

260] *jiāng*: same as *ná* 拿 , 'to take', in modern usage.

§257–68] *nĭ-shuō-de. . . tā:* not in *KMCP*.

慌 張 了 莫 說 自 己 許 了 他

267　huāng-zhāng le. Mò shuō zì-jǐ xǔ-le tā,
became-frantic (P). Not to-say myself [I] promised (P) him,

連 你 也 許 了 他 兒 也 這 也

268　lián nǐ yě xǔ-le tā. Ér yě, zhè yě
even you also [I] promised (P) him. Child (P), this also

是 出 於 無 奈 （ 正 旦 云 ） 婆 婆

269　shì chū-yú wú-nài. (Zhèng dàn yún :) Pó-po,
was out-of no-other-way.' (Principal female-role says:) 'Mother-
in-law,

你 聽 我 說 波 （ 唱 ）

270　nǐ tīng wǒ shuō bo. (Chàng:)
you listen-to me speak (P).' (Sings:)

（ 後 庭 花 ） 避 凶 神 要 擇

271　(Hòu-tíng huā) Bì xiōng shén yào zé
('Backyard Flowers') 'To-avoid evil spirits, [one] must
select

好 日 頭 拜 家 堂 要 將

272　hǎo rì-tou, bài jiā-táng yào jiāng
auspicious days; worshipping-in ancestral-halls, [one] must
(Pr)

香 火 修 梳 着 箇 霜 雪

273　xiāng-huǒ xiū. Shū-zhe ge shuāng-xuě-
incense-burning cultivate. [With your hair] combed-in [a]
(M) frost/snow-

般 白 鬏 髻 怎 將 這 雲

274　bān bái dí-jì, zěn jiāng zhè yún-
like white knot, how (Pr) this cloud/

霞 般 錦 帕 兜 怪 不 的

275　xiá-bān jǐn pà dōu. Guài-bu-de
haze-like silk veil wear? No-wonder:

frantic; and it wasn't just myself I promised them, but you also.
My child, there was nothing else I could do.

TOU O: Mother, you listen to me.

(Sings sixth lyric):

> To avoid evil spirits, one must select auspicious days;
> For a wedding ceremony, one must offer incense-burning.
> Now your knot of hair is as white as snow,
> How can you wear the colorful silk veil?
> No wonder people say,

272] *bài jiā-táng:* 'wedding ceremony' – worshipping (*bài*) ancestors is part of the wedding ceremony, which is held in the family hall (*jiā-táng*).

274-5] *yún-xiá-bān:* used idiomatically to mean 'colorful'. At a Chinese wedding, red is predominantly used, whereas white, traditionally used in a Western wedding, is worn at a Chinese funeral.

§271-2] *Bì xiōng shén. . . rì-tou: Yù shí-chen wǒ tì nǐ yōu* 遇 時 辰 我 替 你 憂 in *KMCP* p.6a

§272-3] *yào jiàng xiāng-huǒ xiū: wǒ tì nǐ chóu* 我 替 你 愁 in *KMCP*, p. 6a.

§274-5] *zěn jiàng zhè. . . dōu: zěn dài nà xiāo jīn jǐn gài-toú* 怎 戴 那 銷 金 錦 蓋 頭 in *KMCP*, p. 6a.

276 女大不中留你如今
nǚ dà bù zhōng liú! Nǐ rú-jīn
"Girl grown, not fit to-keep!" You now

277 六旬左右可不道到
liù-xún zuǒ-yòu kě-bú dào dào
sixty-years left/right; isn't-it said, "[When one] reaches

278 中年萬事休舊恩愛
zhōng nián wàn shì xiū. Jiù ēn-ài
middle age, ten-thousand things are-over?" Old affection

279 一筆勾新夫妻兩意
yì bǐ gōu, xīn fū qī liǎng yì
[with] one stroke [you] mark-off; new husband/wife, both
[their] feelings

280 投枉教人笑破口
tóu. Wǎng jiào rén xiào pò kǒu.
are-congenial. To-no-purpose [you] make people laugh
splitting [their] mouths.'

281 （卜兒云）我的性命都是他
(Bǔ-er yún:) Wǒ-de xìng-mìng dōu shì tā
(Old-woman says:) 'My (P) life entirely is they

282 爺兒兩箇救的事到如今
yé ér liǎng ge jiù-de. Shì dào rú-jīn,
father son two (M) saved (P). Things have-come-to as-of-now,

283 也顧不得別人笑話了（正
yě gù-bu-de bié rén xiào-hua le. (Zhèng
indeed cannot-care other people laugh (P).' (Principal

284 旦唱）
dàn chàng:)
female-role sings:)

285 （青哥兒）你雖然是得
(Qīng-gē-er) Nǐ suí-rán shì dé
('Green-Parrot') 'You although truly-did receive

94

You cannot keep a grown girl at home.
Now you are about sixty years of age,
Isn't it said that 'when middle age arrives, all is over'?
With one stroke, you mark off the memories of former love;
Now you and this man act like newlyweds.
To no purpose you make people split their mouths with laughter.

TS'AI : These two saved my life. Since it has come to this,
I don't care if other people laugh at me.

TOU O (Sings seventh lyric):
Though indeed you had him, had him save you,

276] There is a proverb: *nǔ dà bù zhōng liú, liú lái liú qù liú chéng chóu* 留來留去
留成仇 'A grown girl is not to be kept at home; if you try, you only make an
enemy out of her'.
277] *zuǒ-yòu:* literally 'left/right', meaning 'more or less', 'about'.
285] *shì:* used for emphatic assertion: 'do', 'is'.

§276] Before *nǔ:* *kě zhèng shì* 可正是 in *KMCP*, p. 6a.
§277] *kě-bú dào:* *zán rén* 喈人 in *KMCP*, p. 6a.
§280] *Wǎng jiào rén:* *Wǎng zháo bíe rén* 枉着別人 in *KMCP*, p. 6a.
After *xiào pò kǒu:* *zháo bié rén xiào pò kǒu* 着別人笑破口 *KMCP*, p. 6a
(a repetition).
§281-4] *Bǔ-er yún...dàn chàng:* not in *KMCP*.
§285-6] *Nǐ suī-rán...yíng-jiù: Nǐ bǐ nà shān fén de shēng-shòu* 你比那搧墳的生受
in *KMCP*, p. 6a.

95

286

他 得 他 營 救 須 不 是

tā dé tā yíng-jiù, xū bú-shì

his, receive his rescue, [you] truly are-not

287

筍 條 筍 條 年 幼 剗 的

sǔn-tiáo sǔn-tiáo nián-yòu. Chǎn-de

bamboo-shoot, bamboo-shoot, young-in-years. How

288

便 巧 畫 蛾 眉 成 配 偶

biàn qiǎo huà é-méi chéng pèi-ǒu.

then [can you] skillfully paint moth-eyebrows [and] become mates?

289

想 當 初 你 夫 主 遺 留

Xiǎng dāng-chū nǐ fū-zhǔ yí-liú

Think [how] formerly your husband left/bequeathed [things];

290

替 你 圖 謀 置 下 田 疇

tì nǐ tú-móu; zhì-xià tián-chóu,

for you planned; secured arable-land,

291

蚤 晚 羹 粥 寒 暑 衣 裘

zǎo wǎn gēng-zhōu, hán shǔ yī qiú;

morning/evening soup/gruel, winter/summer clothes/fur-garments;

292

滿 望 你 鰥 寡 孤 獨 無

mǎn wàng nǐ guān guǎ gū dú, wú

fully expecting you widower/widow, orphan/childless, not

293

捱 無 靠 母 子 每 到 白

ai wú kào, mǔ-zǐ-měi dào bái-

to-lean-on, not to-depend-on [anyone]; mother/child (Pl) [would live] till [they have] white

294

頭 公 公 也 則 落 得 乾

tóu. Gōng-gong ye! zé luò-de gān

heads. Father-in-law (P), [it] has-so-turned-out-that in-vain

You are no longer young like a bamboo shoot, like a bamboo shoot;
How can you paint your eyebrows fine to make another match?
Your husband left you his property;
He made plans for you;
He bought fertile land to provide food for morning and evening
And clothing for summer and winter,
Fully expecting his widowed wife and orphaned son,
To remain free and independent till old age.
Oh, father-in-law, you labored for nothing!

287] *Chăn-de:* 'how'; *píng-bái-de* 平白地, 'without reason'.
288] *é-méi:* 'moth eyebrows' – eyebrows which are long, delicate, and curved, like
    moth antennae. Zhāng Chăng 張敞 of the Han Dynasty, in his devotion to
    his wife, painted her eyebrows for her. Although later the allusion 'Zhāng Chăng
    painting eyebrows' is used to signify affection between husband and wife, the
    story, as told in the *History of Han*, always suggests a slightly improper intimacy
    (*Han shu* 漢書, *Po-na* ed., *chüan* 76, p. 18*a*). Since the painting of a wife's eye-
    brows by a husband is considered an excessive gesture according to traditional
    Chinese taste, the thought of Mistress Ts'ai at her age to contemplate such an
    intimate gesture with a stranger is outrageous.
291] *zăo:* same as *zăo* 早, 'morning'.
292] *guăn guă gū dú:* Literally, 'the widower, widow, orphan, and childless', here it
    refers to 'the widow and the orphan'.

§287] *sŭn-tiáo:* not repeated in *KMCP*.
§290] *tú-móu: dān-yōu* 躭憂 in *KMCP*, p. 6*a*.
    zhi-xià tián-chóu: not in *KMCP*.
§291] *zăo wăn: sì shí* 四時 in *KMCP*, p. 6*a*.
    hán shŭ yī qiú: yòu jiē chóu móu 又結綢繆 in *KMCP*, p. 6*b*.
§292] *măn wàng: zhĭ wàng* 指望 in *KMCP*, p. 6*b*.
§294] *zé luò-de: nĭ wèi tā* 你爲他 in *KMCP*, p. 6*b*.

生受
295
shēng-shòu.
[you] suffered.'

（卜兒云）孩兒也他如今只
296
(Bǔ-er yún:) Hái-er ye, tā rú-jīn zhǐ
(Old-woman says:) 'Child (P), they now just

待過門喜事匆匆的教我
297
dài guò-mén, xǐ shì cōng-cōng-de. Jiào wǒ
are-waiting to-pass-the-gate; [for] joyous affair, excited (P).
Ask me

怎生回得他去（正旦唱）
298
zěn-shēng huí-de tā qù? (Zhèng dàn chàng:)
how to-turn them away?' (Principal female-role sings:)

（寄生草）你道他匆匆
299
(Jì-shēng cǎo) Nǐ dào tā cōng-cōng-
('Parasite Grass') 'You say they greatly

喜我替你倒細細愁
300
-xǐ, wǒ tì nǐ dào xì-xì chóu;
are-happy, I for you however particularly worry;

愁則愁興闌刪嚥不
301
chóu zé chóu xìng lán-shān yàn-bú-
[I] worry, just worry [that your] spirit waning, [you]
cannot-swallow-

下交歡酒愁則愁眼
302
xià jiāo-huān jiǔ; chóu zé chóu yǎn
down [the] together-happy wine; [I] worry, just worry,
[that your] vision

昏騰扭不上同心扣
303
hūn-téng niǔ-bu-shàng tóng-xīn kòu;
unclear, [you] cannot-knot-up same-heart button;

98

TS'AI : Child, he is waiting to get married. He is so excited, how can
I refuse him?

TOU O (Sings eighth lyric):

You say that he is excited and happy.
I, however, am worried for your sake.
I worry that you, in waning spirit, cannot swallow the wedding wine;
I worry that you, with failing vision, cannot tie the same-heart knot;

297] *guò-mén:* 'to pass the gate' is an idiom for 'to get married' (used in reference to
females, or to males taken into the wife's family and adopting the wife's family
name after the marriage).

§296–8] *tā rú-jīn. . . tā qù:* not in *KMCP.*
§299–308] *jì-shēng cǎo . . . hòu:* this whole lyric is not in *KMCP.*

愁 則 愁 意 朦 朧 睡 不

304   *chóu zé chóu yì méng-lōng shuì-bu-*
[I] worry, just worry, [that your] mind dim, [you] cannot-
sleep-

穩 芙 蓉 褥 你 待 要 笙

305   *wěn fú-róng rù. Nǐ dài-yào shēng-*
secure [under the] hibiscus quilt. You want music/

歌 引 至 畫 堂 前 我 道

306   *gē yǐn zhì huà-táng qián; wǒ dào*
songs [to] lead [you] to decorated-hall front (L); I say

這 姻 緣 敢 落 在 他 人

307   *zhè yin-yuán gǎn luò zài tā rén*
this match must fall at other people's [marriages]

後

308   *hòu.*
behind (L).'

(卜 兒 云) 孩 兒 也 再 不 要 說

309   *(Bǔ-er yún:) Hái-er ye, zài bú-yào shuō*
(Old-woman says:) 'Child (P), further do-not scold

我 了 他 爺 兒 兩 箇 都 在 門

310   *wǒ le. Tā yé ér liǎng ge dōu zài mén-*
me (P). They father son two (M) all at gate

首 等 候 事 已 至 此 不 若 連

311   *shǒu děng-hòu. Shì yǐ zhì cǐ, bú-ruò lián*
are-waiting. Things have-already come-to this, nothing-like
even

你 也 招 了 女 婿 罷 (正 旦 云)

312   *nǐ yě zhāo-le nǚ-xu ba. (Zhèng dàn yún:)*
you also take (P) [in] husband (P).' (Principal female-role says:)

婆 婆 你 要 招 你 自 招 我 並

313   *Pó-po, nǐ yào zhāo nǐ zì zhāo. Wǒ bìng-*
'Mother-in-law, you want to-take [one], you yourself take [one].
I definitely

I worry that you, sleepy and feeling dim, cannot rest secure under the flower-quilt.

You want to be led by songs and music to the wedding hall;
I would say that this match certainly will fall short of others.

TS'AI: Oh child, scold me no more. They are both waiting at the gate. Since things have come to this, it is better that you too take a husband.

TOU O: If you want to take a husband, go ahead. I definitely do not

305] *rù* [or *ròu*]: *rù* is modern pronunciation; for rhyme it reads *ròu*. *CYYY* in fact gives a second pronunciation, homophonous with *ròu* 肉.

305–6] *shēng-gē*: generally used to mean 'music and songs'. *Shēng* is a small music instrument consisting of pipes.

307] *yīn-yuán*: generally used to mean the fate which brings about a marriage, or which 'causes' a man and a woman to marry. The expression is derived from the Buddhist term *yīn-yuán* 因緣, which was a translation of the Sanskrit term *hetu-pratyaya*, meaning 'cause' and 'condition'. *Hetu* is the primary cause, or internal cause, such as a seed is to a sprout, and *pratyaya* is the condition or secondary cause or causes, such as rain, dew, etc., are to a sprout. (Mochizuki Shinkō, 望月信亨, *Mochizuki Bukkyō daijiten*, 望月佛教大辭典, Tokyo, 1936, vol 1, p. 173.)

309] *zài*: used for emphasis before a negative.

312] *nǚ-xu*: specifically, 'daughter's husband'.

313] *zhāo*: abbreviation of *zhāo zhàng-fu* (see n. 249).

313–4] *bìng-rán*: 'definitely'; cf. *Ǎn shǒu xià bǐng wēi jiàng guǎ, zěn-shēng pò-de Lü Bù; bìng-rán qù bú dé yě*, 俺手下兵微將寡怎生破的呂布並然去不得也, 'Under my command the soldiers are scarce, the generals are few. How can we possibly defeat Lü Bu! Definitely, we should not go there.' *(San Chan Lü Pu* 三戰呂布 [*YCH wai-pien* 外編 no. 129], Act 1, Liu Pei's speech in the opening scene.)

§309–11] *Bǔ-er yún... děng-hòu*: not in *KMCP*.
§312] After *ba*: *Jīn rì jiù dōu guò liǎo mén zhe* 今日就都過了門者 in *KMCP*, p. 6b.

101

314　然不要女壻（卜兒云）那箇

rán bú yào nǚ-xu. (Bǔ-er yún:) Nǎ ge

do-not want husband.' (Old-woman says:) 'Which [one] (M)

315　是要女壻的爭奈他爺兒

shì yào nǚ-xu de? Zhēng-nài tā yé ér

is wanting husband one? What-to-do; they father son

316　兩箇自家捱過門來教我

liǎng ge zì-jiā āi guò mén lái, jiào wǒ

two (M) themselves forced through door (C); ask me

317　如何是好（張驢兒云）我們

rú-hé shì hǎo? (Zhāng Lǘ-er yún:) Wǒ-men

be-like-what would-be best?' (Chang Donkey says:) 'We

318　今日招過門去也帽兒光

jīn-rì zhāo guò mén qù ye. Mào-er guāng-

today are-taken passing gate (C) (P). "Hats bright,

319　光今日做箇新郎袖兒窄

guāng, jīn-rì zuò ge xīn-láng; xiù-er zè-

today be [a] (M) bridegroom; sleeves stylish,

320　窄今日做箇嬌客好女壻

zè, jīn-rì zuò ge jiāo-kè. Hǎo nǚ-xu,

today be [a] (M) handsome guest." Good sons-in-law,

321　好女壻不枉了不枉了（同

hǎo nǚ-xu, bù wǎng le, bù wǎng le. (Tóng

good sons-in-law; not in-vain (P), not in-vain (P).' (With

322　孛老入拜科正旦做不禮

bó-lǎo rù bài kē. Zhèng dàn zuò bù lǐ

old-man, enters, saluting gesture. Principal female-role makes
not-saluting

323　科云）兀那廝靠後（唱）

kē, yún:) Wù-nà sī, kào hòu! (Chàng:)

gesture, says:) 'Hey-there, fellow, [step] toward back!' (Sings:)

want a husband.

TS'AI: Who wants a husband? But what can one do when both, father and son, squeezed past the door of their own accord? What am I to do?

DONKEY CHANG: Today we are going to be married and be taken into our wives' family.

> Bright are our hats,
> Today we are going to be bridegrooms;
> Handsome are our sleeves,
> Today we are going to be guests of honor.

What good husbands, What good husbands! Not bad, not bad! (He and Old Chang enter and salute.)

TOU O (refuses to salute): You wretch, stand back!

(Sings ninth lyric):

318–20] *Mào-er...jiāo-kè:* this verse describing the neatness of a groom's attire and his happy mood appears several times in Yüan plays, usually quoted by others to the groom. Donkey Chang's quoting of the verse in praise of himself and his presumptuous behavior here further expose his boorish character and strengthen the audience's sympathy for Tou O when she rejects him.

319–20] *zè-zè:* usually means 'narrow'; here is used as *zè zè* 仄仄, 'handsome', 'stylish'.

323] *sī:* 'servant'; used here as verbal abuse in the sense of 'wretch'.

§314–7] *Nǎ ge... shì hǎo: Shí xuǎn dìng jīn-rì gǎn dōu gùo-mén lái yě* 實選定今日敢都過門來也 in *KMCP*, p. 6b.

§319] *xiù-er: mào-er mào-er* 帽兒帽兒 in *KMCP*, p. 6b.

§321–3] *Tóng bó-lǎo... bù lǐ kě:* the stage directions here are not in *KMCP*.

（賺煞）我想這婦人每

324 　(*Zhuàn-shā*) *Wǒ xiǎng zhè fù-rén-měi*
　　('Coda') 'I think these women (Pl)

休信那男兒口婆婆

325 　*xiū xìn nà nán-er kǒu, pó-po*
　　should-not believe those men's mouths; mother-in-law

也怕沒的貞心兒自

326 　*ye, pà méi-de zhēn xin-er zì*
　　(P), [I] am-afraid [you] have-no chaste heart yourself

守到今日招着箇村

327 　*shǒu. Dào jin-rì zhāo-zhe ge cūn*
　　to-keep. Comes today, take-in (P) [a] (M) rustic

老子領着箇半死囚

328 　*lǎo-zi, lǐng-zhe ge bàn sǐ qiú.*
　　old-fellow, lead-in (P) [a] (M) half dead convict'.

（張驢兒做嘴臉科云）你看

329 　*(Zhāng Lǘ-er zuò-zuǐ-liǎn kē, yún:) Nǐ kàn*
　　(Chang Donkey making-grimace gesture, says:) 'You see,

我爺兒兩箇這等身段儘

330 　*wǒ yé ér liǎng-ge zhè-děng shēn-duàn, jìn*
　　we father son two (M) [are] such figures, fully

也選得女壻過你不要錯

331 　*yě xuǎn-de nǚ-xu guò. Nǐ bú-yào cuò*
　　(P) for-being-selected as-husbands qualify. You must-not mis-
　　takenly

過了好時辰我和你早些

332 　*guò-le hǎo shí-chen. Wǒ hé nǐ zǎo-xiē-*
　　let-pass (P) good time. I and you a-little-sooner

兒拜堂罷（正旦不禮科唱）

333 　*er bài-táng ba. (Zhèng dàn bù-lǐ kē, chàng:)*
　　worship-in-hall (P).' (Principal female-role not-saluting gesture,
　　sings:)

104

Women should not, I think, believe what men say;
My Mother-in-law, I am afraid, will not maintain her chaste widowhood.
Now she takes as a husband an uncouth old fellow,
Who brings along with him a half-dead convict.

DONKEY CHANG (making a grimace): You can see that we two, father and son, cut such fine figures that we fully qualify for being selected as husbands. Don't let your good days go to waste. You and I, let's get on with the wedding ceremonies.

TOU O (refusing to salute, sings):

331] *guò:* 'to pass the test'; 'to qualify'.

§325-7] *pó-po. . . zì shŏu: kàn nĭ nà tiān cháng dì jiŭ* 看 你 那 天 長 地 久 in *KMCP*, p. 6*b*.

§327] *Dào jīn-rì zhāo-zhe: zhāo-de* 招 的 in *KMCP*, p. 6*b*.

§328] *bàn sĭ qiú: bú lù tóu* 不 律 頭 in *KMCP*, p. 6*b*.

§329-33] *Zhāng Lǘ-er. . . chàng:* not in *KMCP*.

則 被 你 坑 殺 人 燕 侶

334
Zé bèi nǐ kēng-shā rén yàn lǚ
'Only by you hurt-unto-death [other] people – swallow mates,

鶯 儔 婆 婆 也 你 豈 不

335
ying chóu! Pó-po ye, nǐ qǐ bù
oriole companions! Mother-in-law (P), you how not

知 羞 俺 公 公 撞 府 沖

336
zhī xiū! Ǎn gōng-gong chuàng fǔ chōng
feel shame! My father-in-law knocked-around prefectures, wandered-around

州 闖 閭 的 銅 斗 兒 家

337
zhōu, zhēng-zhái de tóng dǒu-er jiā-
counties; labored till [he got] "brass peck" family-property,

緣 百 事 有 想 着 俺 公

338
yuán bǎi shì yǒu. Xiǎng-zhe ǎn gōng-
hundred things included. Recalling (P) [how] my father-in-law

公 置 就 怎 忍 教 張 驢

339
gong zhì-jiù, zěn rěn jiào Zhāng Lǘ-
secured [it], how [can you] bear to-let Chang Donkey

兒 情 受 （ 張 驢 兒 做 扯

340
er qíng-shòu? (Zhāng Lǘ-er zuò chě
enjoy [it]?' (Chang Donkey performs pulling

正 旦 拜 科 正 旦 推 跌 科 唱 ）

341
zhèng dàn bài kē. Zhèng dàn tuī diē kē, chàng :)
principal female-role to-salute action. Principal female-role pushes [him] to-fall action; sings:)

兀 的 不 是 俺 沒 丈 夫

342
Wǔ-de-bú-shì ǎn méi zhàng-fu
'Is-this-not we having-no husband

You really can kill a person!
Swallows and orioles in pairs!
Mother-in-law, don't you feel shame?
My father-in-law worked in different prefectures and states;
He amassed a solid fortune, lacking in nothing.
How can you let the wealth he secured be enjoyed now by Donkey Chang?
(Donkey Chang pulls Tou O to kneel for the wedding ceremony.
Tou O pushes him over.)

TOU O (sings):
Isn't this the outcome of us widowed women! (Exit.)

334] *kēng-shā:* comparable to *hài-sǐ* 害死, 'to entrap'; 'to involve one in great trouble'.
334–5] *yàn lǚ yīng chóu:* 'swallows and orioles in pairs' is a traditional image for happy couples.
336–7] *chuàng fǔ chōng zhōu:* a stock phrase, meaning to go from place to place, working hard to establish oneself.
337] *zhēng-zhái:* same as *zhēng-zhá* 挣扎, 'to struggle', 'to work hard to obtain'; cf. *wú yòng zhēng-zhái* 無用關閿, 'no need to struggle' (*Ku chin hsiao shuo* 古今小說, Shanghai, 1947, vol 3, p. 4a.)
    tóng dǒu-er: 'brass peck' is used as an image of a solid fortune (see Chu Chü-i, *Yüan-chü su-yü fang-yen li-shih*, pp. 288–9).
340] *qíng-shòu:* comparable to *chéng-shòu* 承受, 'to receive, to enjoy', 'to inherit'; e.g., *ǎn gē-ge hé qíng-shòu Hàn-jiā jī-yè* 俺哥哥合情受漢家基業, 'my brother deserves to enjoy the House of Han's property'. (*Tan Tao Hui* 單刀會, Act IV, Song 5, 'Ch'en tsui tung feng' 沉醉東風).

§334–5] *Zé bèi nǐ. . . yīng chóu: Jiù ēn qíng yì bǐ dōu gōu* 舊恩情一筆都勾 in *KMCP*, p. 6b.
§335–6] *Pó-po. . . zhī xiū: Nǐ kě yě zì qióng jiū* 你可也自窮究 in *KMCP*, pp. 6b–7a.
§338] *Xiǎng-zhe: wǔ-di* 兀的 in *KMCP*, p. 7a.
§340–1] *Zhāng Lǚ-er. . . chàng:* the stage direction is not in *KMCP*.
§342–3] *Wǔ-de. . . xià-chǎng-tóu: Zhè dí shì qián rén tián tǔ hòu rén shōu* 這的是前人田土後人收 in *KMCP*, p. 7a.

的婦女下塲頭 (下)

343   *de fù-nǚ xià-chǎng-tóu. (Xià)*
       (P) women's outcome?' (Exit.)

(卜兒云) 你老人家不要惱

344   *(Bǔ-er yún:) Nǐ lǎo-rén-jia bú-yào nǎo-*
       (Old-woman says:) 'You, elderly-man, do-not be-annoyed.

懆難道你有活命之恩我

345   *zào. Nán-dào nǐ yǒu huó mìng zhī ēn, wǒ*
       Impossible-to-say you have rescuing life (P) kindness, I

豈不思量報你只是我那

346   *qǐ bù sī-liàng bào nǐ. Zhǐ shì wǒ nà*
       how-could not think-of rewarding you? Only it-is my that

媳婦兒氣性最不好惹的

347   *xí-fu-er qì-xìng zuì bù hǎo rě-de.*
       daughter-in-law's temperament utmostly not good to-provoke
       (P).

既是他不肯招你兒子敎

348   *Jì-shì tā bù-kěn zhāo nǐ ér-zi, jiào*
       Since she is-not-willing to-take-in your son, ask

我怎好招你老人家我如

349   *wǒ zěn-hǎo zhāo nǐ lǎo-ren-jia? Wǒ rú-*
       me how to-take-in you elderly-person? I now

今拼的好酒好飯養你爺

350   *jin pàn-de hǎo jiǔ hǎo fàn yǎng nǐ yé*
       provide (P) good wine, good meals to-keep you father

兒兩箇在家待我慢慢的

351   *ér liǎng-ge zài jiā. Dài wǒ màn-man-de*
       son two (M) at home. Wait-till I slowly (P)

勸化俺媳婦兒待他有箇

352   *quàn-huà ǎn xí-fu-er. Dài tā yǒu ge*
       persuade/convert my daughter-in-law. Wait-till she has [a] (M)

TS'AI: You, sir, don't be annoyed. You saved my life; I cannot but think of repaying you. Only that daughter-in-law of mine is not to be provoked and easily prevailed upon. Since she does not want to take your son as a husband, how can I take you, sir, as my husband? Now I shall provide good wine and good food to keep you both here at my house. Wait till I take time to persuade my daughter-in-law. When she has changed her mind, we can again

343] xià-cháng-tóu: 'the end', 'outcome'.
344] lǎo-rén-jiā: a courteous address to an elderly person.
345] Nán-dào: 'impossible to say', meaning 'hardly conceivable'; freely translated as 'Do you mean to say...?'
350] pàn: comparable to gē shě 割捨, 'to give up, to relinquish' (see Chang Hsiang, pp. 192–3, and Morohashi v: 12116).

§344–65] Bǔ-er yún... xià: (Bó-lǎo tóng bǔ yún:) Lǎo-er, zán jiā zhōng chī jiǔ qù-lái (xià. Jìng:) Dòu É bù kěn, zé zhè-ban bà-le bù-chéng; hǎo gòng dài yú wǒ zuò ge lǎo-pó. Hé ǎn lǎo-zi chī jiǔ qù-lai (xià). (孛老同卜云) 老兒嗜家中喫酒去來 (下淨) 竇娥不肯則這般罷了不成好共夕與我做箇老婆 和俺老子喫酒去來 (下) in KMCP, p. 7a.

109

回心轉意再作區處（張驢

353   *huí xin zhuǎn yì, zài zuò qū-chù. (Zhāng Lǘ-*
change-of heart, change-of mind, again [we will] make arrangements.' (Chang Donkey

兒云）這歪剌骨便是黃花

354   *er yún:) Zhè wāi-là gǔ, biàn shì huáng huā*
says:) 'This perverse bone, even-if [she] were "yellow flower

女兒 剛 剛 扯 的 一 把 也 不

355   *nǚ-er, gāng-gāng chě-de yì-bǎ yě bù*
girl", [I] just pulled (P) [her] once (M) indeed [she] did-not

消這等使性平空的推了

356   *xiāo zhè děng shǐ xìng, píng-kōng-de tui-le*
need this way to-engage temperament; for-nothing (P) pushed (P)

我一交我肯乾罷就當面

357   *wǒ yì jiāo. Wǒ kěn gān bà! Jiù dāng miàn*
me a fall. I be-willing to-neatly end! Then to [your] face

睹箇誓與你我今生今世

358   *dǔ ge shì yǔ nǐ: Wǒ jin-shēng jin-shì*
[I] make [an] (M) oath with you; [if] I in-this-life, in-this-world

不要他做老婆我也不算

359   *bú yào tā zuò lǎo-po, wó yě bú suàn*
do-not get her to-be wife, I indeed should-not be-considered

好男子（詞云）美婦人我見

360   *hǎo nán-zǐ. (Cí yún:) Měi fù-ren wǒ jiàn-*
proper man.' ([In] verse says:) 'Beautiful women I have-seen

過萬千向外不似這小妮

361   *guò wàn qiān xiàng-wài, bú sì zhè xiǎo ní-*
ten-thousand thousand beyond; [they] are-not as this little girl

子生得十分懶賴我救了

362   *zi shēng-de shí-fēn bèi-lài. Wǒ jiù-le*
grew (P) completely perverse. I saved (P)

110

make arrangements.

DONKEY CHANG: Such a perverse bone! Even if she were a virgin, just to be pulled by someone, she need not be so cross and push me to the ground for no reason. Will I let this go? I shall swear to your face that if I do not get her to be my wife in this life, I shall not be considered a man. (He recites):

> *Beautiful women I have seen by the thousands,*
> *But none so perverse as this wench.*
> *I saved your mother-in-law's life;*

354] *wāi-là:* comparable to the present expression *pō-là* 潑辣, 'perverse'. 'Perverse bone' is conventional abusive language.

354–5] *huáng huā nǔ-er:* a symbolic term for an innocent young girl; virgin.

357] *gān bà:* comparable to *gān xiū* 乾休, 'to end'.

362] *bèi-lài:* comparable to *pō-lài* 潑賴, 'perverse', 'cunning'.

你 老 性 命 死 裏 重 生 怎 割

363   *nǐ lǎo xìng-mìng sǐ li chóng-shēng. Zěn gē-*
your elder's life [so that she from] death (L) was-re-born.
How [can you] to-make-a-sacrifice

捨 得 不 肯 把 肉 身 陪 待 （同

364   *shě-de bù-kěn bǎ ròu shēn péi dài? (Tóng*
be-unwilling – with [your] flesh body to-keep-company, to-serve
[me]?' (Together

下 ）

365   *xià.)*
exeunt.)

第 二 折

366   *Dì-èr Zhé*
Number-two Act

（ 賽 盧 醫 上 詩 云 ） 小 子 太 醫

367   *(Sài Lú-yi shàng; shī yún:) Xiǎo zi tài-yi*
('Rival Lu-Doctor' enters; [in] verse says:) 'Insignificant person
[is a] doctor

出 身 也 不 知 道 醫 死 多 人

368   *chū-shēn. Yě bù zhī-dao yi sǐ duō rén.*
in-origin. Truly do-not know have-doctored to-death how-many
persons.

何 嘗 怕 人 告 發 關 了 一 日

369   *Hé-cháng pà rén gào-fā, guān-le yí rì*
When-have-been afraid people would-bring-accusation, [or]
closed (P) [for] one day

店 門 在 城 有 箇 蔡 家 婆 子

370   *diàn mén? Zài chéng yǒu ge Cài-jiā pó-zi.*
shop door? In city there-is [a] (M) Ts'ai-family woman.

剛 少 的 他 廿 兩 花 銀 屢 屢

371   *Gāng shǎo-de tā niàn liǎng huā-yín. Lǚ-lǚ*
[I] just owed (P) her twenty taels flower-silver. Frequently

How can you be unwilling to make a sacrifice to serve me with your body?
(Exeunt.)

ACT TWO

(Enter Doctor Lu, reciting a verse.)

LU:

I am a physician.
There is no knowing how many have died from my doctoring.
But when have I been afraid of accusation,
And closed my door once for apprehension?

There is a Mistress Ts'ai in town. I owe her twenty taels of silver.

363–4] *Zěn gē-shě-de bù-kěn:* in a more common order, the words would read: *Zěn bù kěn gē-shě-de,* 'how not willing to sacrifice'.

364] *bǎ ròu shēn:* an alternative translation would read: '(Pr) [my] flesh body'.

367] *Xiǎo zi:* 'I', a traditionally humble way for a young man to refer to himself.
     tài-yī: originally means the emperor's doctor, and later is used freely as 'a doctor'.

371] *huā-yín:* literally 'flower silver'; *huā* probably means 'snowflake flower', i.e., 'pure'. (See L. S. Yang, *Money and Credit in China, A Short History*, p. 46, paragraph 5.23.)

§366] *Zhé: Chū* 齣 in *KMCP*, p. 7a.
§367–84] *Xiǎo zi tài-yī. . . jīng-wén:* not in *KMCP*.

113

親 來 索 取 爭 些 撚 斷 脊 筋

372　　*qīn lái suǒ-qǔ; zhēng-xie niǎn-duàn jí jin.*
in-person [she] came to-demand [it]. [I] almost twisted/broke
[her] back tendons.

也 是 我 一 時 智 短 將 他 賺 到

373　　*Yě shì wǒ yì-shí zhì duǎn, jiāng tā zuàn dào*
Also it-was [that] I for-a-moment wits lacking; (Pr) her lured
to

荒 村 撞 見 兩 箇 不 識 姓 名

374　　*huāng cūn. Chuàng-jiàn liǎng ge bú-shì xìng-míng*
deserted village. Bumped-into two (M) [of]-unknown names

男 子 一 聲 嚷 道 浪 蕩 乾 坤

375　　*nán-zǐ. Yì shēng rǎng-dào: "Làng-dàng qián-kūn,*
men. One voice shouted: "[In this] vast-open heaven/earth,

怎 敢 行 兇 撒 潑 擅 自 勒 死

376　　*zěn gǎn xíng xiōng sā-pō, shàn-zì lēi-sǐ*
how dare commit violence, behave-evilly, following-own-will
strangle-to-death

平 民 嚇 得 我 丟 了 繩 索 放

377　　*píng-mín!" Xià-de wǒ diū-le shéng-suǒ, fàng-*
common-citizen!" Frightened (P) me to-let-go (P) rope, set-
loose

開 腳 步 飛 奔 雖 然 一 夜 無

378　　*kāi jiǎo-bù fēi bēn. Suí-rán yí yè wú*
foot-steps, flying-like ran. Although whole night no

事 終 覺 失 精 落 魂 方 知 人

379　　*shì, zhōng jué shi jing luò hún; fāng zhi rén*
incident, in-the-end, feel [as though] lost spirit lost soul. Only-
now realize human

命 關 天 關 地 如 何 看 做 壁

380　　*mìng guān tiān guān dì, rú-hé kàn zuò bì-*
life is-related-to heaven, related-to earth; how regard [it] as
on-the-wall (L)

She has been here often to claim the money. I almost broke her back. Indeed, I was stupid for a moment; I led her to the deserted countryside. Then we ran into two strangers. They shouted, 'Who dares commit a murder, a violent deed, under the open sky, disregard the law and strangle a citizen!' It frightened me so much that I threw away the rope and ran. Although nothing happened during the night, I was scared out of my wits. Now I know that a human life is tied to Heaven and Earth. How can one treat it like mere dust

375] *qián-kūn:* 'heaven/earth'; 'universe'; cf. *Tiān zhūn dì bēi, qián-kūn dìng yǐ,* 天尊 地卑,乾坤定矣 'Heaven is high, earth is low; thus the universe is determined'. (*Chou I* 周易 [*SPTK*] *chüan* 7, p. 1a.)

上 灰 塵 從 今 改 過 行 業 要

381 *shàng huī-chén? Cóng jīn gǎi-guò háng-yè, yào*
dust? From today shall-change profession, wanting

得 滅 罪 修 因 將 以 前 醫 死

382 *dé miè zuì xiū yīn. Jiāng yǐ-qián yī sǐ*
to-succeed-in wiping-out guilt, cultivating "cause". (Pr) formerly doctored to-death

的 性 命 一 箇 箇 都 與 他 一

383 *de xìng-mìng, yí-gè-gè dōu yǔ tā yí-*
(P) lives, [to] each-one, [I] without-exception shall-offer him a

卷 超 度 的 經 文 小 子 賽 盧

384 *juàn chāo-dù de jīng-wén. Xiǎo zǐ Sài Lú-*
volume releasing-soul (P) scripture. Insignificant person "Rival
Lu-

醫 的 便 是 只 爲 要 賴 蔡 婆

385 *yī de biàn shì. Zhǐ wèi yào lài Cài Pó-*
Doctor" (P) then is. Merely because-of wanting to-deny Ts'ai
Mistress

婆 二 十 兩 銀 子 賺 他 到 荒

386 *pó èr-shí liǎng yín-zi, zuàn tā dào huāng-*
twenty taels silver, lured her to deserted

僻 去 處 正 待 勒 死 他 誰 想

387 *pì qù-chù. Zhèng dài lēi-sǐ tā, shéi xiǎng*
place. Just about-to strangle-to-death her, who would-have-
expected [that we]

遇 見 兩 箇 漢 子 救 了 他 去

388 *yù-jian liǎng ge hàn-zi, jiù-le tā qù.*
encountered two (M) men, [who] rescued (P) her (C).

若 是 再 來 討 債 時 節 敎 我

389 *Ruò-shì zài lái tǎo zhài shí-jié, jiào wǒ*
If [she] again comes to-demand debt, [on such] occasion, have
me

116

on the wall? From now on I shall change my profession and try to wipe out my guilt and cultivate a better Karma. For each life that I killed by my doctoring, I shall offer the reading of a scripture to release the soul from suffering. I am Sai Lu-yi. Merely for wanting to default on a loan of twenty taels of silver, I lured Mistress Ts'ai to a deserted place. When I was just about to strangle her to death, two strangers turned up and saved her. If she comes again to ask

382] *yīn*: 'cause'; here it means causes or factors which will lead to a good or bad consequence, or future existence; loosely, 'Karma'.

384] *chāo-dù*: a Buddhist term, meaning 'to release souls from suffering'.

§389–95] *Ruò-shì... gān-jing: Jīn-rì kāi zhè yào-pù, kàn yǒu shém-me rén lái.* 今日開 這藥舖看有甚麼人來, in *KMCP*, p. 7a.

怎 生 見 他 常 言 道 的 好 三
390 zěn-shēng jiàn tā? Cháng-yán dào de hǎo: Sān-
 how to-see her? Proverb says (P) [it] well: "[Of] thirty-

十 六 計 走 爲 上 計 喜 得 我
391 shí-liù jì, zǒu wéi shàng jì. Xǐ-de wǒ
 six schemes, to-go-away is the-best scheme." Fortunately (P) I

是 孤 身 又 無 家 小 連 累 不
392 shì gū shēn, yòu wú jiā-xiǎo lián-lèi. Bú-
 am lone body; moreover have-no family/children to-be-
 involved-with. Nothing-

若 收 拾 了 細 軟 行 李 打 箇
393 ruò shōu-shi-le xì-ruǎn xíng-li, dǎ ge
 like pack-up (P) fine/soft luggage, make [a] (M)

包 兒 悄 悄 的 躲 到 別 處 另
394 bāo-er, qiāo-qiāo-de duǒ dào bié chù, lìng
 bundle, quietly (P) hide to another place, some-other-way

做 營 生 豈 不 乾 淨（張 驢 兒
395 zuò yíng-shēng, qǐ-bù gān-jing? (Zhāng Lǘ-er
 make living. Wouldn't-it be-neat?' (Chang Donkey

上 云）自 家 張 驢 兒 可 奈 那
396 shàng, yún:) Zì-jiā Zhāng Lǘ-er, kě-nài nà.
 enters, says:) 'Myself [is] Chang Donkey. No-way-to-handle
 that

竇 娥 百 般 的 不 肯 隨 順 我
397 Dòu É bǎi bān de bù kěn suí shùn wǒ.
 Tou O, [who is] in-a-hundred ways (P) not willing to-follow/
 to-yield-to me.

如 今 那 老 婆 子 害 病 我 討
398 Rú-jìn nà lǎo pó-zi hài-bìng. Wǒ tǎo
 Now, that old woman is-sick. I shall-ask-for

服 毒 藥 與 他 喫 了 藥 死 那
399 fù dú-yào, yǔ tā chī-le. Yào-sǐ nà
 dose-of poison, give-to her to-eat (P). [If I] poison-to-death that

for her money, how am I to face her? It is well said by the proverb, 'Of the thirty-six schemes, the best is to run away'. Fortunately I am by myself, not burdened by a family. It is better that I pack my valuables and luggage, tie up a bundle and quietly go to another place to hide and to start a new life. Won't that be a clean break? (Enter Donkey Chang.)

DONKEY CHANG: I am Donkey Chang. But alas! Tou O is still unwilling to yield to me. Now the old woman is sick. I shall get a dose of poison to give to her. When the old woman is poisoned, that

---

396] *kě-nài*: same as *wú kě nài-hé* 無可奈何, 'no way to handle'; *nài-hé*, 'to deal with', 'to handle'.

§396] *kě-nài nà*: *yǒu* 有 in *KMCP*, p. 7a.
§397] *bǎi bān de*: not in *KMCP*.
    suí shùn: *tōng shùn* 通順 in *KMCP*, p. 7a–b.

老婆子這小妮子好歹做
400 lǎo pó-zi, zhè xiǎo ní-zi hǎo-dǎi zuò
old woman, this little girl [for] better/worse will-be

我的老婆（做行科云）且住
401 wǒ-de lǎo-po. (Zuò xíng kē, yún:) Qiě zhù.
my (P) wife.' (Performs walking gesture, says:) 'Now stop.

城裏人耳目廣口舌多倘
402 Chéng-lǐ rén ěr mù guǎng, kǒu shé duō. Tǎng
In-the-city (L) people ears/eyes are-extensive, mouths/tongues
are-many. If [they]

見我討毒藥可不嚷出事
403 jiàn wǒ tǎo dú-yào, kě-bù rǎng-chu shì
see me asking-for poison, won't [they] cry-out an incident

來我前日看見南門外有
404 lai? Wǒ qián rì kàn-jian Nán mén wài yǒu
(C)? I previous day saw South Gate outside (L) there-was

箇藥舖此處冷靜正好討
405 ge yào pù, cǐ chù lěng-jìng; zhèng hǎo tǎo
[an] (M) apothecary shop; this place was-deserted/quiet; just
right to-ask-for

藥（做到科叫云）太醫哥哥
406 yào. (Zuò dào kē; jiào yún:) Tài-yi gē-ge,
drug.' (Performs arriving action; shouting, says:) 'Doctor older
brother,

我來討藥的（賽盧醫云）你
407 wǒ lái tǎo yào de. (Sài Lú-yi yún:) Nǐ
I come to-ask-for drug (P).' ('Rival Lu-Doctor' says:) 'You

討甚麽藥（張驢兒云）我討
408 tǎo shém-me yào? (Zhāng Lǘ-er yún:) Wǒ tǎo
are-asking-for what drug?' (Chang Donkey says:) 'I am-asking-
for

120

little wench, for better or for worse, must be my wife. (He walks.)
Wait a bit! There are too many eyes and ears and too much gossip
in town. If they see me buying poison, they will make noise and cause
trouble. The other day I saw an apothecary shop outside the South
Gate, where it was quiet and just right for getting the drug. (He
arrives and calls out.) Brother doctor, I came to get some medicine!
L U: What medicine do you want?
DONKEY CHANG: I want a dose of poison.

403] *kě-bù:* 'won't. . . ?'; a rhetorical question in negative form expecting a positive
answer.
403–4] *chu. . . lai:* a split directional complement (see Chao, *Grammar*, pp. 476–7).

§401–6] *Zuò xíng kē. . . jiào yún:* merely *Zhè li shì yào pù* 這裡是藥舖 in *KMCP*, p. 7b.

121

服毒藥（賽盧醫云）誰敢合

409 *fù dú-yào. (Sài Lú-yi yún:) Shéi gǎn huò*
dose-of poison.' ('Rival Lu-Doctor' says:) 'Who would-dare
mix

毒藥與你這廝好大膽也

410 *dú-yào yǔ nǐ? Zhè si hǎo dà-dǎn yě.*
poison for you? This fellow how bold (P)!'

（張驢兒云）你真箇不肯與

411 *(Zhāng Lǘ-er yún:) Nǐ zhēn-ge bù kěn yǔ*
(Chang Donkey says:) 'You really not willing [to] give

我藥麽（賽盧醫云）我不與

412 *wǒ yào ma? (Sài Lú-yi yún:) Wǒ bù yǔ*
me medicine (P)?' ('Rival Lu-Doctor' says:) '[If] I do-not
give-to

你你就怎地我（張驢兒做

413 *nǐ, nǐ jiù zěn-di wǒ? (Zhāng Lǘ-er zuò*
you, you then would-do-what-toward me?' (Chang Donkey
performs

拖盧云）好呀前日謀死蔡

414 *tuō Lú, yún:) Hǎo ya, qián rì móu sǐ Cài*
dragging Lu, says:), 'Good (P)! Previous day plot to-murder
Ts'ai

婆婆的不是你來你說我

415 *Pó-po de bú-shì nǐ lai? Nǐ shuō wǒ*
P'o-p'o one, wasn't-it you (P)? You say I

不認的你哩我拖你見官

416 *bú rèn-de nǐ li? Wǒ tuō nǐ jiàn guān*
not able-to-recognize you (P)? I will drag you to-see magistrate

去（賽盧醫做慌科云）大哥

417 *qù. (Sài Lú-yi zuò huāng kē, yún:) Dà gē,*
(C).' ('Rival Lu-Doctor' performs panic gesture, says:) 'Big
brother,

LU: Who dares mix poison for you? This wretch certainly has a lot
   of gall!
DONKEY CHANG: You really refuse to give me the medicine?
LU: I will not give it to you. What are you going to do to me?
DONKEY CHANG (seizes Doctor Lu): Fine! Aren't you the one who
   tried to strangle Mistress Ts'ai the other day? Do you think that I
   don't recognize you? I'll take you to the magistrate.
LU (panics): Big brother, let me go. I have the medicine, I have the

410] *dà-dăn: dăn*, the 'gall', is said to be the seat of courage; *dà-dăn*, 'of large gall'
   meaning 'bold'.
411] *zhēn-gè:* same as *zhēn-de* 眞的.

§411–12] *Nǐ zhēn-gè. . . ma: nǐ bù yǔ wǒ zhè yào, nǐ zhēn-gè bù yǔ shì zěm-me?* 你不與我
   這藥, 你眞箇不與是怎麽 in *KMCP*, p. 7*b*.
§414–15] *qián rì. . . nǐ lai: nǐ zài chéng wài jiāng nà pó-zi yào lēi sǐ hǎo de shì nǐ lai* 你
   在城外將那婆子要勒死好的是你來 in *KMCP*, p. 7*b*.

你 放 我 有 藥 有 藥（做 與 藥

418　nǐ fàng wǒ; yǒu yào, yǒu yào. (Zuò yǔ yào
you release me; there-is drug, there-is drug.' (Performs giving
drug

科 張 驢 兒 云）旣 然 有 了 藥

419　kē. Zhāng Lǘ-er yún: Jì-rán yǒu-le yào,
gesture. Chang Donkey says:) 'Since there-is (P) drug,

且 饒 你 罷 正 是 得 放 手 時

420　qiě ráo nǐ ba. Zhèng shì: Dé fàng shǒu shí
for-now shall spare you (P). Exactly is: Can release hands
occasion,

須 放 手 得 饒 人 處 且 饒 人

421　xū fàng shǒu; dé ráo rén chù qiě ráo rén.
should let-loose hands; can spare person situation, for-the-time-
being spare person.'

（下 賽 盧 醫 云）可 不 悔 氣 剛

422　(Xià. Sài Lú-yi yún:) Kě-bù huì-qì! Gāng-
(Exit. 'Rival Lu-Doctor' says:) 'Isn't-it bad-luck! Just-now

剛 討 藥 的 這 人 就 是 救 那

423　gāng tǎo yào de zhè rén, jiù shì jiù nà
asking-for poison (P) this person, exactly was saving that

婆 子 的 我 今 日 與 了 他 這

424　pó-zi de. Wǒ jin-rì yǔ-le tā zhè
woman one. I today gave (P) him this

服 毒 藥 去 了 以 後 事 發 越

425　fù dú-yào qù le; yǐ-hòu shì fā, yuè-
dose-of poison (C) (P); afterward affair comes-to-light, even-
more

越 要 連 累 我 趁 早 兒 關 上

426　yuè yào lián-lèi wǒ. Chèn zǎo-er guān-shàng
will involve me. Taking-advantage-of early-time, [I shall]
close-up

medicine. (Gives him the poison.)

DONKEY CHANG: Since I now have the drug, I will let you off. Indeed, it is: 'When one can set others free, it is better to set them free; when one is able to forgive, it is better to forgive.' (Exit.)

LU: This is surely bad luck. The fellow who has just asked for the medicine is the one who saved that old woman. Now I have given him a dose of poison; if anything happens, I shall be in more trouble. I'd better close this store before it's too late. I'll go to Cho-chou to

---

422] *huì*: usually meaning 'to regret' and in third tone, here it is used as a variant of *huì* 晦 in *huì-qì*, 'bad luck'.

§420–1] *qiě ráo. . . ráo rén: Wǒ wǎng jiā zhōng qù yě* 我往家中去也 in *KMCP*, p. 7*b*.
§422] *Kě-bù huì-qì:* not in *KMCP*.
§422-3] *Gāng-gāng: yuán-lái* 原來 in *KMCP*, p. 7*b*.
§425] *yǐ-hòu shì fā:* not in *KMCP*.
§425–6] *yuè-yuè yào: zhǐ pà* 只怕, in *KMCP*, p. 7*b*.
§426–7] *Chèn zǎo-er. . .yào pù: Wǒ jīn kāi bù chéng yào pù* 我今開不成藥舖 in *KMCP*, p. 8*a*.

藥舖到涿州賣老鼠藥去

427   *yào pù, dào Zhuō-zhōu mài lăo-shŭ-yào qù*
apothecary shop, to Cho-chou to-sell rat-poison will-go

也（下卜兒上做病伏几科

428   *yě. (Xià. Bŭ-er shàng, zuò bìng fú ji kē.*
(P).' (Exit. Old-woman enters; performs sick leaning-onto table gesture.

孛老同張驢兒上云）老漢

429   *Bó-lăo tóng Zhāng Lǘ-er shàng; yún:) Lăo hàn*
Old-man with Chang Donkey enters, says:) 'Old man

自到蔡婆婆家來本望做

430   *zì dào Cài Pó-po jiā lái, běn wàng zuò*
since arriving-at Ts'ai Mistress's house (C), originally hoped to-be

箇接腳却被他媳婦堅執

431   *ge jiē-jiǎo. Què bèi tā xí-fu jiān-chí*
[a] (M) second-husband. However by her daughter-in-law obstinately

不從那婆婆一向收留俺

432   *bù cóng. Nà pó-po yí-xiàng shōu-liú ǎn*
not agreed. That old-woman up-to-the-present has-kept us

爺兒兩箇在家同住只說

433   *yé ér liăng ge zài jiā tóng zhù. Zhǐ shuō*
father son two (M) at house together to-live. [She] just says

好事不在忙等慢慢裏勸

434   *hǎo shì bú zài máng, děng màn-màn-li quàn*
good things do-not rest-on haste; wait [till she] slowly (P) persuades/

轉他媳婦誰想那婆婆又

435   *zhuǎn tā xí-fu. Shéi xiǎng nà pó-po yòu*
brings-around her daughter-in-law. Who would-have-expected that old-woman moreover

sell rat poison. (Exit.)

(Enter Mistress Ts'ai, sick, holding onto a table. Enter Old Chang and Donkey Chang.)

OLD CHANG: I came to the house of Mistress Ts'ai hoping to be her second husband. But her daughter-in-law stubbornly refuses to give in. The old woman has kept the two of us, father and son, here at her house. She keeps on saying that a good thing should not be rushed, and we should wait until she succeeds in persuading her daughter-in-law to change her mind. Who would have thought

431] *jiē-jiǎo*: abbreviation of *jiē-jiǎo-xù* 婿 'following-feet-husband', a man who married into a family after the first husband's death; cf. *(Xú) Yuán-jié wèi Lín Qiáo fá-kē, yì cūn háo jiā wéi jiē-jiǎo xù* (徐) 元 杰 爲 林 喬 伐 柯, 一 村 豪 家 爲 接 腳 婿 'Yuán-jíe performed match-making for Lín Qiáo; he was married into a powerful family in the village'. (Chou Mi 周 密 '*Kuei-hsin tsa-chih pieh-chi*' 癸 辛 雜 識 別 集 [in *Hsüeh-chin t'ao yüan* 學 津 討 原, ser. 19, vol. 6, 1805], p. 12a).

434] *màn-màn-li*: comparable to *màn-màn-de* 的 in modern usage.

§428–9] *Bǔ-er. . . yún*: *bó-lǎo tóng jìng fú bǔ-er shàng* 孛 老 同 淨 扶 卜 兒 上 in *KMCP*, p. 8a.

§430] *běn wàng*: not in *KMCP*.

§431–5] *Què bèi tā. . . xí-fu*: not in *KMCP*.

害 起 病 來 孩 兒 你 可 曾 算

436 *hài-qǐ-bìng-lai. Hái-er, nǐ kě céng suàn*

began-to-be-sick. Child, you possibly have figured-out

我 兩 箇 的 八 字 紅 鸞 天 喜

437 *wǒ liǎng-ge de bá-zi? Hóng luán Tiān xǐ*

we both (M)'s (P) horoscopes? "Red *Luan*-bird," "Heaven's Joy"

幾 時 到 命 哩 (張 驢 兒 云) 要

438 *jǐ-shí dào mìng li? (Zhāng Lǘ-er yún:) Yào*

what-time will-enter [our] lives (P)?' (Chang Donkey says:) 'Expect

看 什 麼 天 喜 到 命 只 睹 本

439 *kàn shém-me tiān xǐ dào mìng? Zhǐ dǔ běn-*

to-see what "Heaven's Joy" coming-into life? Just bet-on ability;

事 做 得 去 自 去 做 (孛 老 云)

440 *shì, zuò-de-qù zì qù zuò. (Bó-lǎo yún:)*

[if you] are-able-to-do [a thing], yourself go to-do [it].' (Old-man says:)

孩 兒 也 蔡 婆 婆 害 病 好 幾

441 *Hái-er yě, Cài Pó-po hài-bìng háo jǐ*

'Child (P), Ts'ai Mistress has-been-sick [for a] good many

日 了 我 與 你 去 問 病 波 (做

442 *rì le, wǒ yǔ nǐ qù wèn bìng bo. (Zuò*

days (P). I and you go to-inquire-after sickness (P).' (Performs

見 卜 兒 問 科 云) 婆 婆 你 今

443 *jiàn bǔ-er wèn kē, yún:) Pó-po, nǐ jin-*

seeing old-woman, inquiring gesture. Says:) 'P'o-p'o, you today

日 病 體 如 何 (卜 兒 云) 我 身

444 *rì bìng tǐ rú-hé? (Bǔ-er yún:) Wǒ shēn-*

sick body like-what?' (Old-woman says:) 'My body

子 十 分 不 快 哩 (孛 老 云) 你

445 *zi shí-fēn bú kuài li. (Bó-lǎo yún:) Nǐ*

very is-not well (P).' (Old-man says:) 'You

128

that the old woman would fall sick? Son, have you had our horoscopes read? When will the lucky star and the auspicious day enter into our life?

DONKEY CHANG: Why wait for the auspicious day to arrive? One can only gamble on his ability. If you are able to do something, go ahead and do it.

OLD CHANG: Son, Mistress Ts'ai has been sick for quite a few days. Let us go inquire after her sickness. (Sees the old woman and inquires.) *P'o-p'o*, how do you feel today?

TS'AI: I don't feel well at all.

437] *Hóng luán:* luán, a fabulous bird; *Hóng luán* is the name of a lucky star.
   Tiān xǐ: certain days in the reckoning of astrologists are considered auspicious and are called *Tiān-xǐ* ('Heaven's Joy').
445] *kuài:* 'feeling well'; see Hsü Chia-jui, *Chin Yüan hsi-ch'ü fang-yen k'ao*, p. 14.

§436] *hài-qǐ-bìng-lai:* yí-xiàng rǎn bìng 一问染病 in *KMCP*, p. 8a.
§436–8] *Hái-er... míng li: Duō shì zì-jǐ bú-xìng* 多是自己不幸 in *KMCP*, p. 8a.
§438–45] *Zhāng Lǘ-er... Bó-lǎo yún:* not in *KMCP*.

可 想 些 甚 麽 吃（卜 兒 云）我

446   *kě xiǎng xie shém-me chī? (Bǔ-er yún:) Wǒ*
possibly want a-little something to-eat?' (Old-woman says:) 'I

思 量 些 羊 腈 兒 湯 吃（孛 老

447   *sī-liàng xiē yáng dǔ-er tāng chī. (Bó-lǎo*
would-like some mutton tripe soup to-eat.' (Old-man

云）孩 兒 你 對 竇 娥 說 做 些

448   *yún:) Hái-er, nǐ duì Dòu É shuō, zuò xiē*
says:) 'Child, you to Tou O say, make some

羊 腈 兒 湯 與 婆 婆 吃（張 驢

449   *yáng dǔ-er tāng yǔ pó-po chī. (Zhāng Lǘ-*
mutton tripe soup to-give-to p'o-p'o to-eat.' (Chang Donkey

兒 向 古 門 云）竇 娥 婆 婆 想

450   *er xiàng gǔ-mén yún:) Dòu É, pó-po xiǎng*
toward stage-door, says:) 'Tou O, p'o-p'o wants

羊 腈 兒 湯 吃 快 安 排 將 來

451   *yáng dǔ-er tāng chī. Kuài ān-pái jiāng lái.*
mutton tripe soup to-eat. Quickly prepare [some and] bring [it] (C).'

（正 旦 持 湯 上 云）妾 身 竇 娥

452   *(Zhèng dàn chí tāng shàng. Yún:) Qiè-shēn Dòu É*
(Principal female-role carrying soup enters. Says:) 'Hand-maiden Tou O

是 也 有 俺 婆 婆 不 快 想 羊

453   *shì yě. Yǒu ǎn pó-po bú kuài, xiǎng yáng*
is (P). It-happens-that my mother-in-law is-not well, wants mutton

腈 湯 吃 我 親 自 安 排 了 與

454   *dǔ-er tāng chī. Wǒ qin-zì ān-pái-le yǔ*
tripe soup to-eat. I personally have-prepared (P) [some] to-give-to

婆 婆 吃 去 婆 婆 也 我 這 寡

455   *pó-po chī qù. Pó-po yě, wǒ zhè guǎ-*
mother-in-law to-eat (C). Mother-in-law (P), we these widows,

OLD CHANG: Would you want a little something to eat?

TS'AI: I'd like to have some mutton tripe soup.

OLD CHANG: Son, you tell Tou O to prepare some mutton tripe soup for *p'o-p'o*.

DONKEY CHANG (calling toward the stage door): *P'o-p'o* would like to have some mutton tripe soup. Hurry to prepare some and bring it here.

(Enter Tou O, carrying the soup.)

TOU O: I am Tou O. My mother-in-law doesn't feel well and she wants to have some mutton tripe soup. I myself have made some for her, and I am going to take it to her now. Mother-in-law, we

447] *dŭ:* the present form is *dŭ* 肚.

450] *gŭ-mén:* same as *gŭ-mén dào* 古門道, 'old doorway' or *guĭ-mén dào* 鬼門道, 'ghost doorway', doors on the stage for exit and entrance. The reason that the doors are so called is that the impersonated individuals who pass through them are usually deceased; cf. Su Tung-p'o's (蘇東坡 1037–1101) line: *bān yăn gŭ rén shì, chū rù guĭ-mén dào* 搬演古人事出入鬼門道, 'To stage the affairs of the people of old; and to pass in and out of the ghost doors.' (Quoted in *T'ai-ho cheng-yin p'u* 太和正音譜 [in *CKKTHCLCCC*, vol. III], p. 54 and p. 213, n. 218.)

§446] After *chī: Nĭ biàn shūo po* 你便說波 in *KMCP*, p. 8a.

§448] *Hái-er: Zhāng Lǘ-er* 張驢兒 in *KMCP*, p. 8a.

§450] *xiàng gŭ-mén yún:* not in *KMCP*.

§452] *chí tāng:* not in *KMCP*.

§455–62] *Pó-po yě... bù jié de:* not in *KMCP*.

婦 人 家 凡 事 也 要 避 些 嫌

456   *fù-rén-jia, fán shì yě yào bì xiē xián-*

in-all things truly need to-avoid some-few suspicions.

疑 怎 好 收 留 那 張 驢 兒 父

457   *yí. Zěn-hǎo shōu-liú nà Zhāng Lǘ-er fù*

How-can [we] keep those Chang Donkey father

子 兩 箇 非 親 非 眷 的 一 家

458   *zǐ liǎng gè? Fēi qin fēi juàn de, yì jiā-*

son two (M)? [They are] neither relatives nor family (P) –
[as] one family

兒 同 住 豈 不 惹 外 人 談 議

459   *er tóng zhù, chǐ-bú rě wài-rén tán-yì?*

with [us] live, how-not provoke outsiders to-talk?

婆 婆 也 你 莫 要 背 地 裏 許

460   *Pó-po ye, nǐ mò-yào bèi-dì-lǐ xǔ-*

Mother-in-law (P), you don't behind-back (L) promise

了 他 親 事 連 我 也 累 做 不

461   *le tā qin-shì; liǎn wǒ yě lèi zuò bù*

(P) him marriage; even I also would-be-involved to-be not

淸 不 潔 的 我 想 這 婦 人 心

462   *qing bù jié de. Wǒ xiǎng zhè fù-rén xin*

pure not clean (P). I think this woman's heart

好 難 保 也 呵 （ 唱 ）

463   *hǎo nán bǎo ye he. (Chàng:)*

very hard to-keep (P) (P)!' (Sings:)

（ 南 呂 一 枝 花 ） 他 則 待

464

  (Nán-lǚ: Yì zhi huā) Tā zé dài

(Nan-lü [mode]: 'One Twig-of Blossoms') 'She just wants

widows should be discreet in all things. How can we keep Donkey Chang and his father, who are not relatives or members of our family, here in the house with us? Won't that make people talk? Mother-in-law, do not promise them your hand secretly and involve me also in impropriety. I can't help thinking how hard it is to keep watch over a woman's heart.

(Sings first lyric):

She wants to rest behind lovebird curtains all her days,

462] *Wŏ xiǎng:* here Tou O turns aside from the immediate situation to a general reflection which will become the subject of the following two arias.

§464] *Nán-lǚ: Nán-gōng* 南 宮 *KMCP,* p. 8a: an abbreviation of *Nán-lǚ-gōng* 南 呂 宮.

465 一生鴛帳眠那裏肯

yì shēng yuān zhàng mián. Nǎ-li kěn

whole life [behind] mandarin-duck curtains to-sleep. Where (L) be-willing

466 半夜空房睡他本是

bàn yè kōng fáng shuì; tā běn shì

[for] half-a night [in] empty chamber slumber? She originally was

467 張郎婦又做了李郎

Zhāng láng fù, yòu zuò-le Lǐ láng

Chang man's woman, again becomes (P) Li man's

468 妻有一等婦女每相

qi. Yǒu yì děng fù-nǚ-měi xiāng

wife. There-is a type-of woman (Pl), [who] each-other

469 隨並不說家克計則

suí, bìng bù shuō jiā-kè-jì, zé

following, absolutely do-not talk-of household-plans; only

470 打聽些閒是非說一

dǎ-ting xiē xián shì-fēi. Shuō yí

inquire-about some idle rights/wrongs. Talk [for] a

471 會不明白打鳳的機

huì bù míng-bai dǎ fèng de ji-

while [of] not comprehensible catching phoenix (P) tricks,

472 關使了些調虛囂撈

guān, shǐ-le xiē tiáo xū-xiāo lāo

display (P) a-little engaging falsehood trapping

473 龍的見識

lóng de jiàn-shì.

dragon (P) knowledge.'

134

Unwilling to sleep in an empty chamber for half a night.
First she was Mr Chang's woman, now she is Mr Li's wife.
There is a type of woman, who, following each other's fashion,
Speak not of household matters, but pick up all idle gossip.
They vaguely talk of catching-phoenix adventures,
And display knowledge of trapping-dragon tricks.

465] *yuān zhàng: yuān*, Mandarin duck, symbol of conjugal love. *Zhàng*, net hanging
   around the bed. Cf. n. 1340.
471-3] *dǎ fèng* and *lǎo lóng:* 'catching a phoenix' or 'trapping a dragon' is usually
   interpreted as 'to hurt a good person'.

§471] *bù míng-bai:* not in *KMCP*; instead *nà zhàng-fu* 那丈夫, p. 8b.
§472] After *xiē: bù zhao* 不着, *KMCP*, p. 8b.
§472-3] *lǎo lóng:* not in *KMCP*.

（梁州第七）這一箇似
474   *(Liáng-zhōu dì qi) Zhè yí ge sì*
('Liang-chou No. Seven':) 'This one (M), as

卓氏般當鑪滌器這
475   *Zhuó-shì bān dāng lú dí qì. Zhè*
Miss-Cho's manner, in-the-presence-of wine-jars washes utensils. This

一箇似孟光般舉案
476   *yí ge sì Mèng Guāng bān jǔ àn*
one (M), as Meng Kuang's manner, raises tray

齊眉說的來藏頭蓋
477   *qí méi; shuō-de-lái cáng tóu gài*
level-with [her] eyebrows; can-talk-so-as to-hide head, to-cover

脚多怜悧道着難曉
478   *jiǎo duó lián-lì. Dào-zhe nán xiǎo,*
feet, how clever! [From] talking (P), hard to-know;

做出纔知舊恩忘却
479   *zuò-chū cái zhi. Jiù ēn wàng-què,*
[from] action, only-then understood. Old love is-forgotten/rejected;

新愛偏宜墳頭上土
480   *xin ài piān-yí. Fén tóu shàng tǔ*
new love is-favored. Grave top (L) earth

脉猶濕架兒上又換
481   *mò yóu shī; jià-er-shàng yòu huàn*
veins still are-wet; on-the-rack (L) [she has] again changed-to

新衣那裏有奔喪處
482   *xin yi. Nǎ-lǐ yǒu bēn-sāng chù*
new clothes. Where (L) is-there [anyone who at a] funeral place

(Sings second lyric):

'*This one is like Lady Cho, who worked in a tavern;*
This one is like Meng Kuang, who raised her tray as high as her eyebrows.'
Behind these clever words they hide their true selves.
Their words do not reveal, only their deeds.
Old love is easily forgotten, and new love is favored.
Upon the grave the earth is still wet;
On the rack new clothes are hung.
Where would one find a woman who would weep down the Great Wall at
her husband's funeral?

475] *Zhuó:* proper name; refers to Zhuó Wén-jūn, the wife of Sī-mǎ Xiàng-rú. When they were poor, they kept a small tavern in Chéng-dū, where she served as a barmaid (see n. 28 on '*Zǐ Xū*').

476–7] *Mèng Guāng bān jǔ àn qí méi:* Mèng was the wife of Liáng Hóng 梁鴻 of the Later Han. She showed her respect and love by bringing in the dinner tray raised as high as her eyebrows (*History of Later Han* [*Hou-Han Shu* 後漢書], *Po-na* ed., *chūan* 83, p. 14*a*).

 Jǔ àn qí méi, 'to raise the dinner tray as high as the eyebrows', is later used to indicate mutual respect and love of husband and wife. There is also a Yüan play by this title, author unknown (*YCH*, no. 53).

477–8] *cáng tóu gài jiǎo:* 'to hide one's head and to cover one's feet', meaning 'to deceive'.

478] *lián-lì:* a variant of *líng-li* 伶俐 'clever' (Morohashi IV: 10461: 4).

480–2] *Fén tóu. . . xīn yī:* before the earth on the late husband's grave has time to dry, the woman already got out her new clothes, eager to seek attention.

§474] *dì qī:* not in *KMCP.*

§477–8] *shuō-de. . . lián-lì: Jìn shí yǒu děng pó niáng měi* 近時有等婆娘每 in *KMCP,* p. 8*b.*

§479] *cái: nán* 難 in *KMCP,* p. 8*b.*

§482] *bēn-sāng chù: zǒu biān tíng* 走邊廷 in *KMCP,* p. 8*b.*

137

哭倒長城那裏有浣

483   *kū dǎo Cháng-chéng? Nǎ-li yǒu huǎn*
will-weep [so-as] to-crumble [the] Great Wall? Where (L)
is-there [anyone who] washing

紗時甘投大水那裏

484   *shā shí gān tóu dà shuǐ? Nǎ-li*
yarn time would-willingly plunge-into great river? Where
(L)

有上山來便化頑石

485   *yǒu shàng shān lái biàn huà wán shí?*
is-there [anyone who would] go-up mountain (C) then
turn-to senseless stone?

可悲可恥婦人家直

486   *Kě-bēi kě-chǐ, fù-ren-jia zhí*
Pitiable, shameful – women simply

恁的無仁義多淫奔

487   *rèn-de wú rén-yì; duō yín-bēn,*
this-way (P) lack kindness/fidelity – have-much wantonness,

少志氣虧殺前人在

488   *shǎo zhì-qì. Kuī-shā qián-rén zài*
have-little purpose. Fortunately, [these] former persons
were

那裏更休說本性難

489   *nà-li, gèng xiu shuō běn xìng nán*
there (L); further do-not say [that people's] basic nature
is-hard

移

490   *yí.*
to-change.'

（云）婆婆羊腅兒湯做成了

491   *(Yún:) Pó-po, yàng dǔ-er tāng zuò-chéng le,*
(Speaks:) 'Mother-in-law, mutton tripe soup is-done (P),

Where would one find a girl who, while washing her yarn, would willingly
plunge into the Big River?
Where would one find a wife turning into stone while waiting for her
husband's return?
How pitiable and shameful!
Women today are not virtuous but wanton and lacking in purpose.
Fortunately, there were faithful women of old;
Thus say not that human nature is hard to change.

(Speaks:) Mother, the mutton tripe soup is ready. How about

483] *kū dǎo Cháng-chéng:* this refers to the folk tale about Mèng Jiāng-nǔ 孟姜女,
whose husband, Fàn Chǐ-liáng 范杞梁 died while a conscript laborer working
on the Great Wall during the reign of the first Emperor of Ch'in 秦. Later
she went to seek her husband and wept so bitterly at the foot of the Wall that
part of it crumbled and exposed her husband's body (Morohashi III: 6960: 53).

484] *gān tóu dà shuǐ:* 'be willing to drown oneself in a big river'. During the Spring
and Autumn period, the minister Wǔ Zǐ-xū 伍子胥 fled from the state of Chǔ to
Wú. A woman washing by the river took pity on the refugee and fed him. Upon
leaving, he asked her not to tell his pursuers which way he had gone. She
drowned herself in the river to assure him that no word of his escape could come
from her. Another reason for her drowning was that although she helped the refugee
out of compassion, she nonetheless failed in chastity in dealing with a man who
was a stranger. ('Wu Tzu-hsü pien-wen' 伍子胥變文, *Tun-huang pien-wen chi*
敦煌變文集 ed., Wang Ch'ung-min 王重民 *et. al.*, [Peking, 1957], pp. 3–8).
Tou O made the allusion here evidently on account of this second reason. In
the Yüan play *Wu yüan ch'ui hsiao* 伍員吹簫 (*YCH*, No. 38), only the first
reason for her drowning is given. The story of Wǔ Zǐ-xū's begging for food on
his flight to Wú is told in the *Historical Records* (*chüan* 66, p. 3b), but there is
no mention of his being fed by a woman who later drowned herself.

485] *huà wán shí:* 'to become a block of insensitive stone'. This refers to a legend that
a faithful wife, during her husband's absence from home, climbed a hill every
day to watch for his return, until finally she was transformed into a large stone,
which was called *Wàng-fū shí* (望夫石 'Watching-for-husband Stone'; see
wàng-fū in Morohashi V: 14368: 129).

489–90] *běn xing nán yí:* 'basic nature hard to change', a stock phrase. Here it means:
'Do not say that women are born to be fickle, because many women in
the old days were chaste and faithful.'

§487] *rén-yi: rén-yi* 人意, *KMCP*, p. 8b.
§489–90] *běn xìng nán yí: bǎi bù xiāng shuí* 百步相隨, *KMCP*, p. 8b.

你 吃 些 兒 波 （ 張 驢 兒 云 ） 等
492　nǐ chi xiē-er bo. (Zhāng Lǘ-er yún:) Děng
you eat some (P).' (Chang Donkey says:) 'Wait-till

我 拿 去 （ 做 接 嘗 科 云 ） 這 裏
493　wǒ ná-qù. (Zuò jiē cháng kē, yún:) Zhè-lǐ-
I take [it] (C).' (Performs taking-over, tasting gesture, says:)
'This (L)

面 少 些 鹽 醋 你 去 取 來 （ 正
494　miàn shǎo xiē yán cù. Nǐ qù qǔ lái. (Zhèng
lacks a-little salt, vinegar. You go to-fetch [them]　(C).'
(Principal

旦 下 張 驢 兒 放 藥 科 正 旦
495　dàn xià. Zhāng Lǘ-er fàng yào kē. Zhèng dàn
female-role exit. Chang Donkey putting-in drug gesture. Principal female-role

上 云 ） 這 不 是 鹽 醋 （ 張 驢 兒
496　shàng yún:) Zhè bú shì yán cù? (Zhāng Lǘ-er
enters, says:) 'This not is salt, vinegar?' (Chang Donkey

云 ） 你 傾 下 些 （ 正 旦 唱 ）
497　yún:) Nǐ qing-xià xiē. (Zhèng dàn chàng:)
says:) 'You pour-in some.' (Principal female-role sings:)

（ 隔 尾 ） 你 說 道 少 鹽 欠
498　(Gé wěi) Nǐ shuō-dào shǎo yán qiàn
('Separate Tail') 'You say [that-it] lacks salt, needs

醋 無 滋 味 加 料 添 椒
499　cù wú zī-wèi, jiā liào tiān jiāo
vinegar, has-no flavor; [if I] add spice, add pepper,

纔 脆 美 但 願 娘 親 蚤
500　cái cuì měi. Dàn yuàn niáng-qin zǎo
only-then be-delicious/good. [I] only wish mother will-
early

140

eating some?

DONKEY CHANG: Let me take it to her. (He tastes the soup.)
There is not quite enough salt and vinegar in this; go get some.
(Exit Tou O. He puts the poison in the soup. Enter Tou O.)

TOU O: Here are the salt and vinegar.

DONKEY CHANG: You put some in the soup.

TOU O (Sings third lyric):

You say that lacking in salt and vinegar, the soup has no taste;
Only if I add spice and pepper will it be good.
All I hope is that mother will soon recover.

§492] *nǐ chī xiē-er: bù miǎn sòng qù* 不免送去 in *KMCP*, p. 8b.
§493] *cháng:* not in *KMCP*.
§495] *xià: xū xià* 虛下 , *KMCP*, p. 8b.

痊濟飲羹湯一杯勝

501　quán-jì. Yǐn gēng-tāng yì bēi, shèng

recover. To-drink soup one cup is-better-than [to-have]

甘露灌體得一個身

502　gān lù guàn tǐ. Dé yí ge shēn-

sweet dew fill body. To-have [your] whole (M) body

子平安倒大來喜

503　zi píng-ān, dào dà-lái xǐ.

well, [I would] after-all greatly rejoice.'

（孛老云）孩兒羊腤湯有了

504　(Bó-lǎo yún:) Hái-er, yáng dǔ tāng yǒu-le

(Old-man says:) 'Child, mutton tripe soup is-here (P),

不曾（張驢兒云）湯有了你

505　bù-céng? (Zhāng Lǘ-er yún:) Tāng yǒu le. Nǐ

[or] not?' (Chang Donkey says:) 'Soup is-here (P). You

拿過去（孛老將湯云）婆婆

506　ná-guò-qù. (Bó-lǎo jiāng tāng yún:) Pó-po,

take-[it]-over-there (C).' (Old-man carrying soup, says:) 'P'o-p'o,

你吃些湯兒（卜兒云）有累

507　nǐ chī xiē tāng-er. (Bǔ-er yún:) Yǒu lèi

you eat some soup.' (Old-Woman says:) 'Have troubled

你（做嘔科云）我如今打嘔

508　nǐ. (Zuò ǒu kē, yún:) Wǒ rú-jīn dǎ-ǒu,

you.' (Performs vomiting gesture, says:) 'I now am-vomiting,

不要這湯吃了你老人家

509　bú yào zhè tāng chī le. Nǐ lǎo-ren-jia

do-not want this soup to-eat (P). You elderly-person

吃罷（孛老云）這湯特做來

510　chī ba. (Bó-lǎo yún:) Zhè tāng tè zuò-lai

eat (P).' (Old-man says:) 'This soup [is] especially made (C)

Drinking one cup of soup is better than filling yourself with medicine;
When you get well, I shall greatly rejoice.

OLD CHANG: Son, is the soup ready?

DONKEY CHANG: Here is the soup. You take it to her.

(Old Chang takes the soup.)

OLD CHANG: Eat some soup, *p'o-p'o.*

TS'AI: Thanks for the trouble. (She vomits.) I feel nauseous; I don't want this soup now. Why don't you eat some?

OLD CHANG: This was prepared especially for you. Even if you don't

502] *gān lù:* 'sweet dew'; listed as a tonic in *Pen Ts'ăo* 本草, an early Chinese study in pharmaceutical material (ed. Chang Shao-t'ang 張紹棠, Ho-fei 合肥, 1885, *chüan* 5, p. 6*b*; cf. n. 106 above).

503] *dà-lái:* greatly; see Hsü Chia-jui, p. 4.

§502–3] *Dé... píng-ān: Nín sān kŏu-er tuán-yuán* 您三口兒團圓 in *KMCP*, p. 9*a*.

§508–10] *Zuò ŏu kē... chī ba: Nĭ xiān chī kŏu-er wŏ chī* 你先吃口兒我喫 in *KMCP* p. 9*a*.

§510–12] *Zhè tāng...yì kŏu-er: Nĭ chī* 你吃 in *KMCP*, p. 9*a*.

與你吃的便不要吃也吃

511   *yǔ nǐ chī de. Biàn bú yào chī, yě chī*
for you to-eat (P). Even-if [you] do-not want to-eat, still eat

一口兒（卜兒云）我不吃了

512   *yì kǒu-er. (Bǔ-er yún:) Wǒ bù chī le.*
one mouthful.' (Old-woman says:) 'I will-not eat (P).

你老人家請吃（孛老吃科

513   *Nǐ lǎo-rén-jiā qǐng chī. (Bó-lǎo chī ke.*
You elderly-person, please eat.' (Old-man performs eating gesture.

正旦唱）

514   *Zhèng dàn chàng:)*
Principal female-role sings:)

（賀新郎）一箇道你請

515   *(Hè xīn-láng) Yí ge dào nǐ qǐng*
('Congratulating Bridegroom') 'One (M) says you please

喫一箇道婆先喫這

516   *chī, yí ge dào pó xiān chī. Zhè*
eat, one (M) says, p'o first eat. This

言語聽也難聽我可

517   *yán-yǔ tīng yě nán tīng. Wǒ kě-*
talk, to-listen-to (P) is-hard to-listen. I should

是氣也不氣想他家

518   *shì qì yě bú qì! Xiǎng tā jiā*
be angry (P), [or] not angry? [I] think their family

與咱家有甚的親和

519   *yǔ zán jiā yǒu shén-de qīn hé*
with our family has what family-relations and

戚怎不記舊日夫妻

520   *qì? Zěn bú jì jiù rì fū qī*
relations-by-marriage? How not remember old days husband/wife

144

feel like it, eat a mouthful anyway.

TS'AI: I don't want it anymore. You eat some. (Old Chang eats.)

TOU O (Sings fourth lyric):

> One says, 'Please eat this.'
> One says, 'You eat first.'
> This kind of talk is hard to take,
> And how can I help getting angry?
> What relation is there between him and us!
> How could she forget the love of her former husband,

516–18] *Zhè...bú qì: yě*, comparable to *ne* 呢 in modern usage, is used for making a pause. The second part is a rhetorical question meaning, 'Can I help getting angry?'

519] *shén-de*: same as *shém-me* 甚麼 in present usage.

§512–13] *Wǒ...qǐng chī: Lǎo-er nǐ xiān chī* 老兒你先吃 in *KMCP*, p. 9a.

§515–16] *nǐ qǐng chī: nǐ yé xiān chī* 你爺先喫 in *KMCP*, p. 9a.

§516] *pó xiān chī: Nǐ niáng chī* 你娘喫 in *KMCP*, p. 9a.

§518–20] *Xiǎng tā jiā...qì:xīn hūn de yīn-juàn piān huān-xǐ* 新婚的姻眷偏歡喜 in *KMCP*, p. 9a.

§520–1] *Zěn...qíng-yì: Bù xiǎng nà jiù rì fū qī dào-lǐ* 不想那舊日夫妻道理 in *KMCP*, p. 9a.

145

情意也曾有百縱千

521 *qíng-yì? Yě céng yǒu bǎi zòng qiān*
affection? [You] also once-did have [your] hundred
indulgences, thousand

隨婆婆也你莫不爲

522 *suí. Pó-po ye, nǐ mò-bú wèi*
followings. Mother-in-law (P), you – isn't-it-not – think
[that]

黃金浮世寶白髮故

523 *huáng jin fú-shì bǎo, bái fǎ gù-*
yellow gold [is] fleeting-worldly treasure, [and] white
haired old-

人稀因此上把舊恩

524 *rén xì; yin-cǐ-shàng bǎ jiù ēn-*
companion [is] rare; therefore (Pr) old affection

情全不比新知契則

525 *qíng, quán bù bǐ xin zhi-qì? Zé*
[you] completely do-not rate-as the-new intimacy? [You]
just

待要百年同墓穴那

526 *dài-yào bǎi nián tóng mù-xuè, nǎ-*
hope-to [after] a-hundred years share [a] grave; where

裏肯千里送寒衣

527 *lǐ kěn qiān lǐ sòng hán yi?*
(L) be-willing [over] a-thousand miles to-deliver winter
clothes?'

（孛老云）我吃下這湯去怎

528 *(Bó-lǎo yún:) Wǒ chi xià zhè tāng qù, zěn*
(Old-man says:) 'I ate (C) this soup (C); how-is-it-that [I]

覺昏昏沈沈的起來（做倒

529 *jué-hūn-hūn-chén-chén-de-chǐ-lai? (Zuò dǎo*
begin-to-feel-dizziness/drowsiness (P)?' (Performs falling

Who used to indulge her many wishes?
Oh, mother, is it because you regard gold but a fleeting treasure,
And a friend in old age a rare thing,
That you value your new find more than your former love?
You want even in death to share a grave with a mate;
Where is any thought of going a thousand miles to deliver winter clothes?

OLD CHANG: After eating the soup, why do I begin to feel dizzy?
(He falls. Mistress Ts'ai panics.)

522] *mò-bú:* see n. 206.
523–4] *huáng jīn. . . xī:* the meaning of these two lines is ambiguous. The saying here
is evidently proverbial, and loosely applicable to the situation; a literary sense
perhaps is not to be looked for. *KMCP* has two lines criticizing her for her
inability to remain faithful (see § 522–4).
526] *bǎi nián:* literally, 'hundred years': a euphemism for 'death'.
527] *lǐ:* a Chinese 'mile', about one-third of an English mile.
  Here Dòu É is contrasting her fickle mother-in-law to the faithful Mèng Jiāng-
nü, who traveled a thousand 'miles' to deliver warm clothing to her conscript
husband in the construction of the Great Wall under the first emperor of Ch'in.
(see n. 483). Mistress Cài evidently wants to enjoy companionship with her
mate even in death, but cannot remain faithful when deprived of the companionship.

§521] *Yě céng yǒu: cháng hǎo shì* 常好是 in *KMCP*, p. 9a.
§522–4] *Pó-po. . . xī: Zhè pó-niáng xīn rú fēng kuā xù; nǎ lǐ kěn shēn huà-zuò wàng-fū-shí?*
這婆娘心如風刮絮 那里肯身化做望夫石 in *KMCP*, p. 9a–b.
§524–5] *yīn-cǐ-shàng. . . zhī-qì: jiù ēn-qíng dào bù bǐ xīn jiā-pèi* 舊恩情倒不比新佳
配 in *KMCP*, p. 9b.
§525–6] *Zé. . . mù xuè: tā zé dài bǎi nián wèi hūn juàn* 他則待百年爲婚眷 in *KMCP*,
p. 9b.
§529] After *chén-chén-de: Lǎo-er, nǐ chī xià zhè tāng qù, zěn-shēng bù hǎo le ye* 老兒 你
吃下這湯去怎生不好了也 in *KMCP*, p. 9b.
§529–30] *Zuò dǎo. . . huāng kē: bǔ jiào* 卜 叫 in *KMCP*, p. 9b.

科卜兒慌科云 ）你老人家

530　kē. Bú-er huāng kē, yún:) Nǐ lǎo-ren-jia
gesture. Old-woman panic gesture, says:) 'You, old-**person,**

放精神着你札掙着些兒

531　fàng-jing-shen zhe. Nǐ zhā-zhēng zhe xiē-er.
be-spirited (P). You struggle (P) a-little.'

（做哭科云 ）兀的不是死了

532　(Zuò kū kē yún:) Wù-de-bú-shì sǐ-le
(Performs weeping gesture.) 'Isn't-this [that he] is **dead** (P)

也（正旦唱 ）

533　ye! (Zhèng dàn chàng:)
(P)!' (Principal female-role sings:)

（鬥蝦蟆 ）空悲戚沒理

534　(Dòu há-ma) Kōng bēi-qì, méi lǐ-
('Fighting Frogs') 'In-vain, [you] grieve; **have-no** understanding [that]

會人生死是輪迴感

535　huì. Rén shēng sǐ, shì lún-huí. Gǎn-
human birth/death are transmigration. Affected-by

着這般病疾值着這

536　zhe zhè bān bìng-jí, zhí-zhe zhè
(P) this kind-of sickness, encounter (P) this

般時勢可是風寒暑

537　bān shí-shì: kě shì fēng-hán shǔ-
kind-of situation: could be chills, rheumatic-

濕或是饑飽勞役各

538　shī, huò shì jī bǎo láo-yì; gè
fever, or be hunger/fullness, hard-work; each

人證候自知人命關

539　rén zhèng-hòu zì zhi. Rén mìng guān
person [his] symptoms himself knows. Human life is
related-to

TS'AI: You, sir, get hold of yourself. Make an effort to stay awake!
   (Cries.) He is dead!
TOU O (Sings fifth lyric):

   It's no use grieving; you really have no understanding.
   Birth and death are part of transmigration.
   Some fall sick, some encounter hard times,
   Some catch a chill, some suffer rheumatic fever,
   Some die of hunger, overeating, or overwork;
   Each knows his own lot.
   Human life is ruled by Heaven and Earth;

539] *zhèng-hòu:* same as 症候.

§530] *Nǐ lǎo-ren-jia: Lǎo-er ye* 老兒也 in *KMCP*, p. 9*b*.
§531] *jīng-shen: jīng-xì* 精細 *KMCP*, p. 9*b*.
§532–3] *Wǔ-de. . .ye:* not in *KMCP* here, but occurs later; cf. § 554.
§534] *Kōng bēi-qì: Wǎng zhao nǐ fán-nǎo* 枉着你煩惱 in *KMCP*, p. 9*b*.
§536] *zhí-zhe: chèn-zhe* 趁着 in *KMCP*, p. 9*b*.
§537] *kě shì: zhí-zhe* 值着 in *KMCP*, p. 9*b*.

540

天關地別人怎生替

tiān guān dì; bié rén zěn-shēng tì-

Heaven, is-related-to Earth; other people how can-substitute?

541

得壽數非干今世相

de? Shòu-shù fēi gān jin shì. Xiāng

Life-span is-not dependent-on this life. [Having] each-other

542

守三朝五夕說甚一

shǒu sān zhāo wǔ xī, shuō shén yì

kept-company [for] three mornings, five evenings, speak-of what "one

543

家一計又無羊酒段

jiā yí jì. Yòu wú yáng jiǔ duàn

family, one idea"? Moreover, there-is-no sheep, wine, sections/

544

匹又無花紅財禮把

pǐ, yòu wú huā-hóng cái-lǐ; bǎ

bolts; moreover, there-is-no money-gifts, money/gifts. To-clench

545

手爲活過日撒手如

shǒu wéi huó guò rì, sā shǒu rú-

[our] hands, make a-living [and] pass the-days; to-loosen the-hands is-

546

同休棄不是竇娥忤

tóng xiū-qì. Bú-shì Dòu É wǔ-

like stopping/giving-up. It-is-not Tou O is-unfilial/

547

逆生怕傍人論議不

nì, shēng-pà páng rén lùn-yì. Bù-

contrary; [but I] fear other people will-discuss [it]. Nothing

548

如聽咱勸你認箇自

rú tīng zá quàn nǐ, rèn ge zì-

is-like listening-to me exhort you: look-on-[it]-as [a] case-of (M) own

How can one substitute years for another person?
Our life-span is not determined in this world.
You and he were together only for a few days;
What is there to speak of in terms of one family?
Besides, there is neither sheep, wine, silk, money, nor other wedding gifts.
Clenching our hands, we work and go on,
Letting loose the hand, it is the end of life.
It is not that I am contrary; only I fear what others may say.
It is better to heed my advice and regard the whole thing as poor luck.

542] *sān zhāo wŭ xī*: a stock phrase meaning 'a few days'.
542–3] *yì jiā yí jì*: 'one family with one idea' – a harmonious family.
543–4] *duàn pĭ*: 'sections and bolts (of fabric)'.
544] *huā-hóng*: an old custom was to decorate with gold flowers (*huā*) and red (*hóng*) coverings during a celebration; *huā-hóng* was used to denote money gifts to servants during such celebrations. Later this term was used to mean money gifts, especially those given as betrothal gifts.
    huā-hóng cái-lĭ: a stock phrase in reference to betrothal gifts, or wedding gifts.
545–6] *sā shŏu. . . xiū-qì*: here 'opening the hand' is compared to 'death'. (Cf. the use of a close-up scene of the opening of a person's hand to indicate his death in today's movies.)

§542] *wŭ xī: wŭ rì* 五 日 in *KMCP*, p. 9*b*.
    shuō shén: cháng hăo 常 好 in *KMCP*, p. 9*b*.
§546] After *xiū-qì: Bú pà páng rén xiào chĭ*, 不 怕 旁 人 笑 恥 in *KMCP*, pp. 9*b*–10*a*.
§547–54] *shēng-pà. . .fū qī: quàn-bù-di jì-jì shì-shì, kū-kū tí-tí, fán tiān năo dì. Pèi, bú sì nĭ shĕ-bù-de nĭ nà cóng xiăo lĭ zhĭ-jiăo-ér fū qī.* 勸 不 的 即 即 世 世 哭 哭 啼 啼 煩 天 惱 地 吥 不 似 你 捨 不 的 你 那 從 小 里 指 脚 兒 夫 妻 in *KMCP*, p. 10*a*.

151

家悔氣割捨的一具
549   *jiā huì-qì. Gē-shě-de yí jù*
bad-luck. Relinquish a (M)

棺材停置幾件布帛
550   *guān-cai, tíng-zhì jǐ jiàn bù bò.*
coffin; prepare several articles-of cloth, silk.

收拾出了咱家門裏
551   *Shōu-shi chū-le zá jiā mén-lǐ,*
Arrange [for him] to-get-out (P) our family gate (L),

送入他家墳地這不
552   *sòng rù tā jiā fén-dì. Zhè bú*
to-escort [him] into his family grave-yard. This [match] not

是你那從小兒年紀
553   *shì nǐ nà cóng xiǎo-er nián-jì*
is [the same as] your that from young age

指脚的夫妻我其實
554   *zhǐ-jiǎo de fū qi. Wǒ qí-shí*
"[tied] by-feet" (P) husband/wife. I really

不關親無半點恓惶
555   *bù guān-qin, wú bàn diǎn xī-huáng*
am-not concerned, have-not half-a drop-of troubled

泪休得要心如醉意
556   *lèi. Xiū-dé yào xin rú zuì, yì*
tears. Don't have [your] heart like drunk, [or your] mind

似癡便這等嗟嗟怨
557   *sì chi biàn zhè děng jiē-jiē yuàn-*
like crazy – then this way sigh, grieve,

怨哭哭啼啼
558   *yuàn, kū-kū tí-tí.*
weep, wail.'

Sacrifice for him a coffin and secure several pieces of cotton and silk;
Get him out of our house and send him to his grave.
This one is not a marriage contracted from your young age;
I really do not care and cannot shed half a drop of tear.
Do not be so overcome with grief,
Sigh or wail like this!

554] *zhǐ-jiǎo de fū qī:* husband and wife who had become engaged or married when young; *zhǐ-jiǎo* means 'on the basis of feet'. The expression may come from the legend that in the T'ang dynasty, Wéi Gù 韋固, while staying in Sùng 宋 City, encountered an old man sitting against a bag, reading in the moonlight. Wéi asked about the red strings in the bag and was told that they were for tying together at birth the feet of those who eventually will become husband and wife. Later, when Wéi went to the market, he saw a blind old woman holding a three-year-old girl in rags. The old man pointed to the girl and said, 'When seventeen, she will become your wife.' Displeased, Wéi tried to have the girl killed, but succeeded only in injuring the girl between the eyebrows. Fourteen years later, after many complications, Wéi became the husband of this same girl, who then constantly wore a floral decoration between her eyebrows because of the scar. Evidently the old man had supernatural powers in binding people's fates together. This legend underlines the belief that men and women were bound somewhat by destiny to be husbands and wives. (See T'ang author Li Fu-yen's 李復言, *Hsü yu kuai lu* 續幽怪錄 [*SPTK hsü-pien*] *chüan* 4, pp. 3–5.)

555] *guān-qīn:* concerned; comparable to *guān-xīn* (see cf. n. §555).

§554] After *fū qī:* (Pó-lǎo sǐ kē. Bǔ yún) zěn-shēng shì hǎo, sǐ liǎo ye. (Dàn) 〔孛老死科卜 云〕怎生是好死了也（且）, in *KMCP*, p. 10a; cf. 11. 532–3.
§555] *qīn: xīn* 心 in *KMCP*, p. 10a.
§557–8] *biàn zhè děng jiē-jiē yuàn-yuàn: hún fēi shǒu huāng jiǎo luàn* 魂飛手荒腳亂 in *KMCP*, p. 10a.

（張驢兒云）好也囉你把我

559　(Zhāng Lǘ-er zuò　Hǎo ye-luo! Nǐ bǎ wǒ

(Chang Donkey says:) 'Fine (P), you (Pr) my

老子藥死了更待乾罷（卜

560　lǎo-zi yào-sǐ-le; gèng dài gān bà! (Bǔ-

father poisoned-to-death (P); [you] still want-to neatly end [it]!' (Old-

兒云）孩兒這事怎了也（正

561　er yún:) Hái-er, zhè shì zěn liǎo yě? (Zhèng

woman says:) 'Child, this matter how to-end (P)?' (Principal

旦云）我有什麼藥在那裏

562　dàn yún:) Wǒ yǒu shém-me yào zài nǎ-lǐ?

female-role says:) 'I had what drug at where (L)?

都是他要鹽醋時自家傾

563　Dōu shì tā yào yán cù shí, zì-jiā qing

All [it was] was [that] he wanted salt, vinegar time, he-himself put [it]

在湯兒裏的（唱）

564　zài tāng-er lǐ de. (Chàng:)

into the-soup (L) (P).' (Sings:)

（隔尾）這廝搬調咱老

565　(Gé wěi) Zhè sī bān-tiáo zá lǎo

('Separate Tail') 'This fellow manipulated my old

母收留你自藥死親

566　mǔ shōu-liú nǐ. Zì yào-sǐ qin

mother to-keep you. You-yourself poisoned-to-death own

爺待要諕嚇誰

567　yé dài yào hǔ-hè shéi?

father, [now you] want-to intimidate whom?'

（張驢兒云）我家的老子倒

568　(Zhāng Lǘ-er yún:) Wǒ jiā de lǎo-zi, dào

(Chang Donkey says:) 'My family (P) old-man – yet

154

DONKEY CHANG: Fine! You have poisoned my father; yet you expect to get out of it clean!

TS'AI: Child, how is this going to end?

TOU O: What poison would I have? When he was asking for salt and vinegar, he put the poison in the soup himself.

(Sings sixth lyric):

This fellow tricked my old mother into keeping you.
You yourself have poisoned your father.
Whom do you think you can frighten?

DONKEY CHANG: My own father – to say that I, the son, poisoned

§561] *zhè shì zěn liǎo: wǒ suí-shùn-le tā ba.* 我隨順了他罷 in *KMCP*, p. 10a.

§562–4] *Wǒ yǒu. . . lǐ de: not in KMCP; instead, Pó-po zěn-shēng shuō zhè bān yán-yǔ* 婆婆
怎生說這般言語 *KMCP*, p. 10a; cf. § 580–2.

§566] *shōu-liú: chéng-hé-le* 成合了 , *KMCP*, p. 10a.

§567] *dài yào: jīn rì* 今日, *KMCP*, p. 10a.

§568–79] *Zhāng Lǘ-er yún. . . ráo-le tā:* this long prose insertion is not in *KMCP; instead,*
merely (*Bǔ*) *Yǔ tā zuò-le hūn-jia ba*(卜)與他做了渾家罷,*KMCP*, p. 10a.

說 是 我 做 兒 子 的 藥 死 了

569 *shuō shì wǒ zuò-ér-zi-de yào-sǐ-le,*
[you] say was I who-was-[a]-son [who] poisoned-[him]-to-death (P),

人 也 不 信 （ 做 叫 科 云 ） 四 鄰

570 *rén yě bú xìn. (Zuò jiào kē, yún:) Sì lín*
people indeed would-not believe [it].' (Performs shouting gesture, says:) 'Four neighbors,

八 舍 聽 着 竇 娥 藥 殺 我 家

571 *bá shè tīng-zhe: Dòu É yào-shā wǒ jiā*
eight houses, listen (P): Tou O poisoned-to-death my family

老 子 哩 （ 卜 兒 云 ） 罷 麼 你 不

572 *lǎo-zi li. (Bǔ-er yún:) Bà ma, nǐ bú-*
old-man (P).' (Old-woman says:) 'Stop (P)! you don't

要 大 驚 小 怪 的 嚇 殺 我 也

573 *yào dà jīng xiǎo guài de. Hè-shā wǒ yě.*
greatly be-alarmed-at small peculiarities (P). Frighten-to-death me (P)!'

（ 張 驢 兒 云 ） 你 可 怕 麼 （ 卜 兒

574 *(Zhāng Lǘ-er yún:) Nǐ kě pà ma? (Bǔ-er*
(Chang Donkey says:) 'You perhaps are-afraid (P)?' (Old-woman

云 ） 可 知 怕 哩 （ 張 驢 兒 云 ） 你

575 *yún:) Kě-zhī pà li. (Zhāng Lǘ-er yún:) Nǐ*
says:) 'Certainly am-afraid (P).' (Chang Donkey says:) 'You

要 饒 麼 （ 卜 兒 云 ） 可 知 要 饒

576 *yào ráo ma? (Bǔ-er yún:) Kě-zhī yào ráo*
want to-be-let off (P)?' (Old-woman says:) 'Indeed want to-be-let-off

哩 （ 張 驢 兒 云 ） 你 教 竇 娥 隨

577 *li. (Zhāng Lǘ-er yún:) Nǐ jiào Dòu É suí-*
(P).' (Chang Donkey says:) 'You ask Tou O to-follow/

him, nobody would believe it. (Shouts.) Neighbors, neighbors, listen! Tou O has poisoned my father!

TS'AI: Stop! Don't get so excited. You scare me to death.

DONKEY CHANG: Are you afraid?

TS'AI: Indeed I am afraid.

DONKEY CHANG: You want to be let off?

TS'AI: Indeed, I want to be let off.

DONKEY CHANG: Then you tell Tou O to give in to me, to call

570–1] *Sì lín bá shè:* 'four neighbors eight houses' – an idiom for 'neighbors'.
573] *dà jīng xiǎo guài:* 'becoming alarmed at trifles', an idiomatic saying, only loosely applicable to the occasion here. Mistress Cài evidently is trying her best to quiet down Donkey Zhāng, telling him not to exaggerate the situation at hand.
575] *Kě-zhī:* 'certainly' (see Chang Hsiang, p. 112).

157

順了我叫我三聲的的親

578 *shùn le wǒ, jiào wǒ sān-shēng dí-dí qín-*
obey (P) me, call me three-times (M) dear/beloved

親的丈夫我便饒了他（卜

579 *qín de zhàng-fu, wǒ biàn ráo-le tā. (Bǔ-*
(P) husband, I then forgive (P) her.' (Old-woman

兒云）孩兒也你隨順了他

580 *er yún:) Hái-er ye, nǐ suí-shùn-le tā*
says:) 'Child (P), you follow/obey (P) him

罷（正旦云）婆婆你怎說這

581 *ba. (Zhèng dàn yún:) Pó-po, ní zěn shuō zhè*
(P).' (Principal female-role says:) 'Mother-in-law, you how-
could utter this

般言語（唱）

582 *bān yán-yǔ? (Chàng:)*
kind-of talk?' (Sings:)

我一馬難將兩鞍鞴

583 *Wǒ yì mǎ nán jiāng liǎng ān bèi.*
'I, one horse, hardly-can (Pr) two saddles wear.

想男兒在日曾兩年

584 *Xiǎng nán-ér zài rì céng liǎng nián*
Think [that your] son was-alive days, [we] were [for] two
years

匹配却教我改嫁別

585 *pǐ-pèi. Què jiào wǒ gǎi-jià bié*
married. Yet [you] ask me to-re-marry another

人其實做不得

586 *rén. Qí-shí zuò-bu-dę.*
person. In-truth, [I am] unable-to-do [it].'

（張驢兒云）竇娥你藥殺了

587 *(Zhāng Lǘ-er yún:) Dòu É, nǐ yào-shā-le*
(Chang Donkey says:) 'Tou O, you poisoned-to-death (P)

me dear, beloved husband three times; then I shall let you off.

TS'AI: Child, you had better give in now.

TOU O: Mother, how can you say such a thing? (Sings.)

> *One horse cannot wear two saddles.*
> *When your son was alive we were married for two years;*
> *Yet now you ask me to marry another.*
> *This is indeed something I cannot do.*

DONKEY CHANG: Tou O, you have poisoned my father. Do you

578–9] *dí-dí qīn-qīn:* probably came from *dí qīn* 嫡親

583] *yì mǎ . . . bèi:* a proverb meaning that one woman cannot serve two husbands; cf. ll. 1108–9.

§580–2] *Hái-er ye . . . yán-yǔ:* not in *KMCP* here, but occurs earlier (see §561 and §562–4).

§584–5] *céng . . . pǐ-pèi: Ān fū qī dào-lǐ* 俺 夫 妻 道 理 in *KMCP*, p. 10a.

§585] *Què: Nǐ* 你 in *KMCP*, p. 10a.

§586] *zuò-bu-de: xià-bu-de* 下 不 的 in *KMCP*, p. 10a.

588 俺老子你要官休要私休

ǎn lǎo-zi, nǐ yào guān xiū? Yào sī xiū?

my old-man, you want officially to-settle [it]? Want privately to-settle [it]?'

589 （正旦云）怎生是官休怎生

(Zhèng dàn yún:) Zěn-shēng shì guān xiū? Zěn-shēng

(Principal female-role says:) 'What is officially to-settle [it]? What

590 是私休（張驢兒云）你要官

shì sī xiū? (Zhāng Lǘ-er yún:) Nǐ yào guān

is privately to-settle [it]?' (Chang Donkey says:) '[If] you want officially

591 休呵拖你到官司把你三

xiū he, tuō nǐ dào guān-si, bǎ nǐ sān

to-settle [it] (P), [I] will-drag you to court; [they will] (Pr) you three [times]

592 推六問你這等瘦弱身子

tui liù wèn. Nǐ zhè-děng shòu ruò shēn-zi,

examine, six [times] question. Your such thin/ frail body,

593 當不過拷打怕你不招認

dāng-bú-guò kǎo-dǎ, pà nǐ bù zhāo-rèn

will-be-unable-to-bear beating; [there is no] fear [that] you will-not confess-to

594 藥死我老子的罪犯你要

yào sǐ wǒ lǎo-zi de zuì-fàn! Nǐ yào

poisoning-to-death my old-man (P) crime! [If] You want

595 私休呵你早些與我做了

sī xiū he, nǐ zǎo-xie yǔ wǒ zuò-le

privately to-settle [it] (P), you soon to me be (P)

596 老婆倒也便宜了你（正旦

lǎo-po, dào yě pián-yi-le nǐ. (Zhèng dàn

wife; [this] on-the-contrary, also would-benefit (P) you. (Principal female-role want to settle the matter officially or privately?

TOU O: What do you mean by officially or privately?

DONKEY CHANG: If you want to settle the matter officially, I shall drag you to court, where you will be thoroughly interrogated. Frail as you are, you will not be able to stand the beating and will have to confess to the murder of my father. If you want to settle privately, you had better become my wife soon. After all, you will benefit.

591–2] *sān tuī liù wèn:* a stock phrase.
592] *tuī:* same as *tuī chiú* 推求, 'to examine'.

§591–3] *bǎ nǐ. . . kǎo-dǎ:* not in *KMCP.*
§595] *zǎo-xiē:* not in *KMCP.*
§596] *dào yě piàn-yi-le nǐ: Wǒ biàn ráo-le nǐ* 我便饒了你 in *KMCP,* p. 10b.

云) 我 又 不 曾 藥 死 你 老 子

597   *yún:) Wǒ yòu bù céng yào-sǐ nǐ lǎo-zi;*
      says:) 'I moreover not have poisoned-to-death your old-man;

情 願 和 你 見 官 去 來 (張 驢

598   *qíng-yuàn hé nǐ jiàn guān qù lai. (Zhāng Lǘ-*
      am-willing with you to-see official to-go (P).' (Chang Donkey

兒 拖 正 旦 卜 兒 下 淨 扮 孤

599   *er tuō zhèng dàn bǔ-er xià. Jìng bàn gū*
      drags principal female-role, old-woman; exeunt. *Ching*-role in-
      make-up-of official

引 祇 候 上 詩 云) 我 做 官 人

600   *yǐn zhǐ-hòu shàng. Shī yún:) Wǒ zuò guān-rén*
      leading attendant enters. [In] verse says:) 'I as official

勝 別 人 告 狀 來 的 要 金 銀

601   *shèng bié rén. Gào-zhuàng-lái-de yào jin yín.*
      am-better-than other people. The-ones-who-come-to-file-suit
      are-demanded gold, silver.

若 是 上 司 當 刷 卷 在 家 推

602   *Ruò-shì shàng-si dāng shuā-juàn, zài jiā tuī*
      If [my] superior act-as inspector, [I] remain-at home, using-
      excuse-of

病 不 出 門 下 官 楚 州 太 守

603   *bìng bù chū mén. Xià guān Chǔ-zhōu tài-shǒu*
      sickness, do-not go-out-of door. Humble official Ch'u-chou
      prefect

桃 杌 是 也 今 早 升 廳 坐 衙

604   *Táo Wù shì ye. Jin zǎo shēng ting zuò yá.*
      T'ao Wu is (P). This morning [I] ascend hall to-sit-at court.

左 右 喝 攛 廂 (祇 候 么 喝 科

605   *Zuǒ-yòu, hē-cuān-xiāng. (Zhǐ-hòu yāo-he kē.*
      Attendants, call-aloud-to-the-chambers.' (Attendants calling
      gesture.

TOU O: I did not poison your father. I am willing to go with you to see the magistrate.

(Donkey Chang drags Tou O and the old woman out. Enter the prefect with an attendant.)

PREFECT (recites):

I am a better official than many another.
Whoever comes to file a suit is asked to pay in gold and silver.
If a superior official comes to investigate,
I stay at home, pretending to be under the weather.

I am the prefect of Ch'u-chou. My name is T'ao Wu. This morning I am holding court. Attendants, summon the court.

(Attendant shouts. Enter Donkey Chang dragging in Tou O and

599] *gū*: a role which usually appears as an official in Yüan drama (see Hu Chi 胡忌 *Sung Chin tsa-chü k'ao* 宋金雜劇攷, Shanghai, 1957, pp. 136–7).

600] *zhǐ-hòu*: in the Sung times, *zhǐ-hòu* was an official in the service of court ceremonies. (*History of Sung* [*Sung Shih* 宋史, Po-na ed.], *chüan* 166, p. 10b.) Later the term was used freely for an attendant to a high official.

602] *shuā-juàn*: 'to review records or court cases'; literally, 'to brush off the documents'.

605] *Zuŏ-yòu*: 'left/right' is used to denote attendants because they usually stay on either side of the master.

    hē-cuān-xiāng: 'to call the court to order'. There are two interpretations of this expression. One is that when the court opened, the yamen runners cried aloud (喝攛 *hē cuān*, 'to call', 'to urge') at both wings (*xiāng* 廂) of the courtroom to add to the dignity of the occasion. Another interpretation is that the yamen runners cried aloud (*hē*) while fetching (*cuān*) written papers which had been deposited by the people in court boxes (*xiāng* 箱) (see Chang Hsiang, p. 712).

§597] *Wŏ... lăo-zi: wŏ xīn shàng wú shì*, 我心上無事 in *KMCP*, p. 10b.

§599–600] Before *Jìng bàn gū... shàng: Dì-sān chū* 第三齣 in *KMCP*, p. 10b; the Third Act in *YCH* occurs much later in l. 718 below.

§599] *Jìng bàn gū: chŏu bàn guān rén* 丑扮官人 in *KMCP*, p. 10b.

§605] *Zhǐ-hòu: Zhāng Qiān* 張千 in *KMCP*, p. 10b; and same difference hereafter.

163

張驢兒拖正旦卜兒上云）
606 *Zhāng Lǘ-er tuō zhèng dàn bǔ-er shàng, yún:)*
Chang Donkey, dragging principal female-role, old-woman,
enters, says:)

告狀告狀（祇候云）拿過來
607 *Gào-zhuàng, gào-zhuàng. (Zhǐ-hòu yún:) Ná guò-lai.*
'Lodge-a-charge, lodge-a-charge.' (Attendant says:) 'Bring [them]
over (C).'

（做跪見孤亦跪科云）請起
608 *(Zuò guì jiàn. Gū yì guì kē, yún:) Qǐng qǐ.*
(Performs kneeling, presenting-self. Official also kneeling
gesture, says:) 'Please arise.'

（祇候云）相公他是告狀的
609 *(Zhǐ-hòu yún:) Xiàng-gōng, tā shì gào-zhuàng-de.*
(Attendant says:) 'Sir, he is one-who-files-a-charge.

怎生跪着他（孤云）你不知
610 *Zěn-shēng guì-zhe tā? (Gū yún:) Nǐ bù zhī-*
Why kneel (P) [to] him?' (Official says:) 'You don't know,

道但來告狀的就是我衣
611 *dao, dàn lái-gào-zhuàng-de, jiù-shì wǒ yī*
merely come-to-file-suit-ones then are my clothing [and]

食父母（祇候幺喝科孤云）
612 *shí fù mǔ. (Zhǐ-hòu yāo-he kē. Gū yún:)*
food father/mother.' (Attendants shouting action. Official says:)

那箇是原告那箇是被告
613 *Nǎ-ge shì yuán-gào? Nǎ-ge shì bèi-gào?*
'Which (M) is complainant? Which (M) is accused?

從實說來（張驢兒云）小人
614 *Cóng shí shuō lái. (Zhāng Lǘ-er yún:) Xiǎo rén*
According-to truth speak (C).' (Chang Donkey says:) 'Insignificant person

是原告張驢兒告這媳婦
615 *shì yuán-gào Zhāng Lǘ-er, gào zhè xí-fu-*
is complainant Chang Donkey, [who] accuses this woman

Mistress Ts'ai.)

DONKEY CHANG: I want to lodge a charge! I want to lodge a charge!

ATTENDANT: Then bring them over here.

(Donkey Chang kneels; the prefect also kneels.)

PREFECT: Please rise.

ATTENDANT: Your honor, he is the plaintiff. Why do you kneel to him?

PREFECT: Don't you know that these who come to file a suit are like my parents who pay for my clothing and food?

(Attendants shout.)

OFFICIAL: Which of you is the plaintiff? Which is the defendant? Now tell the truth.

DONKEY CHANG: I am the plaintiff, Chang Lü-er, who accuses this

---

609] *Xiàng-gōng:* a courteous respectful address to a young man.

§610] *Gū: chǒu* 丑, *KMCP*, p. 11*a*; and same difference hereafter.
§612] *yāo-he: dá yìng* 答 應, in *KMCP*, p. 11*b*.
§613] *bèi-gào: bèi-hài* 被 害 in *KMCP*, p. 11*b*.

616 兒 喚 做 竇 娥 合 毒 藥 下 在
er, huàn-zuo Dòu É, huò dú-yào xià zài
called Tou O of-mixing poison, putting [it] into

617 羊 腸 湯 兒 裏 藥 死 了 俺 的
yáng dǔ tāng-er lǐ, yào sǐ le ǎn-de
mutton tripe soup (L), poisoning to-death (P) my (P)

618 老 子 這 個 喚 做 蔡 婆 婆 就
lǎo-zi. Zhè ge huàn-zuò Cài Pó-po, jiù
old-man. This [one] (M) is-called Ts'ai P'o-p'o; exactly

619 是 俺 的 後 母 望 大 人 與 小
shì ǎn-de hòu-mǔ. Wàng dà rén yǔ xiǎo
is my (P) step-mother. [I] hope great person for insignificant

620 人 做 主 咱 （ 孤 云 ） 是 那 一 箇
rén zuò zhǔ za. (Gū yún:) Shì nǎ yí ge
person will-make decision (P).' (Official says:) '[It] was which
one (M)

621 下 的 毒 藥 （ 正 旦 云 ） 不 干 小
xià-de dú-yào? (Zhèng dàn yún:) Bù gān xiǎo
[who] put-in (P) poison?' (Principal female-role says:) 'Has-
nothing to-do-with insignificant

622 婦 人 事 （ 卜 兒 云 ） 也 不 干 老
fù-ren shì. (Bǔ-er yún:) Yě bù gān lǎo
woman's affairs.' (Old-woman says:) 'Also has-nothing to-do-
with old

623 婦 人 事 （ 張 驢 兒 云 ） 也 不 干
fù-ren shì. (Zhāng Lǘ-er yún:) Yě bù gān
woman's affairs.' (Chang Donkey says:) 'Also has-nothing to-
do-with

624 我 事 （ 孤 云 ） 都 不 是 敢 是 我
wǒ shì. (Gū yún:) Dōu bú-shì. Gǎn-shì wǒ
my affairs.' (Official says:) 'All [of you] are-not [the one].
Must-be [that] I

young woman, called Tou O, of preparing poison, putting it into mutton tripe soup and poisoning my father. This one is Mistress Ts'ai, who is my stepmother. I ask your honor to render a decision on my behalf.

PREFECT: Which one of you put in the poison?

TOU O: It had nothing to do with me.

TS'AI: And it had nothing to do with me.

DONKEY CHANG: It had nothing to do with me either.

PREFECT: It wasn't any of you. It must have been I who put in

§616] huàn-zuò Dòu É: not in KMCP.
§616–7] xià zài. . . lǐ: not in KMCP.
§618–19] Zhè ge huàn-zuò Cài Pó-po, jiù shì ān-de hòu-mǔ: not in KMCP.
§619–20] xiǎo rén: hái-er 孩兒 in KMCP, p. 11a.

下 的 毒 藥 來 （ 正 旦 云 ） 我 婆

625   *xià-de dú-yào lai? (Zhèng dàn yún:) Wǒ pó-*
put-in (P) poison (P)? (Principal female-role says:) 'My mother-in-law

婆 也 不 是 他 後 母 他 自 姓

626   *po yě bú-shì tā hòu-mǔ. Tā zì xìng*
moreover is-not his step-mother. He himself is-surnamed

張 我 家 姓 蔡 我 婆 婆 因 爲

627   *Zhāng, wǒ jiā xíng Cài. Wǒ pó-po yīn-weı*
Chang, my family is-surnamed Ts'ai. My mother-in-law because

與 賽 盧 醫 索 錢 被 他 賺 到

628   *yǔ Sài Lú-yi suǒ qián, bèi tā zuàn dào*
from "Rival Lu-Doctor" asked-for money, by him was-lured to

郊 外 勒 死 我 婆 婆 却 得 他

629   *jiāo-wài lēi-sǐ. Wǒ pó-po què dé tā*
countryside to-strangle-to-death. My mother-in-law however had these

爺 兒 兩 箇 救 了 性 命 因 此

630   *yé ér liǎng ge jiù-le xìng-mìng. Yīn-cǐ*
father son two (M) save (P) [her] life. Because-of this,

我 婆 婆 收 留 他 爺 兒 兩 箇

631   *wǒ pó-po shōu-liú tā yé ér liǎng ge*
my mother-in-law kept them father son two (M)

在 家 養 膳 終 身 報 他 的 恩

632   *zài jiā yǎng-shàn zhōng shēn bào tā de ēn-*
at home to-provide [for them] whole life to-requite their (P) kindness.

德 誰 知 他 兩 箇 倒 起 不 良

633   *dé. Shéi zhi tā liǎng ge dào qǐ bù-liáng*
Who could-have-known they two (M) however began-to-have no-good

the poison?

TOU O: My mother-in-law is not his stepmother either. His family
name is Chang; ours is Ts'ai. When my mother-in-law was asking
a loan back from Doctor Lu, she was led by him to the countryside
to be strangled. However, my mother-in-law's life was saved by
these two, father and son. Therefore my mother-in-law took both
father and son into our house to stay permanently as a reward for
their favor. Who could have known that the two of them would

629] *jiāo-wài:* 'outside the environment' – 'countryside', 'suburbs' (see Chao
Grammar, p. 624).

§625–48] *Zhèng dàn yún . . . za:* the recapitulation of the story is not in *KMCP*.

之 心 冒 認 婆 婆 做 了 接 脚

634   *zhī xīn. Mào rèn pó-po zuò-le jiē-jiǎo,*

(P) intention. [One] falsely claimed [my] mother-in-law, acted-
as (P) [her] second-husband;

要 逼 勒 小 婦 人 做 他 媳 婦

635   *yào bī-lè xiǎo fù-ren zuò tā xí-fu.*

[one] wanted to-force insignificant woman to-be his wife.

小 婦 人 元 是 有 丈 夫 的 服

636   *Xiǎo fù-ren yuán shì yǒu-zhàng-fu-de, fú-*

Insignificant woman formerly was one-who-had-a-husband;
wearing-

孝 未 滿 堅 執 不 從 適 值 我

637   *xiào wèi mǎn. Jiān-zhí bù cóng. Shì zhí wǒ*

mourning was-not-yet complete; obstinately did-not comply.
Just so-happened my

婆 婆 患 病 着 小 婦 人 安 排

638   *pó-po huàn-bìng, zháo xiǎo fù-ren ān-pái*

mother-in-law was-sick, asked insignificant woman to-prepare

羊 賭 湯 兒 喫 不 知 張 驢 兒

639   *yáng dǔ tāng-er chī. Bù zhī Zhāng Lǘ-er*

mutton tripe soup to-eat. [I] do-not know Chang Donkey

那 裏 討 得 毒 藥 在 身 接 過

640   *nǎ-lǐ tǎo-dé dú-yào zài shēn. Jiē guò*

where got (P) poison on [his] person. [He] took over

湯 來 只 說 少 些 鹽 醋 支 轉

641   *tāng lái, zhǐ shuō shǎo xiē yán cù, zhī-zhuǎn*

soup (C); only saying [it] lacked some salt, vinegar, [he] sent-
away

小 婦 人 闇 地 傾 下 毒 藥 也

642   *xiǎo fù-ren, àn-dì qīng-xià dú-yào. Yě*

insignificant woman; secretly (P) put-in poison. Also

是 天 幸 我 婆 婆 忽 然 嘔 吐

643   *shì tiān xìng; wǒ pó-po hū-rán ǒu-tù,*

was heavenly luck; my mother-in-law suddenly vomited,

begin to have evil thoughts? One boldly claimed to be my mother-in-law's second husband; the other wanted to force me to become his wife. I had a husband, and my mourning for him was not yet over. I firmly refused the proposal. It just happened that my mother-in-law was sick and asked me to prepare some mutton tripe soup. I don't know where Donkey Chang got the poison which he carried with him. He took the soup, and saying that it lacked salt and vinegar, he managed to send me away. Meanwhile he secretly put the poison in the soup. It was indeed a piece of heaven-sent good fortune that my mother-in-law suddenly began vomiting. She didn't want the

644 不要湯吃讓與他老子吃
bú yào tāng chī, ràng yǔ tā lǎo-zi chī.
did-not want soup to-eat; gave [it] to his father to-eat.

645 纔吃的幾口便死了與小
Cái chī-de jǐ kǒu, biàn sǐ le. Yú xiǎo
Just ate (P) several mouthfuls, then died (P). With insignificant

646 婦人並無干涉只望大人
fù-ren bìng wú gān-shè. Zhǐ wàng dà rén
woman absolutely had-no connection. Only hope great person

647 高檯明鏡替小婦人做主
gāo tái míng jìng, tì xiǎo fù-ren zuò zhǔ
high raise clear mirror, on-behalf-of insignificant woman make decisions

648 咱（唱）
za. (Chàng:)
(P).' (Sings:)

649 （牧羊關）大人你明如
(Mù-yáng guān) Dà rén, nǐ míng rú
('Pasturing-Sheep Pass') 'Great person, you are-bright as

650 鏡清似水照妾身肝
jìng, qīng sì shuǐ, zhào qiè-shēn gān
mirror, clear as water; illuminate handmaiden's liver/

651 膽虛實那羹本五味
dǎn xū shí. Nà gēng běn wǔ wèi
gall's falseness/truth. That soup originally five flavors

652 俱全除了外百事不
jù quán. Chú-le-wài bǎi shì bù
all were-complete. Except-(P)-this, hundred things [I] do-not

653 知他推道嘗滋味喫
zhī. Tā tuī dào cháng zī-wèi. Chī
know. He made-excuse saying [he was] tasting flavor. Swallowed [it]

172

soup anymore. She gave it to his father to eat. No sooner had he eaten a few mouthfuls than he died. His death had absolutely nothing to do with me. I hope your honor will raise high the clear mirror and act on my behalf for justice.

(Sings seventh lyric):

> *Your honor, you, bright as a mirror and clear as water,*
> *Can discern whether I am inwardly true or false.*
> *The soup had the five flavors all properly blended;*
> *Besides this I know nothing else.*
> *He pretended to taste it;*
> *His father swallowed it and became unconscious.*

646] *bìng: bìng-rán* (cf. n. 313–14).
647] *gāo tái míng jìng:* 'to hold high a clear mirror' is an idiom for politely asking an official 'to discern wrongs and justice'. As a clear mirror reflects things lucidly, a discerning judge sees through motivation, and can detect false intentions. A clear mirror is thus associated with a wise judge; cf. ll. 649–50 and l. 1384 of the concluding couplet of the play.

§653] *dào: qù* 去 , *KMCP*, p. 11a.

654
下去便昏迷不是妾

xià qù biàn hūn-mí. Bú-shì qiè

down (C); then fainted. It-is-not handmaiden

655
訟庭上胡支對大人

sòng-tíng-shàng hú zhī-duì. Dà rén

in-court (L) nonsensically answer. Great person

656
也却敎我平白地說

ye, què jiào wǒ píng-bái-di shuō

(P), instead, would-have me groundlessly (P) say

657
甚的

shén-de.

what.'

658
(張驢兒云) 大人詳情他自

(Zhāng Lǘ-er yún:) Dà rén xiáng qíng: Tā zì

(Chang Donkey says:) 'Great person, carefully-examine situation: She herself

659
姓蔡我自姓張他婆婆不

xìng Cài, wǒ zì xìng Zhāng. Tā pó-po bù

is-surnamed Ts'ai; I myself am-surnamed Chang. [If] her mother-in-law did-not

660
招俺父親接脚他養我父

zhāo ǎn fù-qin jiē-jiǎo, tā yǎng wǒ fù

take-in my father [as a] second-husband, she provided-for us father

661
子兩箇在家做甚麼這媳

zǐ liǎng ge zài jiā zuò-shém-me? Zhè xí-

son two (M) at home to-do-what? This woman's

662
婦年紀兒雖小極是箇賴

fu nián-jì-er suí xiǎo, jí shì ge lài-

age although is-small, [she] very-much is [a] (M) bad-

663
骨頑皮不怕打的 (孤云) 人

gǔ wán pí, bú-pà-dǎ-de. (Gū yún:) Rén

boned, stubborn skinned, one-not-afraid-of-beating.' (Official says:) 'People

It is not that I answer evasively in court,
Your honor, what could I say groundlessly when I am innocent?

DONKEY CHANG: Your honor, please examine the matter carefully. Her name is Ts'ai and my name is Chang. If her mother-in-law did not take my father as her second husband, why did she keep us two, father and son, in her house? This woman, though young, is bad and stubborn, unafraid of a beating.

PREFECT: People are mean worms. If you don't beat them, they

656–7] This foreshadows her later forced confession and suggests that she senses that the case will go against her.

§655] *Dà rén: xiàng-gōng* 相 公 in *KMCP*, p. 11a.
§658–63] *Zhāng Lǘ-er... dǎ-de:* not in *KMCP*.

175

是 賤 虫 不 打 不 招 左 右 與
664　shì jiàn chóng, bù dǎ bù zhāo. Zuǒ-yòu, yǔ
　　are mean worms, not beaten, not confess. Attendants, for

我 選 大 棍 子 打 着 （ 祗 候 打
665　wǒ xuǎn dà gùn-zi dǎ zhe. (Zhǐ-hòu dǎ
　　me select big stick to-beat (P).' (Attendants beat

正 旦 三 次 噴 水 科 正 旦 唱 ）
666　zhèng dàn; sān cì pēn shuǐ kē. Zhèng dàn chàng:)
　　principal female-role; three times sprinkle water [on her]
　　gesture. Principal female-role sings:)

（ 罵 玉 郎 ） 這 無 情 棍 棒
667　(Mà Yù-láng) Zhè wú-qíng gùn-bàng
　　('Scold Jade-man') 'This un-feeling stick

敎 我 捱 不 的 婆 婆 也
668　jiào wǒ ái-bù-de. Pó-po ye,
　　makes me unable-to-endure. Mother-in-law (P),

須 是 你 自 做 下 怨 他
669　xū shì nǐ zì zuò-xià, yuàn tā-
　　certainly it-is you yourself did [this]; blame whom?

誰 勸 普 天 下 前 婚 後
670　shéi? Quàn pǔ tiān-xià qián hūn hòu
　　[I] urge all under-heaven first married, later

嫁 婆 娘 每 都 看 取 我
671　jià pó-niáng-měi, dōu kàn-qǔ wǒ
　　wedded women (Pl) all to-take-note-of my

這 般 傍 州 例
672　zhè bān páng zhōu lì.
　　this kind-of other district example.'

（ 感 皇 恩 ） 呀 是 誰 人 唱
673　(Gǎn Huáng ēn) Yā! Shì shéi rén chàng
　　('Thanking Imperial Favor') "Ah, it-is which person crying/

will not confess. Attendants, select a heavy stick and beat her.
(The attendants beat Tou O. Three times they sprinkle water on
her to revive her.)

TOU O (Sings eighth lyric):

> *This heartless stick is more than I can endure.*
> *Oh mother, this indeed is your own doing;*
> *Who else can be blamed?*
> *Here I urge all women in the world, married or remarried,*
> *To take note of my case as a precedent.*

(Ninth lyric):

> *Ah! Who is shouting so fiercely?*

665] *zhe:* a final particle (see pp. 17).

669–70] *tā-shéi:* comparable to *shéi* 誰, 'who'; e.g., *bǎ gǔ jīn yí hèn xiàng tā-shéi shuō*
把古今遺恨向他誰說, 'my regrets old and new to whom could I tell?'
(*Hsin Ch'i-chi* 辛棄疾, 'Man chiang hung' 滿江紅, *Chia hsüan tz'u* 稼軒詞
[in *Sung liu-shih ming-chia tz'u* 宋六十名家詞, *SPPY* ed.], *chüan* 2, p. 1*b*.)

672] *páng zhōu lì:* In making sentences, magistrates, besides resorting to the law of
the land, often used decisions made in other district courts as precedents. Later
páng zhōu lì, 'example from other districts' is used to mean 'example'; cf. Officer
Li: '*Wǒ quàn nǐ zhè yì huǒ liáng lì, zài xiū bǎ jì-nǔ qǔ wéi chī, zé wǒ shì páng·zhōu*
lì 我勸你這一火良吏 再休把妓女娶爲妻 則我是傍州例, I urge
you good officials, do not marry prostitutes as wives – I am an example here for
you.' (*Huan lao mo* 還牢末 [*YCH*, no. 92], Act I, Song 9, '*Ch'ing-ke-er*' 青哥兒).

§667] *Zhè:* not in *KMCP*.

叫揚疾不由我不魄

674 *jiào yáng jí, bù yóu wǒ bú pò*
calling loud, fast? Not controllable-by me not-to-have [my] spirit

散魂飛恰消停纔蘇

675 *sàn hún fēi. Qià xiāo-tíng, cái sū-*
scatter, [my] soul flies-out. As-soon-as [it] stops, as-soon-as [I]

醒又昏迷捱千般打

676 *xǐng, yòu hūn-mí. Ái qiān bān dǎ-*
revive, again [I] faint. [I] suffer thousand sorts beating,

拷萬種凌逼一杖下

677 *kǎo, wàn zhǒng líng-bī, yí zhàng xià,*
ten-thousand kinds punishment. One blow falls –

一道血一層皮

678 *yí dào xuě, yì céng pí.*
one streak blood, one layer skin.'

（探茶歌）打的我肉都

679 *(Çǎi chá gē) Dǎ de wǒ ròu dōu*
('Picking Tea Song') '[I am] beaten until my flesh all

飛血淋漓腹中寃枉

680 *fēi, xuě lín-lí. Fù zhōng yuān-wang*
flies [about, my] blood drips. Belly within (L) grievances,

有誰知則我這小婦

681 *yǒu shéi zhī! Zé wǒ zhè xiǎo fù-*
there-is who [that] would-know! Only [with] me this insignificant woman,

人毒藥來從何處也

682 *ren dú-yào lái cóng hé-chù yě?*
poison [could] come from what-place (P)?

I cannot help being frightened out of my wits.
No sooner does the noise stop and scarce do I revive,
Than once again I faint.
A thousand beatings and ten thousand punishments;
One blow falls – one streak of blood, one layer of skin!

(Sings tenth lyric):

They beat me till pieces of my flesh fly about,
And I am dripping with blood.
Who knows the bitterness in my heart?
Where could I, this insignificant woman, have secured poison?

674-5] *pò sàn hún fěi:* a stock phrase. 'Soul flies out of one's body' means 'frightened out of one's wits'.

§674-5] *bú pò sàn hún fěi: kū-kū tí-tí* 哭哭啼啼 in *KMCP*, p. 11b.
§675] *Qià xiāo-tíng: wǒ qià huán-hún* 我恰還魂 in *KMCP*, p. 11b.
§677] *wàn zhǒng líng-bǐ: jiàn xiān xuě lín-lí* 見鮮血淋漓 in *KMCP*, p. 11b.
§679-80] *ròu dōu fěi: Pò sàn hún fěi* 魄散魂飛 in *KMCP*, p. 11b.
§680] *xuě lín-lí: mìng yǎn quán shí* 命掩泉石 in *KMCP*, p. 11b.
§681-2] *Zé wǒ... hé-chù yě: Wǒ bù céng yào sǐ gōng-gong dāng zuì zé* 我不曾藥死公公當罪責 in *KMCP*, p. 12a.

179

天那怎麼的覆盆不

683 *Tiān na! Zěm-me-de fú pén bú*
Heaven, ah! How-is-it overturned tub is-not

照太陽暉

684 *zhào tài-yáng huī!*
shined-upon-by sun's light!'

（ 孤云 ）你招也不招（ 正旦云 ）

685 *(Gū yún) Nǐ zhāo yě bù zhāo? (Zhèng dàn yún:)*
(Official says:) 'You confess or not confess?' (Principal female-role says:)

委的不是小婦人下毒藥

686 *Wěi-de bú-shì xiǎo fù-ren xià dú-yào*
'Really not was insignificant person [who] put-in poison

來（ 孤云 ）旣然不是你與我

687 *lai. (Gū yún:) Jì-rán bú-shì nǐ, yǔ wǒ*
(P).' (Official says:) 'Since not was you, for me

打那婆子（ 正旦忙云 ）住住

688 *dǎ nà pó-zi. (Zhèng dàn máng yún:) Zhù, zhù,*
beat that old-woman.' (Principal female-role quickly says:) 'Stop, stop,

住休打我婆婆情願我招

689 *zhù, xiū dǎ wǒ pó-po; qíng-yuàn wǒ zhāo-*
stop, don't beat my mother-in-law; am-willing I confess

了罷是我藥死公公來（ 孤

690 *le ba. Shì wǒ yào-sǐ gōng-gong lai. (Gū*
(P) (P). [It] was I [who] poisoned-to-death father-in-law (P).' (Official

云 ）旣然招了着他畫了伏

691 *yún:) Jì-rán zhāo-le, zháo tā huà-le fú-*
says:) 'Since [she] confessed (P), have her mark (P) confession

狀將枷來枷上下在死囚

692 *zhuàng, jiāng jiā lái jiā-shang, xià zài sǐ-qiú*
form, bring cangue (C) to-lock-[her]-up, send-[her]-down to condemned-convict

> *Oh Heaven, why don't the sun's rays*
> *Ever reach underneath an overturned tub?*

PREFECT: Are you going to confess or not?

TOU O: Really, I did not put in the poison.

PREFECT: Since it wasn't you, let's just beat the old woman.

TOU O (hastily): Stop! Stop! Stop! Do not beat my mother-in-law; rather, I'll confess. It was I who poisoned my father-in-law.

PREFECT: Since she has confessed her crime, have her make her mark on her confession. Fasten her in the cangue and throw her in the

---

683–4] *fú pén. . . huī:* 'under an overturned tub shines no sunlight' meaning justice does not exist in a dark court. A wrong sentence is sometimes referred to as *fú-pén zhī yuān* 覆 盆 之 寃, 'overturned tub grievance'.

692] *jiā:* 'cangue', a frame used to confine the neck and hands: an old Chinese punishment. The English and French 'cangue' is from the Portugese *canga*, which in turn is from the Vietnamese *gông*, 'yoke'.

§683–4] *Tiān na. . . tài-yáng huī: gào nǐ ge xiàng-gōng míng jīng chá xū shí* 告 你 箇 相 公 明 鏡 察 虛 實 in *KMCP*, p. 12a.

691–2] *Jì-rán. . . zhuàng:* not in *KMCP*.

693　牢裏去到來日判箇斬字
láo li qù. Dào lái-rì pàn ge zhǎn zì,
cell (L) (C). Comes tomorrow, [I shall] sentence [her with one]
(M) "decapitate" word;

694　押付市曹典刑（ 卜兒哭科
yā-fù shì-cáo diǎn-xíng. (Bǔ-er kū kē,
send-[her]-under-guard-to market-place [for] statutory-pen-
alty.' (Old-woman crying gesture,

695　云) 竇娥孩兒這都是我送
yún:) Dòu É hái-er, zhè dōu shì wǒ sòng-
says:) 'Tou O, child, this all is me giving

696　了你性命兀的不痛殺我
le nǐ xìng-mìng. Wù-de bú tòng shā wǒ
(P) [away] your life. Does-this not pain to-death me

697　也（ 正旦唱 ）
yě! (Zhèng dàn chàng:)
(P)!' (Principal female-role sings:)

698　（ 黃鍾尾 ）我做了箇銜
(Huáng-zhōng wěi) Wǒ zuò-le ge xián
('Yellow-bell Coda') '[When] I become (P) (M) carrying

699　冤負屈沒頭鬼怎肯
yuān fù qū méi tóu guǐ, zěn kěn
grievance burdened-with injustice no head ghost, how
[shall I] be-willing-to

700　便放了你好色荒淫
biàn fàng-le nǐ hào-sè huāng-yín
then let-go (P) you, lustful, lecherous,

701　漏面賊想人心不可
lòu-miàn zéi? Xiǎng rén xīn bù kě
exposing-face thief? [I] think [how] human heart not may

cell for the condemned. Tomorrow I shall sentence her to death and
have her taken to the marketplace to be executed.

TS'AI (weeps): Tou O, it is I who am costing you your life. Oh,
this pains me to death!

TOU O (Sings eleventh lyric):

> *When I become a headless ghost, suffering great injustice,*
> *Do you think I would spare you,*
> > *A lustful, lecherous, brazen-faced thief?*
> *Men cannot be long deceived;*

694] *diǎn-xíng: cháng xíng* 常 刑, 'statutory penalty'.
696–7] *Wǔ-de bú tòng shā wǒ yě:* a stock phrase often used in Yüan drama (see n. 66–7).

§693] *pàn ge zhǎn zì:* not in *KMCP*.
§694] *kū kē:* not in *KMCP*.
§695–7] The two sentences here are reversed in *KMCP*, p. 12a.
§698] *Huáng-zhōng wěi: Wěi-shēng* 尾 聲 in *KMCP*, p. 12a.
§699–700] *zěn kěn biàn fàng-le:* bù zǒu le 不 走 了 in *KMCP*, p. 12a.
§701–2] After *zéi: xiǎng qīng-tiān bù kě qī* 想 青 天 不 可 欺 in *KMCP*, p. 12a.

欺 冤 枉 事 天 地 知 爭
702　　*qi. Yuān-wang shì tiān dì zhī. Zhēng*
be-cheated; unjust matters Heaven/Earth know-of. [I have] struggled

到 頭 競 到 底 到 如 今
703　　*dào tóu, jìng dào dǐ. Dào rú-jīn*
to the-end; fought to the-finish; come-to now,

待 怎 的 情 願 認 藥 殺
704　　*dài zěn-de? Qíng-yuàn rèn yào shā*
wait-for what? Am-willing to-admit poisoning/killing

公 公 與 了 招 罪 婆 婆
705　　*gōng-gong; yǔ-le zhāo-zuì. Pó-po*
father-in-law; have-submitted (P) confession. Mother-in-law

也 我 若 是 不 死 呵 如
706　　*ye, wǒ ruò-shì bù sǐ he, rú-*
(P), I if do-not die (P), how

何 救 得 你（隨 祇 候 押
707　　*hé jiù-de nǐ? (Suí zhǐ-hòu yā*
can-save you?' (Following attendant, in-custody,

下 ）
708　*xià)*
exit.)

（ 張 驢 兒 做 叩 頭 科 云 ） 謝 青
709　*(Zhāng Lǘ-er zuò kòu-tóu kē, yún:) Xiè qing-*
(Chang Donkey performs kowtowing action, says:) 'Thank blue-

天 老 爺 做 主 明 日 殺 了 竇
710　*tiān lǎo-ye zuò zhǔ! Míng-rì shā-le Dòu*
Heaven Old-lord [for] making decision! Tomorrow kill (P) Tou

娥 纔 與 小 人 的 老 子 報 的
711　*É, cái yǔ xiǎo rén de lǎo-zi bào-de*
O, only-then for insignificant person's (P) father will-avenge (P)

184

Injustice escapes not the eyes of Heaven and Earth.
I struggled to the end and fought to the finish,
Now why should I wait any longer?
I willingly admit poisoning my father-in-law and sign a confession.
Oh mother, if I do not die,
How can I save your life?

(Exit Tou O following the attendant.)

DONKEY CHANG (kowtows): Thank you, heavenly magistrate, for acting on my behalf. When Tou O is executed tomorrow, my father's death finally will be avenged.

705] *zhāo-zuì:* comparable to *fú-biàn,* 服辯 (see n. 1131).
709] *kòu-tóu:* 'to prostrate oneself and to knock one's head on the ground in reverence'; 'to do obeisance'. The word has been taken into the English language and is spelled 'kowtow'.

§704] *dài zěn-de?: shuō shén-de yuān,* 說甚的冤 in *KMCP,* p. 12a.
　　Qíng-yuàn rèn: Wǒ biàn 我便, *KMCP,* 12a.
§705-7] After *zhāo-zuì: pó-po wǒ dào bǎ nǐ lái biàn dǎ-de dǎ-de lái rèn-de* 婆婆我到把你來便打的打的來恁的 in *KMCP,* p. 12b.
§709-10] *zuò kòu-tóu... zuò zhǔ:* not in *KMCP.*
§711-12] *cái yǔ...yuān:* not in *KMCP;* instead, *wǒ qiě suí yá tīng hòu* 我且隨衙聽候, *KMCP,* p. 12b.

185

冤 (卜兒哭科云) 明日市曹

712　*yuān. (Bǔ-er kū kē, yún:) Míng-rì shì-cáo-*
wrongs.' (Old-woman weeping action, says:) 'Tomorrow in-
the-market-place

中殺竇娥孩兒也兀的不

713　*zhōng shā Dòu É hái-er ye. Wù-de bú*
(L) [they will] kill Tou O child(P). [Does] this not

痛殺我也 (孤云) 張驢兒蔡

714　*tòng-shā wǒ yě! (Gū yún:) Zhāng Lǘ-er, Cài*
pain-to-death me (P)!' (Official says:) 'Chang Donkey, Ts'ai

婆婆都取保狀着隨衙聽

715　*Pó-po, dōu qǔ bǎo-zhuàng, zháo suí-yá tīng-*
P'o-p'o, all fetch security-papers; [I] would-have [you] be-close-
to-court to-listen-for-call.

候左右打散堂鼓將馬來

716　*hòu. Zuǒ-yòu, dǎ sàn táng gǔ. Jiāng mǎ lái*
Attendants, beat dismiss court drum. Bring horse (C).

回私宅去也 (同下)

717　*huí sī zhái qù ye. (Tóng xià)*
[I] am-returning-to private residence (C) (P).' (Together
exeunt.)

第三折

718　*Dì-sān Zhé*
Number-three Act

(外扮監斬官上云) 下官監

719　*(Wài bàn jiān zhǎn guān shàng, yún:) Xià guān jiān*
(*Wai*-role in-make-up-of overseeing execution official enters;
says:) 'Humble official overseeing

斬官是也今日處決犯人

720　*zhǎn guān shì yě. Jīn-rì chǔ-jué fàn-ren;*
execution official is (P). Today execute criminal;

TS'AI (weeps): Tomorrow at the marketplace they are going to kill
Tou O, my child. Oh, this pains me to death!
PREFECT: Donkey Chang and Mistress Ts'ai, get yourselves
securities. I would have you at the court's disposal at all times.
Attendant, sound the drum for the court's dismissal. Bring my horse.
I am going home.
(Exeunt.)

ACT THREE

(Enter the officer in charge of execution.)
OFFICER: I am the officer in charge of execution. Today we are

---

715] *suí-yá:* to be at court or close to it; see Hsü Chia-jui, p. 48.
719] *Wài:* a role in Yüan drama usually acting the part of a dignified person.

§712] After *yuān: xià* 下, *KMCP*, p. 12b.
§714] After *yě: xià* 下, *KMCP*, p. 12b.
§714–7] *Gū yún. . . qù ye: Dào míng-rì diǎn-xíng Dòu É; jīn-rì wú shì; jiāng mǎ lái hòu
zhái qù chī jiǔ* 到 明 日 典 刑 竇 娥 今 日 無 事 將 馬 來 後 宅 去 喫 酒，
KMCP, p. 12b.
§717] *Tóng xià: xià* 下, *KMCP*, p. 12b.
§718] *Dì-sān Zhé:* not in *KMCP* here; *Dì-sān chū* appears earlier in *KMCP*, on p.
10b. (see § 599–600).

着做公的把住巷口休放

721 *zháo zuò-gōng-de bǎ-zhù xiàng kǒu, xiū fàng*
order officers to-guard lane entrance, not let

往來人閒走（淨扮公人皷

722 *wǎng lái rén xián zǒu. (Jìng bàn gōng-rén, gǔ*
going/coming persons idly walk.' (*Ching*-role in-make-up-of
officer, performs-drumming

三通鑼三下科劊子磨旗

723 *sān tòng, luó sān xià kē. Kuài-zi mò qí,*
three times, beating-gong three strokes gesture. Executioner
waving flag,

提刀押正旦帶枷上劊子

724 *tí dāo, yā zhèng dàn dài jiā shàng. Kuài-zi*
carrying sword, guarding principal female-role, wearing
cangue, enters. Executioner

云）行動些行動些監斬官

725 *yún:) Xíng-dòng xiē, xíng-dòng xiē, jiān zhǎn guān*
says:) 'Move a-little, move a-little, overseeing execution official

去法場上多時了（正旦唱）

726 *qù fǎ-chǎng shàng duō-shí le. (Zhèng dàn chàng:)*
has-gone-to execution-ground (L) long time (P).' (Principal
female-role sings:)

（正宮端正好）沒來由

727 *(Zhèng-gōng: Duān-zhèng hǎo) Méi lái-yóu*
(*Cheng-kung* [mode]: 'Proper/Good') 'No reason

犯王法不隄防遭刑

728 *fàn wáng fǎ, bù-tí-fáng zāo xíng-*
sinned-against Imperial law, unexpectedly suffered punishment.

憲叫聲屈動地驚天

729 *xiàn. Jiào shēng qū, dòng dì jing tiān.*
Utter [a] cry (M) [of] injustice; stirs Earth, startles Heaven.

putting a criminal to death. Officers, guard the roads. Do not let any passers-by loiter.

(Enter attendant. They beat the drum and gong three times. The executioner enters, waving a flag, carrying a sword, and guarding Tou O in a cangue.)

EXECUTIONER: Move faster, move faster! The officer in charge of execution has long since gone to the place of execution.

TOU O (Sings first lyric):

> For no reason, I am found guilty by Imperial law;
> Unexpectedly, I suffer punishment.
> My cry of injustice startles Heaven and Earth!

721] *zuò-gōng-de:* same as *gōng-rén* 公人, a general term for yamen runners.

722] *gǔ:* same as *gǔ* 鼓, 'a drum', 'to drum'.

723] *tòng:* read in the fourth tone when used as a measure word for drum beating; ordinarily it is read in the first tone.

Kuài-zi (or guì-zi): *kuài* is 'to cut', and *zi* here is a nominalizing suffix, not the familiar redundant suffix added to the nouns, as in *er-zi.*

mò qí (mó qí): same as *yáo qí* 搖, 'to wave a flag'; cf. *Mò chí-zhì máng shōu duì-wǔ; jī jīn zhēng jù diǎn bīng-zú* 磨 旗 幟 忙 收 隊 伍 擊 金 鉦 聚 點 兵 卒. 'Waving the flags, they quickly collected the army; striking the gongs, they reassembled the soldiers.' ('*Tou an-ch'un*': '*Chan Yen Liang*' 鬥 鵪 鶉 斬 顏 良 in *Yung-hsi yüeh-fu,* 雍 熙 樂 府 [*SPTK hsü-pien*], *chüan* 13, p. 28*a.*)

729] *dòng dì jīng tiān:* a comparable phrase appears in the title and the concluding couplet of the play.

§721] *zháo zuò-gōng-de:* not in *KMCP.*

§722] *Jìng bàn gōng-rén:* *chǒu* 丑, *KMCP*, p. 12*a.*

§723–4] *Kuài-zi mò qí tí dāo:* *kuài-zi mò dāo kē, kuài-zi mò qí kē, dìng tóu tòng luó gǔ kē* 劊 子 磨 刀 科 劊 子 磨 旗 科 定 頭 通 鑼 鼓 科 in *KMCP*, p. 12*b.*

§725–6]*jiǎn zhǎn guān. . . duō-shí le:* not in *KMCP;* instead, *bǎ zhù xiàng kǒu* 把 住 巷 口 in *KMCP*, p. 12*b.*

§728] *bù-tí-fáng:* *hú-lu-tí* 葫 蘆 提 in *KMCP*, p. 12*b.*

頃刻間遊魂先赴森

730 *Qǐng-kè jiān yóu hún xiān fù Sēn-*
Instant-moment (L) drifting soul first goes-to Yama's

羅殿怎不將天地也

731 *luó diàn. Zěn bù jiāng tiān dì yě*
palace. How not (Pr) [toward] Heaven/Earth also

生埋怨

732 *shēng mái-yuàn?*
beget harbored-resentment?'

（滾繡球）有日月朝暮

733 *(Gǔn xiù qiú) Yǒu rì yuè zhāo mù*
('Rolling Embroidered Ball') 'There-are sun [and] moon
morning/evening

懸有鬼神掌著生死

734 *xuán; yǒu guǐ shén zhǎng-zhu shēng sǐ*
hang; there-are ghosts, spirits control (P) life/death

權天地也只合把清

735 *quán. Tiān dì yě, zhǐ hé bǎ qīng*
power. Heaven/Earth (P), only should (Pr) pure,

濁分辨可怎生糊突

736 *zhuó fēn-biàn; kě zěn-shēng hú-tu-*
foul distinguish; instead, how confused

了盜跖顏淵為善的

737 *le dào Zhí Yán Yuān. Wéi shàn de*
(P) Bandit Chih, Yen Yüan. Do good [deeds] ones

受貧窮更命短造惡

738 *shòu pín-qióng gèng mìng duǎn; zào è*
suffer poverty, moreover life short; do evil

190

In a moment, my drifting soul goes to Yama's palace.
Why shouldn't I blame Heaven and Earth?
(Sings second lyric):
The sun and moon hang aloft by day and by night;
Ghosts and spirits hold the power over our lives and deaths.
Heaven and Earth should distinguish the pure from the foul;
But how they have mixed up Bandit Chih and Yen Yüan!
The good suffer poverty and short life;
The wicked enjoy wealth, nobility, and long life.

730–1] *Sēn-luó diàn:* the palace of Yama, king of the nether world in popular Bud-
dhism. Morohashi gives Yama as a meaning not for *sēn-luó* itself, but only as
it occurs in the compound with 'palace' (VI: 14974: 31).

736] *hú-tu:* same as *hú-tu* 糊塗, 'confused', 'mixed-up'.

737] *dào Zhí Yán Yüán:* both were of the Spring and Autumn period. Zhí was a
notorious robber; and Yán Yüán, a Confucian disciple, was a virtuous person
who died young in poverty (*Historical Records, chüan* 61, p. 8*b*). Later these
two persons represented the extreme good and bad.

§730–1] *Qǐng-kè jiān. . . luó diàn:* not in *KMCP*.
§731–2] *Zěn bù. . . mái-yuàn: wǒ jiāng tiān dì hé mái-yuàn. Tiān yě, nǐ bù yǔ rén wéi
fāng-biàn,* 我將天地合埋怨天也你不與人爲方便, in *KMCP*, p. 13*a*.
§734] *xuán: xiǎn* 顯 in *KMCP*, p. 13*a*.
§734–5] *yǒu guǐ shén. . . quán: yǒu shān hé jīn gǔ jiān* 有山河今古監 in *KMCP*, p. 13*a*.
§735 and 740] *dì:* not in *KMCP*.
§735] *zhǐ hé: què bú* 却 不 in *KMCP*, p. 13*a*.
§736–7] *kě zěn-shēng hú-tu-le: kě zhī dào cuò kàn le* 可 知道錯看了 in *KMCP*, p. 13*a*.
§737] *Wéi shàn: yǒu dé de* 有 德 的 in *KMCP*, p. 13*a*.

191

的 享 富 貴 又 壽 延 天

739   *de xiǎng fú guì yòu shòu yán. Tiān*
ones enjoy wealth, nobility; moreover life-span extensive.
Heaven/

地 也 做 得 箇 怕 硬 欺

740   *dì yě zuò-de ge pà yìng qī*
Earth too have-so-acted-that [theirs is a] case-of (M) fear
the-strong, oppress

軟 却 元 來 也 這 般 順

741   *ruǎn; què yuán-lái yě zhè bān shùn*
the-weak; contrary [to expectations], after-all, also this
way follow

水 推 船 地 也 你 不 分

742   *shuǐ tuī chuán. Dì yě, nǐ bù fēn*
current push boat. Earth (P), [if] you do-not distinguish

好 歹 何 爲 地 天 也 你

743   *hǎo dǎi hé wéi dì? Tiān yě, nǐ*
good, evil, how be Earth? Heaven (P), [if] you

錯 勘 賢 愚 枉 做 天 哎

744   *cuò kān xián yú wǎng zuò tiān! Āi!*
mistakenly examine virtuous, foolish, in-vain be Heaven.
Alas!

只 落 得 兩 淚 漣 漣

745   *zhǐ luò-de liǎng lèi lián-lián.*
only reduced-to two [streams of] tears flowing-unceasingly.'

（ 劊 子 云 ） 快 行 動 些 悮 了 時

746   *(Kuài-zi yún:) Kuài xíng-dòng xiē, wù-le shí-*
(Executioner says:) 'Quickly move some, have-missed (P) time

辰 也 （ 正 旦 唱 ）

747   *chén ye. (Zhèng dàn chàng:)*
(P).' (Principal female-role sings:)

Even Heaven and Earth have come to fear the strong and oppress the weak.
They, after all, only push the boats following the current.
Oh Earth, as you fail to discriminate between good and evil,
 How can you function as Earth?
Oh Heaven, in mistaking the sage and the fool,
 You are called Heaven in vain!

EXECUTIONER: Move on faster; we are late.

TOU O (Sings third lyric):

741–2] *shùn shuǐ tuī chuán:* 'to push the boat that follows the current', meaning 'to
 help without sincerity, to offer help to those who are already lucky'.
744] *cuò kǎn xián yú:* 'to misjudge the virtuous and the foolish'.

§741] *què yuán-lái yě zhè bān: bù-xiǎng tiān dì yě* 不 想 天 地 也 in *KMCP*, p. 13*a*.
§743] *hé: nán* 難, *KMCP*, p. 13*a*.
§743–5] *nǐ . . . lián-lián: wǒ jīn-rì fù qū xián yuān āi gào tiān; kūng jiào wǒ dú yǔ dú yán*
 我 今 日 負 屈 銜 冤 哀 告 天 空 敎 我 獨 語 獨 言, in *KMCP*, p. 13*a*.

（倫秀才）則被這枷紐

748　*(Tăng xiù-cai) Zé bèi zhè jiā niŭ-*
　　('Surprised Scholar') 'Only by this cangue twisted-

的我左側右偏人擁

749　*de wŏ zuŏ cè yòu piān, rén yōng-*
　　till I to-left tilt, to-right stagger; people crowded-

的我前合後偃我竇

750　*de wŏ qián hé hòu yàn. Wŏ Dòu*
　　till I forward bend, backward incline. I, Tou

娥向哥哥行有句言

751　*É xiàng gē-ge xíng yŏu jù yán.*
　　O, toward brother (L) have (M) words.'

（劊子云）你有甚麼話說(正

752　*(Kuài-zi yún:) Nĭ yŏu shém-me huà shuō? (Zhèng*
　　(Executioner says:) 'You have what words to-say?' (Principal

旦唱）

753　*dàn chàng:)*
　　female-role sings:)

前街裏去心懷恨後

754　*Qián jiē li qù xīn huái hèn; hòu*
　　'Front street (L) go, heart holds grudge; back

街裏去死無冤休推

755　*jiē li qù sĭ wú yuān. Xiū tuī-*
　　street (L) go, to-die have-no grievance. Do-not make-
　　excuse-of

辭路遠

756　*cí lù yuăn.*
　　road being-distant.'

（劊子云）你如今到法場上

757　*(Kuài-zi yún:) Nĭ rú-jīn dào fă-chăng shàng-*
　　(Executioner says:) 'You now go-to execution-ground (L),

194

I am twisted by this cangue

Till I tilt to the left and stagger to the right;

The crowd pushes me backward and forward.

I, Tou O, wish to say something to you, brother.

EXECUTIONER: What do you want to say?

TOU O (sings):

If we go through the main street, I shall bear you a grudge;

If we go through the back street,

I will have no grievance, though I die.

Do not refuse me by saying, 'The back road is too long.'

EXECUTIONER: Now that you are going to the execution ground,

749] *de*: 'till', introducing resultative clause.

751] *xíng* (or *háng*): in Sung and Yüan language, *xíng* sometimes is used in locative
expressions. It may be freely translated as 'place'; e.g. *Nĭ zài wŏ xíng kŏu qiáng,
yìng dĭ-zhe tóu-pí chuàng* 你在我行口强 硬抵着頭皮撞 , 'At my place, you
talk big, and stubbornly fight with your skull' (*The Romance of the Western
Chamber*, Part I, Act II, Song no. 12, 'Ch'ao t'ien-tzu' 朝天子); also *Dī shēng
wèn xiàng shéi xíng sù, chéng shàng yĭ sān gēng* 低聲問向誰行宿，城上已三更
'I quietly asked at whose place I may stay; they have already sounded the
third-watch over the city' (Chou Pang-yen 周邦彥, 'Shao-nien yu' 少年遊,
Sung liu-shih ming-chia tz'u 宋六十名家詞 [*SPPY*] vol. II, p. 11a). This usage
is frequent in the interlinear Chinese translation in the *Yüan-ch'ao pi-shih* 元
朝秘史.

The graph 行 has two pronunciations in *CYYY*, appearing in both 'gēng-
qīng' 庚青 and 'jiāng-yáng' 江陽 rhyme groups.

§754] *xīn huái hèn: zhōng yŏu yuàn* 中有怨 in *KMCP*, p. 13a.

§755–6] *Xiū...yuàn: Fĕi shì wŏ zì-zhuān* 非是我自專 in *KMCP*, p. 13a.

§757–9] *Nĭ rú-jīn...hăo: Nĭ dāng xíng, rú-jīn lái fù fă-chăng yŏu shèn qīn-juàn* 你當
刑如今來赴法塲有甚親眷 in *KMCP*, p. 13b.

195

面 有 甚 麽 親 眷 要 見 的 可

758   *miàn, yŏu shém-me qin-juàn yào jiàn-de, kĕ*
have what relatives/family [whom you] want to-see (P), [you]
may

教 他 過 來 見 你 一 面 也 好

759   *jiào tā guò-lai jiàn nĭ yí-miàn yĕ hăo.*
ask them come-over to-see you once (M) also all-right.'

（ 正 旦 唱 ）

760   *(Zhèng dàn chàng:)*
(Principal female-role sings:)

（ 叨 叨 令 ） 可 憐 我 孤 身

761   *(Dāo-dāo lìng) Kĕ-lián wŏ gū shēn*
('Chattering Song') 'Pitiable I, lonely body,

隻 影 無 親 眷 則 落 的

762   *zhĭ yĭng wú qin-juàn; zé luò-de*
single shadow, have-no relative/family; thus so-reduced-
that

吞 聲 忍 氣 空 嗟 怨

763   *tūn shēng rĕn qì kōng jiē yuàn.*
[I] swallowing voice, restraining anger, in-vain sigh/grieve.'

（ 劊 子 云 ） 難 道 你 爺 娘 家 也

764   *(Kuài-zi yún:) Nán-dào nĭ yé-niáng-jiā yĕ*
(Executioner says:) 'Do-you-mean-to-say you father/mother
even

沒 的 （ 正 旦 云 ） 止 有 箇 爹 爹

765   *méi-de? (Zhèng dàn yún:) Zhĭ yŏu ge diē-die,*
have-none (P)?' (Principal female-role says:) 'Only have (M)
father,

十 三 年 前 上 朝 取 應 去 了

766   *shí-sān nián qián shàng cháo qŭ-yìng qù le.*
thirteen years ago to court to-take-examination went (P).

if you have any relatives you would like to see, it would be all right for you to see them.

TOU O (Sings fourth lyric):

Unhappily I am all alone and have no relatives;
So I can only endure in silence, and sigh in vain.

EXECUTIONER: Do you mean to say that you don't even have parents?

TOU O: I have only a father, who went to the capital thirteen years ago to take the Examination. There has not been any word from

759] *yí-miàn: miàn*, literally meaning 'face', here is used as an auxiliary noun for the verb 'to see' (see Chao, *Grammar*, pp. 615–20).

763] *tūn shēng rěn qì:* 'to restrain one's temper in silence'; 'to endure'.

§761–2] *Kě-lián... qīn-juàn: Nǐ dào wǒ dāng xíng fù fǎ-chǎng hé qīn-juàn* 你道 我當刑赴法塲何親眷 in *KMCP*, p. 13*b* (1st line in *Dǎo-dǎo lìng*). In the first part of this song, the prose interpolation in the texts differs; corresponding lines with end rhymes *juàn, yuàn, miàn,* and *jiàn* in *YCH*, and *juàn miàn, yuàn,* and *jiàn* in *KMCP* are identified here and in notes §762–3, § 768–9, §773–4.

§762–3] *Zé luò-de... yuàn: Qián jiē lǐ qù gào nín kàn xie yán miàn* 前 街裡 去 告 您 看 些 顔面, *KMCP*, p. 13*b* (2nd line of *Dǎo-dǎo lìng*). In *KMCP* between these 1st and 2nd lines there is a prose interpolation: *Nǐ qián jiē qù shì zěn-shēng, hòu jiē qù shì rú-hé* 你 前 街 去 是 怎 生 後 街 去 是 如 何, *KMCP*, p. 13*b*.

§764–7] *Kuài-zi yún... yīn-xìn:* not in *KMCP*.

197

至今杳無音信（唱）

767　*Zhì jin yǎo wú yin-xìn. (Chàng:)*
Till now obscure, has-no news.' (Sings:)

蚤已是十年多不覩

768　*Zǎo yǐ-shì shí nián duō bù dǔ*
'Already has-been ten years and-more not see

爹爹面

769　*diē-die miàn.*
father's face.'

（劊子云）你適纔要我往後

770　*(Kuài-zi yún:) Nǐ shì-cái yào wǒ wǎng hòu*
(Executioner says:) 'You just-now wanted me toward back

街裏去是什麼主意（正旦

771　*jiē li qù. Shì shém-me zhǔ-yi? (Zhèng dàn*
street (L) go. Is what intention?' (Principal female-role

唱）

772　*chàng:)*
sings:)

怕則怕前街裏被我

773　*Pà zé pà qián jiē li bèi wǒ*
'Fear then fear, front street (L) by my

婆婆見

774　*pó-po jiàn.*
mother-in-law seen.'

（劊子云）你的性命也顧不

775　*(Kuài-zi yún:) Nǐ-de xìng-mìng yě gù-bu-*
(Executioner says:) 'Your (P) life even cannot-care-for.

得怕他見怎的（正旦云）俺

776　*dé, pà tā jiàn zěn-de? (Zhèng dàn yún:) Ǎn*
fear her see [you], why?' (Principal female-role says:) 'My

198

him since. (Sings).

I have not seen my father for over ten years.

EXECUTIONER: Just now you asked me to take you by the back
street. What is your reason?

TOU O (sings):

I fear that on the main street my mother-in-law would see me.

EXECUTIONER: You cannot even take care of your own life now.
Why should you worry about her seeing you?

TOU O: If my mother-in-law sees me in a cangue and lock, going to

767] *yīn-xìn:* *yīn,* 'sound', and *xìn,* 'letter': *yīn-xìn* is 'news'.

773] *Pà zé pà:* 'as to what I fear, it's that I fear. . .'

§768–9] *Zǎo yǐ-shì. . . miàn: Wǒ wǎng hòu jiē lǐ qù he, bù bǎ gē-ge yuàn,* 我往後街
裡去呵不把哥哥怨 in *KMCP,* p. 13*b* (3rd line in *Dāo-dāo lìng*).

§770–2] *Kuài-zi yún. . . chàng:* not in *KMCP.*

§773–4] *Pà zé pà. . . jiàn: qián jiē lǐ qù zhǐ kǒng-pà ǎn pó-po jiàn* 前街里去只恐怕
俺婆婆見, *KMCP,* p. 13*b* (4th line in *Dāo-dāo lìng*).

199

婆 婆 若 見 我 披 枷 帶 鎖 赴
777 *pó-po ruò jiàn wǒ pēi jiā dài suǒ fù*
mother-in-law if sees me wearing cangue, carrying lock, to

法 場 飡 刀 去 呵 （ 唱 ）
778 *fǎ-chǎng cān dāo qù he, (chàng:)*
execution-ground to-eat knife going (P)', (sings:)

枉 將 他 氣 殺 也 麼 哥
779 *Wǎng jiāng tā qì shā yě mo-ge!*
'In-vain (Pr) her would-anger to-death (P) (P)!

枉 將 他 氣 殺 也 麼 哥
780 *Wǎng jiāng tā qì shā yě mo-ge!*
In-vain (Pr) her would-anger to-death (P) (P)!

告 哥 哥 臨 危 好 與 人
781 *Gào gē-ge, lín wéi hǎo yǔ rén*
Tell older-brother, on-the-brink-of danger is-good for people

行 方 便
782 *xíng fāng-biàn.*
to-render convenience.'

（ 卜 兒 哭 上 科 云 ） 天 那 兀 的
783 *(Bǔ-er kū shàng kē, yún:) Tiān na, wǔ-de*
(Old-woman crying, entering gesture, says:) 'Heaven (P)! this

不 是 我 媳 婦 兒 （ 劊 子 云 ） 婆
784 *bú shì wǒ xí-fù-er? (Kuài-zi yún:) Pó-*
not is my daughter-in-law?' (Executioner says:) 'Old-woman,

子 靠 後 （ 正 旦 云 ） 旣 是 俺 婆
785 *zi kào hòu. (Zhèng dàn yún:) Jì-shì ǎn pó-*
[step] toward back.' (Principal female-role says:) 'Since my mother-

婆 來 了 叫 他 來 待 我 囑 付
786 *po lái-le, jiào tā lái. Dài wǒ zhǔ-fu*
in-law has-come (P), ask her to-come [to me]. Wait-till I tell

200

the execution ground to be killed, (sings)

> *Won't she die from anger for nothing?*
> *Won't she die from anger for nothing?*
> *I tell you, brother,*
> *It is good to do favors for people in times of peril.*

TS'AI: Oh Heaven, isn't this my daughter-in-law?

EXECUTIONER: Old woman, stand back.

TOU O: Since my mother-in-law is here, ask her to come closer. Let

779] *yě mo-ge:* this appears in the songs with the melody *Dāo-dāo ling*, and always towards the end of the song. *Mo-ge* is an interrogative particle used in a rhetorical question. A comparable interrogative particle *me-ge* 嗎哥 is still used in the district south of Tientsin, Hopei (see Sun K'ai-ti, *Ts'ang-chou chi*, p. 589).

§784] After *xí-fù-er: Wǒ ér yě, bú tòng-shā wǒ yě* 我兒也不痛殺我也 in *KMCP*, p. 13*b*.

787 他 幾 句 話 咱 （ 劊 子 云 ） 那 婆
tā jǐ jù huà za. (Kuài-zi yún:) Nà pó-
her several (M) words (P).' (Executioner says:) 'Hey-there old-woman,

788 子 近 前 來 你 媳 婦 要 囑 付
zi jìn qián lái. Nǐ xí-fu yào zhǔ-fu
near front come (C). Your daughter-in-law wants to-tell

789 你 話 哩 （ 卜 兒 云 ） 孩 兒 痛 殺
nǐ huà li. (Bǔ-er yún:) Hái-er, tòng shā
you words (P).' (Old-woman says:) 'Child, pains to-death

790 我 也 （ 正 旦 云 ） 婆 婆 那 張 驢
wǒ ye! (Zhèng dàn yún:) Pó-po, nà Zhāng Lǘ-
me (P)!' (Principal female-role says:) 'Mother-in-law, that Chang Donkey

791 兒 把 毒 藥 放 在 羊 賭 兒 湯
er bǎ dú-yào fàng zài yáng dǔ-er tāng
(Pr) poison put in mutton tripe soup

792 裏 實 指 望 藥 死 了 你 要 覇
li, shí zhǐ-wàng yào-sǐ-le nǐ, yào bà
(L), really expected to-poison-to-death (P) you, wanting by-force

793 佔 我 爲 妻 不 想 婆 婆 讓 與
zhàn wǒ wéi qi. Bù xiǎng pó-po ràng yǔ
to-seize me to-be wife. Did-not expect P'o-po give [it] to

794 他 老 子 吃 倒 把 他 老 子 藥
tā lǎo-zi chī, dào bǎ tā lǎo-zi yào-
his father to-eat; instead, (Pr) his father poisoned-

795 死 了 我 怕 連 累 婆 婆 屈 招
sǐ-le. Wǒ pà lián-lèi pó-po, qū-zhāo-
to-death (P). I was-afraid to-involve mother-in-law, under-pressure-confessed

me say a few words to her.

EXECUTIONER: You old woman over there, come near. Your daughter-in-law wants to say something to you.

TS'AI: My child, this pains me to death!

TOU O: Mother, when Donkey Chang put the poison in the mutton-tripe soup, he really wanted to kill you and then force me to be his wife. He never expected you to give the soup to his father to eat, and thus kill him instead. Because I was afraid you would get into trouble, I confessed, under pressure, to murdering my father-in-law.

787] *Nà: nà* in direct address here functions as *wŭ-nà* ('hey', 'you over there') to attract the addressee's attention (see n. 139); *nà pó-zi* could also mean 'that woman over there'.

795] *qū-zhāo:* 'to confess under pressure when one is not guilty'.

§790–2] *Pó-po. . . li: Pó-po dōu zhǐ wèi nǐ shēn-zi bú kuài, sī-liàng yáng-dǔ-er tāng chī. Wǒ ān-pái le, yòu dào shǎo yán cù; bèi Zhāng Lǘ-er zuàn de wǒ qǔ yán cù qù; tā jiāng dú-yào fàng zài tāng lǐ, kě zháo wǒ ná guò qù yǔ nǐ chī. Shéi xiǎng nǐ ràng yǔ tā lǎo-zi chī* 婆婆都只爲你身子不快思量羊肚兒湯吃我安排了又道少鹽醋被張驢兒賺的我取鹽醋去他將毒藥放在湯里可着我拿過去與你吃誰想你讓與他老子吃 in *KMCP,* p. 14*a.*

§793–4] *pó-po. . . dào:* not in *KMCP.*

§795] after *sĭ-le: yīn bào qián chóu bǎ wǒ tuō qù guān-sī* 因報前讐把我拖去官司 in *KMCP,* p. 14*a.*

203

了 藥 死 公 公 今 日 赴 法 場

796   *le yào-sǐ gōng-gong. Jìn-rì fù fǎ-chǎng*
(P) poisoning-to-death father-in-law. Today go-to execution-
ground

典 刑 婆 婆 此 後 遇 着 冬 時

797   *diǎn-xíng. Pó-po, cǐ-hòu yù-zhe dōng shí*
to-be-executed. Mother-in-law, here-after encountering winter
time,

年 節 月 一 十 五 有 灆 不 了

798   *nián jié, yùe yi shí-wǔ, yǒu jiān-bù-liǎo-*
New-Year/festivals, month's first, fifteenth, [if] there-be
not-completely-poured

的 漿 水 飯 灆 半 碗 兒 與 我

799   *de jiāng-shuǐ fàn, jiān bàn-wǎn-er yǔ wǒ*
(P) gruel rice, pour half-a bowl for me

吃 燒 不 了 的 紙 錢 與 竇 娥

800   *chī, shāo-bù-liǎo de zhǐ-qián, yǔ Dòu É*
to-eat, not-completely-burned-up (P) paper-money, for Tou O

燒 一 陌 兒 則 是 看 你 死 的

801   *shāo yí-mò-er. Zé shì kàn nǐ sǐ-de*
burn a-hundred. Only is to-have-regard-for your dead (P)

孩 兒 面 上 （ 唱 ）

802   *hái-er miàn shang. (Chàng:)*
child's face (L).' (Sings:)

（ 快 活 三 ） 念 竇 娥 葫 蘆

803   *(Kuài-huó sān) Niàn Dòu É hú-lu-*
('Happy Three') 'Think-of Tou O, [due to] confusion,

提 當 罪 愆 念 竇 娥 身

804   *ti dāng zuì-qiān, niàn Dòu É shēn*
bore sin/guilt; think-of Tou O body/

首 不 完 全 念 竇 娥 從

805   *shǒu bù wán quán, niàn Dòu É cóng*
head not whole; think-of Tou O formerly,

Today I am going to the execution ground to be killed. Mother, in the future, during the winter season, on New Year and other festivals, and on the first and fifteenth of each month, if you have any spare gruel, pour half a bowl for me; and if you have paper money to spare, burn some for me. Do this for the sake of the personal dignity of your late son.

(Sings fifth lyric):

> Think of Tou O, who wrongly was found guilty;
> Think of Tou O, whose head and body were severed;
> Think of Tou O, who, in the past, worked in your house.

802] *miàn*: 'face', to the Chinese, has a special connotation. There is no English equivalent to it. It may be understood as 'personal dignity'.

803–4] *hú-lu-tí*: as *hú-tu* 糊塗, 'confused', 'foolish'; cf. *Dàn zūn zhōng yǒu jiǔ, xīn-tóu wú shì, hú-lu-tí guò,* 但 樽 中 有 酒 心 頭 無 事 葫 蘆 提 過, 'If only there is wine in the cup, and no cares in the mind, I just muddle through my days.' (Sung poet Li P'in-shan 李 屏 山, 'Shui lung yin' 水 龍 吟 in *Hua ts'ao ts'ui pien* 花 草 粹 編, ed. Ch'en Yao-wen 陳 耀 文, Ming Wan-li period, *chüan* 11, p. 34*a*; see also Wu Hsiao-ling, *Hsiao-shuo hsi-ch'ü lun-chi,* 小 說 戲 曲 論 集 pp. 84–5 and Sun K'ai-ti, *Ts'ang-chou chi*, pp. 623–5.)

§797–8] *cǐ-hòu... shí-wǔ*: not in *KMCP.*
§803] *Niàn*: *kàn* 看, *KMCP*, p. 14*a.*
§804] *niàn*: *zháo* 着, *KMCP*, p. 14*a.*
§805] *niàn*: *xiǎng* 想, *KMCP*, p. 14*a.*

前 已 往 幹 家 緣 婆 婆
806　*qián yǐ-wǎng gàn jiā-yuán. Pó-po*
in-the-past, did household-work. Mother-in-law

也 你 只 看 竇 娥 少 爺
807　*ye, nǐ zhǐ kàn Dòu É shǎo yé*
(P), you only have-regard-for Tou O lacking father

無 娘 面
808　*wú niáng miàn.*
have-no mother sake.'

（ 鮑 老 兒 ）念 竇 娥 伏 侍
809　*(Bāo lǎo-er) Niàn Dòu É fú-shì*
('Bao Old-man') 'Think-of Tou O served

婆 婆 這 幾 年 遇 時 節
810　*pó-po zhè jǐ nián. Yù shí-jié*
mother-in-law these few years. Come-upon festivals,

將 碗 涼 漿 奠 你 去 那
811　*jiāng wǎn liáng jiāng diàn; nǐ qù nà*
(Pr) bowlful-of cold gruel offer-as-sacrifice; you go-to that

受 刑 法 屍 骸 上 烈 些
812　*shòu xíng-fǎ shī-hái shàng liè xiē*
endured penalty corpse/skeleton (L), burn some

紙 錢 只 當 把 你 亡 化
813　*zhǐ qián. Zhǐ dàng bǎ nǐ wáng-huà-*
paper money. Only regard-as (Pr) your dead

的 孩 兒 薦
814　*de hái-er jiàn.*
(P) child being-offered-sacrifice.'

（ 卜 兒 哭 科 云 ）孩 兒 放 心 這
815　*(Bǔ-er kū kē, yún:) Hái-er fàng-xin. Zhè-*
(Old-woman weeping gesture, says:) 'Child, set-mind-at-ease.
This

206

Oh mother, do all of these for the sake of Tou O's face,
   Since she has no father or mother.
(Sings sixth lyric):
   Think of Tou O, who served you all these years;
   At festivals, offer me a bowl of cold gruel,
   Burn some paper money for my headless corpse.
   Regard this as offering sacrifice to your own late son.
TS'AI (weeping): Child, don't worry. I shall remember all this. Ah

---

809] *Bāo lǎo-er:* 'old man Bao'; or the title of a role (see n. 4 on *bǔ-er*).

814] *jiàn:* to offer a sacrifice in which no animal is used. *Jiàn xiū* 羞 is sacrificial food; before offering, it is called *jiàn*, and after offering, it is called *xiū*.

§811] After *liáng jiāng diàn:* (*bǔ*) *hái-er fàng-xīn, wǔ-de bú tòng-sha wǒ yě* (卜) 孩兒放心兀的不痛殺我也 in *KMCP*, p. 14*b*.

§813–14] *Zhǐ dàng...jiàn: Kàn nǐ nà huà qù hái-er miàn* 看你那化去孩兒面 in *KMCP*, p. 14*b*.

§815–17] *Bǔ-er...wǒ ye:* not in *KMCP* here, but a comparable passage occurs earlier (see §811).

816 箇 老 身 都 記 得 天 那 兀 的
ge lǎo-shēn dōu jì-de. Tiān na, wǔ-de
(M) old-self all remember. Heaven (P), [does] this

817 不 痛 殺 我 也 （ 正 旦 唱 ）
bú tòng-shā wǒ ye! (Zhèng dàn chàng:)
not pain-to-death me (P)!' (Principal female-role sings:)

818 婆 婆 也 再 也 不 要 啼
Pó-po ye, zài-yě bú-yào tí-
'Mother-in-law (P), (intensifier) do-not cry/

819 啼 哭 哭 煩 煩 惱 惱 怨
tí kū-kū, fán-fán nǎo-nǎo, yuàn-
weep, be-troubled, fret – grievance

820 氣 衝 天 這 都 是 我 做
qì chōng tiān. Zhè dōu shì wǒ zuò-
rushing-to heaven. This all is I, who-am-

821 竇 娥 的 沒 時 沒 運 不
Dòu-É-de méi shí méi yùn, bù
Tou-O, have-no opportunity, have-no luck – not

822 明 不 闇 負 屈 銜 寃
míng bú àn, fù qū xián yuān.
clearly, not darkly, bearing injustice, harboring grievance.'

823 （ 劊 子 做 喝 科 云 ） 兀 那 婆 子
(Kuài-zi zuò hē kē, yún:) Wǔ-na pó-zi
(Executioner performs calling gesture, says:) 'Hey-there, old woman,

824 靠 後 時 辰 到 了 也 （ 正 旦 跪
kào hòu. Shí-chén dào-le ye. (Zhèng dàn guì
[step] toward back. The-time has-come (P) (P)!' (Principal female-role kneeling

825 科 劊 子 開 枷 科 正 旦 云 ） 竇
kē. Kuài-zi kāi jiā kē. Zhèng-dàn yún:) Dòu
gesture. Executioner opening cangue gesture. Principal female-role says:) 'Tou

Heaven, this kills me.

TOU O (sings):

Oh mother, do not cry or fret or complain to high Heaven.
It is I, Tou O, who has no luck,
And who has to suffer in confusion such great injustice.

EXECUTIONER (shouts): You old woman over there, stand back! The hour has come.

(Tou O kneels and the executioner unlocks the cangue.)

TOU O: I wish to say to your honor, that if you would agree to one

818] *zài-yé:* here used as an intensifier for a negative.

§818] *Pó-po ye, zài-yě bú-yào:* not in *KMCP.*
§820–1] *Zhè dōu shì. . . méi yùn:* not in *KMCP;* instead, *wǒ bù fēn shuō* 我 不 分 說 in *KMCP*, p. 14*b.*
§823] *zuò hē kě, yún:* not in *KMCP.*

娥告監斬大人有一事肯

826   *É gào jiān zhǎn dà rén, yǒu yí shì kěn*

O tells overseeing execution great person, there-is one thing, be-willing

依竇娥便死而無怨（ 監斬

827   *yī Dòu É, biàn sǐ ér wú yuàn. (Jiān zhǎn*

to-grant Tou O, even to die, however, would-have-no grievance.' (Overseeing execution

官云）你有什麼事你說（ 正

828   *guān yún:) Nǐ yǒu shém-me shì? Nǐ shuō. (Zhèng*

official says:) 'You have what matter? You tell.' (Principal

旦云）要一領淨席等我竇

829   *dàn yún:) Yào yì lǐng jìng xí, děng wǒ Dòu*

female-role says:) 'Want one (M) clean mat, wait-for me Tou

娥站立又要丈二白練挂

830   *É zhàn-lì. Yòu yào zhàng-èr bái liàn, guà*

O to-stand-on. Also want ten-feet-two white silk to-hang

在旗鎗上若是我竇娥委

831   *zài qí qiāng shàng. Ruò-shì wǒ Dòu É wěi-*

on flag staff (L). If I Tou O truly

實宛枉刀過處頭落一腔

832   *shí yuān-wang, dāo guò chù tóu luò, yì qiāng*

am-wronged, knife passing place, head falls, one chestful-of

熱血休半點兒沾在地下

833   *rè xuě xiū bàn diǎn-er zhān zài dì xia;*

hot blood not half drop sprinkle on ground (L);

都飛在白練上者（ 監斬官

834   *dōu fēi zài bái liàn shàng zhe. (Jiān zhǎn guān*

all fly onto white silk (L) (P).' (Overseeing execution official

云）這箇就依你打甚麼不

835   *yún:) Zhè-ge jiù yī nǐ. Dǎ shém-me-bù-*

says:) 'This then grant you, makes whatever-no-

210

thing, I would die content.

EXECUTION OFFICER: Say what you have on your mind.

TOU O: I want a clean mat to stand on. Also, I want a piece of white silk, twelve feet long, to hang on the flagpole. If I have really been wronged, where the knife strikes and my head falls, a chestful of warm blood, without a drop staining the ground, will fly up to the piece of white silk.

EXECUTION OFFICER: I agree to this; it's nothing of importance.

830] *liàn:* white dressed silk.

835-6] *Dǎ shém-me-bù-jǐn:* same as 打甚麼緊 'nothing important'. It is comparable to the present usage *yǒu shém-me yào jǐn* 有甚麼要緊 'has what importance?' meaning 'has no importance'. Cf. *Dàn-er yún:* '*Ruò kěn ráo le ǎn xìng-mìng he, zhè-ge dǎ shém-me bù jǐn . . . (Zuò yǔ shǒu-shì kē)*, 旦兒云若肯饒了俺性命呵這個打甚麼不緊 . . . (做 與 首 飾 科), Female-role says, 'If you spare my life, of what importance is this?' . . . (Hands over the jewelry.) (*Hòu tíng hūa* 後 庭 花, [*YCH*, no. 54], Act I, following Song 'Chin chan-erh' 金 盞 兒; see also Lu Tan-an, p. 168.)

§826] *dà rén: guān* 官 in *KMCP*, p. 14*b*.
    yì: sān jiàn 三 件 in *KMCP*, p. 14*b*.
§827-9] *Jiān zhǎn. . . Zhèng dàn yún:* not in *KMCP*.
§829] *Yào yì. . . xì:* this phrase occurs earlier in *KMCP*, following *gào jiān zhǎn dà rén* [*guān*] in l. 826.
§829-30] *děng wǒ. . . zhàn-lì:* not in *KMCP*.
§831-2] *Ruò-shì. . . yuān-wang:* not in *KMCP*.
§834-51] *Jiān zhǎn guān. . . rén:* not in *KMCP*; a whole lyric, ll. 838-47, is absent.

211

緊（劊子做取席站科又取

836 jǐn (Kuài-zi zuò qǔ xí zhàn kē; yòu qǔ
importance.' (Executioner performs fetching mat; [Tou O
performs] standing [on it] gesture; [he] also [performs] fetching

白練挂旗上科正旦唱）

837 bái liàn guà qí shàng kē. Zhèng dàn chàng:)
white silk, hanging-on flag (L) gesture. Principal female-role
sings:)

（耍孩兒）不是我竇娥

838 (Shuǎ hái-er) Bú shì wǒ Dòu É
('Playing Dolls') 'Not is I, Tou O,

罰下這等無頭願委

839 fá-xià zhè-děng wú tóu yuàn; wěi-
issue (C) this-manner no head wishes; truly

實的冤情不淺若沒

840 shí-de yuān-qíng bù qiǎn. Ruò méi
(P) grievance not shallow. If there-is-not

些兒靈聖與世人傳

841 xiē-er líng-shèng yǔ shì rén chuán,
some spirit-divine to world people transmit,

也不見得湛湛青天

842 yě bú jiàn-dé zhàn-zhàn qīng tiān.
also unable to-show deep-clear blue Heaven.

我不要半星熱血紅

843 Wǒ bú yào bàn xīng rè xuě hóng
I do-not want half speck hot blood red

塵灑都只在八尺旗

844 chén sǎ; dōu zhǐ zài bā chǐ qí
dust sprinkle; all solely onto eight foot flag

鎗素練懸等他四下

845 qiāng sù liàn xuán. Děng tā sì-xià
staff white silk hang. Wait-till they four-directions

212

(The executioner fetches the mat, and Tou O stands on it. He also fetches a piece of white silk and hangs it on the flagpole.)

TOU O (Sings seventh lyric):

It is not that I, Tou O, make irrational wishes;
Indeed the wrong I suffer is profound.
If there is no miraculous sign to show the world,
Then there is no proof of a clear, blue Heaven.
I do not want half a drop of my blood to stain the earth;
All of it will go to the white silk hanging on the eight-foot flagpole.
When people see it from four sides,

839] *fá:* a variant of *fǎ* 發 'to issue'.

    wú tóu: comparable to the present usage *méi tóu méi nǎo de* 沒 頭 沒 腦 的 'having no head no brain', meaning 'irrational, incomprehensible, or inconceivable'.

裏皆瞧見這就是咱

846 *li jiē qiáo-jiàn, zhè jiù shì za*
(L) all see, this then is I, [as]

莨弘化碧望帝啼鵑

847 *Cháng Hóng huà bì, Wàng-dì tí juān.*
Ch'ang Hung transformed-into green-stone, Wang-ti
[turned into] crying cuckoo.'

（劊子云）你還有甚的說話

848 *(Kuài-zi yún:) Nǐ hái yǒu shén-de shuō-huà,*
(Executioner says:) 'You still have whatever words-to-say,

此時不對監斬大人說幾

849 *cǐ shí bú duì jiān zhǎn dà rén shuō, jǐ-*
this time not to overseeing execution great person say, what-

時說那（正旦再跪科云）大

850 *shí shuō na? (Zhèng dàn zài guì kē, yún:) Dà*
time say (P)?' (Principal female-role again kneeling gesture,
says:) 'Great

人如今是三伏天道若竇

851 *rén, rú-jìn shì sān fú tiān-dào. Ruò Dòu*
person, now is third *fu* season. If Tou

娥委實寃枉身死之後天

852 *É wěi-shí yuān-wang, shēn sǐ zhī hòu, tiān*
O truly is-wronged, body died (P) afterward, Heaven

降三尺瑞雪遮掩了竇娥

853 *jiàng sān chǐ ruì xuě, zhē-yǎn-le Dòu É*
sends-down three feet auspicious snow to-cover (P) Tou O's

屍首（監斬官云）這等三伏

854 *shī-shou. (Jiān zhǎn guān yún:) Zhè děng sān fú*
corpse.' (Overseeing execution official says:) 'This manner
third *fu*

天道你便有衝天的怨氣

855 *tiān-dào, nǐ biàn yǒu chōng tiān de yuàn-qì,*
season, you even-if have rushing-to heaven (P) grievance,

214

> *It will be the same as the blood of Ch'ang Hung turning into a green stone,*
> *Or the soul of Wang-ti residing in a crying cuckoo.*

EXECUTIONER: What else do you have to say? If you don't tell his honor now, when are you going to tell?

TOU O (kneels again): Your honor, this is the hottest time of summer. If Tou O has been truly wronged, after her death Heaven will send down three feet of auspicious snow to cover her corpse.

EXECUTION OFFICER: In such hot weather, even if you had

847] *Cháng Hóng huà bì:* Cháng Hóng was an official of the Chou dynasty who was unjustly killed. According to legend, after his death, his blood turned into a green stone. (*Wang Chia* 王嘉, *Shih yi chi* 拾遺記 [*Pi shu nien-yi chung* 秘書廿一種] *chüan* 3, p. 6b.)

    Wàng-dì: according to legend, Dù Yǔ 杜宇, styled Wàng-dì, was king of the Shǔ 蜀 state toward the end of the Chou 周 dynasty. He abdicated in favor of his prime minister because of the latter's success in controlling the flood; he himself then retired to the Western Mountain and later turned into a cuckoo which cries in the spring, and people grieve for it. Ch'in ching 禽經 [in *Han wei ts'ung shu* 漢魏叢書], pp. 8a–8b.)

    Tso Ssu 左思 (250?–*ca.* 306) also uses these allusions in his *Shu tu fu* 蜀都賦: *Bì chū Cháng Hóng zhī xuě, niǎo shēng Dù Yǔ zhī pò*, 碧出萇弘之血，鳥生杜宇之魄, 'A green stone came from Ch'ang Hung's blood, a bird was born of Tu Yü's spirit.' (Hsiao T'ung 蕭統 ed., *Wen hsüan* 文選 [*SPTK*] *chüan* 4, p. 32b.)

851] *sān fú:* in the Chinese concept, *fú*-days consist of thirty days divided into three ten-day periods – the first *fú*, the second *fú*, and the third *fú*; they are the hottest days of the summer. *Sān* being 'three' or 'third', *sān fú* can be the whole three-*fú* period or the third ten-day period.

    Comparable to the *sān fú* is the *jiǔ jiǔ* (nine nines) in the winter. Starting from the day after the winter solstice, there is an eighty-one day period, divided into nine nine-day periods, which are considered as the coldest time of the year. There is a proverb, '*Lěng zài sān jiǔ, rè zài sān fú* 冷在三九熱在三伏, 'The coldest weather is in the "third-nine" period, and the hottest weather is in the "third *fú*" period.'

    tiān-dào: 'weather', 'season'; cf. *Jīn-rì yù-zhe mù dōng tiān-dào...* 今日遇着暮冬天道 ...'Today encountering the late winter weather...' (*Yü ch'iao chi* 漁樵記 [*YCH*, no. 50], Act I, opening speech).

§853] *sān:* not in *KMCP*.
§854–69] *Jiàn zhǎn guān...hòu:* not in *KMCP*; a whole lyric in ll. 858–66 is missing.

856 也召不得一片雪來可不
yě zhāo-bù-dé yí piàn xuě lai. Kě-bù
still cannot-summon one flake snow (C). Isn't-it

857 胡說（正旦唱）
hú shuō! (Zhèng dàn chàng:)
foolish talk!' (Principal female-role sings:)

858 （二煞）你道是暑氣暄
(Èr shà) Nǐ dào shì shǔ qì xuān,
('Secondary Coda') 'You say [this] is summer weather warm;

859 不是那下雪天豈不
bú shì nà xià xuě tiān. Qǐ bù
not is that falling snow weather. How not

860 聞飛霜六月因鄒衍
wén fēi shuāng liù-yuè yīn Zōu Yǎn?
heard-of flying frost [in the] Sixth Month because-of Tsou Yen?

861 若果有一腔怨氣噴
Ruò guǒ yǒu yì qiāng yuàn qì pēn
If indeed there-be one chestful-of wronged feeling spurt

862 如火定要感的六出
rú huǒ, dìng yào gǎn-de liù-chū
like fire, certainly will move-till six-pointed

863 冰花滾似綿免着我
bīng huā gǔn sì mián, miǎn-zhe wǒ
ice flowers roll as cotton, to-avoid my

864 屍骸現要什麼素車
shī-hái xiàn. Yào shém-me sù chē
corpse/skeleton being-exposed. Need what white carriage,

865 白馬斷送出古陌荒
bái mǎ, duàn-sòng chū gǔ mò huāng
white horse to-escort-funeral off-to ancient path, wild

216

grievances reaching to Heaven, you still couldn't call down one snowflake. Surely this is talking nonsense!

TOU O (Sings eighth lyric):

You say that hot summer is not a time for snow.
Have you not heard that frost formed in June because of Tsou Yen?
If I have a chestful of wronged feelings that spurt like fire,
It will move snow to tumble down like cotton,
And keep my corpse from exposure.
What need is there of white horses and a white carriage,
To escort my funeral through the ancient path and wild trail?

860] *fēi shuāng liù-yuè yīn Zōu Yǎn:* frost formed in the sixth month of the year because of Zōu Yǎn's unjust death. Zōu Yǎn was a loyal official of the Warring States period. When he suffered unjust imprisonment, he cried to Heaven; frost occurred – even in the warm month of June. This unnatural event is understood to be a sign of Heaven's displeasure (see p. 5 above).

864–5] *sù chē bái mǎ:* 'white carriage and white horse'. In the Later Han Dynasty, Zhāng Shào 張 劭 died, and his friend Fàn Shì 范 式 attended the funeral from afar in a white carriage drawn by a white horse. (Biography of Fan Shih in *History Of The Later Han, chüan* 71, p. 15*a*.) Later this allusion comes to mean a funeral.

865] *duàn-sòng:* same as *sòng zàng,* 送 葬 'to escort a funeral' (see Chang Hsiang, p. 694).

865–6] *mò... qiān:* usually appearing as *qiān-mò,* it is reversed here because of rhyme. *Qiān* is the road leading north and south, and *mò* is the raised path going east and west; *qiān mò* is used to mean 'roads in all directions'.

阡

866   *qiān?*
        trail?'

（正旦再跪科云）大人我竇

867   *(Zhèng dàn zài guì kē, yún:) Dà rén, wǒ Dòu*
    (Principal female-role again kneeling gesture, says:) 'Great
    person, I, Tou

娥死的委實宽枉從今以

868   *É sǐ-de wěi-shí yuān-wang; cóng jīn yǐ-*
    O, die (P) truly unjustly; from now (P) afterward,

後着這楚州亢旱三年（監

869   *hòu zháo zhè Chǔ-zhōu kàng hàn sān nián. (Jiān*
    have this Ch'u-chou [suffer] severe drought three years.'
    (Overseeing

斬官云）打嘴那有這等說

870   *zhǎn guān yún:) Dǎ zuǐ! Nǎ yǒu zhè děng shuō-*
    execution official says:) 'Slap mouth! Where is this kind talk!'

話（正旦唱）

871   *huà! (Zhèng dàn chàng:)*
    (Principal female-role sings:)

（一煞）你道是天公不

872   *(Yí shà) Nǐ dào shì tiān gōng bù*
    ('Penultimate Coda') 'You say it-is-true Heavenly lord is-
    not

可期人心不可憐不

873   *kě qī, rén xīn bù kě lián; bù*
    possible to-be-counted-on, human heart is-not to-be-pitied;
    not

知皇天也肯從人願

874   *zhī Huáng tiān yě kěn cóng rén yuàn.*
    know August Heaven also is-willing to-follow human
    wishes.

(Tou O again kneels.)

Your honor, I, Tou O, truly die unjustly. I ask that from this day this Ch'u-chou District should suffer from drought for three years.

EXECUTION OFFICER: Slap her! What a thing to say!

TOU O (Sings ninth lyric):

> *You say that Heaven cannot be counted on,*
> *It has no sympathy for the human heart;*
> *You don't know that Heaven does answer men's prayers.*

§869–70] *Jiăn zhăn guān yún: Kuài-zi* 刽 子 in *KMCP*, p. 14*b*.
§871] *Zhèng dàn chàng:* not in *KMCP*.
§872–80] *Yí shà. . . nán yán:* the whole lyric is not in *KMCP*.

219

做甚麼三年不見甘
875   *Zuò-shém-me sān nián bú jiàn gān*
    Why three years did-not see sweet

霖降也只爲東海曾
876   *lín jiàng. Yě zhǐ wèi Dōng-hǎi céng*
    rain fall? Also only because East-Sea once

經孝婦寃如今輪到
877   *jīng xiào fù yuān. Rú-jīn lún dào*
    experienced filial woman's injustice. Now turned to

你山陽縣這都是官
878   *nǐ Shān-yáng xiàn. Zhè dōu shì guān-*
    you Shan-yang District. This all is officials/

吏每無心正法使百
879   *lì-měi wú xīn zhèng fǎ, shǐ bǎi-*
    clerks (Pl) have-no intention to-uphold law, causing people

姓有口難言
880   *xìng yǒu kǒu nán yán.*
    having mouth, hard to-speak-out.'

（劊子做磨旗科云）怎麼這
881   *(Kuài-zi zuò mò qí kē, yún:) Zěm-me zhè*
    (Executioner performs waving flag action, says:) 'How this

一會兒天色陰了也（內做
882   *yì huì-er tiān sè yīn le ye? (Nèi zuò*
    one moment sky color has-darkened (P) (P)?' (Inside performs

風科劊子云）好冷風也（正
883   *fēng kē. Kuài-zi yún:) Hǎo lěng fēng ye! (Zhèng*
    wind movement. Executioner says:) 'Extremely cold wind (P)!'
    (Principal

且唱）
884   *dàn chàng:)*
    female-role sings:)

Otherwise, why did sweet rain fail to fall for three years?
It was all because of the wrong suffered by the filial daughter at Tung-hai.
Now is the turn of your Shan-yang District!
It is all because officials care not for justice,
People in turn are afraid to speak out.

EXECUTIONER (waving a flag): Why is the sky suddenly overcast?
  (Sound of wind is heard from backstage.) What cold wind!
TOU O (Sings tenth lyric):

877] *xiào fù:* 'a filial woman'. For her story, see pp. 4–5 above.
879–80] *bǎi-xing:* 'the people'; literally, 'a hundred surnames'.
§881–3] *Ƶĕm-me. . . lĕng fēng ye:* not in *KMCP*; instead, a comparable scene is given
    later; see § 888–9.

885
(煞尾) 浮雲爲我陰悲

(Shà-wěi) Fú yún wèi wǒ yin, bēi

('Coda') 'Floating clouds for me darken; grieving

886
風爲我旋三椿兒誓

fēng wèi wǒ xuán. Sān zhuāng-er shì-

wind for me whirls. Three (M) oaths

887
願明題徧

yuàn míng tí biàn.

make-clear the-theme completely.'

888
(做哭科云) 婆婆也直等待

(Zuò kū kē, yún:) Pó-po ye, zhí děng-dài

(Performs weeping gesture says:) 'Mother-in-law (P), just wait [till]

889
雪飛六月亢旱三年呵 (唱)

xuě fēi liù yuè, kàng hàn sān nián he; (chàng:)

snow flies [in the] Sixth Month, severe drought three years (P);'
(sings:)

890
那其間纔把你個屈

Nà qí-jiān cái bǎ nǐ ge qū

'That moment only-then (Pr) you (M) unjustly

891
死的寃魂這竇娥顯

sǐ de yuān hún zhè Dòu É xiǎn.

slain (P) wronged ghost, this Tou O, reveal.'

892
(劊子做開刀正旦倒科監

(Kuài-zi zuò kāi dāo; zhèng dàn dǎo kē. Jiān

(Executioner performs wielding sword; principal female-role falling gesture. Overseeing

893
斬官驚云) 呀眞箇下雪了

zhǎn guān jing yún:) Yā! Zhēn-ge xià xuě le.

execution official is-startled, says:) 'Ya! Really falls snow (P).

The wandering clouds darken for my sake,
The mournful wind whirls on my behalf.
My three prayers will make things completely clear.

(Weeps.) Mother, wait till snow falls in June and drought lasts for three years; (sings.)

Then, and only then, the innocent soul of Tou O will be revealed.

(The executioner strikes, and Tou O falls.)

EXECUTION OFFICER:. What! It is indeed snowing. How strange!

§885] *Shà-wěi: Wěi shēng* 尾 聲, *KMCP*, p. 15a.

§885–7] *Fú yún. . . tí biàn: Dāng rì ge yǎ fù hán yào fǎn shòu yāng, gēng niú wèi zhǔ zāo biān* 當 日 箇 啞 婦 含 藥 反 受 殃 耕 牛 爲 主 遭 鞭, in *KMCP*, p. 15a.

§888–9] *Zuò kū kē, yún. . . chàng:* not in *KMCP*; instead (*Kuài-zi*) *Tiān sè yīn le ya, xià xuě le. (Kuài-zi shān xuě tiān fā yuàn kē. Mò qí kuài-zi zhē zhù kē. Dàn)* (劊 子) 天 色 陰 了 呀 下 雪 了 (劊 子 搧 雪 天 發 願 科 磨 旗 劊 子 遮 住 科 旦) in *KMCP*, p. 15a; cf. ll. 881–3.

§890–1] *Nà qí-jiān. . . xiǎn: Shuāng jiàng shǐ zhī shuō Zōu Yǎn. Xuě fēi fāng biǎo Dòu É yuān* 霜 降 始 知 說 鄒 衍 雪 飛 方 表 竇 娥 冤 in *KMCP*, p. 15a.

§892–905] *Kuài-zi. . . tái shī xià: (Xíng rèn Kuài-zi kāi dāo zhāo tóu; fù jìng cuàn shī. Kuài-zi yún). Hǎo miào shǒu ye. Zá chī jiǔ qù-lái. (Zhòng hé xià, tái shī xià)* (行 刄 劊 子 開 刀 劊 頭 付 淨 攛 尸 劊 子 云) 好 妙 手 也 咱 喫 酒 去 來) (衆 和 下 抬 尸 下) in *KMCP*, p. 15a.

有這等異事（劊子云）我也
894　*Yǒu zhè-děng yì shì! (Kuài-zi yún:) Wǒ yě*
There-is such strange thing!' (Executioner says:) 'I also

道平日殺人滿地都是鮮
895　*dào píng rì shā rén mǎn dì dōu shì xiān*
say, ordinary days kill people, whole ground all is fresh

血這個竇娥的血都飛在
896　*xuě. Zhè-ge Dòu É de xuě dōu fēi zài*
blood. This (M) Tou O's (P) blood all flew onto

那丈二白練上並無半點
897　*nà zhàng-èr bái liàn shang; bìng wú bàn diǎn*
that ten-feet-two white silk (L); absolutely not half drop

落地委實奇怪（監斬官云）
898　*luò dì. Wěi-shí qí-guài. (Jiān zhǎn-guān yún:)*
fell-on ground. Truly is-strange!' (Overseeing execution official
says:)

這死罪必有冤枉早兩椿
899　*Zhè sǐ-zuì bì yǒu yuān-wang. Zǎo liǎng zhuāng-*
'This capital-punishment must involve injustice. Already two
(M)

兒應驗了不知亢旱三年
900　*er yìng-yàn-le. Bù zhī kàng hàn sān nián*
have-come-true (P). Not know severe drought three years

的說話准也不准且看後
901　*de shuō-huà, zhǔn yě bù zhǔn; qiě kàn hòu-*
(P) talk, true (P), not true; further see later-on

來如何左右也不必等待
902　*lái rú-hé. Zuǒ-yòu, yě bú bì děng-dài*
like-what. Attendants, also do-not need to-wait-for

雪晴便與我擡他屍首還
903　*xuě qíng; biàn yǔ wǒ tái tā shī-shou huán-*
snow to-clear; [now] then for me carry her corpse, return

EXECUTIONER: I, for my part, say that usually when I execute people, the ground is full of blood. The blood of this Tou O, however, all flew onto the twelve feet of white silk and not a single drop is on the ground. This is truly wondrous.

EXECUTION OFFICER: There must be injustice in this death sentence. Two of her wishes have already come true. There is no knowing whether her talk of a three-year drought will come true or not. We shall wait and see how it turns out. Attendants, there is no need to wait for the snow to stop; now take her corpse away and return it to Mistress Ts'ai.

了那蔡婆婆去罷（衆應科

904 *le nà Cài Pó-po qù ba. (Zhòng yìng kē,*
(P) [it to] that Ts'ai *P'o-p'o* (C) (P).' (All answering gesture;

擡屍下）

905 *tái shi xià.)*
carry corpse, exeunt.)

第四折

906 *Dì-sì Zhé*
Number-four Act

（竇天章冠帶引丑張千祗

907 *(Dòu Tiān-zhāng guān dài yǐn chǒu Zhāng Qiān zhǐ-*
(Tou T'ien-chang in-cap, sash, leading clown Chang Ch'ien,
attendants,

從上詩云）獨立空堂思黯

908 *cóng shàng. Shī yún:) Dú lì kōng táng sī àn-*
enters. [In] verse says:) 'Alone stand-in empty hall, thoughts
dark.

然高峯月出滿林煙非關

909 *rán. Gāo fēng yuè chū mǎn lín yān. Fēi guān*
Towering peak, moon appears, whole forest mist. Not because-
of

有事人難睡自是驚魂夜

910 *yǒu shì rén nán shuì; zì shì jīng hún yè*
having cares, person hard to-sleep; self being startled spirit
at-night

不眠老夫竇天章是也自

911 *bù mián. Lǎo fū Dòu Tiān-zhāng shì yě. Zì*
cannot sleep. Old man Tou T'ien-chang is (P). Since

離了我那端雲孩兒可蚤

912 *lí-le wǒ nà Duān-yún hái-er, kě zǎo*
left (P) my that Tuan-yün child indeed already

226

(All answer. Exeunt, carrying the corpse.)

ACT FOUR

(Enter Tou T'ien-chang in cap and sash, followed by Chang Ch'ien and attendants.)

T O U (recites):

As I stand alone in this empty hall, my thoughts are dark.
The moon appears above the cliff-top, the woods are shrouded in mist.
It is not because of cares that I cannot sleep;
It's just that my startled spirit cannot rest at night.

I am Tou T'ien-chang. It has been sixteen years since I left my child

907] *Zhāng Qiān:* a conventional name for a male servant in Yüan drama.
907–8] *zhǐ-cóng:* 'attendant' (Morohashi VIII: 24665: 24).
910] *zì shì:* may be a variant of *zhǐ shì* 只 是, 'it is just'.
910–11] *zì shì. . . bù mián:* he is probably haunted, as his next reference to his daughter indicates.

§906] *Dì-sì Zhé: KMCP* also has *Zhé* here, though *Chū* is used for the three earlier divisions (see § 3, 366, 599–600).
§907–9] *Dòu Tiān-zhāng. . . Shī yún: Wài shàng* 外 上 in *KMCP*, p. 15*a*.
§908–11] *Dú lì. . . bù mián:* the quatrain is not in *KMCP*.

227

十 六 年 光 景 老 夫 自 到 京
913   *shí-liù nián guāng-jīng. Lǎo fū zì dào jing-*
sixteen years time. Old man since arrived-at capital,

師 一 舉 及 第 官 拜 參 知 政
914   *shī, yì jǔ jí-dì. Guān-bài cān-zhī-zhèng-*
one try passed-examination. Was-granted-official-post Councilor-for-State-

事 只 因 老 夫 廉 能 清 正 節
915   *shì. Zhǐ yin lǎo fū lián néng qing zhèng, jié*
Affairs. Only because old man incorruptible/able, pure/just, moderate/

操 堅 剛 謝 聖 恩 可 憐 加 老
916   *cāo jiān gāng, xiè shèng ēn kě-lián, jiā lǎo*
restrained, firm/strong, thanks-to Imperial favor showing-kindness, bestowed-concurrently-upon old

夫 兩 淮 提 刑 肅 政 廉 訪 使
917   *fū liǎng Huái tí-xíng-sù-zhèng-lián-fǎng shǐ*
man Two Huai Surveillance Commissioner

之 職 隨 處 審 囚 刷 卷 體 察
918   *zhī zhí. Suí-chù shěn qiú shuā-juàn, tǐ-chá*
(P) post. All-places inspect prisons, review-cases; seek-out

濫 官 汚 吏 容 老 夫 先 斬 後
919   *làn guān wū lì. Róng lǎo fū xiān zhǎn hòu*
corrupt officials, foul clerks. Allow old man first execute, later

奏 老 夫 一 喜 一 悲 喜 呵 老
920   *zòu. Lǎo fū yì xǐ yì bēi. Xǐ he, lǎo*
report-to-the-throne. Old man [about] one [thing] happy, [about] one [thing] sad. Happy (P), old-

夫 身 居 臺 省 職 掌 刑 名 勢
921   *fū shēn jū tái shěng; zhí zhǎng xíng-míng, shì*
man body dwells-in Censorate, Secretariat; post administers criminal-law; [with] authority

228

Tuan-yün. I went to the capital, passed the Imperial Examination on the first try, and was made a State Councilor in the Secretariat. Because I am incorruptible, able, moderate, and strong, the Emperor kindly appointed me concurrently to the post of Surveillance Commissioner to the two circuits of the Huai River area. I have traveled from place to place to inspect prisons, check court records, and to discover and investigate corrupt officials. I have been given authority to execute the guilty before reporting to the throne. I am both happy and sad. I am happy because I hold high posts in the Censorate and Secretariat and have the power to see that justice is done. With

914] *Guān-bài:* *guān* is 'official post'; *bài* usually means 'to do obeisance', and here means *bài mìng* 拜 命, 'by Imperial order'.

914–15] *cān-zhī-zhèng-shì:* 'State Councilor' (Kracke in his *Civil Service in Early Sung China*, p. 229, translates this as Second Privy Councilor).

917] *liǎng Huái:* refers to *Huái xī jiāng běi dào* 淮 西 江 北 道, 'the Circuit to the west of the Huai River and north of the Yangtze River' and *jiāng běi Huái dōng dào* 江 北 淮 東 道, 'the Circuit to the east of the Huai River and north of the Yangtze River' (*History of Yüan,* [*Yüan shih* 元 史, *Po-na* ed.], *chüan* 59, pp. 16*b*, 19*b*).

tí-xíng-sù-zhèng-lián-fǎng shǐ: in the Yüan dynasty, the Provincial Surveillance Office, first called *tí-xíng-àn-chá sī* 提 刑 按 察 司, was changed in the year 1291 to *sù-zhèng-lián-fǎng sī* 肅 政 廉 訪 司, and the Surveillance Commissioner's title was changed from *tí-xíng-àn-chá shǐ* 提 刑 按 察 使 to *sù-zhèng-lián-fǎng shǐ* 肅 政 廉 訪 使 (Biography of Emperor Shih-tzu 世 祖, *History of Yüan, chüan* 16, p. 15*a*).

919–20] *xiān zhǎn hòu zòu:* note here the extraordinary power given to Dou to carry out a death sentence without the usual mandatory review by a higher (in this case the central) judicial authority.

921] *tái shěng:* *tái* refers to *yù shǐ tái* 御 史 臺, the Censorate, to which the *lián-fǎng shǐ* (Surveillance Commissioner) belonged; *shěng* refers to *zhōng shū shěng* 中 書 省 (Grand Council), to which the *cān-zhī-zhèng-shì* (State Councilor) belonged.

xíng-míng: same as *xíng fǎ* 刑 法, 'criminal law', 'criminal code'.

921–2] *shì jiàn jīn pái:* symbols of power given by the emperor. *Shì jiàn* was the sword of authority empowering the receiver to execute without permission from above. *Jīn pái* was a golden tablet worn by high-ranking officials in the Yüan dynasty.

§913] *shí-liù nián: shí-sān nián* 十 三 年 in *KMCP,* p. 15*a*. Sixteen is the correct number: Tou O was separated from her father when she was seven (l. 177); she got into trouble with the Changs at 20 (l. 182); and there has been a three-year drought after her death (l. 932, *KMCP,* p. 15*b*).

§918] After *shuā-juàn: chì cì shì jiàn jīn pái* 勅 賜 勢 劍 金 牌 in *KMCP,* p. 15*b*.

§921–2] *shì-jiàn. . . wàn lǐ:* in *KMCP* earlier; cf. § 918.

劍 金 牌 威 權 萬 里 悲 呵 有

922   *jiàn jīn pái, wēi-quán wàn lǐ. Bēi he, yǒu*
sword, golden tally, [my] power/authority [extend over] ten-thousand 'miles'. Sad (P), there-was

端 雲 孩 兒 七 歲 上 與 了 蔡

923   *Duān-yún hái-er, qī-suì-shàng, yǔ-le Cài*
Tuan-yün child at-seven-years-of-age (L) was-given-to (P) Ts'ai

婆 婆 爲 兒 媳 婦 老 夫 自 得

924   *Pó-po wéi ér xí-fu. Lǎo fū zì dé*
P'o-p'o to-be son's wife. Old man since obtained

官 之 後 使 人 往 楚 州 問 蔡

925   *guān zhī hòu, shǐ rén wǎng Chǔ-zhōu wèn Cài*
official-post (P) - sent persons to-go-to Ch'u-chou to-ask-about Ts'ai

婆 婆 家 他 隣 里 街 坊 道 自

926   *Pó-po jiā. Tā lín-lǐ-jiē-fang dào, zì*
P'o-p'o family. Her neighbors said, since

當 年 蔡 婆 婆 不 知 搬 在 那

927   *dāng nián Cài Pó-po bù zhī bān zài nǎ-*
that-same year Ts'ai *P'o-po* not know moved to where

裏 去 了 至 今 音 信 皆 無 老

928   *lǐ qù le. Zhì jīn yin-xìn jiē wú. Lǎo*
(L) (C) (P). Till now news entirely is-lacking. Old

夫 爲 端 雲 孩 兒 啼 哭 的 眼

929   *fū wèi Duān-yún hái-er, tí-kū de yǎn-*
man for Tuan-yün child cried till eyes

目 昏 花 憂 愁 的 鬚 髮 班 白

930   *mù hūn-huā, yōu-chóu de xū fǎ bān bái.*
dim; worried till beard/hair streaked white.

今 日 來 到 這 淮 南 地 面 不

931   *Jīn-rì lái dào zhè Huái Nán dì-miàn, bù*
Today came to this Huai South area, do-not

the sword from the Emperor and a golden tablet, my authority is extensive. I am unhappy because of my child, Tuan-yün. When she was seven years old, I gave her to Mistress Ts'ai to be her daughter-in-law. After I had become an official, I sent messengers to Ch'u-chou for news of Mistress Ts'ai. Her neighbors said that she moved away that same year; no one knew where she went, and there had been no word since. I have wept for my child, Tuan-yün, till my eyes are dim and blurred, and I have worried so much that my hair has turned white. I have come south of the Huai River and I

926] *jiē-fang*: *jiē* means 'street', and *fáng*, 'neighborhood'. *Jiē-fang* is an idiom for 'neighbors'.

§925] After *Chŭ-zhōu*: *Shăn-yáng jùn* 山 陽 郡 in *KMCP*, p. 15*b*.
§931] *di-miàn*: *Yáng-zhōu ye* 楊 州 也 in *KMCP*, p. 15*b*.

知 這 楚 州 爲 何 三 年 不 雨

932   *zhī zhè Chŭ-zhōu wèi-hé sān nián bù yŭ.*

know this Ch'u-chou for what three years not rained.

老 夫 今 在 這 州 廳 安 歇 張

933   *Lăo fū jīn zài zhè zhōu tīng ān-xiē. Zhāng*

Old man now at this district hall rest. Chang

千 說 與 那 州 中 大 小 屬 官

934   *Qiān, shuō yŭ nà zhōu zhōng dà xiăo shŭ guān,*

Ch'ien, tell to those district (L) big/small subordinate officials,

今 日 免 參 明 日 蚤 見 （ 張 千

935   *jīn-rì miăn cān; míng-rì zăo jiàn. (Zhāng Qiān*

today [they] are-excused-from attendance; tomorrow early be-present.' (Chang Ch'ien

向 古 門 云 ） 一 應 大 小 屬 官

936   *xiàng gŭ-mén yún:) Yì-yìng dà xiăo shŭ guān,*

towards stage-door says:) 'All big/small subordinate officials,

今 日 免 參 明 日 蚤 見 （ 竇 天

937   *jīn-rì miăn cān, míng-rì zăo jiàn. (Dòu Tiān-*

today [you] are-excused-from attendance; tomorrow early be-present.' (Tou T'ien-

章 云 ） 張 千 說 與 那 六 房 吏

938   *zhāng yún:) Zhāng Qiān, shuō yŭ nà liù fáng lì-*

chang says:) 'Chang Ch'ien, tell to those six departments clerks/

典 但 有 合 刷 照 文 卷 都 將

939   *diăn, dàn yŏu hé shuā-zhào wén-juàn, dōu jiāng*

secretaries, only-if there-are ought-to-be reviewed cases, all bring [them]

來 待 老 夫 燈 下 看 幾 宗 波

940   *lái, dài lăo fū dēng xià kàn jĭ zōng bo.*

(C); let old man lamp below (L) look-at several (M) (P).'

（ 張 千 送 文 卷 科 竇 天 章 云 ）

941   *(Zhāng Qiān sòng wén-juàn kē. Dòu Tiān-zhāng yún:)*

(Chang Ch'ien brings-over documents gesture. Tou T'ien-chang says:)

wonder why it hasn't rained here in Ch'u-chou for three years. Today I shall rest in this district office. Chang Ch'ien, tell the local officials they need not call today. I shall see them early tomorrow.

CHANG CH'IEN (calling toward the stage door): Officials of all ranks! You are excused from attendance today; his honor will see you early tomorrow.

TOU: Chang Ch'ien, tell the secretaries of the six departments to bring over all the files that ought to be reviewed. I shall study some under the lamp.

(Chang Ch'ien hands him the files.)

939] *shuā-zhào*: *shuā*, 'to brush (off dust)', *zhào*, 'to cast light on'; *shuā-zhào* then is an idiom for 'to review' court cases.

§933] *zhōu tīng*: *Yáng-zhōu fǔ hòu tīng* 楊州府後廳 in *KMCP*, p. 15*b*.

§934] *zhōu zhōng*: *Yáng-zhōu* 楊州 in *KMCP*, p. 15*b*.

§936] *xiàng gǔ-mén yún*: not in *KMCP*.

    After *shǔ guān*: *bìng lì-diǎn* 并吏典 in *KMCP*, pp. 15*b*–16*a*.

張 千 你 與 我 掌 上 燈 你 每

942 Zhāng Qian, nǐ yǔ wǒ zhǎng-shàng dēng. Nǐ-měi

'Chang Ch'ien, you for me light lamp. You (Pl)

都 辛 苦 了 自 去 歇 息 罷 我

943 dōu xin-kǔ le, zì qù xiē-xi ba. Wǒ

all worked-hard (P); self go to-rest (P). [If] I

喚 你 便 來 不 喚 你 休 來 （ 張

944 huàn nǐ biàn lái, bú huàn nǐ xiū lái. (Zhāng

call you, then come; [if I] do-not call you, don't come.' (Chang

千 點 燈 同 祗 從 下 竇 天 章

945 Qiān diǎn dēng tóng zhǐ-cóng xià. Dòu Tiān-zhāng

Ch'ien lights lamp, with attendants, exit. Tou T'ien-chang

云 ） 我 將 這 文 卷 看 幾 宗 咱

946 yún:) Wǒ jiāng zhè wén-juàn kàn jǐ zōng za.

says:) 'I (Pr) these documents look-at several (M) (P).

一 起 犯 人 竇 娥 將 毒 藥 致

947 Yì qǐ fàn-rén Dòu É, jiāng dú-yào zhì

A (M) criminal Tou O used poison, brought-about

死 公 公 我 纔 看 頭 一 宗 文

948 sǐ gōng-gong. Wǒ cái kàn tóu-yì zōng wén-

death [of] father-in-law. I just look-at first (M) document,

卷 就 與 老 夫 同 姓 這 藥 死

949 juàn, jiù yǔ lǎo fū tóng xìng. Zhè yào-sǐ

then as old man has-same surname. This poisoning-to-death

公 公 的 罪 名 犯 在 十 惡 不

950 gōng-gong de zuì-míng fàn zài shí-è bú

father-in-law (P) criminal-charge, a-violation within "ten evils not

赦 俺 同 姓 之 人 也 有 不 畏

951 shè. Ăn tóng xìng zhi rén yě yǒu bú wèi

pardonable". [Of] my same surname (P) persons, also there-is not fearing

234

TOU: Chang Ch'ien, light the lamp for me. You must be tired; you may retire now. You need not come unless I call. (Chang Ch'ien lights the lamp. He leaves with other attendants.) Let me go through a few cases. Here is a criminal by the name of Tou O who poisoned her father-in-law. This is the first thing I read and I come upon someone with the same family name as my own. To poison one's father-in-law is one of the ten unpardonable crimes. Thus among my clan too, there are some who are lawless. Since this is a case

946] *zōng:* a measure word for files.

947] *Yì qǐ:* one group; cf. *nán yì qǐ nǚ yì qǐ, yì qǐ yì qǐ jù xíng guò-le lǐ,* 男一起女一起, 一起一起俱行過了禮 'the men in one group, the women in one group; group by group they made their obeisance'. (*Hung lou meng* 紅樓夢 *Dream of the Red Chamber,* Peking, 1957, chap. 53, p. 667). The phrase *yì qǐ fàn rén* seems to mean 'one group of criminals [relating to one court case]'. (I am obliged to Dr Hsia Tao-t'ai, the Chinese Law Research Division, Library of Congress, for this interpretation); thus the expression *yì qǐ* can be used in reference to one criminal (as here and also ll. 995–6), or a group of criminals (as in ll. 1204–5 and l. 1336).

950] *shí-è:* the ten crimes. The Criminal Law Section in the *History of Yüan* lists the 'ten crimes' as the following:

(1) *móu fǎn* 謀反, 'to contemplate rebellion': 謂謀危社稷, that is, to conspire against and to put into danger the gods of soil and grain [to endanger one's country];

(2) *móu dà nì* 謀大逆 'to contemplate a greatly subversive act': 謂謀毀宗廟山陵及宮闕, that is, to conspire to destroy the imperial ancestral temples, tombs, and palaces;

(3) *móu pàn* 謀叛, 'to contemplate treason': 謂謀背國, 從偽 that is, to renounce one's country and to put oneself in the service of a foreign power;

(4) *è nì* 惡逆, 'a detestable, subversive act': 謂毆及謀殺祖父母, 父母, 殺伯叔父母, 姑, 兄, 姊, 外祖父母, 夫, 夫之祖父母父母者, that is, to beat or murder grandparents or parents; to kill a paternal uncle, paternal uncle's wife, paternal aunt, older brother, older sister, maternal grandparents, husband, husband's grandparents, or husband's parents;

(5) *bú dào* 不道, 'to lack moral rules': 謂殺一家非死罪三人, 及支解人, 造畜蠱毒魘魅, that is, to massacre three persons of one family not guilty of a capital crime; to mutilate someone [for making medicine]; to concoct violent poisons and to conjure up evil spirits;

(6) *dà bú jìng* 大不敬, 'to be extremely disrespectful': 謂盜大祀神御之物, 乘輿服御物, 盜及偽造御寶, 合和御藥誤不如本方, 及封題誤, 若造御膳, 誤犯食禁, 御幸舟船誤不牢固..., that is, to steal any of the sacred vessels consecrated to divine purpose, the ornaments on carriages or sedan chairs and other objects used by the Emperor; to steal or to counterfeit the imperial seal; to make a mistake in a remedy prepared for the Emperor, not following the prescriptions of the formula; to present things erroneously in the secret reports to the Emperor; in the preparation of the Emperor's meals, to present him forbidden food [because of religion or of health]; or to put at

——→

§942–3] *Nǐ-měi dōu: Nǐ* 你 in *KMCP*, p. 16a.
§945] *tóng zhī-cóng:* not in *KMCP*.
§948] After *gōng-gong: hǎo shì qí-guài yě* 好是奇怪也 in *KMCP*, p. 16a.
§950–1] *bú shè:* not in *KMCP*.

法度的這是問結了的文
952   *fă-dù de. Zhè shì wèn-jié-le de wén-*
law one. This is examined/concluded (P) (P) case,

書不看他罷我將這文卷
953   *shū, bú kàn tā ba. Wŏ jiāng zhè wén-juàn*
not look-at it (P). I (Pr) this case

壓在底下別看一宗咱（做
954   *yā zài dĭ-xià, bié kàn yì zōng za. (Zuò*
stick in underneath (L); separately look-at one (M) (P).'
(Performs

打呵欠科云）不覺的一陣
955   *dă-hē-qiàn kē, yún:) Bù-jué-de yí zhèn*
yawning gesture, says:) 'Unconsciously (P), one spell (M) [of]

昏沉上來皆因老夫年紀
956   *hūn-chén shàng-lai. Jiē yin lăo fū nián-jì*
dizziness comes-up. All because-of old man age

高大鞍馬勞困之故待我
957   *gāo-dà ān-mă láo-kùn zhi gù. Dài wŏ*
advanced, saddle/horse fatigue (P) reason. Wait-till I

搭伏定書案歇息些兒咱
958   *dā-fú dìng shū-àn, xiē-xi xiē-er za.*
lean on writing-desk, rest a-little (P).'

（做睡科魂旦上唱）
959   *(Zuò shuì kē. Hún dàn shàng. Chàng:)*
(Performs sleeping gesture. Ghost female-role enters. Sings:)

that has been closed, I shall not read any more of it. I shall put this at the bottom of the pile, and look at another case. (Yawns.) I am drowsy. It must be that I am getting old and tired from traveling. Let me lean on the desk and take a little rest. (Sleeps. Enter the ghost of Tou O.)

the Emperor's disposal boats that are not strong. . . .

(7) *bú xiào* 不孝, 'to lack filial piety': 謂告言詛詈祖父母，父母，夫之祖父母父母，及祖父母父母在，別籍異財，若奉養有缺，居父母喪身自嫁娶，若作樂，釋服從吉，聞祖父母父母喪，匿不舉哀，詐稱祖父母父母死 that is, to accuse in court, or curse and revile one's grandparents, father, or mother, or the husband's grandparents, father, or mother; while one's grandparents and parents are still living, to establish a different household and to store property there; to be lacking in providing for one's parents; during the mourning period for one's father or mother, to marry, to make music, or to discard mourning clothes; upon learning of the death of one's grandparents, father, or mother, to feign ignorance and abstain from showing grief; to falsely report the death of one's grandparents, father, or mother.

(8) *bú mù* 不睦, 'to lack concord': 謂謀殺及賣緦麻以上親，毆告夫及大功以上尊長，小功尊屬, that is, to contemplate the murder or the sale of a relative for whose death one should wear fifth degree mourning; to beat, or to accuse in court one's husband, or a relative of an older generation for whom one should wear third degree mourning, or a relative of an older generation for whose death one should wear fourth degree mourning.

(9) *bú yì* 不義, 'unrighteousness': 謂部民殺本屬知府知州知縣，軍士殺本管官吏，卒殺本部五品以上長官，若殺見受業師，及聞夫喪匿不舉哀，若作樂釋服從吉及改嫁. that is, the crime of a subordinate who kills his prefect, governor, or magistrate; the crime of a soldier who kills his officer; the crime of a clerk or employee of a court of justice who kills an official of the fifth or higher rank; the crime of a disciple who kills his teacher; the crime of a wife, who, learning of the death of her husband, feigns ignorance, and abstains from showing grief, finds joy in music, discards mourning clothing, and remarries.

(10) *nèi luàn* 內亂, 'incest': 謂姦小功以上親父祖妾及與和者, that is, to have carnal relations with relatives for whose death one should wear fourth degree mourning, with the concubines of one's father or grandfather, or with any other woman with whom the father or grandfather has had intimate relations. (*History of Yüan, chüan* 102, pp. 3b-5b).

This translation is made in reference to the original Chinese version, the French translation (*Manuel du Code Chinois*, trans. P. Gui Boulais, S.J., Shanghai, 1923, pp. 28-30) and the English translation (*Ta Tsing Leu Lee; Being the Fundamental Laws, and a Selection from the Supplementary Statutes, of the Penal Code of China*, trans. Sir George T. Staunton, London, 1810, pp. 3-4).

Tou O was accused of the crime of *è nì*, listed as Item (4) here.

956-7] *Jiē yīn. . . zhī gù:* a split adverbial phrase, which reads 'all because of. . .'s reason', meaning 'all because of'; not in *KMCP*.

958] *dā-fú ding:* 'to lean on'. *Dā-fú* is the same as *fú;* *dā*, generally meaning 'to lay across', is used with certain verbs, the action of which goes from the doer to the receiver as in *dā-jiu* 搭救, *dā shi* 搭識, or *dā pèi* 搭配.

959] *Hún dàn:* the female-role as a ghost.

§954-5] *Zuò dā-hē-qiàn kē:* qiè zhù 且住 in *KMCP*, p. 16a.

§959] *Hún dàn: dàn hún* in *KMCP*, p. 16a; hereafter referred to in *KMCP* as *hún, dàn* or *hún dàn.*

237

（雙調新水令）我每日
960 *(Shuāng-dìao: Xīn shuǐ lìng) Wǒ měi rì*
(Shuang-tiao [mode]: 'New Water Song') 'I every day

哭啼啼守住望鄉臺
961 *kū-tí-tí shǒu-zhù Wàng xiāng tái,*
cry, keep-to Gazing-toward Native-place Terrace;

急煎煎把讐人等待
962 *jí-jiān-jiān bǎ chóu-rén děng-dài.*
anxiously (Pr) enemy wait-for.

慢騰騰昏地裏走足
963 *Màn-téng-téng hūn-dì-li zǒu, zú-*
Slowly in-dark-place (L) walk; quickly

律律旋風中來則被
964 *lǜ-lǜ xuán-fēng-zhōng lái; zé bèi*
amidst-the-whirl-wind (L) come; only by

這霧鎖雲埋攛掇的
965 *zhè wù suǒ yún mái; cuān-duo de*
this fog locked, cloud buried – so-hastened-that [I came]

鬼魂快
966 *guǐ-hún kuài.*
ghost fast.'

（魂旦望科云）門神戶尉不
967 *(Hún dàn wàng kē, Yún:) Mén shén hù wèi bú*
(Ghost female-role looks-around gesture. Says:) 'Gate god, door
guardian do-not

放我進去我是廉訪使竇
968 *fàng wǒ jìn-qù; wǒ shì lián-fǎng shǐ Dòu*
let me enter (C); I am Surveillance Commissioner Tou

天章女孩兒因我屈死父
969 *Tiān-zhāng nǚ-hái-er. Yīn wǒ qū sǐ, fù-*
T'ien-chang's daughter. Because I unjustly died, father

238

TOU O (Sings first lyric):

> *Daily I weep at the Homegazing Terrace;*
> *Anxiously I await my enemy.*
> *Slowly I pace in darkness,*
> *And quickly I am borne along by the whirlwind;*
> *Enveloped in fog and clouds,*
> *I come fast as a ghost.*

(The ghost of Tou O looks about her.)

The door-guards will not let me pass. I am Surveillance Commissioner Tou T'ien-chang's daughter. Because I died unjustly, and my father

961] *Wàng xiāng tái:* according to Chinese folklore, there is a terrace in the nether world for the dead to ascend to watch their families in the human world.

963] *Màn-téng-téng: màn,* 'slowly', *téng-téng,* an adverbial suffix for emphasis.

963-4] *zú-lù-lù:* 'quickly'; an onomatopoeic expression, also written as *chì-li-li* 赤力力.

965] *cuān-duo:* 'to urge'; 'to incite to evil'.

967] *Mén shén hù wèi:* on the New Year, pictures of *mén shén* (god of the left door) and of *hù wèi* (god of the right door) are hung to ward off evil spirits.

§963] *dì: wù* 霧 in *KMCP,* p. 16*b.*
§964] *zhōng: ér* 兒 in *KMCP,* p. 16*b.*
§967] *kē: kōng* 空 in *KMCP,* p. 16*b.*

親 不 知 特 來 託 一 夢 與 他
970   *qin bù zhī, tè lái tuō yí mèng yǔ tā*
does-not know, especially come by-means-of a dream [to
communicate] with him

咱 （ 唱 ）
971   *za.*   *(Chàng:)*
(P).' (Sings:)

（ 沉 醉 東 風 ） 我 是 那 提
972   *(Chén-zuì dōng fēng) Wǒ shì nà tí-*
('Intoxicated [in] East Wind') 'I am that Surveillance

刑 的 女 孩 須 不 比 現
973   *xíng de nǔ-hái; xū bù bǐ xiàn*
Commissioner's (P) daughter, should not be-compared-
with appearing [in]

世 的 妖 恠 怎 不 容 我
974   *shì de yāo-guài. Zěn bù róng wǒ*
world (P) evil-apparition. Why not allow me

到 燈 影 前 却 攔 截 在
975   *dào dēng yǐng qián, què lán-jiē zài*
to-reach lamp shadow front; however, stop [me] at

門 桯 外
976   *mén-yíng wài.*
door-sill outside (L).'

（ 做 叫 科 云 ） 我 那 爺 爺 呵 （ 唱 ）
977   *(Zuò jiào kē, yún:) Wǒ nà yé-ye he. (Chàng:)*
(Performs calling gesture, says:) 'My that father (P)!' (Sings:)

枉 自 有 勢 劔 金 牌 把
978   *Wǎng zì yǒu shì jiàn jīn pái. Bǎ*
'In-vain self possesses authority sword, golden tally. (Pr)

俺 這 屈 死 三 年 的 腐
979   *ǎn zhè qū-sǐ sān nián de fǔ*
my this wrongly-slain three year-old (P) rotting

does not know it, I come especially to visit him in his dreams.
(Sings second lyric):

> *I am the executed daughter of the Surveillance Commissioner;*
> *I am not an evil spirit.*
>
> *Why prevent me from going near the lamp shadow?*
> *Why do you stop me outside the gate?*

(Calls.) Oh, that father of mine,

> *Useless are his powerful sword and golden tally.*
> *How is he to redeem my innocent, three-year rotting bones,*

970] *tuō yí mèng:* '[to communicate] by means of a dream'.

972–3] *tí-xíng:* abbreviation of *tí-xíng-àn-chá shǐ*.

976] *mén-yíng (or mén-xíng):* comparable to the present expression *mén kǎn* 門檻, 'doorsill'; cf. *Zuò-zhe mén-yíng; pī-zhe tóu shāo* 坐着門程，披着頭梢 'Sit at the doorsill, with hair hanging down on the shoulders' (*Táo huā nǚ* 桃花女 [*YCH*, no. 59], *Hsieh-tzu* 楔子, Song '*Duān zhèng hǎo*' 端正好); see also Hsü Chia-jui, p. 20.

§971–81] *Chàng. . . kǔ hǎi:* The whole lyric is not in *KMCP*.

骨骸怎脱離無邊苦

980 gǔ-hái, zěn tuō-lí wú biān kǔ
bones/skeleton, how to-redeem-from no bound bitter

海

981 hǎi?
sea?'

（ 做入見哭科竇天章亦哭

982 (Zuò rù jiàn kū kē. Dòu Tiān-zhāng yì kū
(Performs entering, seeing [her father, and] weeping gesture.
Tou T'ien-chang also weeps

科云 ）端雲孩兒你在那裏

983 kē, yún:) Duān-yún hái-er, nǐ zài nǎ-lǐ
gesture, says:) 'Tuan-yün child, you are-at where

來 （ 魂旦虛下竇天章做醒

984 lái? (Hún dàn xū-xià. Dòu Tiān-zhāng zuò xǐng
(P)?' (Ghost female-role feigns-exit. Tou T'ien-chang performs
awaking

科云 ）好是奇怪也老夫纔

985 kē, yún:) Hǎo-shì qí-guài ye! Lǎo-fū cái
gesture, says:) 'Really-is strange (P)! Old-man just

合眼去夢見端雲孩兒恰

986 hé yǎn qù, mèng-jiàn Duān-yún hái-er, qià-
closed eyes (C), dreamed-of Tuan-yün child exactly

便似來我跟前一般如今

987 biàn sì lái wǒ gēn-qián yì-bān. Rú-jīn
as coming-to my front (L) like. Now

在那裏我且再看這文卷

988 zài nǎ-lǐ? Wǒ qiě zài kǎn zhè wén-juàn
is-at where (L)? I for-now again look-at these documents

咱 （ 魂旦上做弄燈科竇天

989 za. (Hún dàn shàng, zuò nòng dēng kē. Dòu Tiān-
(P).' (Ghost female-role enters, performs adjusting lamp
gesture. Tou T'ien-

242

From the boundless sea of sufferings?

(She enters the gate, weeping. Tou T'ien-chang also weeps.)

T O U : Tuan-yün, my child, where are you?

(Tou O's ghost vanishes. Tou T'ien-chang wakes up.) How strange! As soon as I closed my eyes, I dreamed of Tuan-yün, my child, who seemed to appear right in front of me. Where is she now? Let me go on with these cases.

(Tou O's ghost enters and adjusts the lamp.)

984] *xū-xià:* 'false exit', that is, for a stage character to turn his back toward the audience to indicate exit; often a stage character needs to be temporarily absent for a scene, but if he exits and re-enters, the movement may disturb the smoothness of the scene.

§987-8] *Rú-jīn zài nǎ-lǐ:* not in *KMCP.*

§989] *shàng: guò* 過 in *KMCP*, p. 16b.

章云 ）奇怪我正要看文卷
990　zhāng yún:) Qí-guài. Wǒ zhèng yào kàn wén-juàn,
chang says:) 'Strange. I just about-to look-at files,

怎生這燈忽明忽滅的張
991　zěn-shēng zhè dēng hū míng hū miè de! Zhāng
how-is-it this lamp suddenly brightens, suddenly dims (P).
Chang

千也睡着了我自己剔燈
992　Qiān yě shuì-zháo-le. Wǒ zì-jǐ tī dēng
Ch'ien also has-fallen-asleep (P). I myself trim lamp

咱（ 做剔燈魂旦翻文卷科
993　za. (Zuò tī dēng. Hún dàn fān wén-juàn kē.
(P).' (Performs trimming lamp. Ghost female-role rearranging
file gesture.

竇天章云 ）我剔的這燈明
994　Dòu Tiān-zhāng yún:) Wǒ tī de zhè dēng míng
Tou T'ien-chang says:) 'I trimmed till this lamp is-bright

了也再看幾宗文卷一起
995　le ye, zài kàn jǐ zōng wén-juàn. Yì qǐ
(P) (P), again look-at several (M) files: "A (M)

犯人竇娥藥死公公（ 做疑
996　fàn-rén Dòu É yào-sǐ gōng-gong. (Zuò yí-
criminal Tou O poisoned-to-death father-in-law."' (Performs
wondering

怪科云 ）這一宗文卷我爲
997　guài kē. Yún:) Zhè yì zōng wén-juàn, wǒ wéi
gesture. Says:) 'This one (M) file, I, as

頭看過壓在文卷底下怎
998　tóu kàn-guo, yā zài wén-juàn dǐ-xià, zěn-
first-one, have-looked-at, stuck at files underneath (L), how-is-it

生又在這上頭這幾時問
999　shēng yòu zài zhè shàng-tou? Zhè jǐ-shí wèn-
again is on this (L)? This sometime-ago examined/

244

TOU: How strange! I was just about to read a case when the lamp flickered. Chang Ch'ien is asleep. I had better fix the lamp myself. (He trims the lamp. Tou O's ghost rearranges the file.) Now the lamp is brighter. I shall read a few more cases: 'A certain criminal, Tou O, who poisoned her father-in-law. . .' (He is puzzled.) I read this case first, and put it under the other documents. How has it again come to the top? Since this case has already been closed, let me

§993] *Zuò:* not in *KMCP*.

Before *tī dēng: wàng dōng biān* 往 東 邊 in *KMCP*, p. 17*a*; same addition in *KMCP,* pp. 17a-b.
§996–7] *Zuò yí. . . Yún:* not in *KMCP;* instead, *hǎo shì qí-guài yě* 好 是 奇 怪 也, *KMCP*, p. 17*a*.

結了的還壓在底下我別
1000　*jié le de, hái yā zài dǐ-xià. Wǒ bié*
concluded (P) one, again stick [it] underneath (L). I separately

看一宗文卷波（　魂旦再弄
1001　*kàn yì zōng wén-juàn bo. (Hún dàn zài nòng*
look-at a (M) file (P).' (Ghost female-role again adjusting

燈科竇天章云）怎麼這燈
1002　*dēng kē. Dòu Tiān-zhāng yún:) Zěm-ma zhè dēng*
lamp gesture. Tou T'ien-chang says:) 'How-is-it this lamp

又是半明半闇的我再剔
1003　*yòu shì bàn míng bàn àn de. Wǒ zài tī*
again is half bright, half dim (P). I again trim

這燈咱（　做剔燈魂旦再翻
1004　*zhè dēng za. (Zuò tī dēng. Hún dàn zài fān*
this lamp (P).' (Performs trimming lamp. Ghost female-role again turning

文卷科竇天章云）我剔的
1005　*wén-juàn kē. Dòu Tiān-zhāng yún:) Wǒ tī de*
file gesture. Tou T'ien-chang says:) 'I trimmed till

這燈明了我另拿一宗文
1006　*zhè dēng míng le, wǒ lìng ná yì zōng wén-*
this lamp is-bright (P); I separately take one (M) file

卷看咱一起犯人竇娥藥
1007　*juàn kàn za. Yì qǐ fàn-rén Dòu É yào*
to-look-at (P). "A (M) criminal Tou O poisoned

死公公呸好是奇怪我纔
1008　*sǐ gōng-gong. Pēi! Hǎo-shì qí-guài! Wǒ cái*
to-death father-in-law." P'ei! Really-is strange! I just-now

將這文書分明壓在底下
1009　*jiāng zhè wén-shū fēn-míng yā zài dǐ-xià,*
(Pr) this file clearly stuck at underneath (L);

again put it at the bottom and study a different one. (Tou O's ghost again adjusts the lamp.) Why is this light flickering again? I shall trim it once more. (He trims the light. Tou O's ghost again turns over the file.) Now I have made the lamp brighter. Let me read another case. 'A criminal Tou O poisoned her father-in-law'. Ah! How strange. I had definitely put this paper at the bottom of the file, and I have

§1002] Before *Zěm-ma: hǎo shì, qí-guài yě* 好 是 奇 怪 也 in *KMCP*, p. 17a.
§1003] After *zài: zì-jǐ* 自 己 *KMCP*, p. 17a.

剛剔了這燈怎生又翻在

1010 *gāng tī-le zhè dēng, zěn-shēng yòu fān zài*
   just trimmed (P) this lamp, how-is-it again replaced at

面上莫不是楚州後廳裏

1011 *miàn-shang? Mò-bú-shì Chǔ-zhōu-hòu-tīng-li*
   top (L)? Not-unlikely-is in-Ch'u-chou-back-hall (L)

有鬼麼便無鬼呵這樁事

1012 *yǒu guǐ ma? Biàn wú guǐ he, zhè zhuāng shì*
   there-is ghost (P)? Even-if there-is-no ghost (P), this (M) affair

必有冤枉將這文卷再壓

1013 *bì yǒu yuān-wang. Jiāng zhè wén-juàn zài yā*
   must involve injustice. (Pr) this file again place

在底下待我另看一宗如

1014 *zài dǐ-xia. Dài wǒ lìng kàn yì-zōng, rú-*
   at bottom (L). Wait-till I separately look-at one (M), like-

何（魂旦又弄燈科竇天章

1015 *hé? (Hún dàn yòu nòng dēng kē. Dòu Tiān-zhāng*
   what?' (Ghost female-role again adjusting lamp action. Tou
   T'ien-chang

云）怎生這燈又不明了敢

1016 *yún:) Zěn-shēng zhè dēng yòu bù míng le? Gǎn*
   says:) 'How-is-it this lamp again not bright (P)? Must-be

有鬼弄這燈我再剔一剔

1017 *yǒu guǐ nòng zhè dēng. Wǒ zài tī-yi-tī*
   there-is ghost adjusting this lamp. I again trim once [M]

去（做剔燈科魂旦上做撞

1018 *qù. (Zuò tī dēng kē. Hún dàn shàng. Zuò chuàng-*
   (C).' (Performs trimming lamp gesture. Ghost female-role
   enters. Performs colliding/

見科竇天章舉劍擊桌科

1019 *jiàn kē. Dòu Tiān-zhāng jǔ jiàn jī zhuō kē,*
   seeing gesture. Tou T'ien-chang raising sword, striking desk
   gesture,

just trimmed the lamp. How is it again put on the top? Can it be
that there is a ghost in the hall? Even if there is no ghost, there
must be some injustice involved in this case. Let me again place
this underneath and read another case. (Tou O's ghost again
adjusts the lamp.) How is it that the light dims again? It must be a
ghost who is adjusting this light. Let me again trim the wick.
(He trims the wick. Tou O's ghost enters. They unexpectedly see each
other. Tou T'ien-chang takes out his sword and strikes the desk.)

§1011] *Chǔ-zhōu*: *Yáng-zhōu fǔ* 楊州府 in *KMCP*, p. 17*b*.
§1012] *Biàn*: *gèng* 更 *KMCP*, p. 17*b*.
§1016] Before *Zěn-shēng*: *Shí shì qí-guài yě* 實是奇恠也 in *KMCP*, p. 17*b*.
       After *bù míng le*: *Yòu zhè děng hū míng hū àn de* 又這等忽明忽暗的
       in *KMCP*, p. 17*b*.
§1018] *Hún dàn shàng*: *huāng huí kē*; *hún fān wén-juàn kē* 荒回科魂番文卷科, *KMCP*,
       p. 17*b*.
§1019] *jǔ jiàn jī zhuō*: *zhàng jiàn* 仗劍, *KMCP*, p. 17*b*.

云 ）呸 我 說 有 鬼 兀 那 鬼 魂

1020　yún:) Pèi! Wǒ shuō yǒu guǐ! Wǔ-nà guǐ-hún,
　　　says:) 'P'ei! I said, "There-is ghost!" Hey-there, ghost,

老 夫 是 朝 庭 欽 差 帶 牌 走

1021　lǎo fū shì cháo-tíng qin-chāi dài pái zǒu
　　　old man is Court Imperially-sent carrying tally, travelling-on-

馬 肅 政 廉 訪 使 你 向 前 來

1022　mǎ sù-zhèng-lián-fǎng shǐ. Nǐ xiàng qián lái,
　　　horse Surveillance Commissioner. [If] you toward front ad-
　　　vance,

一 劍 揮 之 兩 段 張 千 虧 你

1023　yí jiàn hui zhi liǎng duàn. Zhāng Qiān, kui nǐ
　　　[with] one [stroke of the] sword, sweep you [into] two pieces.
　　　Chang Ch'ien, fortunate-for you,

也 睡 的 着 快 起 來 有 鬼 有

1024　yě shuì-de-zháo. Kuài qǐ-lai. Yǒu guǐ, yǒu
　　　still to-have-been-able-to-sleep. Quickly get-up (C). There-is
　　　ghost. There-is

鬼 兀 的 不 嚇 殺 老 夫 也 （ 魂

1025　guǐ. Wǔ-de bú xià-shā lǎo fū ye! (Hún
　　　ghost. [Would] this not frighten-to-death old man (P)!' (Ghost

旦 唱 ）

1026　dàn chàng:)
　　　female-role sings:)

（ 喬 牌 兒 ）則 見 他 疑 心

1027　(Qiáo pái-er) Zé jiàn tā yí xin-
　　　('Lofty Sign') 'Only see [that] he, [with] doubting heart,

兒 胡 亂 猜 聽 了 我 這

1028　er hú-luàn cāi, ting-le wǒ zhè
　　　at-random guesses; hearing (P) my this

哭 聲 兒 轉 驚 駭 哎 你

1029　kū shēng-er zhuǎn jing-hài. Ai! Nǐ
　　　crying voice, changes-to being-startled/frightened. Ah! You

250

Ah! I said, 'There is a ghost.' Hey, you ghost over there, I am the
Imperial Surveillance Commissioner, who wears the golden tally
and has access to the government's horses and posting stations. If
you advance towards me, I shall cut you in two with my sword.
Chang Ch'ien, how can you be sound asleep? Get up at once.
There is a ghost. There is a ghost. This frightens me to death!

TOU O'S GHOST (Sings third lyric):

> *Full of doubts, he makes random guesses;*
> *Upon hearing my cry, he becomes frightened.*
> *You, Tou T'ien-chang, are indeed powerful;*

1021–2] *dài pái zŏu mă:* *pái* is *jīn pái*, a symbol of power, which enables an official
to execute first and report to the throne later (see n. 921–2). *Zŏu mă* is 'to
ride horses, which were provided by official posting stations (*yì zhàn* 驛站)'.
1029–30] *Nĭ ge Dòu Tiān-zhāng:* the daughter would not, in actual speech, pronounce
her father's given name, especially in his presence; nor would she use the
pronoun '*ni*'. This is a license allowed in arias; it could also be a freedom
accorded a ghost.

§1024] *Kuài: dòu* 都 in *KMCP*, p. 17*b*.
§1027] *Qiáo pái-er: Yàn-ér luò* 鴈兒落 in *KMCP*, p. 17*b*; song titles differ, but contents
are comparable.
　　　Zé: wo 我, *KMCP*, p. 17*b*.
§1028] *hú-luàn: zhuăn-zhuăn* 轉 轉 in *KMCP*, p. 17*b*.
　　　tīng-le: not in *KMCP*.
§1029] *zhuăn jīng-hài: tiān jīng-guài* 添 驚 怪 in *KMCP*, p. 17*b*.

個竇天章直恁的威
1030 *ge Dòu Tiān-zhāng zhí rèn-de wēi-*
(M) Tou T'ien-chang really this-way power

風大且受我竇娥這
1031 *fēng dà. Qiě shòu wǒ Dòu É zhè*
great. For-now accept my, Tou O's this

一拜
1032 *yí bài.*
one salute.'

（竇天章云）兀那鬼魂你道
1033 *(Dòu Tiān-zhāng yún:) Wǔ-nà guǐ-hún, nǐ dào*
(Tou T'ien-chang says:) 'Hey-there, ghost, you say

竇天章是你父親受你孩
1034 *Dòu Tiān-zhāng shì nǐ fù-qin, shòu nǐ hái-*
Tou T'ien-chang is your father, should-accept your child

兒竇娥拜你敢錯認了也
1035 *er Dòu É bài. Nǐ gǎn cuò rèn-le ye.*
Tou O's salute. You must-have mistakenly identified (P) (P).

我的女兒叫做端雲七歲
1036 *Wǒ-de nǔ-er jiào-zuo Duān-yún, qí-suì*
My (P) daughter was-called Tuan-yün; at-seven-years-of-age

上與了蔡婆婆爲兒媳婦
1037 *shàng yǔ-le Cài Pó-po wéi ér xí-fu.*
(L) was-given-to (P) Ts'ai P'o-p'o to-be son's wife.

你是竇娥名字差了怎生
1038 *Nǐ shì Dòu É; míng-zi chà le. Zěn-shēng*
You are Tou O; name differs (P). How-can

是我女孩兒（魂旦云）父親
1039 *shì wǒ nǔ-hái-er? (Hún dàn yún:) Fù-qin,*
be my daughter?' (Ghost female-role says:) 'Father,

252

Let me, Tou O, bow to you.

TOU: Ghost, you say that Tou T'ien-chang is your father and should receive the greetings of his child, Tou O. You must be mistaken. My daughter was called Tuan-yün. When she was seven, I gave her to Mistress Ts'ai to be her daughter-in-law. You are Tou O; the name is different. How can you be my daughter?

TOU O'S GHOST: Father, after you gave me to Mistress Ts'ai, she

1030] *ge:* an abbreviation of *zhè ge* 這 個, used here for emphasis.
1031] *dà: dà* is the modern pronunciation; for rhyme it may read *dài.*

§1030] After *Dòu Tiān-zhāng: lǎo fù-qīn* 老 父 親 in *KMCP*, p. 18a.
§1030-1] *zhí. . . dà:* not in *KMCP.*
§1031-2] *Qiě. . . yí bài: Shòu Dòu É hái-er shèn-shèn bài* 受 竇 娥 孩 兒 深 深 拜 in *KMCP*, p. 18a.

你將我與了蔡婆婆家改

1040　*nǐ jiāng wǒ yǔ-le Cài Pó-po jiā, gǎi*

you (Pr) me gave-to (P) Ts'ai *P'o-p'o*'s family; changed

名做竇娥了也（竇天章云）

1041　*míng zuò Dòu É le ye. (Dòu Tiān-zhāng yún:)*

name to-be Tou O (P) (P).' (Tou T'ien-chang says:)

你便是端雲孩兒我不問

1042　*Nǐ biàn shì Duān-yún hái-er? Wǒ bú wèn*

'You then are Tuan-yün child? I not ask

你別的這藥死公公是你

1043　*nǐ bié-de. Zhè yào-sǐ gōng-gong shì nǐ*

you anything-else. This poisoning-to-death father-in-law was you,

不是（魂旦云）是你孩兒來

1044　*bú shì? (Hún dàn yún:) Shì nǐ hái-er lai.*

not was?' (Ghost female-role says:) 'Was your child (P).'

（竇天章云）噤聲你這小妮

1045　*(Dòu Tiān-zhāng yún:) Jìn shēng! Nǐ zhè xiǎo ní-*

(Tou T'ien-chang says:) 'Silence voice! You this little girl!

子老夫爲你啼哭的眼也

1046　*zi. Lǎo fū wèi nǐ tí-kū de yǎn yě*

Old man for you cried till eyes even

花了憂愁的頭也白了你

1047　*huā le, yōu-chóu de tóu yě bái le. Nǐ*

dim (P), worried till head even white (P). You

劃地犯下十惡大罪受了

1048　*chǎn-dì fàn-xià shí-è dà zuì, shòu-le*

how committed "ten-evil great crime", suffered (P

典刑我今日官居臺省職

1049　*diǎn-xíng. Wǒ jin-rì guān jū tái shěng, zhí*

penalties. I today office is-in Censorate, Secretariat; post changed my name to Tou O.

TOU: You are then my child Tuan-yün. Let me ask you this: Was it you who poisoned your father-in-law?

TOU O'S GHOST: It was.

TOU: Be quiet, you wretched girl! I have wept for you till my eyes have grown dim, and I have worried for you till my hair has turned white. How did you come to commit one of the ten unpardonable crimes and be executed? Now I hold high official posts in the

---

1045–6] *xiǎo nī-zi :* literally 'little girl', it is used in an abusive sense here (cf. § 1045–6).

§1043] After *gōng-gong : shòu le diǎn-xíng* 受 了 典 刑 in *KMCP*, p. 18a.

§1045–6] *xiǎo nī-zi : xiǎo jiàn-rén* 小 賤 人 in *KMCP*, p. 18a.

掌 刑 名 來 此 兩 淮 審 囚 刷

1050   *zhǎng xíng-míng. Lái cǐ Liǎng Huái shěn qiú shuā*

controls criminal-law. Come-to this Two Huai to-investigate prisons, to-review

卷 體 察 濫 官 污 吏 你 是 我

1051   *juàn, tǐ-chá làn guān wū lì. Nǐ shì wǒ*

files, to-uncover corrupt officials, foul clerks. You are my

親 生 之 女 老 夫 將 你 治 不

1052   *qīn shēng zhī nǚ. Lǎo fū jiāng nǐ zhì-bu-*

own born (P) daughter. Old man (Pr) you unable-to-govern,

的 怎 治 他 人 我 當 初 將 你

1053   *dè, zěn zhì tā rén? Wǒ dāng-chū jiāng nǐ*

how govern other people? I formerly (Pr) you

嫁 與 他 家 呵 要 你 三 從 四

1054   *jià yǔ tā jiā he, yào nǐ sān cóng sì*

married to their family (P), expected-of you "Three Obediences", "Four

德 三 從 者 在 家 從 父 出 嫁

1055   *dé. Sān cóng zhě, zài jiā cóng fù, chū-jià*

Virtues". "Three Obediences (P)": at home obey father; married,

從 夫 夫 死 從 子 四 德 者 事

1056   *cóng fū, fū sǐ cóng zǐ. Sì dé zhě, shì*

obey husband; husband dies, obey son. "Four Virtues (P)": serve

公 姑 敬 夫 主 和 妯 娌 睦 街

1057   *gōng gū, jìng fū-zhǔ, hé zhú-li, mù jiē-*

father-in-law/mother-in-law, respect husband, get-along-with sisters-in-law, live-in-peace-with neighbors.

坊 今 三 從 四 德 全 無 剗 地

1058   *fang. Jīn sān cóng sì dé quán wú, chǎn-dì*

Now "Three Obediences", "Four Virtues" entirely have-not; how

Censorate and the Secretariat, and am in charge of criminal law. I have come here to the Huai River area to investigate criminal cases and to expose corrupt officials. You are my own daughter. If I could not govern you, how can I govern others? When I gave you in marriage to that family, I expected you to observe the Three Obediences and the Four Virtues. The Three Obediences are obedience to your father before marriage, obedience to your husband after marriage, and obedience to your son after your husband's death. The Four Virtues are service to your parents-in-law, respect for your husband, being on good terms with your sisters-in-law, and living in peace with your neighbors. You have disregarded the Three Obediences and the Four Virtues, and on the contrary, have

§1050] *Lái cǐ Liǎng Huái: tiān xià* 天 下, *KMCP*, p. 18a.
§1052] After *zhī nǚ:* xiān fàn xià shí è dà zuì 先 犯 下 十 惡 大 罪 in *KMCP*, p. 18b.
§1056] After *cóng zǐ: cǐ nǎi wéi zhī sān cóng* 此 乃 爲 之 三 從 in *KMCP*, p. 18b.
§1058] After *fang: cǐ nǎi wéi zhī sì dé* 此 乃 爲 之 四 德 in *KMCP*, p. 18b.

犯了十惡大罪我竇家三

1059　*fàn-le shí è dà zuì. Wǒ Dòu jiā sān*

committed (P) "ten-evil great crime"? My Tou family three

輩無犯法之男五世無再

1060　*bèi wú fàn fǎ zhī nán, wǔ shì wú zài*

generations have-no violating laws (P) male; five generations have-no re-

婚之女到今日被你辱沒

1061　*hūn zhī nǔ. Dào jīn-rì bèi nǐ rǔ-mò*

married (P) female. Till today by you disgraced/negated

祖宗世德又連累我的清

1062　*zǔ-zōng shì dé, yòu lián-lèi wǒ-de qīng-*

ancestors, generations-of virtue; moreover implicate my (P) pure

名你快與我細吐眞情不

1063　*míng. Nǐ kuài yǔ wǒ xì tǔ zhēn qíng, bú-*

name. You quickly to me in-detail spit-out true situation, do-not

要虛言支對若說的有半

1064　*yào xū yán zhī-duì; ruò shuō-de yǒu bàn-*

[with] false words evasively-answer. If statements have half

釐差錯牒發你城隍祠內

1065　*lí chā-cuò, dié fā nǐ chéng huáng cí nèi,*

particle difference/mistake, by-official-document send you [to] city god temple (L),

着你永世不得人身罰在

1066　*zhāo nǐ yǒng-shì bù dé rén shēn, fá zài*

make you permanently not gain human body; as-penalty, be-confined-at

陰山永爲餓鬼（魂旦云）父

1067　*yīn shān yǒng wéi è guǐ. (Hún dàn yún:) Fù-*

dark mountain, forever be hungry ghost.' (Ghost female-role says:) 'Father,

258

committed one of the ten unpardonable crimes. In our Tou family for three generations there has been no male who has broken the law, and for five generations there has been no woman who has remarried. Now you have disgraced our ancestors and dishonored my good name. Tell me at once the truth in detail, and do not try to make excuses. If your account varies in the slightest from the truth, I shall send you to the temple of the city god, and you will never be able to re-enter human form, and will be exiled to a dark mountain and remain forever a hungry ghost.

TOU O'S GHOST: Father, please, for the time being, rest your anger

§1059] After *dà zui: cháng yán dào, shì yào qián sī, miǎn láo hòu-huǐ* 常 言 道 事 要
前 思 免 勞 後 悔 in *KMCP*, p. 18*b*.

§1061] After *zhī nǚ: Jì jiāng nǐ chū jià cóng fū, biàn xí xué lián chǐ rén yì. Quán bù sī
jiǔ liè sān zhēn, dào fàn le shí è dà zui* 旣 將 你 出 嫁 從 夫 便 習 學 廉 恥 仁
義 全 不 思 九 烈 三 貞 到 了 犯 了 十 惡 大 罪 in *KMCP*, p. 18*b*.

§1061-3] *Dào jìn-rì... qīng-míng: Nǐ rǔ-mò zǔ-shàng jiā-mén, yòu bǎ wǒ qīng míng lián-lèi*
你 辱 沒 祖 上 家 門 又 把 我 清 名 連 累 in *KMCP*, p. 18*b*.

§1064] *ruò: mò* 莫 in *KMCP*, p. 18*b*.

親 停 嗔 息 怒 暫 罷 狼 虎 之
1068 qīn tíng chēn xí nù, zhàn bà láng hǔ zhī
stop scolding, cease anger, temporarily end wolf/tiger (P)

威 聽 你 孩 兒 慢 慢 的 說 一
1069 wēi. Tīng nǐ hái-er màn-màn-de shuō yí
terror. Listen-to your child slowly (P) tell [it] one

徧 咱 我 三 歲 上 亡 了 母 親
1070 biàn za. Wǒ sān-suì-shàng wáng-le mǔ-qin,
time (M) (P). I at-three-years-of-age (L) lost (P) mother,

七 歲 上 離 了 父 親 你 將 我
1071 qí-suì-shàng lí-le fù-qin. Nǐ jiāng wǒ
at-seven-years-of-age (L), parted-from (P) father. You (Pr) me

送 與 蔡 婆 婆 做 兒 媳 婦 至
1072 sòng yǔ Cài Pó-po zuò ér-xí-fu. Zhì
sent to Ts'ai P'o-p'o to-be son's-wife. Reaching

十 七 歲 與 夫 配 合 纔 得 兩
1073 shí-qí suì yǔ fū pèi-hé. Cái-dé liǎng
seventeen years-of-age, with husband mated. Just-about two

年 不 幸 兒 夫 亡 化 和 俺 婆
1074 nián, bú-xìng ér fū wáng-huà, hé ǎn pó-
years, unfortunately daughter's husband died; with my mother-
in-law

婆 守 寡 這 山 陽 縣 南 門 外
1075 po shǒu guǎ. Zhè Shān-yáng xiàn Nán-mén wài
observed widowhood. This Shan-yang District South Gate
outside,

有 箇 賽 盧 醫 他 少 俺 婆 婆
1076 yǒu ge Sài Lú-yī. Tā shǎo ǎn pó-po
there-was [a] (M) "Rival Lu-Doctor". He owed my mother-in-
law

二 十 兩 銀 子 俺 婆 婆 去 取
1077 èr-shí liǎng yín-zi. Ǎn pó-po qù qǔ
twenty taels silver. My mother-in-law went to-demand [it];

260

and your 'wolf and tiger' -like bearing. Listen to me tell the whole story slowly. At three I lost my mother, and at seven I was separated from my father. You gave me to Mistress Ts'ai to be her future daughter-in-law. At seventeen I married. Unfortunately, after two years, my husband died. I remained a widow and lived with my mother-in-law. Outside the South Gate of the Shan-yang District there was a Sai Lu-yi. He owed my mother-in-law twenty taels of silver. When my mother-in-law went to ask for the money,

§1069] *hái-er : nǚ-er* 女兒, *KMCP*, p. 19a.
§1072] After *ér-xí-fu : gǎi míng Dòu É* 改名竇娥 in *KMCP*, p. 19a.
§1073–4] *Cái-dé liǎng nián :* not in *KMCP.*
§1074] After *bú-xìng : dāng nián* 當年 in *KMCP*, p. 19a.
§1075] *Zhè. . . wài : Chǔ-zhōu chéng lǐ* 楚州城里 in *KMCP*, p. 19a.

1078 討 被 他 賺 到 郊 外 要 將 婆
tăo, bèi tā zuàn dào jiāo-wài, yào jiāng pó-
by him lured to countryside, wanting-to (Pr) mother-in-law

1079 婆 勒 死 不 想 撞 見 張 驢 兒
po lēi sĭ. Bù-xiăng chuàng-jiàn Zhāng Lǘ-er
strangle to-death. Unexpectedly bumped-into Chang Donkey

1080 父 子 兩 箇 救 了 俺 婆 婆 性
fù zĭ liăng ge, jiù-le ăn pó-po xìng-
father son two (M); saved (P) my mother-in-law's life.

1081 命 那 張 驢 兒 知 道 我 家 有
mìng. Nà Zhāng Lǘ-er zhĭ-dao wŏ jiā yŏu
That Chang Donkey knew my family had

1082 個 守 寡 的 媳 婦 便 道 你 婆
ge shŏu guă de xí-fu, biàn dào: Nĭ pó-
an observing widowhood (P) daughter-in-law; then said,
"You mother-in-law/

1083 兒 媳 婦 既 無 丈 夫 不 若 招
er xí-fu jì wú zhàng-fu, bú-ruò zhāo
daughter-in-law since have-no husbands, nothing-like taking-in

1084 我 父 子 兩 個 俺 婆 婆 初 也
wŏ fù zĭ liăng ge. Ăn pó-po chū yě
us father son two (M)." My mother-in-law at-first also

1085 不 肯 那 張 驢 兒 道 你 若 不
bù kěn. Nà Zhāng Lǘ-er dào: Nĭ ruò bù
was-not willing. That Chang Donkey said, "You if not

1086 肯 我 依 舊 勒 死 你 俺 婆 婆
kěn, wŏ yī-jiù lēi-sĭ nĭ. Ăn pó-po
be-willing, I still strangle-to-death you." My mother-in-law

1087 懼 怕 不 得 已 含 糊 許 了 只
jù-pà. Bù-dé-yĭ hán-hu xŭ-le; zhĭ
was-afraid. Had-no-other-way-out, ambiguously consented (P);
only

262

she was lured by him to the country, where he intended to strangle her to death. Unexpectedly Donkey Chang and his father came upon them. The two of them saved my mother-in-law's life. When Donkey Chang learned that there was a young widow in our family, he said, 'You two, mother-in-law and daughter-in-law, do not have husbands. Why don't you two marry us, father and son?' My mother-in-law was unwilling at first. Donkey Chang said, 'If you refuse, I shall strangle you again.' My mother-in-law was afraid. Because there was no way out, she haphazardly consented and

1087] *Bù-dé-yǐ*: 'unable to cease'; an idiom for 'cannot but' or 'to have no other way out'.

§1078] After *bèi tā: jiǎng ǎn pó-po* 將 俺 婆 婆 in *KMCP*, p. 19*a*.
§1081–4] *Nà Zhāng Lǘ-er . . . liǎng ge: Nà lǎo Zhāng wèn dào, Pó-po, Nǐ jiā-li yǒu shém-me rén. Pó-po dào, ǎn jiā wú rén, zhǐ yǒu ge shǒu guǎ de xí-fu, huàn zuò Dòu-É. Lǎo Zhāng dào, Nǐ jiā-zhōng jì wú rén, wǒ zhāo yǔ nǐ zuò fū-zhǔ. Nǐ yì xià rú-hé?* 那老張問道婆婆你家里有甚麼人 婆婆道俺家 無人 止有箇守寡的媳婦喚做竇娥老張道你家中既無人 我 招 與 你 做 夫 主 你 意 下 如 何. in *KMCP*, pp. 19*a*–*b*.
§1084] *chū yě: jiān-zhí* 堅執 in *KMCP*, p. 19*b*.
§1085] *Nà Zhāng Lǘ-er dào: nà lǎo Zhāng fù zǐ liǎng ge dào* 那老張父子兩個道 in *KMCP*, p. 19*b*.
§1087] *hán-hu*: not in *KMCP*.
     After *xǔ-le: shí shì hǔ-hè chéng-qīn* 實 是 唬 嚇 成 親 in *KMCP*, p. 19*b*.

1088 得 將 他 父 子 兩 個 領 到 家
dé jiāng tā fù zi liǎng ge lǐng dào jiā
could (Pr) these father son two (M) lead to house

1089 中 養 他 過 世 有 張 驢 兒 數
zhōng, yǎng tā guò-shì. Yǒu Zhāng Lǘ-er shù-
(L) to-provide-for them [till they] pass-away. There-was Chang Donkey several

1090 次 調 戲 你 女 孩 兒 我 堅 執
cì tiáo-xì nǐ nǚ-hái-er. Wǒ jiān-zhí
times flirted-with your daughter. I stubbornly

1091 不 從 那 一 日 俺 婆 婆 身 子
bù cóng. Nà yí rì ǎn pó-po shēn-zi
did-not yield. That one day my mother-in-law body

1092 不 快 想 羊 膪 兒 湯 喫 你 孩
bú kuài, xiǎng yáng dǔ-er tāng chī. Nǐ hái-
not well, wanted mutton tripe soup to-eat. Your child

1093 兒 安 排 了 湯 適 值 張 驢 兒
er ān-pái-le tāng. Shì zhí Zhāng Lǘ-er
prepared (P) soup. Just happened Chang Donkey

1094 父 子 兩 個 問 病 道 將 湯 來
fù zi liǎng ge wèn bìng, dào: Jiāng tāng lái.
father son two (M) inquired-about sickness; said, "Bring soup (C).

1095 我 嘗 一 嘗 說 湯 便 好 只 少
Wǒ cháng-yì-cháng. Shuō tāng biàn hǎo, zhǐ shǎo
[Let] me have-a-taste." Said soup then was-fine, only lacked

1096 些 鹽 醋 賺 的 我 去 取 鹽 醋
xiē yán cù. Zuàn-de wǒ qù qǔ yán cù,
some salt, vinegar. Tricked (P) me to-go to-fetch salt, vinegar;

1097 他 就 闇 地 裏 下 了 毒 藥 實
tā jiù àn-dì-lǐ xià-le dú-yào, shí
he then secretly (P) (L) put (P) [in] poison, actually

brought the two of them, father and son, home, to provide for them for life. Donkey Chang tried several times to flirt with your daughter and to seduce her. I firmly resisted him. One day my mother-in-law was not well and wanted some mutton tripe soup. When I had the soup ready, Donkey Chang happened to be there with his father to inquire after my mother-in-law's sickness. He said, 'Bring the soup and let me taste it.' Then he said there was not enough salt and vinegar. Having tricked me into fetching salt and vinegar, he secretly put poison in the soup. He actually expected to poison my

1089] *guò-shì*: literally 'pass out of the world': 'to die'.

§1089] *yǎng tā guò-shì*: *guò qí rì-yuè* 過 其 日 月 in *KMCP*, p. 19*b*.
§1093-4] *Shì zhí . . . dào*: *Zhāng Lü-er yán dào* 張 驢 兒 言 道 in *KMCP*, p. 19*b*.
§1097] *àn-dì-lǐ*: not in *KMCP*.
§1097-9] *shí zhǐ-wàng . . . chéng-qīn*: not in *KMCP*; instead, *tā yòu jiào wǒ jiāng qù* 他 又 教 我 將 去, p. 19*b*.

指望藥殺俺婆婆要強逼

1098 zhǐ-wàng yào-shā ǎn pó-po, yào qiáng-bī
expected to-poison-to-death my mother-in-law, wanting-to force

我成親不想俺婆婆偶然

1099 wǒ chéng-qīn. Bù-xiǎng ǎn pó-po ǒu-rán
me into-marrying. Unexpectedly, my mother-in-law by-chance

發嘔不要湯吃却讓與老

1100 fā-ǒu. Bú yào tāng chī, què ràng yǔ Lǎo
vomited. Did-not want soup to-eat; instead give [it] to Old

張吃隨即七竅流血藥死

1101 Zhāng chī. Suí-jì qī qiào liú xuě yào-sǐ
Chang to-eat. Immediately seven apertures issued blood; poisoned-to-death

了張驢兒便道竇娥藥死

1102 le. Zhāng Lǘ-er biàn dào: Dòu É yào-sǐ
(P). Chang Donkey then said, "Tou O poisoned-to-death

了俺老子你要官休要私

1103 le ǎn lǎo-zi. Nǐ yào guān xiū yào sī
(P) my old-man. You want-to officially settle [it], want to privately

休我便道怎生是官休怎

1104 xiū? Wǒ biàn dào: Zěn-shēng shì guān xiū? Zěn-
settle [it]?" I then said, "How is officially to-settle? How

生是私休他道要官休告

1105 shēng shì sī xiū? Tā dào: Yào guān xiū, gào
is privately to-settle?" He said, "Want to officially settle, appeal

到官司你與俺老子償命

1106 dào guān-si; nǐ yǔ ǎn lǎo-zi cháng-mìng.
to court; you for my old-man pay-life-for-life.

若私休你便與我做老婆

1107 Ruò sī xiū, nǐ biàn yǔ wǒ zuò lǎo-po.
If privately settle, you then to me be wife."

266

mother-in-law and to force me into marrying him. Quite unexpectedly, however, my mother-in-law started to vomit. Not wanting the soup any more, she gave it to Old Chang to eat. Then blood spurted from the old man's mouth, nostrils, ears, and eyes, and he died. Donkey Chang then said, 'Tou O poisoned my father. Do you want to settle this officially or privately?' I then said, 'What do you mean by settling this officially or privately?' He said, 'If you want it settled officially, I shall take the case to court, and you will pay for my father's death with your life. If you want it settled privately, then be my wife.' Your child then said, 'A good horse will

1101] *qī qiào liú xuě:* a stock phrase usually used to describe someone who has been poisoned.

§1099–101] *Bù-xiǎng. . . chī: Ǎn pó-po ràng Lǎo Ƶhāng xiān chī* 俺 婆 婆 讓 老 張 先 喫 in *KMCP*, p. 19*b*.

你 孩 兒 便 道 好 馬 不 鞴 雙

1108   *Nǐ hái-er biàn dào: Hǎo mǎ bú bèi shuāng*

Your child then said, "Good horse does-not carry two

鞍 烈 女 不 更 二 夫 我 至 死

1109   *ān. Liè nǚ bù gēng èr fū. Wǒ zhì sǐ*

saddles. Chaste woman does-not change-for second husband."
I till death

不 與 你 做 媳 婦 我 情 願 和

1110   *bù yǔ nǐ zuò xí-fu. Wǒ qíng-yuàn hé*

would-not to you be wife. I am-willing with

你 見 官 去 他 將 你 孩 兒 拖

1111   *nǐ jiàn guān qù. Tā jiāng nǐ hái-er tuō*

you see official go." He (Pr) your child dragged

到 官 中 受 盡 三 推 六 問 吊

1112   *dào guān-zhōng. Shòu jìn sān tui, liù wèn, diào*

to court (L). Suffered utmostly "three examining, six questioning", hanging,

拷 綳 扒 便 打 死 孩 兒 也 不

1113   *kǎo bēng pá. Biàn dǎ-sǐ hái-er, yě bù*

beating, stretching, stripping. Even beaten-to-death, child still
was-not

肯 認 怎 當 州 官 見 你 孩 兒

1114   *kěn rèn. Zěn dāng zhōu-guān jiàn nǐ hái-er*

willing to-confess. How withstand [it, when] prefect saw your
child

不 認 便 要 拷 打 俺 婆 婆 我

1115   *bú rèn, biàn yào kǎo-dǎ ǎn pó-po. Wǒ*

would-not confess, then was-going-to beat my mother-in-law? I

怕 婆 婆 年 老 受 刑 不 起 只

1116   *pà pó-po nián lǎo, shòu-xíng-bù-chǐ, zhǐ*

feared mother-in-law in-years old, unable-to-suffer-torture, only not have two saddles; a chaste woman will not serve two husbands. I would rather die than be your wife. I would rather go to court.' He dragged me to court, where I was questioned again and again, hung, beaten, stripped, and bound. I would rather have died than make a false confession. How could I stand it when the prefect, seeing that your child would not confess, was going to beat my mother-in-law? I was afraid that she was too old to stand the torture,

1108–9] *Hǎo mǎ . . . èr fū:* a proverb; cf. l. 583.
1112] *diào:* hanging for inquisition (not for execution).

§1108] After *biàn dào: Ǎn jiā sān bèi-er wú fàn fǎ zhī nán, wǔ shì wú zài hūn zhī nǔ* 俺家三輩兒無犯法之男五世無再婚之女 in *KMCP*, p. 20a.
§1110] After *Wǒ: xīn shàng wú shì* 心上無事 in *KMCP*, p. 20a.
§1111] After *qù: Bù-yóu fēn-shuō* 不由分說 in *KMCP*, p. 20a.
§1112] *Shòu jìn: nǐ ér zěn dàng tā* 你兒怎當他, *KMCP*, p. 20a.
§1114] *Zěn dāng zhōu-guān: Tā* 他 in *KMCP*, p. 20a.

得屈認了因此押赴法塲
1117 dé qū-rèn-le. Yīn-cǐ yā-fù fǎ-chǎng,
    could confess-with-grievance (P). Because-of-this was-sent-
    under-guard-to execution-ground;

將我典刑你孩兒對天發
1118 jiāng wǒ diǎn-xíng. Nǐ hái-er duì tiān fā-
    (Pr) me executed. Your child toward Heaven issued

下三椿誓願第一椿要丈
1119 xià sān zhuāng shì-yuàn. Dì-yī zhuāng, yào zhàng-
    (C) three (M) vows. First (M), asked ten-feet-

二白練掛在旗鎗上若係
1120 èr bái liàn guà zài qí qiāng shàng, ruò xì
    two white silk to-be-hung on flag staff (L); if there-be

冤枉刀過頭落一腔熱血
1121 yuān-wang, dāo guò tóu luò, yì qiāng rè xuě
    injustice, knife passes, head falls, one chestful hot blood

休滴在地下都飛在白練
1122 xiū dì zài dì xià, dōu fēi zài bái liàn
    not drop on ground (L); all fly onto white silk

上第二椿現今三伏天道
1123 shang. Dì-èr zhuāng, xiàn-jīn sān fú tiān-dào,
    (L). Second (M), now third fu weather,

下三尺瑞雪遮掩你孩兒
1124 xià sān chǐ ruì xuě, zhē-yǎn nǐ hái-er
    send-down three feet auspicious snow to-cover your child's

屍首第三椿着他楚州大
1125 shī-shou. Dì-sān zhuāng, zháo tā Chǔ-zhōu dà-
    corpse. Third (M), make their Ch'u-chou [suffer] severe

旱三年果然血飛上白練
1126 hàn sān nián. Guǒ-rán xuě fēi shàng bái liàn;
    drought three years. Indeed blood flew onto white silk;

270

so I could not but make a false confession. Thereupon they took me to the execution ground and executed me. Your child made three vows to Heaven. First, I asked for a twelve-foot piece of white silk to be hung on a flagpole. I swore that if I was falsely accused, when the knife struck and my head fell, a chestful of warm blood would not stain the ground, but would fly up to the white silk. Second, I asked that although it was mid-summer, Heaven would send down three feet of snow to cover my corpse. Third, I vowed that this Ch'u-chou would suffer three years of severe drought. Indeed, my blood flew up to the white silk, snow fell in June, and there was no

1117] *qū-rèn*: same as *wū-fú*, 誣服、於服 'to confess under torture when not guilty'. See n. 1131 below on *fú-biàn* and n. 1356 on *wū-fú*.

§1118] After *diàn-xíng*: *Wǒ dào-de fǎ-chǎng* 我到的法塲 in *KMCP*, p. 20a.
§1119] *Dì-yì zhuāng*: not in *KMCP*.
§1120–1] *ruò xì. . . tóu luò*: *Ruò dāo guò qù* 若刀過去 in *KMCP*, p. 20a.
§1123] *Dì-èr zhuāng*: not in *KMCP*; instead *guǒ xì yuān-wang* 果係冤枉, p. 20a.
§1124–5] *zhē-yàn. . . shī shou*: *zhē le nǐ nǚ-er shēn shī* 遮了你女兒身尸 in *KMCP*, p. 20b.
§1125] *Dì-sān zhuāng*: not in *KMCP*; instead, *guǒ shì yuān-wang-le nǐ nǚ-er* 果是冤枉了你女兒, p. 20b.

六 月 下 雪 三 年 不 雨 都 是

1127   *Liù yuè xià xuě, sān nián bù yǔ; dōu shì*

[in] Sixth Month [there] fell snow; [for] three years did-not
rain – all were

爲 你 孩 兒 來 （ 詩 云 ） 不 告 官

1128   *wèi nǐ hái-er lai. (Shī yún:) Bú gào guān-*

because-of your child (P).' ([In] verse says:) 'Not appeal-to
court,

司 只 告 天 心 中 怨 氣 口 難

1129   *si zhǐ gào tiān. Xīn zhōng yuàn-qì kǒu nán*

only appeal-to Heaven. Heart within (L) wronged-feeling,
mouth hard

言 防 他 老 母 遭 刑 憲 情 願

1130   *yán. Fáng tā lǎo mǔ zāo xíng-xiàn, qíng-yuàn*

to-tell. To-prevent her, old mother, [from] suffering punishment,
was-willing

無 辭 認 罪 愆 三 尺 瓊 花 骸

1131   *wú cí rèn zuì-qiān. Sān chǐ qióng huā hái*

without words to-admit guilt. Three feet jade flowers skeleton/

骨 掩 一 腔 鮮 血 練 旗 懸 豈

1132   *gǔ yǎn. Yì qiāng xiān xuě liàn qí xuán. Qǐ*

bones covered. A chestful fresh blood [onto] silk flag hung.
How [say]

獨 霜 飛 鄒 衍 屈 今 朝 方 表

1133   *dú shuāng fēi Zōu Yǎn qū? Jīn-zhāo fāng biǎo*

only frost flew [for] Tsou Yen's wrongs? Today has-just revealed

竇 娥 冤 （ 唱 ）

1134   *Dòu É yuān. (Chàng:)*

Tou O's Injustice.' (Sings:)

（ 鴈 兒 落 ） 你 看 這 文 卷

1135   *(Yàn-er Luò) Nǐ kàn zhè wén-juàn*

('Wild-Goose Descends') 'You look, this record

rain for three years. All these came to pass because of your child.
(Recites.)

> I appealed not to the court, but to Heaven.
> The grievance in my heart cannot be put into words.
> To save my old mother from torture,
> Without argument I willingly confessed to the crime.
> Three feet of snow fell to cover my corpse;
> A chestful of blood stained the silk streamer.
> Not only did frost fly because of Tsou Yen's wrong,
> Today the injustice to Tou O is also revealed.

(Sings fourth lyric):

> Look at the record and see whether it reveals anything!

1131] *wú cí*: 'without words' means 'without protest or argument'; 'willingly'.

    wú cí rèn zuì-qiān is the same as *fú biàn* 服辯. 'According to the T'ang penal code, if a case involved penal servitude, exile, or the death penalty, the criminal should be asked to sign a *fu-pien* 服辯 to indicate that he accepted the verdict and wanted no further argument or explanation. Such a document is known as *fu-pien wen chuang* 服辯文狀 in the *Yüan tien-chang* 元典章 (12.4*a*). The signing of such a document deprives the criminal of any right of appeal. Apparently, the *pien-chuang* and the *fu-pien wen-chuang* were related to the same concept of argument, explanation, and appeal.' (Lien-sheng Yang, 'Notes on Maspero's *Les documents chinois de la troisième expédition de Sir Aurel Stein en Asie centrale*', *HJAS*, XVIII, 154.)

§1127] After *bù yǔ: cùn cǎo bù shēng* 寸草不生 in *KMCP*, p. 20*b*.

§1128] *Shī yún:* not in *KMCP*.

§1130] *Fáng. . . xíng-xiàn: shòu xíng wèi mǔ dāng xíng xiào* 受刑爲母當行孝 in *KMCP*, p. 20*b*.

§1130–1] *qíng-yuàn. . . zuì-qiān: jìn mìng yīn fū kě dāng xián* 盡命因夫可當賢 in *KMCP*, p. 20*b*.

§1131–2] *qióng huā. . . yān: ruì xuě mái sù tǐ* 瑞雪埋素體 in *KMCP*, p. 20*b*.

§1132] *liàn qí xuán: rǎn bái liàn* 染白練 in *KMCP*, p. 20*b*.

§1132–4] *Qǐ dú. . . yuān: shuāng jiàng shǐ zhī Zōu Yǎn qū; xuě fēi fāng biǎo Dòu É yuān* 霜降始知鄒衍屈，雪飛方表竇娥冤 in *KMCP*, p. 20*b*. Except for one character, the couplet is the same as in an earlier lyric (*KMCP*, p. 15*a*; see §890–1).

§1135–6] *Nǐ kàn . . . dào lái: Nǐ hái-er shì zuò lái bù céng zuò lái* 你孩兒是做來不曾做來 in *KMCP*, p. 20*b*.

曾 道 來 不 道 來 則 我

1136

céng dào lái bú dào lái. Zé wǒ

has stated (C), not stated (C). Only my

這 寃 枉 要 忍 耐 如 何

1137

zhè yuān-wang yào rěn-nài, rú-hé

this injustice [even if I] want to-endure, how

耐 我 不 肯 順 他 人 倒

1138

nài? Wǒ bù kěn shùn tā rén, dào

to-endure? I was-not willing to-yield-to other person; instead,

着 我 赴 法 塲 我 不 肯

1139

zháo wǒ fù fǎ-chǎng. Wǒ bù kěn

had me go-to execution-ground. I was-not willing

辱 祖 上 倒 把 我 殘 生

1140

rǔ zǔ-shàng, dào bǎ wǒ cán-shēng

to-disgrace ancestors; instead, (Pr) my rest-of-life

壞

1141

huài.

ruined.'

（ 得 勝 令 ） 呀 今 日 簡 搭

1142

(Dé-shèng lìng) Ȳā, jin-rì-ge dā-

('Victory Song') 'Ya, today leaning

伏 定 攝 魂 臺 一 靈 兒

1143

fú dìng Shè-hún tái, yì líng-er

on Summoning-souls Terrace, whole spirit

怨 哀 哀 父 親 也 你 現

1144

yuàn āi-āi. Fù-qin ye, nǐ xiàn

grievous, sad. Father, ah, you now

How am I to endure this injustice?
I would not yield to another;
Instead, I was sent to the execution ground.
I refused to disgrace my ancestors;
Instead, I lost my life.
(Sings fifth lyric):
Ah! Today I lean on the Summoning-souls Terrace,
A lonely spirit, grievous and sad.
Ah, father, you have the law in your hand

1142] *jīn-rì-ge:* comparable to the modern Northern expression *jīn-er-ge* 今兒個.
1143] *Shè-hún tái: shè-hún* is to summon one's soul either alive or dead (Morohashi v: 13010: 21); *Shè-hún tái* seems to be a place where ghosts may stay.

§1137–8] *yào... nài: Wú biān dà* 無邊大 in *KMCP*, p. 20*b*.
§1142–3] *Yā... Shè-hún tái: Wǒ měi-rì shǒu dìng Wàng-xiāng-tái* 我每日守定望鄉臺 in *KMCP*, p. 20*b*.
§1144–5] *nǐ... xíng-míng shì: nǐ shì jiàn chuī máo kuài* 你勢劍吹毛快 in *KMCP*, p. 20*b*.

掌着刑名事親蒙聖
1145　zhǎng-zhe xíng-míng shì, qin méng shèng
administer (P) legal affairs, personally by sage

主差端詳這文册那
1146　zhǔ chāi. Duān-xiáng zhè wén-cè. Nà
lord sent. Examine-carefully this document. That

斯亂綱常當合敗便
1147　sī luàn gāng-cháng dāng-hé bài. Biàn
fellow violated moral-order, deserves ruin. Even

萬剮了喬才還道報
1148　wàn guǎ-le qiáo-cái, hái dào bào
ten-thousand-times cut (P) evil-person, still say in-avenging

宛讐不暢懷
1149　yuān-chóu bú chàng-huái.
grievances, not satisfied.'

（竇天章做泣科云）哎我那
1150　(Dòu Tiān-zhāng zuò qì kē, yún:) Āi! Wǒ nà
(Tou T'ien-chang performs weeping gesture, says:) 'Alas! My that

屈死的兒則被你痛殺我
1151　qū-sǐ-de ér. Zé bèi nǐ tòng-shā wǒ
wrongly-slain (P) child. Only by you pains-to-death me

也我且問你這楚州三年
1152　ye! Wǒ qiě wèn nǐ zhè Chǔ-zhōu sān nián
(P)! I now ask you: this Ch'u-chou, three years

不雨可真個是爲你來（魂
1153　bù yǔ kě zhēn-ge shì wèi nǐ lai? (Hún
not rain may-be really is because-of you (P)?' (Ghost female-

旦云）是爲你孩兒來（竇天
1154　dàn yún:) Shì wèi nǐ hái-er lai. (Dòu Tiān-
role says:) 'Is because-of your child (P).' (Tou T'ien-

And are sent by the Emperor;
Study this case with care.
That wretch, violating the moral order, deserves ruin;
Even if he is cut into pieces,
My wrongs can never be fully avenged.

TOU (weeps): Ah, my wrongly slain child. For you, I shall die from grief. Let me ask you this: is it really because of you that Ch'u-chou has had no rain for three years?

TOU O'S GHOST: It is because of your child.

1147] *bài*: as *bài lù* 敗露, 'to be ruined by discovery'.
1148] *guǎ*: 'to cut a criminal to pieces', same as *líng-chí* (see n. 1365).
1149] *chàng-huái*: 'expansive feeling', 'cheerful', 'gratified'.

§1145] After *xíng-míng shì*: *jīn-rì-ge* 今日箇 in *KMCP*, p. 20*b*.
§1146] *Duān-xiáng zhè wén-cè*: *shěn-wèn-de míng-bái* 審問的明白 in *KMCP*, p. 20*b*.
§1147] *gāng-cháng*: *rén-lún* 人倫 in *KMCP*, pp. 20*b*–21*a*.
§1148–9] *hái dào...chàng-huái*: *Fù-qin, nǐ jiāng wǒ zhāo-zhuàng-er gǎi jiāng guò-lái* 父親你將我招狀兒改將過來 in *KMCP*, p. 21*a*.
§1152] *Wǒ qiě wèn nǐ*: *Wǒ bú wèn nǐ bié-de* 我不問你別的 in *KMCP*, p. 21*a*.
§1153] *kě zhēn-ge shì wèi nǐ lai*: *kě shì wèi shém-me lái* 可是爲甚麼來 in *KMCP*, p. 21*a*.

277

章 云 ）有 這 等 事 到 來 朝 我

1155   *zhāng yún:) Yǒu zhè-děng shì! Dào lái-zhāo wǒ*
chang says:) 'There-are such things! When-it-gets-to-be to-morrow-morning, I

與 你 做 主 （ 詩 云 ）白 頭 親 苦

1156   *yǔ nǐ zuò zhǔ. (Shī yún:) Bái tóu qin kǔ*
for you make decision.' ([In] verse says:) 'White head parent bitter,

痛 哀 哉 屈 殺 了 你 箇 青 春

1157   *tòng āi-zāi. Qū shā-le nǐ ge qing-chūn*
painful, sad (P). Wrongly killed (P) you (M) young

女 孩 只 恐 怕 天 明 了 你 且

1158   *nǚ-hái. Zhǐ kǒng-pà tiān míng le, nǐ qiě*
girl. Only fear sky is-brightening (P); you temporarily

回 去 到 來 日 我 將 文 卷 改

1159   *huí qù. Dào lái-rì wǒ jiāng wén-juàn gǎi*
return (C). When-it-gets-to-be tomorrow, I (Pr) file change-to

正 明 白 （ 魂 旦 暫 下 竇 天 章

1160   *zhèng míng-bái. (Hún dàn zhàn xià. Dòu Tiān-zhāng*
correct, clear.' (Ghost female-role temporarily exits. Tou T'ien-chang

云 ）呀 天 色 明 了 也 張 千 我

1161   *yún:) Yā, tiān sè míng le ye. Zhāng Qiān, wǒ*
says:) 'Ya, sky color brightens (P) (P). Chang Ch'ien, I

昨 日 看 幾 宗 文 卷 中 間 有

1162   *zuó-rì kàn jǐ zōng wén-juàn; zhōng-jiān yǒu*
yesterday looked-at several (M) files; in-the-midst (L) [of doing it], there-was

一 鬼 魂 來 訴 冤 枉 我 喚 你

1163   *yì guǐ-hún lái sù yuān-wang. Wǒ huàn nǐ*
one ghost came to state grievances. I called you

TOU: That such things could happen! Wait until tomorrow; I shall
act on your behalf. (Recites.)

> *A white-headed father is suffering great pain,*
> *Because you, a young girl, have been wrongly slain.*
> *I am afraid that dawn is breaking, and you had better go.*
> *Tomorrow I shall set right your case and make it plain.*

(Tou O's ghost leaves.)

TOU: Ya! It's dawn. Chang Ch'ien, last night when I was reading
these cases, a ghost came to complain of her grievance. I called you

1157] *qīng-chūn: qīng*, 'green', *chūn*, 'spring': *qīng-chūn*, an idiom for 'youth' or 'young.'

§1155] *Yŏu zhè-dĕng shì:* not in *KMCP*, which has instead, *Yuán-lái shì wèi nǐ lái.*
Bù-yīn wŏ nǚ-er zhè yí jiàn shì, gǎn qǐ yì zhuāng gù-shi. 原來是爲你來不
因我女兒這一件事感起一椿故事 pp. 21*a–b*. Then Dòu Tiān-zhāng
tells the story of the filial daughter-in-law of Dŏng-hăi – the story which
appears in ll. 1193–1202 below; the wording in these two versions is more
or less the same.

§1156] *Shī yún:* not in *KMCP*.

§1158] *Zhǐ kŏng-pà:* not in *KMCP*.

§1160–383] *Hún dàn zhàn xià. . .yuān:* from l. 1160 on, the two texts, *YCH* and
KMCP, differ considerably. Here in *YCH*, the ghost retires at the father's
bidding (l. 1160), and later reappears at court (l. 1233), also at the
father's request, to confront the malefactors. She not only helps Dòu
Tiān-zhāng get the confession from them, she also sings four lyrics
(nos. 6–9) to retell the wrongs she suffered. The second half of this fourth
act consists of a lengthy court scene (ll. 1169–383).

In *KMCP*, the fourth act is much shorter; ll. 1160–336 are absent in
KMCP except for the story of the filial woman of Dŏng-hăi (p. 21*a*).
The ghost, just before she retires, tells her father to punish the guilty,
to take care of Mistress Cài, and to rectify the daughter's record (p. 21*b*).
The ghost never reappears; thus in *KMCP*, there is no elaborate confronta-
tion of the malefactors, and no lengthy court scene. After the ghost dis-
appears, Dòu Tiān-zhāng simply summons the criminals, deals them the
sentences, and promises to rectify the deceased daughter's record and
to offer a Buddhist sacrifice to release her soul from suffering (p. 22*a*).

279

1164 好 幾 次 你 再 也 不 應 直 恁

hǎo jǐ cì, nǐ zài-yě bú yìng. Zhí rèn-

[a] good many times, you (intensifier) did-not respond. Really such

1165 的 好 睡 那 （ 張 千 云 ） 我 小 人

de hǎo shuì na. (Zhāng Qiān yún:) Wǒ xiǎo rén

sound sleep (P).' (Chang Ch'ien says:) 'I insignificant person

1166 兩 個 鼻 子 孔 一 夜 不 曾 閉

liǎng ge bí-zi-kǒng yí yè bù-céng bì.

two (M) nostrils all night never closed.

1167 並 不 聽 見 女 鬼 訴 什 麼 寃

Bìng bù tīng-jiàn nǚ guǐ sù shém-me yuān

Absolutely did-not hear female ghost complain-of any grievance

1168 狀 也 不 曾 聽 見 相 公 呼 喚

zhuàng; yě bù-céng tīng-jiàn xiàng-gong hū-huàn.

case; also never heard sir call [me].'

1169 （ 竇 天 章 做 叱 科 云 ） 呸 今 蚤

(Dòu Tiān-zhāng zuò chì kē, yún:) Tuì! Jīn zǎo

(Tou T'ien-chang performs scolding gesture, says:) 'T'ui! This morning

1170 升 廳 坐 衙 張 千 喝 攛 廂 者

shēng tīng zuò yá. Zhāng Qiān, hē-cuān-xiāng zhe.

[I] ascend hall to-sit-at court. Chang Ch'ien, call-to-chambers (P).'

1171 （ 張 千 做 么 喝 科 云 ） 在 衙 人

(Zhāng Qiān zuò yāo-he kē, yún:) Zài yá rén

(Chang Ch'ien performs calling gesture, says:) 'At courthouse, people,

1172 馬 平 安 擡 書 案 （ 禀 云 ） 州 官

mǎ píng-ān. Tái shū àn. (Bǐng yún:) Zhōu-guān

horses, be-still. Carry writing desk.' (Reporting, says:) 'Magistrate several times, but you did not answer. You really slept well!

CHANG CH'IEN: I never closed my nostrils all night long. However, I did not hear any woman ghost complain of her grievance, nor did I hear your honor call me.

TOU (scolding): Be quiet. The court is to be in session this morning. Call the court to order.

CHANG CH'IEN (speaking aloud): People and horses in this courthouse be still; bring in the desk. (To the Commissioner:) The magistrate presents himself. (The magistrate enters and presents

1166] *bí-zi-kŏng. . . bí:* possibly means 'all night long breathed through the nose: did not snore or sleep soundly'.

1171–2] *Zài yá . . . shū àn:* these words were announced as part of the formality in the opening of a court session. Sometimes only the first phrase *zài yá rén mǎ píng-ān* is used, as in the court scene in *The Butterfly Dream (Hu-tieh Meng* 蝴蝶夢 [*YCH*, no. 37], Act II, opening scene).

Whereas *píng-ān* usually means 'peaceful and well', here it may mean 'be still'.

見（外扮州官入參科張千

1173 jiàn. (Wài bàn zhōu-guān rù cān kē. Zhāng Qiān
presents-himself.' (Wai-role in-make-up-of Magistrate enters,
doing-obeisance gesture. Chang Ch'ien

云）該房吏典見（丑扮吏入

1174 yún:) Gāi fáng lì-diǎn jiàn. (Chǒu bàn lì rù
says:) 'Proper department clerk presents-himself.' (Clown in-
make-up-of clerk enters,

參見科竇天章問云）你這

1175 cān jiàn kē. Dòu Tiān-zhāng wèn yún:) Nǐ zhè
doing-obeisance, presenting-himself gesture. Tou T'ien-chang
asking, says:) 'You this

楚州一郡三年不雨是爲

1176 Chǔ-zhōu yí jùn sān nián bù yǔ, shì wèi-
Ch'u-chou whole prefecture three years not rain, is because-of

着何來（州官云）這個是天

1177 zhe hé lai? (Zhōu-guān yún:) Zhè-ge shì tiān-
what (P)?' (Magistrate says:) 'This is heaven-decreed

道亢旱楚州百姓之灾小

1178 dào kàng hàn, Chǔ-zhōu bǎi-xìng zhī zāi. Xiǎo
severe drought, Ch'u-chou people's (P) disaster. Insignificant

官等不知其罪（竇天章做

1179 guān děng bù zhī qí zuì. (Dòu Tiān-zhāng zuò
officials (Pl) are-not aware-of the wrongs.' (Tou T'ien-chang
acts

怒云）你等不知罪麼那山

1180 nù yún:) Nǐ děng bù zhī zuì ma? Nà Shān-
angry, says:) 'You (Pl) not know wrongs (P)? That Shan-

陽縣有用毒藥謀死公公

1181 yáng xiàn yǒu yòng dú-yào móu sǐ gōng-gong
yang District had using poison to-plot to-murder father-in-law

犯婦竇娥他問斬之時曾

1182 fàn fù Dòu É. Tā wèn-zhǎn zhī shí, céng
criminal woman Tou O. She being-executed (P) time did

282

himself.) The clerk presents himself.

(The clerk enters and presents himself.)

TOU: Why is it that there has been no rain in Ch'u-chou for three years?

MAGISTRATE: This is a drought decreed by Heaven. It is a calamity of the people of Ch'u. We know no guilt.

TOU (angrily): You know no guilt? In the Shan-yang District there was a criminal, Tou O, who poisoned her father-in-law. When she was executed, she made a vow that if she were wrongly accused,

1183　發 願 道 若 是 果 有 冤 枉 着
fā yuàn dào: Ruò-shi guǒ yǒu yuān-wang, zháo
make vows, saying, "If indeed there-was injustice, make

1184　你 楚 州 三 年 不 雨 寸 草 不
nǐ Chǔ-zhōu sān nián bù yǔ, cùn cǎo bù
your Ch'u-chou three years not rain, inch-of grass not

1185　生 可 有 這 件 事 來（州官云）
shēng. Ké yǒu zhè jiàn shì lai? (Zhōu-guān yún:)
grow." May-be there-was this (M) case (P)?' (Magistrate says:)

1186　這 罪 是 前 陞 任 桃 州 守 問
Zhè zuì shì qián shēng-rèn Táo zhōu-shǒu wèn
'This crime was formerly promoted-in-office T'ao Prefect examined/

1187　成 的 現 有 文 卷（竇天章云）
chéng de. Xiàn yǒu wén-juàn. (Dòu Tiān-zhāng yún:)
concluded one. Now there-are documents.' (Tou T'ien-chang says:)

1188　這 等 糊 突 的 官 也 着 他 陞
Zhè děng hú-tu de guān, yě zháo tā shēng
'This manner foolish (P) official, also let him be-promoted

1189　去 你 是 繼 他 任 的 三 年 之
qù! Nǐ shì jì tā rèn de. Sān nián zhī
(C)! You are succeeding-to his office one. Three-years (P)

1190　中 可 曾 祭 這 冤 婦 麼（州官
zhōng, kě céng jì zhè yuān fù ma? (Zhōu-guān
midst (L) may have offered-sacrifice-to this wronged woman (P)?' (Magistrate

1191　云）此 犯 係 十 惡 大 罪 元 不
yún:) Cǐ fàn xì shí è dà zuì, yuán bù
says:) 'This crime belongs-to "ten-evil great crimes"; originally never

1192　曾 有 祠 所 以 不 曾 祭 得（竇
céng yǒu cí, suó-yi bù céng jì-de. (Dòu
has been sacrifice; therefore not have offered-sacrifice.' (Tou

284

there would be no rain in Ch'u-chou for three years, and not an inch of grass would grow on the ground. Is this true or not?

MAGISTRATE: This conviction of the criminal was effected by the former magistrate T'ao who has since been promoted to the position of prefect. We have the documents.

TOU: That such a muddle-headed official should have been promoted! You are his successor. During these three years, have you offered any sacrifice to the wronged woman?

MAGISTRATE: Her crime was one of the ten gravest. No one has ever performed sacrificial services for a person guilty of such a crime; so I have not made sacrificial offerings to her.

天章云）昔日漢朝有一孝

1193   *Tiān-zhāng yún:) Xí rì Hàn cháo yǒu yí xiào*
T'ien-chang says:) 'Former days Han Dynasty had a filial

婦守寡其姑自縊身死其

1194   *fù shǒu guǎ. Qí gū zì yì shēn sǐ. Qí*
woman observing widowhood. Her mother-in-law self hanged,
body-died. Her

姑女告孝婦殺姑東海太

1195   *gū nǚ gào xiào fù shā gū. Dōng-hǎi tài-*
mother-in-law's daughter brought-accusation-that filial woman
murdered mother-in-law. East-Sea prefect

守將孝婦斬了只爲一婦

1196   *shǒu jiāng xiào fù zhǎn-le. Zhǐ wèi yí fù*
(Pr) filial woman executed (P). Only because-of one woman

含寃致令三年不雨後于

1197   *hán yuān, zhì-lìng sān nián bù yǔ. Hòu Yú*
harboring grievance, caused three years not rain. Later Yü

公治獄彷彿見孝婦抱卷

1198   *gōng zhì yù, fǎng-fú jiàn xiào fù bào juàn*
Lord examined prisons, seemed to-see filial woman holding
papers

哭於廳前于公將文卷改

1199   *kū yú tīng qián. Yú gōng jiāng wén-juàn gǎi-*
weeping at hall front (L). Yü Lord (Pr) records rectified.

正親祭孝婦之墓天乃大

1200   *zhèng. Qīn jì xiào fù zhī mù. Tiān nǎi dà*
Personally offered-sacrifice [at] filial woman's (P) grave.
Heaven then greatly

雨今日你楚州大旱豈不

1201   *yǔ. Jīn-rì nǐ Chǔ-zhōu dà hàn. Qǐ-bú*
rained. Today your Ch'u-chou [suffers] severe drought. Isn't-it

正與此事相類張千分付

1202   *zhèng yǔ cǐ shì xiāng lèi? Zhāng Qiān, fēn-fù*
precisely with this affair of-the-same kind? Chang Ch'ien, order

TOU: Formerly in the Han Dynasty there was a widow who showed great filial piety. When her mother-in-law hanged herself, the mother-in-law's daughter brought accusation that this widow was the murderess. The governor of Tung-hai had the woman executed. Because she was wronged, for three years there was no rain in the district. Later, when Lord Yü was reviewing cases of persons confined in the prisons in the area, he seemed to see the widow weeping in front of the courthouse, with papers in her hands. After Lord Yü rectified her court records and personally offered sacrifice to her in front of her grave, rain poured down. Now your Ch'u-chou is suffering severe drought. Isn't the situation comparable to the Han case? Chang Ch'ien, ask the Department to sign a warrant and go

§1193–202] *Xí rì . . . xiāng lèi:* this story of the filial woman was told earlier in *KMCP*, pp. 21*a–b* (see §1155); cf. ll. 1377–81.

該 房 僉 牌 下 山 陽 縣 着 拘

1203   *gāi fáng qiān pái xià Shān-yáng xiàn, zháo jū*
proper department sign warrant, go-down-to Shan-yang District,
have [them] arrest

張 驢 兒 賽 盧 醫 蔡 婆 婆 一

1204   *Zhāng Lǘ-er, Sài Lú-yi, Cài Pó-po yi-*
Chang Donkey, "Rival Lu-Doctor", Ts'ai Mistress – one

起 人 犯 火 速 解 審 毋 得 違

1205   *qǐ rén-fàn. Huǒ-sù jiè shěn, wù-dé wéi-*
group (M) [of] criminals. Fire-quick, arrest for-trial. Do-not
disobey/

惧 片 刻 者 （ 張 千 云 ） 理 會 得

1206   *wù piàn-kè zhe. (Zhāng Qiān yún:) Lǐ-huì-de.*
neglect a-single-moment (P).' (Chang Ch'ien says:) 'Understand.'

（ 下 丑 扮 解 子 押 張 驢 兒 蔡

1207   *(Xià. Chǒu bàn jiè-zi yā Zhāng Lǘ-ér, Cài*
(Exit. Clown in-make-up-of guard escorting Chang Donkey,
Ts'ai

婆 婆 同 張 千 上 禀 云 ） 山 陽

1208   *Pó-po tóng Zhāng Qiān shàng. Bǐng yún:) Shān-yáng*
mistress, with Chang Ch'ien, enters. Reporting, says:) 'Shan-
yang

縣 解 到 審 犯 聽 點 （ 竇 天 章

1209   *xiàn jiè dào shěn-fàn tīng diǎn. (Dòu Tiān-zhāng*
District has-brought-under-guard here criminals waiting-for
roll-call.' (Tou T'ien-chang

云 ） 張 驢 兒 （ 張 驢 兒 云 ） 有 （ 竇

1210   *yún:) Zhāng Lǘ-er. (Zhāng Lǘ-er yún:) Yǒu. (Dòu*
says:) 'Chang Donkey.' (Chang Donkey says:) 'Present.' (Tou

天 章 云 ） 蔡 婆 婆 （ 蔡 婆 婆 云 ）

1211   *Tiān-zhāng yún:) Cài Pó-po. (Cài Pó-po yún:)*
T'ien-chang says:) 'Ts'ai P'o-p'o.' (Ts'ai P'o-p'o says:)

to the Shan-yang District to arrest criminals Donkey Chang, Sai Lu-yi, and Mistress Ts'ai. Quickly bring them here for questioning. Do not delay.

CHANG CH'IEN: Yes, your honor. (Leaves.)

(Enter the guard, escorting prisoners Donkey Chang and Mistress Ts'ai, accompanied by Chang Ch'ien.)

OFFICER: The Shan-yang District has arrested and brought here the criminals, waiting to be called.

TOU: Donkey Chang.

DONKEY CHANG: Present.

TOU: Mistress Ts'ai.

1206] *zhe:* a final particle (see pp. 17).

有（竇天章云）怎麼賽盧醫

1212 yǒu. (Dòu Tiān-zhāng yún:) Zěm-ma Sài Lú-yi

'Present.' (Tou T'ien-chang says:) 'Why "Rival Lu-Doctor" [who]

是緊要人犯不到（解子云）

1213 shì jǐn-yào rén-fàn bú dào? (Jiè-zi yún:)

is urgently-wanted criminal is-not present?' (Guard says:)

賽盧醫三年前在逃一面

1214 Sài Lú-yi sān nián qián zài-táo. Yí miàn

'"Rival Lu-Doctor" three years ago fled. One side

着廣捕批緝拿去了待獲

1215 zháo guǎng bǔ-pi qì-ná qù le. Dài huò

has-requested widely to-search-with-court-order to-arrest (C) (P). Wait-till [he is] taken

日解審（竇天章云）張驢兒

1216 rì jiè shěn. (Dòu Tiān-zhāng yún:) Zhāng Lǘ-er,

day, will-be brought for-trial.' (Tou T'ien-chang says:) 'Chang Donkey,

那蔡婆婆是你的後母麼

1217 nà Cài Pó-po shì nǐ-de hòu-mǔ ma?

that Ts'ai P'o-p'o is your step-mother (P)?'

（張驢兒云）母親好冒認的

1218 (Zhāng Lǘ-er yún:) Mǔ-qin hǎo mào rèn de?

(Chang Donkey says:) 'Mother can-be falsely claimed (P)?

委實是（竇天章云）這藥死

1219 Wěi-shí shì. (Dòu Tiān-zhāng yún:) Zhè yào-sǐ

Truly is!' (Tou T'ien-chang says:) '[As to] this poisoned-to-death

你父親的毒藥卷上不見

1220 nǐ fù-qin de dú-yào, juàn-shang bú jiàn

your-father (P) poison, on-the-record (L) [one] does-not see [that]

290

TS'AI: Present.

TOU: How is it that Sai Lu-yi, who is a key criminal, is not here?

OFFICER: Sai Lu-yi fled three years ago. An order has been issued to search widely for him and to arrest him. As soon as he is taken, he will be brought here for trial.

TOU: Donkey Chang, is Mistress Ts'ai your stepmother?

DONKEY CHANG: How can a mother be falsely claimed? She is truly my stepmother.

TOU: In the court file there is no mention of the person who mixed

1218] *hǎo:* here is used as *zěm-me hǎo* 怎 麼 好, 'how can?'

有合藥的人是那個的毒

1221 *yǒu huò yào de rén. Shì nǎ-ge-de dú-*
there-is mixed poison (P) person. Was whose (M) (P) poison?'

藥（張驢兒云）是竇娥自合

1222 *yào? (Zhāng Lǘ-er yún:) Shì Dòu É zì huò-*
(Chang Donkey says:) 'Was Tou O herself mixed

就的毒藥（竇天章云）這毒

1223 *jiù de dú-yào. (Dòu Tiān-zhāng yún:) Zhè dú-*
(P) poison.' (Tou T'ien-chang says:) 'This poison

藥必有一箇賣藥的醫舖

1224 *yào bì yǒu yí ge mài yào de yī pù.*
must have a (M) selling drug (P) doctor's shop.

想竇娥是箇少年寡婦那

1225 *Xiǎng Dòu É shì ge shào-nián guǎ-fù, nǎ-*
Consider Tou O was [a] (M) young widow; where

裏討這藥來張驢兒敢是

1226 *lǐ tǎo zhè yào lái? Zhāng Lǘ-er, gǎn shì*
got this drug (C)? Chang Donkey, could-it be

你合的毒藥麼（張驢兒云）

1227 *nǐ huò de dú-yào ma? (Zhāng Lǘ-er yún:)*
you mixed (P) poison (P)?' (Chang Donkey says:)

若是小人合的毒藥不藥

1228 *Ruò-shi xiǎo rén hùo de dú-yào, bú yào*
'If insignificant person mixed (P) poison, not poisoned

別人倒藥死自家老子（竇

1229 *bié rén, dào yào-sǐ zì-jiā lǎo-zi? (Dòu*
other person; instead, would-poison-to-death own father?' (Tou

天章云）我那屈死的兒嚛

1230 *Tiān-zhāng yún:) Wǒ nà qū-sǐ de ér luo,*
T'ien-chang says:) 'My that wrongly-slain (P) child (P),

這一節是緊要公案你不

1231 *zhè yì jié shì jǐn-yào gōng àn. Nǐ bú*
this one section (M) is important court case. You not

the poison which killed your father. Whose poison was it?

DONKEY CHANG: It was the poison mixed by Tou O herself.

TOU: There must be an apothecary shop which sold this poison. Tou O was a young widow; where could she have gotten it? Donkey Chang, could it be that you mixed the poison?

DONKEY CHANG: If I had mixed the poison, why didn't I poison someone else instead of my own father?

TOU: My wrongly slain child, this is an important court case. If you

自來折辯怎得一箇明白

1232　*zì lái zhé-biàn, zěn dé yí ge míng-bái?*
yourself come to-argue, how to-get a (M) clearing?

你如今寃魂却在那裏（魂

1233　*Nǐ rú-jīn yuān hún què zài nǎ-lǐ? (Hún-*
You now wronged ghost yet are-at where (L)?' (Ghost

旦上云）張驢兒這藥不是

1234　*dàn shàng. Yún:) Zhāng Lǘ-er, zhè yào bú shì*
female-role enters. Says:) 'Chang Donkey, this drug not was

你合的是那個合的（張驢

1235　*nǐ-huò-de, shì nǎ-ge-huò-de? (Zhāng Lǘ-*
you-mixed-one, was who-(M)-mixed-one?' (Chang Donkey

兒做怕科云）有鬼有鬼撮

1236　*er zuò pà kē, yún:) Yǒu guǐ, yǒu guǐ. Cuō*
performs terrified gesture, says:) 'There-is ghost, there-is ghost.
Take-a-little

鹽入水太上老君急急如

1237　*yán rù shuǐ. Tài shàng lǎo jūn, jí jí rú*
salt [and put it] into water. "Supremely high old lord, quickly,
quickly, as

律令勒（魂旦云）張驢兒你

1238　*lǜ-lìng. Chì. (Hún dàn yún:) Zhāng Lǘ-er, nǐ*
official-order. Decree".' (Ghost female-role says:) 'Chang
Donkey, you

當日下毒藥在羊腊兒湯

1239　*dāng rì xià dú-yào zài yáng dǔ-er tāng*
that day put poison into mutton tripe soup

裏本意藥死俺婆婆要逼

1240　*lǐ, běn yì yào-sǐ ǎn pó-po, yào bī-*
(L), original intention [was] to-poison-to-death my mother-in-
law, wanting to-force

勒我做渾家不想俺婆婆

1241　*lè wǒ zuò hún-jiā. Bù-xiǎng ǎn pó-po*
me to-be wife. Unexpectedly, my mother-in-law

do not come to defend yourself, how can things be made clear? Where is your wronged ghost anyway?

(Enter the ghost of Tou O.)

TOU O'S GHOST: Donkey Chang, if you did not mix the poison, who mixed it?

DONKEY CHANG (terrified): There is a ghost! There is a ghost! Put salt in the water. 'God on high! Come quickly, as commanded. An Imperial Order'.

TOU O'S GHOST: Donkey Chang, when you put the poison in the mutton tripe soup, you planned to kill my mother-in-law and force me to be your wife. Unexpectedly my mother-in-law did not

1236–8] *Yŏu guǐ... Chì:* for a comparable later talisman exorcising demons, see Henri Doré, *Recherches sur les Superstitions en Chine*, part 1, vol. 1, no. 2, Shanghai, 1911, p. 152 and its facing page.

1237] *Tài shàng lǎo jūn:* the Taoist god, leader of the Taoist immortals.

1237–8] *rú lǜ-lìng:* this phrase, used at the end of official documents during the Han dynasty, was adopted by the Taoists in their charms.

1242　不吃讓與你父親吃被藥
　　　bù chī, ràng yǔ nǐ fù-qīn chī. Bèi yào-
　　　did-not eat [it]; gave [it] to your father to-eat. Was poisoned-

1243　死了你今日還敢賴哩（唱）
　　　sǐ le. Nǐ jīn-rì hái gǎn lài li! (Chàng:)
　　　to-death (P). You today still dare to-deny (P)?' (Sings:)

1244　（川撥棹）猛見了你這
　　　(Chuān bō zhuō) Měng jiàn-le nǐ zhè
　　　('Stream Stirs Oar') 'Suddenly seeing (P) you this

1245　喫敲材我只問你這
　　　chī qiāo cái, wǒ zhǐ wèn nǐ zhè
　　　deserve-to-suffer beating material, I only ask you this

1246　毒藥從何處來你本
　　　dú-yào cóng hé chù lái? Nǐ běn
　　　poison from what place came? You originally

1247　意待闇裏栽排要逼
　　　yì dài àn-lǐ zāi-pái, yào bī-
　　　intend to-wait secretly (L) to-plot/arrange, wanting to-
　　　force

1248　勒我和諧倒把你親
　　　lè wǒ hé-xié, dào bá nǐ qīn-
　　　me to-be-harmonious; however (Pr) your own

1249　爺毒害怎教咱替你
　　　yé dú-hài. Zěn jiào zá tì nǐ
　　　father poisoned/harmed. How asked me for you

1250　躭罪責
　　　dān zuì-zé?
　　　to-bear guilt/blame?'

1251　（魂旦做打張驢兒科張驢
　　　(Hún dàn zuò dǎ Zhāng Lǘ-er kē. Zhāng Lǘ-
　　　(Ghost female-role performs beating Chang Donkey gesture.
　　　Chang Donkey

296

eat the soup and gave it to your father. He then died of poisoning.
How dare you deny this today?

(Sings sixth lyric):

Suddenly I see you, cursed knave.

I only want to know where the poison came from.

Your original scheme was to secretly arrange things, forcing me to marry;

However, you poisoned your own father.

How could you have let me shoulder your guilt?

(Tou O's ghost strikes Donkey Chang.)

1248] *hé-xié* (*or hé-xiái*): here refers to 'conjugal harmony'; *hé-xié* is modern pronunciation; for rhyme it reads *hé-xiái*.

1250] *zui-zé* (*or zui-zái*): *zé* is modern pronunciation; for rhyme it reads *zái*.

297

兒 做 避 科 云 ） 太 上 老 君 急

1252 *er zuò bì kē. Yún:) Tài shàng lǎo jūn, jí*
performs dodging gesture. Says:) ' "Supremely high old lord, quickly

急 如 律 令 勒 大 人 說 這 毒

1253 *jí rú lü-lìng. Chì. Dà rén shuō zhè dú-*
quickly, as official-order. Decree." Great Person said this poison

藥 必 有 箇 賣 藥 的 醫 舖 若

1254 *yào bì yǒu ge mài yào de yi pù. Ruò*
must-have had [a] (M) selling drug (P) doctor's shop. If

尋 得 這 賣 藥 的 人 來 和 小

1255 *xún-dé zhè mài yào de rén lái hé xiǎo*
can-find this selling drug (P) person to-come with insignificant

人 折 對 死 也 無 詞 （ 丑 扮 解

1256 *rén zhé-duì, sǐ yě wú cí. (Chǒu bàn jiè-*
person confront, to-die even have-no words.' (Clown in-make-up-of guard

子 解 賽 盧 醫 上 云 ） 山 陽 縣

1257 *zi jiè Sài Lú-yi shàng. Yún:) Shān-yáng xiàn*
escorting 'Rival Lu-Doctor' enters. Says:) 'Shan-yang District

續 解 到 犯 人 一 名 賽 盧 醫

1258 *xù jiè dào fàn-rén yì míng Sài Lú-yi.*
continues bringing-under-guard here criminal one (M) "Rival Lu Doctor".'

（ 張 千 喝 云 ） 當 面 （ 竇 天 章 云 ）

1259 *(Zhāng Qiān hē yún:) Dāng-miàn! (Dòu Tiān-zhāng yún:)*
(Chang Ch'ien shouts, saying:) 'Face-front.' (Tou T'ien-chang says:)

你 三 年 前 要 勒 死 蔡 婆 婆

1260 *Nǐ sān nián qián yào lēi-sǐ Cài Pó-po,*
'You three years ago wanted to-strangle-to-death Ts'ai *P'o-p'o*

賴 他 銀 子 這 事 怎 麼 說 （ 賽

1261 *lài tā yín-zi. Zhè shì zěm-me shuō? (Sài*
to-deny her silver. This thing how to-explain?' ('Rival

298

DONKEY CHANG (dodging): 'God on high! Come quickly, as commanded. An Imperial order.' Your honor has just said that there must have been a store which sold the poison. If your honor can find the seller to confront me, I shall die without further words. (Enter the clown as guard, escorting Sai Lu-yi.)

OFFICER: The Shan-yang District has brought here under guard another criminal, Sai Lu-yi.

CHANG CH'IEN (calls): Face His Honor!

TOU: Three years ago you wanted to strangle Mistress Ts'ai to escape a debt. How are you going to explain this?

1256] *zhé-duì*: 'to argue face to face', 'to argue in person'.

1259] *Dāng-miàn*: when a criminal is brought to court, the court attendants shout at him, *Dāng miàn!* ('Face [His Honor]!'), and the criminal kneels in front of the magistrate; later it becomes the substitute for 'kneel' (see Chu Chü-i, p. 263).

盧醫叩頭科云）小的要賴

1262   *Lú-yi kòu-tóu kē. Yún:) Xiǎo de yào lài*
Lu-Doctor' kowtowing gesture, says:) 'Insignificant one wanting
to-deny

蔡婆婆銀子的情是有的

1263   *Cài pó-po yín-zi de qíng shì yǒu de.*
Ts'ai P'o-p'o's silver (P) affair indeed did-happen (P).

當被兩個漢子救了那婆

1264   *Dāng bèi liǎng ge hàn-zi jiù-le, nà pó-*
Same [time] by two (M) men rescued (P); that old-woman

婆並不曾死（竇天章云）這

1265   *po bìng bù-céng sǐ. (Dòu Tiān-zhāng yún:) Zhè*
however did-not die.' (Tou T'ien-chang says:) 'These

兩箇漢子你認的他叫做

1266   *liǎng ge hàn-zi, nǐ rèn-de tā? Jiào-zuò*
two (M) men, [do] you recognize them? Are-called

什麼名姓（賽盧醫云）小的

1267   *shém-me míng-xìng? (Sài Lú-yi yún:) Xiǎo de*
what given-names, surnames?' ('Rival Lu-Doctor' says:)
'Insignificant one

認便認得慌忙之際可不

1268   *rèn biàn rèn-de. Huāng-máng zhi jì, kě bù*
[as to] recognizing [them], then able-to-recognize. Excited (P)
moment, however not

曾問的他名姓（竇天章云）

1269   *céng wèn-de tā míng xìng. (Dòu Tiān-zhāng yún:)*
have asked their given-names, surnames.' (Tou T'ien-chang
says:)

現有一個在階下你去認

1270   *Xiàn yǒu yí ge zài jiē xià. Nǐ qù rèn*
'Now there-is one (M) at stairs below (L). You go to-identify

DOCTOR LU (kowtows): It is true that I attempted to escape the debt that I owed Mistress Ts'ai, but two men rescued the old woman; she did not die.

TOU: As to these two men, could you recognize them? What are their names?

DOCTOR LU: I would recognize them all right. But in that moment of excitement, I did not ask their names.

TOU: There is one at the foot of the stairs. Go and identify him.

1264] *Dāng:* may be an abbreviation of *dāng shí* 當時, 'at the same time', or *dāng chǎng* 當場, 'at the same place'.

1266] The punctuation mark after *tā* may be omitted; in that case, *tā* becomes the subject of the following clause. Either reading is acceptable.

來（賽盧醫做下認科云）這
1271 *lai. (Sài Lú-yī zuò xià rèn kē, yún:) Zhè*
(P).' ('Rival Lu-Doctor' performs going-down identifying gesture, says:) 'This

個是蔡婆婆（指張驢兒云）
1272 *ge shì Cài Pó-po. (Zhǐ Zhāng Lǘ-er yún:)*
(M) is Ts'ai P'o-p'o.' (Pointing-at Chang Donkey, says:)

想必這毒藥事發了（上云）
1273 *Xiǎng bì zhè dú-yào shì fā-le. (Shàng yún:)*
'[I] think [it] must-be this poison case has-been-discovered (P).' (To-above, says:)

是這一個容小的訴稟當
1274 *Shì zhè yí ge. Róng xiǎo de sù-bǐng: Dāng*
'Is this one (M). Allow insignificant one to-respectfully-report: The-same

日要勒死蔡婆婆時正遇
1275 *rì yào lēi-sǐ Cài Pó-po shí, zhèng yù-*
day wanting to-strangle-to-death Ts'ai P'o-po time, just encountered

見他爺兒兩個救了那婆
1276 *jiàn tā yé ér liǎng ge, jiù-le nà pó-*
them father son two (M), saved (P) that old-woman

婆去過得幾日他到小的
1277 *po qù. Guò-de jǐ rì, tā dào xiǎo de*
(C). Passed (P) several days, he came to insignificant one's

舖中討服毒藥小的是念
1278 *pù zhōng, tǎo fù dú-yào. Xiǎo de shì niàn*
store (L) to-demand dose-of poison. Insignificant one is chanting

佛吃齋人不敢做昧心的
1279 *fó chī zhāi rén, bù gǎn zuò mèi xīn de*
Buddha's-name eating vegetarian-food person, not dare to-do suppressing conscience (P)

302

(Sai Lu-yi goes down to identify.)

DOCTOR LU: This is Mistress Ts'ai. (Pointing at Donkey Chang, he says:) I think it must be that the poison case has been discovered. (Speaks to the official.) It is this one. Let me respectfully report to your honor the story. That day when I was going to strangle Mistress Ts'ai, those two, father and son, came upon us and rescued the old woman. A few days later, he came to my store asking for a dose of poison. I am one who is devoted to reciting Buddha's name and who observes a vegetarian diet; I did not dare to do anything against my conscience. I said to him that we only had legal medicine

1278–9] *niàn fó chī zhāi:* comparable to the Roman Catholic piety expressed in saying the rosary and not eating meat on Fridays.

事 說 道 舖 中 只 有 官 料 藥
1280   *shì. Shuō-dào: Pù zhōng zhǐ yǒu guān-liào yào;*
things. Said: "Store (L) only has officially-sanctioned-in-
gredient drugs;

並 無 什 麼 毒 藥 他 就 睜 着
1281   *bìng wú shém-me dú-yào. Tā jiù zhēng-zhe*
definitely, there-is-no whatever poison." He then opening-wide
(P)

眼 道 你 昨 日 在 郊 外 要 勒
1282   *yǎn dào: Ní zuó-rì zài jiāo-wài yào lēi-*
[his] eyes, said: "You yesterday at countryside (L) wanted to-
strangle-

死 蔡 婆 婆 我 拖 你 見 官 去
1283   *sǐ Cài Pó-po. Wǒ tuō nǐ jiàn guān qù.*
to-death Ts'ai P'o-p'o. I drag you to-see official (C)."

小 的 一 生 最 怕 的 是 見 官
1284   *Xiǎo de yì shēng zuì-pà-de shì jiàn guān;*
Insignificant one whole life what-is-dreaded-most is seeing
official;

只 得 將 一 服 毒 藥 與 了 他
1285   *zhǐ dè jiāng yí fù dú-yào yǔ le tā*
only could (Pr) one dose-of poison, give (P) him

去 小 的 見 他 生 相 是 個 惡
1286   *qu. Xiǎo de jiàn tā shēng xiàng shì ge è*
(C). Insignificant one saw his natural appearance was an evil

的 一 定 拿 這 藥 去 藥 死 了
1287   *de; yí-dìng ná zhè yào qù yào-sǐ le*
one; certainly would-take this drug [and] go to-poison-to-death
(P)

人 久 後 敗 露 必 然 連 累 小
1288   *rén. Jiu hòu bài-lù, bì-rán lián-lèi xiǎo*
people. Long afterward discovered, must involve insignificant

的 一 向 逃 在 涿 州 地 方 賣
1289   *de, yí-xiàng táo zài Zhuō-zhōu dì-fang mài*
one; for-sometime-now, [I] have-fled to Cho-chou area to-sell

304

in the store; we did not have any poison. He opened his eyes wide and said, 'Yesterday in the country you wanted to strangle Mistress Ts'ai. I shall drag you to see the magistrate.' All my life what I have dreaded the most is seeing an official. There was nothing I could do but give him the poison. I saw that he had an evil look and surely would use the poison to kill someone. For fear that later the murder would be exposed and I would be involved, I fled to the Cho-chou area, where I sold rat poison. It is true that recently I

些 老 鼠 藥 剛 剛 是 老 鼠 被

1290　*xie lǎo-shǔ-yào. Gāng-gāng shì lǎo-shǔ bèi*

　　　a-little rat-poison. Just-recently, it-is-true rats were

藥 殺 了 好 幾 個 藥 死 人 的

1291　*yào-shā le hǎo jǐ gè; yào sǐ-rén de*

　　　poisoned-to-death (P) [a] good many (M); poisoning-to-death

　　　people (P)

藥 其 實 再 也 不 曾 合 （ 魂 旦

1292　*yào qí-shí zài-yě bù céng huò. (Hún dàn*

　　　drugs truly (intensifier) not have mixed.' (Ghost female-role

唱 ）

1293　*chàng:)*

　　　sings:)

（ 七 弟 兄 ） 你 只 為 賴 財

1294　*(Qī dì-xiong) Nǐ zhǐ wèi lài cái*

　　　('Seven Brothers') 'You merely for denying money

放 乖 要 當 災

1295　*fàng-guāi yào dāng zāi.*

　　　indulged-in-deception, should suffer disaster.'

（ 帶 云 ） 這 毒 藥 呵 （ 唱 ）

1296　*(Dài-yún:) Zhè dú-yào he (Chàng:)*

　　　(Speaks:) 'This poison (P)' (sings:)

原 來 是 你 賽 盧 醫 出

1297　*yuán-lái shì nǐ Sài Lú-yī chū-*

　　　'after-all was you, "Rival Lu-Doctor" sold,

賣 張 驢 兒 買 沒 來 由

1298　*mài Zhāng Lǘ-er mǎi. Méi lái-yóu*

　　　Chang Donkey bought. [For] no reason,

填 做 我 犯 由 牌 到 今

1299　*tián zuò wǒ fàn yóu pái. Dào jīn-*

　　　filled-in as my "criminal cause plaque". Comes today,

poisoned quite a few rats, but in all truth, I have never even once mixed poison for killing people.

TOU O'S GHOST (Sings seventh lyric):

> *Merely to escape a debt, you employed deception;*
> *You deserve to be punished.*

(Speaks:) Oh, this poison! (Sings.)

> *It was sold by Sai Lu-yi and bought by Donkey Chang.*
> *For no reason at all,*
> *They wrote the crime on my criminal plaque.*
> *Now the judge is gone, only the courthouse remains.*

1296] *Dài-yún:* a technical term in Yüan drama indicating the insertion of a brief prose passage in the midst of a lyric (cf. l. 1354); when the prose passage is not short, it is usually introduced by *yún* only (see ll. 1344–9).

1299] *fàn yóu pái:* a plaque on which is stated the criminal charges (Morohashi, VII: 20238: 7)

§1299–300] *Dào jīn-rì . . . zài:* not in *KMCP*.

日官去衙門在

1300   *rì guān qù yá-men zài.*
        officials are-gone, courthouse remains.'

（竇天章云）帶那蔡婆婆上

1301   *(Dòu Tiān-zhāng yún:) Dài nà Cài Pó-po shàng*
        (Tou T'ien-chang, says:) 'Bring that Ts'ai P'o-p'o up

來我看你也六十外人了

1302   *lai. Wǒ kàn nǐ yě liù-shí-wài rén le;*
        (C). I see you also sixty-[years]-beyond person (P);

家中又是有錢鈔的如何

1303   *jiā zhōng yòu shì yǒu qián-chāo de. Rú-hé*
        family (L) moreover is having money one. Why

又嫁了老張做出這等事

1304   *yòu jià-le Lǎo Zhāng, zuò-chū zhè děng shì*
        again married (P) Old Chang, did this kind thing

來（蔡婆婆云）老婦人因為

1305   *lai? (Cài Pó-po yún:) Lǎo fù-ren yīn-wèi*
        (C)?' (Ts'ai P'o-p'o says:) 'Old woman because

他爺兒兩個救了我的性

1306   *tā yé ér liǎng ge jiù-le wǒ-de xìng-*
        they father son two (M) saved (P) my (P) life,

命收留他在家養膳過世

1307   *mìng, shōu-liú tā zài jiā yǎng shàn guò shì.*
        kept them at home to-care to-feed [till] pass-out-of the-world.

那張驢兒常說要將他老

1308   *Nà Zhāng Lǘ-er cháng shuō yào jiāng tā lǎo-*
        That Chang Donkey often said [that I] should (Pr) his old-

子接腳進來老婦人並不

1309   *zi jiē-jiǎo jìn-lai. Lǎo fù-ren bìng bù*
        man as-second-husband take in. Old woman absolutely not

TOU: Bring Mistress Ts'ai up here. I see that you are over sixty years of age; your family is quite well off. How is it that you were married to Old Chang and were involved in all this?

TS'AI: Because the two of them, father and son, saved my life, I took them home to provide them with food and lodging for life. Donkey Chang often suggested that I marry his father, but I never

曾許他（竇天章云）這等說
1310　céng xǔ tā. (Dòu Tiān-zhāng yún:) Zhè děng shuō,
　　　had promised him.' (Tou T'ien-chang says:) 'This way speaking,

你那媳婦就不該認做藥
1311　nǐ nà xí-fu jiù bù gāi rèn-zuò yào-
　　　your that daughter-in-law then not should confess poisoning-

死公公了（魂旦云）當日問
1312　sǐ gōng-gong le. (Hún dàn yún:) Dāng rì wèn-
　　　to-death father-in-law (P)!' (Ghost female-role says:) 'The-
　　　same day examining

官要打俺婆婆我怕他年
1313　guān yào dǎ ǎn pó-po, wǒ pà tā nián
　　　official wanted to-beat my mother-in-law, I feared she in-age

老受刑不起因此喒認做
1314　lǎo shòu xíng bù-qǐ; yīn-cǐ zán rèn-zuò
　　　old, suffer penalty not-able; because-of-this, I confessed-to

藥死公公委實是屈招箇
1315　yào-sǐ gōng-gong. Wěi-shí shì qū-zhāo ge.
　　　poisoning-to-death father-in-law. Truly was forced-confession
　　　(P).'

（唱）
1316　(Chàng:)
　　　(Sings:)

（梅花酒）你道是咱不
1317　(Méi huā jiǔ) Nǐ dào shì zá bù-
　　　('Plum Blossom Wine') 'You say it-is [that] I not

該這招狀供寫的明
1318　gāi zhè zhāo-zhuàng gòng-xiě de míng
　　　should this confession-form, have-written (P) clearly.

白本一點孝順的心
1319　bai. Běn yì diǎn xiào-shùn de xīn-
　　　Originally a little filial-piety (P) feeling;

310

consented to it.

TOU: In that case, your daughter-in-law should not have confessed to poisoning her father-in-law.

TOU O'S GHOST: At the time the judge wanted to beat my mother-in-law. I was afraid that she was too old to stand torture, so I confessed to poisoning my father-in-law. It was truly a false confession made under pressure.

(Sings eighth lyric):

You say that I should not have signed the confession.
It all started with my feeling of filial piety,

懐倒做了惹禍的胚

1320   *huái; dào zuò-le rě huò de pēi*
however, became (P) provoking trouble (P) embryo.

胎我只道官吏每還

1321   *tāi. Wǒ zhǐ dào guān-lì-měi hái*
I only was-saying officials (Pl) yet

覆勘怎將咱屈斬首

1322   *fù-kàn. Zěn jiāng zá qū zhǎn shǒu*
would-re-examine. How (Pr) me unjustly cut-off head

在長街第一要素旗

1323   *zài cháng jiē? Dì-yī yào sù qí*
at long street? Number-one, wanted [on] white flag

鎗鮮血灑第二要三

1324   *qiāng xiān xuě sǎ, dì-èr yào sān*
staff, fresh blood shed; number-two, wanted three

尺雪將死屍埋第三

1325   *chǐ xuě jiāng sǐ shī mái; dì-sān*
feet snow (Pr) dead corpse bury; number-three,

要三年旱示天灾咱

1326   *yào sān-nián hàn shì tiān zāi. Zá*
wanted three-year drought to-show heaven [decreed] calamity. My

誓願委實大

1327   *shì-yuàn wěi-shí dà.*
vows truly were-comprehensive.'

（收江南）呀這的是衙

1328   *(Shōu jiāng nán) Yā, zhè dí shì yá-*
('Recovering River's South') 'Ya, this truly is courthouses

門從古向南開就中

1329   *men cóng gǔ xiàng nán kāi. Jiù-zhōng*
since of-old toward south open. Therein

Which, however, became the root of all my troubles.
I thought the officials would re-examine the case;
How could I know they would wrongly execute me in the street?
First, I vowed my blood would stain the white silk flying on the flagpole;
Second, I vowed that three feet of snow would cover my corpse;
Third, I vowed a three-years drought would visit as a divine punishment.
My vows were indeed comprehensive.

(Sings ninth lyric):

Ah, it is true that from olden times, courthouses have faced the south,

1323] *jiē* (*or jiái*): *jiē* is modern pronunciation; for rhyme it reads *jiái*.
1324] *să* (*or săi*): *să* is modern pronunciation; for rhyme it reads *săi*.
1328] *dí shì*: comparable to *dí què shì* 的確是 'indeed it is' (see Chang Hsiang, pp. 297-8).
1328–30] There is a Chinese jingle reflecting the people's cynical attitude toward the court:
> *Yá-men kŏu xiàng nán kāi*; 衙門口向南開;
> *Yŏu lĭ wú qíng ná qián lái.* 有理無情拿錢來
> Courthouses open to the south,
> Whether you are right or wrong,
> Just bring the money along!

無個不宛哉痛殺我

1330 　wú ge bù yuān zāi. Tòng-shā wǒ
no one is-not wronged (P). Pains-to-death my

嬌姿弱體閉泉臺蚤

1331 　jiāo zī ruò tǐ bì quán tái, zǎo
frail physique, weak body, shut-inside spring terrace
already

三年以外則落的悠

1332 　sān-nián-yǐ-wài. Zé luò-de yōu-
over-three-years (L). Only am-reduced-to-such-a-state-
that [my] long-lasting

悠流恨似長淮

1333 　yōu liú hèn sì cháng Huái.
flowing regret is-like long Huai.'

（竇天章云）端雲兒也你這

1334 　(Dòu Tiān-zhāng yún:) Duān-yún ér ye, nǐ zhè
(Tou T'ien-chang says:) 'Tuan-yün child (P), your this

冤枉我已盡知你且回去

1335 　yuān-wang, wǒ yǐ jìn zhi. Nǐ qiě huí-qù.
grievance I already completely know. You for-now return (C).

待我將這一起人犯并原

1336 　Dài wǒ jiāng zhè yì qǐ rén-fàn bìng yuán
Wait-till I (Pr) this one group (M) [of] criminals and original

問官吏另行定罪改日做

1337 　wèn guān-lì, lìng xíng dìng-zuì, gǎi rì zuò
examining official/clerks, separately pass sentences; another
day conduct

個水陸道塲超度你生天

1338 　ge shuǐ lù dào-chǎng, chāo-dù nǐ shēng tiān
(M) water land Buddhist-sacrifice-service to-release you to-
ascend heaven,

None inside has not suffered injustice.
It pains me that for over three years,
My fragile body has been locked in the nether world.
All I have left is my deep sorrow flowing on like the long Huai River.

TOU: Tuan-yün, my child, I am fully aware of the injustice you have suffered. Now you had better return. After I sentence these criminals and the officials who originally handled your case, I shall offer a Buddhist sacrifice to release your soul from suffering and enable you to ascend to Heaven.

1331] *quán tái*: 'spring terrace' – a euphemism for 'grave' (cf. *jiŭ-quán* in ll. 1347–8).
1338] *shuĭ lù dào-chăng*: Buddhist ceremony for offering sacrifice to the spirits of creatures on water and on land.
   shēng: as *shēng* 升, 'to ascend'.

§1337-9] *găi ri. . . biàn liăo*: a comparable statement occurs at the end of the *KMCP* text: *zuò yí ge shuĭ lù dà jiāo chāo-dù wǒ nǚ-er shēng tiān* 做 一 箇 水 陸 大 醮 超 度 我 女 兒 生 天 (p. 22a; cf. §1160–383).

315

便了（魂旦拜科唱）

1339   biàn liǎo. (Hún dàn bài kē, chàng:)
     then end.' (Ghost female-role saluting gesture, sings:)

（鴛鴦煞尾）從今後把

1340   (Yuān-yang shā-wěi) Cóng jin-hòu bǎ
     ('Mandarin-Ducks Coda') 'From hereafter (Pr)

金牌勢劍從頭擺將

1341   jin pái shì jiàn cóng tóu bǎi, jiāng
     golden tally, authority sword, from first-place display; (Pr)

濫官污吏都殺壞與

1342   làn guān wū lì dōu shā huài. Yǔ
     corrupt officials, foul clerks, all kill/destroy. With

天子分憂萬民除害

1343   tiān-zǐ fēn yōu, wàn mín chú hài.
     Heaven's-son share worries, [for] myriad people rid evils.'

（云）我可忘了一件爹爹俺

1344   (Yún:) Wó kě wàng-le yí jiàn. Diē-die, ǎn
     (Speaks:) 'I, however, forgot (P) one item (M). Father, my

婆婆年紀高大無人侍養

1345   pó-po nián-jì gāo-dà, wú rén shì yǎng,
     mother-in-law age advanced, has-no person to-serve, to-
     provide-for [her];

你可收恤家中替你孩兒

1346   nǐ kě shōu xù jiā-zhōng, tì nǐ hái-er
     you might keep [her] out-of-compassion in-the-house (L); for
     your child

盡養生送死之禮我便九

1347   jin yǎng-shēng sòng-sǐ zhi lǐ. Wǒ biàn jiǔ-
     fulfill take-care-in-life/send-off-in-death (P) propriety. I then
     nine-

泉之下可也瞑目（竇天章

1348   quán zhi xià, kě yě míng mù. (Dòu Tiān-zhāng
     springs (P) beneath may also close eyes.' (Tou T'ien-chang

TOU O'S GHOST (Sings tenth lyric):

Hereafter the golden tally and the sword of authority
Are to be displayed prominently in the first place.
They are to kill corrupt officials and dishonest clerks,
To relieve the Son of Heaven of his worries,
And to rid the people of evils. (Speaks.)

I almost forgot one thing. Father, my mother-in-law is old and has no one to look after her. Please, out of compassion, keep her in your house and provide her with her daily needs and give her a funeral on behalf of your child. Then I shall be able to close my eyes in peace in my grave.

1340] *Yuān-yang*: usually translated as 'Mandarin ducks'. The male and female *yuān-yang* are noted for amity and will not survive separation (*Ku chin chu* 古今注, ed., *Ts'ui Pao* 崔豹 [*SPTK san-pien*], *chüan* 2, pp. 6*b*–7*a*); therefore they are used as symbols for conjugal affection (see n. 465).

1347] *yǎng-shēng*: 'to take care of someone while he is alive'; cf. the note on *sòng sǐ* below.

sòng-sǐ: 'to show proper concern for the deceased' – 'to give a proper funeral'.

1347–8] *jiǔ-quán*: 'graveyard'; the term is derived from *Jiǔ Yuán* 九原, which was the graveyard for nobles of the Chin 晉 State in the Warring States period (Morohashi 1: 167: 416).

1348] *míng mù*: 'to close eyes' (the Chinese believe that a person would not close his eyes in death if there is a regret).

§1340] *Yuān-yang shā-wěi*: *Wěi-shēng* 尾聲 in *KMCP*, p. 21*b*.
§1340–1] *Cóng jīn-hòu*...*bǎi*: which corresponds approximately to the second line of the lyric in *KMCP*: *chì cì jīn pái shì jiàn chuī máo kuài* 敕賜金牌勢劍吹 毛快, *KMCP*, p. 21*b*.
§1343] *tiān-zǐ*: *yì-rén* 一人 in *KMCP*, p. 21*b*.
§1344] before *Yún*: *Zuò huí shēn kē* 做回身科, *KMCP*, p. 21*b*.
Diē-die: *Fù-qin* 父親 in *KMCP*, p. 21*b*.
§1346–8] *nǐ kě*...*míng mù*: not in *KMCP*.

云) 好孝順的兒也 (魂旦唱)

1349　yún:) *Hǎo xiào-shùn de ér ye!* (*Hún dàn chàng:*)
　　　says:) 'Extremely filial (P) child (P).' (Ghost female-role sings:)

囑付你爹爹收養我

1350　*Zhǔ-fu nǐ diē-die, shōu-yǎng wǒ*
　　　'Tell you, father, to-receive/to-provide-for my

妳妳可憐他無婦無

1351　*nǎi-nai. Kě-lián tā wú fù wú*
　　　mother-in-law. Take-pity-of her having-no daughter-in-
　　　law, no

兒誰管顧年衰邁再

1352　*ér, shéi guǎn-gù nián shuāi-mài? Zài*
　　　son; who takes-care/looks-after [her], in-age feeble/old?
　　　Again

將那文卷舒開

1353　*jiāng nà wén-juàn shū kāi,*
　　　(Pr) that file spread open.'

(帶云) 爹爹也把我竇娥名

1354　(*dài-yún:*) *Diē-die, yě bǎ wǒ Dòu É míng*
　　　(Speaks:) 'Father, also (Pr) my Tou O's name

下 (唱)

1355　*xià, (chàng:)*
　　　beneath (L), (sings:)

屈死的於伏罪名兒

1356　*Qū-sǐ de wū-fú zuì míng-er*
　　　Wrongly-slain one's falsely-confessed criminal charges

改 (下)

1357　*gǎi.* (*Xià*)
　　　change.' (Exit.)

(竇天章云) 喚那蔡婆婆上

1358　(*Dòu Tiān-zhāng yún:*) *Huàn nà Cài Pó-po shàng*
　　　(Tou T'ien-chang says:) 'Call that Ts'ai *P'o-p'o* up

TOU: What a filial and obedient daughter!

TOU O'S GHOST (sings):

I ask you, father, to care for my mother-in-law;
Take pity on her who has no son or daughter-in-law.
Who is to care for her, old and feeble?
Furthermore, re-open my case. (Speaks.)

Father, also under my name Tou O, (sings)

Clear the criminal charges of the wrongly executed one,
Who had confessed under torture. (Exit.)

TOU: Call Mistress Ts'ai to come up here. Do you recognize me?

1352] *mài:* 'old'; 'having passed the time of youth'.

1354] *yě: yě* here is ambiguous: it could be 'also', or a particle.

1356] *wū-fú:* same as *wū-fú* 誣 服, 'to confess under torture when not guilty'; cf. nn. 1117, 1131.

§1350–1] *shōu-yǎng wǒ: qiān zàng le* 遷 葬 了 in *KMCP*, p. 21*b*.

§1351] After *nǎi-nai: ēn yǎng ǎn pó-po* 恩 養 俺 婆 婆 in *KMCP*, p. 21*b*.

§1351–2] *wú fù. . . nián shuāi-mài: tā nián-jì gāo-dà* 他 年 紀 高 大 in *KMCP*, p. 21*b*.

§1354–5] *dài-yún. . . chàng:* not in *KMCP*.

§1356–7] *Qū-sǐ. . . gǎi: Jiāng ǎn qū sǐ de zhāo fú zuì míng-er gǎi* 將 俺 屈 死 的 招 伏 罪 名 兒 改 in *KMCP*, p. 21*b*.

§1358–9] *Huàn nà. . . lai:* not in *KMCP*; instead, *Tiān sè míng le, nǐ jiāng nà Yáng-zhōu-fǔ guān-lì nǎ jǐ gè shì wèn Dòu É dè dōu yǔ wǒ ná-jiāng shàng-lái* 天 色 明 了 你 將 那 楊 州 府 官 吏 那 幾 箇 是 問 竇 娥 的 都 與 我 拿 將 上 來, pp. 21*b*–22*a*; cf. §1160–383.

來你可認的我麼（蔡婆婆

1359　lai. Nǐ kě rèn-de wǒ ma? (Cài Pó-po
　　　(C). You might recognise me (P)?' (Ts'ai P'o-p'o

云）老婦人眼花了不認的

1360　yún:) Lǎo fù-ren yǎn huā le, bú rèn-de.
　　　says:) 'Old woman vision is-blurred (P), do-not recognize
　　　[you].'

（竇天章云）我便是竇天章

1361　(Dòu Tiān-zhāng yún:) Wǒ biàn shì Dòu Tiān-zhāng.
　　　(Tou T'ien-chang says:) 'I then am Tou T'ien-chang.

適纔的鬼魂便是我屈死

1362　Shì-cái de guǐ-hún biàn shì wǒ qū-sǐ
　　　Just-now (P) ghost then is my wrongly-slain

的女孩兒端雲你這一行

1363　de nǚ-hái-er Duān-yún. Nǐ zhè yì xíng
　　　(P) daughter Tuan-yün. You this one group (M) [of]

人聽我下斷張驢兒毒殺

1364　rén, tīng wǒ xià duàn: Zhāng Lǘ-er dú shā
　　　people, listen-to me hand-down verdict: Chang Donkey
　　　poisoned-to-death

親爺姦佔寡婦合擬凌遲

1365　qīn yé, jiān zhàn guǎ-fu, hè-nǐ líng-chí,
　　　own father, seduced, took-by-force widow, should-be-sentenced-
　　　to "slicing/lingering-death";

押付市曹中釘上木驢剐

1366　yā-fù shì-cáo zhōng, dīng shàng mù lǘ, guǎ
　　　send-under-guard-to market-place (L); nail upon "wooden
　　　donkey"; slice

一百二十刀處死陞任州

1367　yì bǎi èr-shí dāo chǔ sǐ. Shēng rèn zhōu-
　　　one hundred twenty cuts to-put-to death. Promoted in-office
　　　governor

TS'AI: My eyes are bad; I do not recognize you.

TOU: I am Tou T'ien-chang. The ghost who has just been here is my wrongly slain daughter Tuan-yün. Now all of you listen to the sentence. Donkey Chang, who murdered his own father and attempted to seduce a widow, deserves to be sentenced to 'slicing alive'. Take him to the marketplace, nail him on a 'wooden donkey,' and let him be sliced one hundred twenty times and die. T'ao Wu, who has been promoted to the post of governor, and the clerks in

1364] *duàn*: abbreviation for *pàn duàn* 判 斷, 'court sentence'.

1365] *líng-chí*: the penalty of death by slicing the limbs before beheading. Same as *guǎ* (see n. 1148).

1366] *mù lǘ*: literally 'wooden donkey', a wooden stake used as an implement of cruel punishment (see Chu Chü-i, pp. 53–4) The 'Donkey's' being punished by a 'donkey' may be meant as an ironic twist.

§1359] After *lai*: *(Zhāng Qiān:) Lǐ-huì-de. (Yā guān-lì, bǔ, jìng shàng; jiān guì kē. Tiān-zhāng:) Cài pò-po,* (張 千) 理 會 的 (押 官 吏 卜 净 上 見 跪 科 天 章) 蔡 婆 婆, *KMCP*, p. 22a.

§1362–3] *Shì-cái... Duàn-yún:* not in *KMCP*.

§1365] *jiān zhàn guǎ-fu: qī-piàn liáng rén* 欺 騙 良 人 in *KMCP*, p. 22a.

§1365–7] *hé-nǐ... chǔ sǐ: Shì-cáo zhōng míng zhèng diǎn-xíng* 市 曹 中 明 正 典 刑 in *KMCP*, p. 22a.

§1367–8] *Shēng rèn... lì-diǎn: Yáng-zhōu guān-lì* 楊 州 官 吏 in *KMCP*, p. 22a.

守 桃 杌 幷 該 房 吏 典 刑 名

1368   *shǒu Táo Wù, bìng gāi fáng lì-diǎn, xíng-míng*

T'ao Wu, and same department clerks/secretaries, criminal-law

違 錯 各 杖 一 百 永 不 敘 用

1369   *wéi-cuò, gè zhàng yì bǎi, yǒng bú xù-yòng.*

mismanage, each beat-with-stick one hundred, forever not to-be-employed.

賽 盧 醫 不 合 賴 錢 勒 死 平

1370   *Sài-Lú-yī bù hé lài-qián, lēi-sǐ píng-*

"Rival Lu-Doctor" not should repudiate-debt, strangle-to-death common-

民 又 不 合 修 合 毒 藥 致 傷

1371   *mín; yòu bù hé xiū-huò dú-yào, zhì shāng*

citizen; also not should prepare/mix poison, causing destruction-of

人 命 發 烟 障 地 面 永 遠 充

1372   *rén mìng, fā yān zhàng dì-miàn, yǒng-yuǎn chōng-*

human life; send-to vaporous malarial place, forever to-do-forced-labor-

軍 蔡 婆 婆 我 家 收 養 竇 娥

1373   *jūn. Cài pó-po wǒ jiā shōu-yǎng. Dòu É*

in-the-army. Ts'ai P'o-p'o my family keep/provide-for. Tou O's

罪 改 正 明 白 (詞 云) 莫 道 我

1374   *zuì gǎi-zhèng míng-bai. (Cí yún:) Mò dào wǒ*

criminal-charges corrected, made-clear.' ([In] verse says:) 'Do-not say I

念 亡 女 與 他 滅 罪 消 愆 也

1375   *niàn wáng nǚ yǔ tā miè zuì xiāo qiān; yě*

think-of deceased daughter, for her wipe-out guilt, cancel wrongs; also

只 可 憐 見 楚 州 郡 大 旱 三

1376   *zhǐ kě-lián-jiàn Chǔ-zhōu jùn dà hàn sān-*

only took-pity-on Ch'u-chou Prefecture's severe draught three

322

his department, all responsible for the wrong handling of criminal law, should each receive a hundred strokes and never again be employed in the government service. Sai Lu-yi should not have repudiated his debt, tried to strangle a citizen, or mixed poison which cost a human life. He is to be permanently exiled to a malarial district to work under the surveillance of military authority. Mistress Ts'ai is to come to stay in my house. The guilt of Tou O is to be cleared. (Recites.)

Say not that for the thought of my late daughter,
I wipe out her guilt and wrongs;
It was only because of the pity for Ch'u-chou Prefecture,
Which has suffered a severe three-year drought.

1372-3] *chōng-jūn:* 'to do forced labor under the surveillance of military authority'. This was part of a banishment sentence, and hence the term evokes the idea of banishment.

1376] *kě-lián-jiàn:* same as *kě-lián* 可憐 'to take pity', 'to like'; cf. Sùng Jiāng's 宋江 plea when a boatman threatened to kill him and his two escorts: *Nǐ rú-hé kě-lián-jiàn, ráo-le wǒ sān-ge,* 你如何可憐見饒了我三個, 'Please no matter what take pity and spare the three of us!' (*Shui-hu ch'üan chuan* 水滸全傳, chap. 37, p. 585).

§1370-1] *bù hé. . . yòu bù hé:* not in *KMCP.*
§1371-2] *zhì shāng rén mìng:* not in *KMCP.*
§1372-3] *fā yān zhàng. . . chōng-jūn: Yún-yáng shì liàng jué yì dāo* 雲陽市量決一 刀 in *KMCP*, p. 22a.
§1374-83] *Cí yún. . . yuān:* not in *KMCP*; instead *Wèi yīn rú-cǐ, jiāng Zhāng Lǘ-er zhǎn shǒu jiē qián, jiāng guān-lì bà zhí chú guān* 爲因如此將張驢兒斬首 街前將官吏罷職除官, p. 22a (see §1160-1383).

1377 年 昔 于 公 曾 表 白 東 海 孝
    nián. Xí Yú gōng céng biǎo bái Dōng-hǎi xiào
    years. Formerly Yü Lord once-did reveal clearly Eastern-Sea
    filial

1378 婦 果 然 是 感 召 得 靈 雨 如
    fù, guǒ-rán shì gǎn-zhāo de líng yǔ rú
    woman; indeed truly moved/summoned till divine rain [fell] like

1379 泉 豈 可 便 推 諉 道 天 灾 代
    quán. Qǐ kě biàn tuī-wěi dào tiān-zāi dài
    fountain. How may then make-excuse, saying natural-disaster
    generation

1380 有 竟 不 想 人 之 意 感 應 通
    yǒu, jìng bù xiǎng rén zhī yì gǎn-yìng tōng
    has, plainly not think human (P) will in-moving-to-respond
    extends-to

1381 天 今 日 個 將 文 卷 重 行 改
    tiān. Jīn-rì-ge jiāng wén-juàn chóng-xíng gǎi
    Heaven. Today (Pr) file anew change-to

1382 正 方 顯 的 王 家 法 不 使 民
    zhèng, fāng xiǎn-de wáng-jiā fǎ bù shǐ mín
    correct; then reveal (P) Royal law not allow people

1383 寃
    yuān.
    to-suffer-injustice.'

1384 **題目**　**秉 鑑 持 衡 廉 訪 法**
    Tí-mu　*Bǐng jiàn chí héng lián-fǎng fǎ.*
    Theme:　Holding mirror carrying scale [is] Surveillance-
    Commissioner's way.

1385 **正名**　**感 天 動 地 竇 娥 寃**
    Zhèng-míng　*Gǎn tiān dòng dì Dòu É yuān.*
    Proper-title:　Arousing Heaven stirring Earth [is] Tou O's
    injustice.

324

Formerly Lord Yü revealed the innocence of the filial daughter of Tung-hai;
Then rain was moved to fall like a fountain.
Do not make the excuse that natural disaster occurs in every generation;
The will of man can move Heaven to respond.
Today I shall correct the records,
To show that Royal law allows no one to suffer injustice.

Theme: Holding a mirror and carrying a scale is the way of the
Surveillance Commissioner.
Title: Arousing Heaven stirring Earth is Tou O's Injustice.

1380] *găn-yìng*: to move others to respond through an appeal to emotions.
1384] *Bĭng jiàn chí héng*: 'holding a mirror' and 'carrying a scale' are images associated
with a discerning and just law officer.
fă: 'law', 'way'. Here the word is used to mean both: the 'way' the
Surveillance Commissioner carries out the 'law'.
1384–5] *Tí-mu. . . Zhèng-míng*: at the conclusion of a Yüan play, two or four seven-
character lines are used to give a brief summary of the story. *Tí-mu* generally
gives the theme of the story and *zhèng-míng*, the title of the play.

§1384–5] There is a quatrain instead of a couplet in *KMCP*, pp. 22*a–b*:
  Hoù jià pó-po tè xīn piān;
  Shŏu zhì liè-nǚ yì zì jiān.
  Tāng fēng mào xuě méi tóu guĭ;
  Găn tiān dòng dì Dòu É yuān.

  後 嫁 婆 婆 忒 心 偏
  守 志 烈 女 意 自 堅
  湯 風 冒 雪 沒 頭 鬼
  感 天 動 地 竇 娥 冤

325

Caption in the upper righthand corner: 'Holding a mirror and carrying a scale is the Surveillance Commissioner's way' (l. 1384 in the text). From *Yüan ch'ü hsüan*, 1616; courtesy of the Syndics of the Cambridge University Library.

PART THREE

APPENDICES

GLOSSARY: *TOU O YÜAN*

The characters are arranged alphabetically according to modern Mandarin pronunciation in the *Pin-yin* system. Entries of the same sound are arranged by tones, with first single-character entries and then multi-character entries. The four tones are marked by ‾ , ′ , ˘ , ‵ , and the neutral tone goes without marking. For words with identical tones, the entry which appears first in the text is listed first. Derivatives are indented, and so are phrases beginning with the same word as the preceding entries. In a few cases where words are represented by identical graphic symbols but have different meanings and no clear semantic relation, they are listed as separate entries.

The meanings listed are those which the words have in the context of the play. They are not necessarily the most common meanings, as these are entries in a vocabulary list, not a dictionary. Asterisks (*) indicate more detailed notes in the main text. Words which are not part of the meaning of an entry but which provide added information are italicized.

āi [挨 捱]	to lean on 293
āi guo [挨 過]	to force through 316
āi [哎]	alas 744
āi-āi [哀 哀]	sad 1144
āi-zāi [哀 哉]	sad; alas 1157
ái [捱]	to endure 668
ài [愛]	love 480
ān [安]	peaceful 6
ān-pái [安 排]	to prepare 451
ān-xiē [安 歇]	to rest 933
ān [鞍]	saddles 583
ǎn [俺]	I; my; we; our 10
àn [闇]	pale 93; darkly 822
àn-dì-li [闇 地 裏]	secretly 1097
àn [按]	to suppress 200
àn [案]	tray, table 476
àn rán [黯 然]	dark; gloomy 908–9
bā, bá [八]	eight 10
bá-zì-er [八 字 兒]	horoscope; fate 206–7*
bá [拔]	to draw 213
bá zhe duǎn chóu [拔着 短 籌]	to draw a short lot 213*

329

bǎ [把]	*a pre-transitive:* to take hold of 42; M *for articles with handles* 355; to guard 721
bà [罷]	no more; the end 114,* 173*; to end 357
bà-zhàn [霸佔]	to seize by force; to usurp 792–3
ba [罷]	*final particle for a tentative statement:* . . . I suppose; how about it? 133*. *See p.* 17
bái [白]	white 274
bái tóu [白頭]	white haired 293–4
bái-zhòu [白晝]	daytime 193
bǎi [百]	hundred 338
bǎi-nián [百年]	*a euphemism for* death 526*
bǎi-xìng [百姓]	common people 879–80*
bǎi [擺]	to display 1341
bài [拜]	to worship; to salute 272
bài jiā-táng [拜家堂]	wedding ceremony 272*
bài-táng [拜堂]	to worship in a hall at a wedding 333
bài [敗]	ruined 1147*
bài-lù [敗露]	to be ruined by discovery; evil deed is discovered 1288
bān [般]	manner; ways 51
bān [搬]	to move 118
bān-tiáo [搬調]	to manipulate 565
bān. . . jū zhù [搬. . .居住]	to move to. . . to live 118–19*
bān-bái [斑白]	streaked with white 930
bàn [扮]	in the makeup of; impersonating 25*
bàn [半]	half 328
bàn yè [半夜]	half a night 466
bǎng [榜]	name list 45*
bāo-er [包兒]	bundle 394
Bāo lǎo-er [鮑老兒]	*title of a melody:* 'Old Man Bao' 809*
bǎo [飽]	to be full from eating 31
bǎo [保]	to keep 463
bǎo-zhuàng [保狀]	security papers 715
bǎo [寶]	treasure 523
bào [報]	reward; to reward 73; to avenge 711
bào [抱]	to hold 1198
bēi [悲]	grieving 86
bēi-qì [悲戚]	to grieve 534
bēi [杯]	cup 501
bèi [備]	to make ready 164
bèi [背]	back 172
bèi-dì [背地]	behind the back 460
bèi-yún [背云]	to speak in an aside 172*
bèi [被]	by 254
bèi-gào [被告]	defendant 613
bèi [鞴]	to wear saddles 583
bèi [輩]	generation 1060
bèi-lài [憊賴]	perverse 362*
bēn [奔]	to run 378

bēn-sāng [奔 喪]	to attend a funeral 482
běn [本]	originally 430
Běn-cǎo [本 草]	*an early study in materia medica* 106*
běn-lì [本 利]	capital and interest 14
běn-shi [本 事]	ability 439–40
běn-xìng nán yí [本 性 難 移]	*see note at* 489–90
bēng [繃]	to stretch 1113
bī [逼]	to force 1098
bī lè [逼 勒]	to force 635
bí-zi-kǒng [鼻 子 孔]	nostrils 1166
bí-zi-kǒng... bì [鼻 子 孔... 閉]	*see note at* 1166
bǐ [比]	comparable to 82
bǐ [筆]	a stroke of the writing brush 279
bì [壁]	wall 88
bì [避]	to avoid 271
bì [碧]	green stone 847
bì [閉]	to close 1166; to shut in 1331
bì-dāng [必 當]	must 73
bì-rán [必 然]	must 1288
biān [邊]	boundary 980
biàn [便]	then 54; convenience 20
biàn [徧]	completely 887; time: *a measure word* 1070
biǎo [表]	to express 1133
biǎo-bái [表 白]	to reveal clearly 1377
bié [別]	other 283; separately 954
bīng [冰]	ice 863
bǐng [稟]	to report to a superior 1172
bǐng [秉]	to hold 1384
bǐng jiàn chí héng [秉 鑑 持 衡]	*see note at* 1384
bìng [幷]	and 247
bìng [病]	sick 428
bìng-jí [病 疾]	sickness 536
bìng [並]	however 469; definitely 646*
bìng-rán [並 然]	definitely 313–14*
bó [薄]	thin; unworthy; slight 74
bó-lǎo [孛 老]	old man 141*
bò [帛]	silk 550
bo [波]	*a final particle* 232*; *see p.* 17
bū, bú, bù [不]	no 5
bú guò [不 過]	*negative resultative complement:* cannot get by 254
bú kuài [不 快]	to feel unwell 445
bú-ruò [不 若]	nothing better than; not equal to 158
bú-xìng [不 幸]	unfortunately 8
bú-yào [不 要]	do not 101
bù-dé-yǐ [不 得 已]	to have no other way out 1087*
bù-jué-de [不 覺 的]	unconsciously; not aware 955
bù-tí-fáng [不 提 防]	unexpectedly 728
bù-tōng [不 通]	not prosperous 31

bù-xiāo [不消]	no need 76
bǔ, bǔ-er [卜兒]	old woman 4*
bǔ-pī [捕批]	to search with a court order 1215
bù [布]	cloth 550
cāi [猜]	to guess 1028
cái [纔]	only then 479; just 645
cái [財]	money 544
Cǎi chá gē [採茶歌]	title of a melody: 'Picking Tea Song' 679
Cài Pó [蔡婆]	Mistress Ts'ai 4
cān [飡]	to eat 193
cān [參]	to visit a superior 937; doing obeisance 1173
cān-zhī-zhèng-shì [參知政事]	State Councilor 914–15*
cán-shēng [殘生]	remaining years of one's life 1140
cáng [藏]	to hide 477
cáng tóu gài jiǎo [藏頭蓋腳]	to deceive 477–8*
cǎo [草]	grass 1184
cè [側]	to incline 749
céng [曾]	once; before 39
céng-jīng [曾經]	once; before 876–7
céng [層]	layer 678
chā, chà [差]	to differ 1038
chā-cuò [差錯]	differences, or mistakes 1065
chāi [差]	to send 1146
chǎn-de [剗的 剗地]	how 287*
cháng [長]	always 5; long 1323
Cháng-ān [長安]	Ch'ang-an: the capital of Han, Sui, and T'ang dynasties 30*
Cháng-chéng [長城]	the Great Wall 483
cháng [腸]	intestines 198*
cháng [嘗]	once; ever 369
cháng [嘗]	to taste 493
cháng [常]	often 43
cháng-yán [常言]	proverb; common saying 390
Cháng Hóng huà bì [萇弘化碧]	see note at 847
cháng-mìng [償命]	to pay life for life 1106
chàng [唱]	to sing 86
chàng-huái [暢懷]	pleased 1149*
chāo-dù [超渡]	to release souls from suffering 384*
cháo-tíng [朝庭]	Imperial Court 1021
chē [車]	vehicle 864
chě [扯]	to pull 340
chè [徹]	completely 201
chēn [嗔]	to scold 1068
chén [塵]	dust 91
chén-chén [沈沈]	drowsiness; very heavy 529
Chén-zuì dōng fēng [沈醉東風]	title of a melody: 'Intoxicated in the East Wind' 972
chèn [趁]	to take advantage of 426

chéng [承]	to receive 28
chéng [城]	city 110
chéng-huáng cí [城隍祠]	temple of the city god 1065
chéng [成]	to become 288; to have achieved 491
chéng-qīn [成親]	to become wedded 181
chī [吃]	to eat 85
chī-zhāi [吃齋]	to observe a vegetarian diet as a religious ordinance 1279
chī, chí [癡]	crazy 557
chí [持]	to carry 452
chǐ [恥]	shame 486
chǐ [尺]	foot: *a measure word* 844
chì [叱]	to scold 1169
chì [勅]	Imperial decree 1238
chōng [衝]	to rush 820
chōng-shàng [衝上]	to rush on 142
chōng-jūn [充軍]	*see note at* 1372–3
chōng-mò [沖末]	supporting male role 24*
chóng [重]	again 4
chóng [虫]	worms 664
chóu [愁]	sorrow 189; worried 300
chóu [籌]	a tally 213
chóu [儔]	companions 335
chóu-rén [讐人]	enemy 962
chóu-xiè [酬謝]	to reward 260
chǒu [醜]	ashamed; ugly 242*
chǒu [丑]	clown 907
chū [初]	first; beginning 1084
chū-jià [出嫁]	to marry (a husband) 1055
chū-mài [出賣]	to sell 1297–8
chū-shēn [出身]	to begin life; to enter public service; in origin 368
chū-shì [出事]	to create an incident 403
chū-yú [出於]	out of 47
chū-yú wú-nài [出於無奈]	there is no other way out 47*
chú [除]	*see note at* 126; to rid 1343
chú-le-wài [除了外]	besides 652
chú-le [除了]	to remove 126
chǔ-fèn [處分]	to punish; to rebuke lightly 81*
chǔ-jué [處決]	to execute 720
chǔ-sǐ [處死]	to put to death 1367
Chǔ-zhōu [楚州]	*a place name:* Ch'u-chou 7
chù [處]	place 90
chu-lai, chu...lai [出來]	a directional complement 403–4*
chuān [穿]	to wear 253
Chuān bō zhuō [川撥棹]	*title of a melody:* 'Stream Stirs Oar' 1244
chuán [船]	boat 742
chuán [傳]	to transmit 841
chuàng fǔ [撞府]	to knock around prefectures 336

333

chuàng fǔ chōng zhōu

[撞府冲州] to go from place to place 336–7*

chuàng-jiàn [撞見] to meet accidentally 1018–19

chūn-bǎng [春榜] spring list 45*

    chūn-bǎng...kāi [春榜...開] the spring examination is about to take place 45*

cí [詞] verse 360

cí [辭] words 1131

cí [祠] sacrificial service 1192

cǐ [此] here 63; this 72

  cǐ-jiān [此間] here 37

cì [次] time: *a measure word* 14

cōng-cōng [匆匆] excited, hurried 297

cóng [從] since 12; to yield to; to obey 432

cù [醋] vinegar 496

cuān-duo [攛掇] to urge; to hasten 965*

cuī [催] to hasten 196

  cuī-bī [催逼] to press 254

cuì [脆] delicious 500*

cūn [村] rustic 327; village 374

cùn [寸] inch 1184

cuō, cuò [撮] to take up with fingers 1236

cuò [錯] mistakenly 744

  cuò guò [錯過] to miss 331–2

  cuò kàn xián yú [錯勘賢愚] to misjudge the virtuous and the foolish 744*

dā-dā-de [耷耷的] *an adverbial modifier* 239*

dā-fú dìng [搭伏定] to lean on 958*

dǎ [打] to beat 80; to make 393; to catch 471

  dǎ-kǎo [打拷] to beat 676–7

  dǎ-ǒu [打嘔] to vomit 508

  dǎ shém-me bù jǐn

    [打甚麼不緊] nothing important 835–6*

  dǎ-ting [打聽] to make inquiries 470

dà, dài [大] grown 276; big 484; greatly 573, 1031*

  dà-dǎn [大膽] bold 410*

  dà hàn [大旱] severe drought 1201

  dà-lái [大來] greatly 503*

  dà jīng xiǎo guài [大驚小怪] to become alarmed at trifles 573*

  dà rén [大人] great person; your honor 826

  dà zuì [大罪] severe crimes 1048

  dà-dōu-lái [大都來] generally 194*

dāi-chí [呆癡] dumb; silly 74

dǎi [歹] evil 743

dài [待] to wait 46; to want 464

dài [帶] to carry 139; to wear 724; sash 907

  dài pái zǒu mǎ [帶牌走馬] *see note at* 1021–2

  dài yún [帶云] to speak an interpolated line or phrase in a lyric 1296*

334

dài [代]	generation 1379
dān [䏢]	to bear 1250
dǎn [膽]	gall 651
dàn [但]	only 53; merely 611
dàn-shì [但 是]	but 257
dāng [當]	to be in the presence of 28; to deserve 81; to withstand; to bear 593; to act as 602; in the very same. . . 927, 1264*
dāng-chū [當 初]	in the beginning; formerly 289
dāng-hé [當 合]	to deserve 1147
dāng-miàn [當 面]	face-to-face 357; 'kneel' 1259*
dāng nián [當 年]	the very same year 927
dāng rì [當 日]	the very same day 1239
dàng [當]	to regard as 100
dāo [刀]	sword; knife 724; to slash 1367
Dāo-dāo lìng [叨 叨 令]	*title of a melody:* 'Chattering Song' 761
dào [到]	up-to; to; to reach 40
dào-tóu [到 頭]	to the end 703
dào [道]	to say 108; a streak 678
dào-chǎng [道 場]	Buddhist ceremony 1338*
dǎo [倒]	to crumble 483
dào [倒]	however; yet; on the contrary 300
Dào Zhí Yán Yuān [盜跖顏淵]	*see note at* 737
dé [得]	to receive; to obtain 53
Dé-shèng lìng [得 勝 令]	*title of a melody:* 'Victory Song' 1142
dé [德]	virtue 1056
de, di [得, 的]	*a particle, which with a resultative complement forms a descriptive complement* 17*
de, di [的]	*a subordinate particle translatable by an adjectival ending, prepositional phrase, or relative pronoun* 67
de, di [的]	*a subordinate particle translatable as '-ly' to form an adverb* 78*
de, di [得, 的]	*a potential complement:* -able, can 83*
de, di [得, 的]	'to' *as applied to extent or degree:* so (to such a degree). . . that, so. . . as, as, till 92*
de, di [的]	*a nominalizer:* one, -er; *the nominalizing de is a morpheme* 106*
de, di [的]	*a subordinate particle translatable as* ''s' *or* 'of' *to indicate possessive case* 167
děi [得]	to have to 47
dēng [燈]	lamp 940
děng [等]	way; kind 65; *a plural suffix* 1180
děng [等]	to wait for 138
děng-hòu [等 候]	to wait for 23
dī [滴]	drop 1122
dī-jī [鬆 髻]	knot; dressed hair 274
dí [滌]	to wash 475
dí-dí qīn-qīn [的 的 親 親]	*see note at* 578–9

335

dí-qīn [嫡 親]   close relation 7
dí-shì [的 是]   truly is 1328*
dǐ [底]   end 703
   dǐ-xià [底 下]   bottom 954
dì [地]   earth 1
   dì-fāng [地 方]   area 1289
   dì-miàn [地 面]   area 931
dì [第]   *placed before numbers to form ordinal numbers* 104
diǎn [點]   a drop 234; to light 945; to call roll 1209
   Diǎn jiàng chún [點 絳 唇]   *title of a melody:* 'Painting Lips Red' 188
diǎn-xíng [典 刑]   statutory penalty 694*; to be executed 797; to execute 1118

diàn [店]   shop 370
diàn [殿]   palace 731
diàn [奠]   to offer as a sacrifice 811
diào [吊 (弔)]   to hang 1112*
diē [跌]   to fall 341
diē, diē-die [爹 爹]   father 97
dié [牒]   by official document 1065
dīng [釘]   to nail 1366
dìng [定]   certainly 862
   dìng-zhǔn [定 准]   sure 92
   dìng-zuì [定 罪]   to sentence 1337
diōu [丟]   to discard 377
dōng [東]   east 137
   Dōng-hǎi [東 海]   *name of a place* 876
   dōng-xi [東 西]   things 53
dōng-shí [冬 時]   winter 797
dòng [動]   to move 1
   dòng dì jīng tiān [動 地 驚 天]   *see note at* 729
dōu [都]   all 71
dōu [兜]   to wear 275
Dòu [竇]   *a surname:* Tou 29
   Dòu É [竇 娥]   *the name of a young widow:* Tou O 1
   Dòu Tiān-zhāng [竇 天 章]   *Tou O's father:* Tou T'ien-chang 25
Dòu há-ma [鬭 蝦 蟆]   *title of a melody:* 'Fighting Frogs' 534
dú [讀]   to study 26
dú [獨]   childless 292; alone 908
   dú-yào [毒 藥]   poison 399
dǔ [賭]   to gamble on 439
   dǔ-shì [賭 誓]   to make an oath 358
dǔ [膳 (肚)]   tripe 447*
dǔ [覩]   to see 768
duān-de [端 的]   really 215*
duān-xiáng [端 祥]   to examine carefully 1146
Duān-yún [端 雲]   *given name of Tou O:* Tuan-yün 25
duān-zhèng [端 正]   proper 727
duǎn [短]   short 213
duàn [斷]   to break 198; verdict 1364*

duàn sòng [斷 送]	to escort a funeral 865*
duàn [段]	piece; section 1023
duàn pǐ [段 匹]	sections and bolts 543–4*
duì [對]	to match 265; to; toward 448; to answer 1064
duì-huán [對 還]	to pay back double amount 40*
duō [多]	much 57
duǒ [躲]	to hide 394
é-méi [蛾 眉]	eyebrows like moth's antennae 288*
è [惡]	evil 738
è [餓]	hungry 1067
ēn [恩]	favor 73; love 479*
ēn-ài [恩 愛]	affection 278
ēn-dé [恩 德]	favor 632–3
ēn-qíng [恩 情]	affection 524–5
ēn-zhāo [恩 召]	to be graciously summoned by the emperor 28
ér [兒]	In Mandarin, 'er' is often added to nouns and pronouns as a suffix 4; child 85
ér-xí-fu [兒 媳 婦]	daughter-in-law 44*
ér-zi [兒 子]	son 247
ěr [耳]	ear 402
èr [二]	two 366
Èr shā [二 煞]	title of a melody: 'Secondary Coda' 858
èr-shí [二 十]	twenty 13
fā [發]	to occur, to issue, to break out 425; to send 1065
fā-ǒu [發 嘔]	to vomit 1100
fā-yuàn [發 願]	to make vows 1183
fá [罰]	penalty 1066
fá-xià [罰 下]	to make (a vow) 839*
fǎ [髮]	hair 523
fǎ [法]	law 728; way 1384*
fǎ-chǎng [法 場]	execution ground 726
fǎ-dù [法 度]	law 952
fān [翻]	to re-arrange; to turn 993
fán [凡]	all 456
fán-fán [煩 煩]	troubled 819
fán-nǎo [煩 惱]	troubled 243
fàn [飯]	rice; meals 230
fàn [犯]	to sin; to commit a crime 728
fàn-fù [犯 婦]	a criminal woman 1182
fàn-ren [犯 人]	criminal 720
fàn-yóu-pái [犯 由 牌]	criminal charge plaque 1299*
fāng [方]	just now 379; then 1382
fāng-biàn [方 便]	convenience 782
fáng [房]	chamber 214; department 1174
fáng [防]	to prevent 1130

337

fǎng-fu [彷彿]	as if 1198
fàng [放]	to let by 420; to put into 495
fàng-guāi [放乖]	to indulge in deception 1295
fàng-jīng-shen zhe [放精神着]	be spirited 531
fàng-kāi [放開]	to set loose 377–8
fàng-xīn [放心]	to set one's mind at ease 78
fēi [飛]	to fly 378
fēi shuāng liù-yuè yīn Zōu Yǎn [飛霜六月因鄒衍]	see note at 860
fēi [非]	is not 458
fèi [費]	expense 54
fèi [廢]	to do without 194
fēn, fèn [分]	apart 90; to distinguish 742; to divide 1343
fēn-biàn [分辨]	to distinguish 736
fēn-fù [分付]	to order 1202
fēn-lí [分離]	to separate 211
fēn-míng [分明]	clearly 50
fèn-wài [分外]	in addition to 52–3
fén [墳]	grave 480
fén-dì [墳地]	graveyard 552
fén tóu. . . xīn yī [墳頭. . . 新衣]	see note at 480–2
fēng [風]	wind 883
fēng-hán [風寒]	chills 537
fēng [峯]	peak of a hill 909
fèng [鳳]	phoenix 471
fó [佛]	Buddha 1279
fǒu [否]	not 189
fū [夫]	husband 180
fū-zhǔ [夫主]	husband 8
fú [服]	dose: a *measure word* 399
fú-xiào [服孝]	in mourning 125
fú [伏]	to lean onto 428
fú-shì [伏侍]	to serve 809
fú-zhuàng [伏狀]	confession paper 691–2
fú [浮]	floating 885
fú-shì [浮世]	transient 523
fú pén [覆盆]	overturned tub 683*
fú pén. . . huī [覆盆. . . 輝]	see note at 683–4
fú-róng [芙蓉]	hibiscus 305
fǔ [腐]	to rot 979
fù [富]	to be rich 6
fù [腹]	belly 188*
fù [婦]	woman 467, 1351*
fù-ren [婦人]	woman 324
fù-rén-jia [婦人家]	woman 486
fù [負]	to carry 699
fù [赴]	to go to 777
fù-jìng [副淨]	supporting *ching*-role 141*

fù-kàn [覆 勘]	to re-examine 1322
fù mǔ [父 母]	parents 612
fù-qin [父 親]	father 178
gāi [該]	to owe 14; ought to 40; to deserve 80; the same 1174
gǎi [改]	to change 121; another 1337
gǎi-jià [改 嫁]	(for a woman) to remarry 585
gǎi-zhèng [改 正]	to rectify 1199–1200
gài [蓋]	to cover 477
gān [乾]	in vain 294; neatly 357
gān-bà [乾 罷]	to terminate neatly 357*
gān-jing [乾 淨]	neat 395
gān [甘]	willingly 484; sweet 875
gān lù [甘 露]	sweet dew 502*
gān tóu dà shuǐ [甘投大水]	*see note at* 484
gān [干]	related 541
gān-shè [干 涉]	connection; concern 646
gān [肝]	liver 650
gǎn [感]	to touch 1; to be affected by 535; to move 862
gǎn-yìng [感 應]	to move one to respond 1380*
Gǎn Huáng ēn [感 皇 恩]	*title of a melody:* 'Thanking Imperial Favor' 673
Gǎn tiān dòng dì Dòu É yuān [感天動地竇娥寃]	*see note at* 1
gǎn [敢]	dare 60; must 165
gǎn-dài [敢 待]	most likely 24*
gǎn-shì [敢 是]	probably 1226
gàn [幹]	to do 806
gāng [剛]	just 371; strong 916
gāng-gāng [剛 剛]	just 355
gāng-cháng [綱 常]	moral order 1147
gāo [高]	high; towering 647
gāo-dà [高 大]	advanced 255
gāo tái míng jìng [高擡明鏡]	to hold high a clear mirror 647*
gào [告]	to accuse 615; to appeal 1105
gào-fā [告 發]	to inform 369
gào-zhuàng [告 狀]	to file suit 601; to lodge a charge 607
gào-zhuàng-de [告 狀 的]	plaintiff 609
gē [哥]	older brother 417
gē-ge [哥 哥]	older brother 154*
gē-shě-de [割 捨 的]	to cut loose and give up; to sacrifice; to relinquish 89*
Gé wěi [隔 尾]	*title of a melody:* 'Separate Coda' 498
gè [各]	each 538
gè [個]	*a general measure word:* one 9; a case of 147; *an abreviation of zhè-ge* 1030*
gēn [跟]	with 101
gēn-qián [跟 前]	front; presence 82

gēng [羹]	soup 651
gēng-tāng [羹 湯]	soup 501
gēng-zhōu [羹 粥]	gruel 291
gēng [更]	to change 1109
gèng [更]	further 489
gōng [公]	lord 872
gōng-àn [公 案]	court case 1231
gōng-gong [公 公]	father-in-law 294
gōng gū [公 姑]	father-in-law and mother-in-law 1057
gōng-rén [公 人]	officer 722
gōng míng [功 名]	achievement and fame 32
gòng-xiě [供 寫]	to confess and to write 1318
gōu [勾]	to mark off (with a brush) 279
gòu [勾]	*a variant of* 夠: enough 53*
gū [孤]	orphan 292; lone 392; *a technical term for an official in Yüan drama* 599*
gū [姑]	mother-in-law 1194
gǔ [骨]	bone 101
gǔ-hái [骨 骸]	skeleton 980
gǔ [鼓 皷]	drum 716; to beat a drum 722*
gǔ [古]	ancient 865
gǔ-mén [古 門]	door on stage 450*
gù [顧]	to care for 775
gù [故]	reason 957
gù-rén [故 人]	old companion 523-4
gù-yì [故 意]	intentionally 166
guǎ [寡]	widow 149
guǎ-fu [寡 婦]	widow 1225
guǎ-fu rén-jia [寡 婦 人 家]	widow 455-6
guǎ [剮]	to slice 1148*
guà [掛]	to hang 199
guài [怪, 恠]	strange 573
guài-bù-de [怪 不 得]	no wonder 275
guān [關]	*a surname* 2; to close 369; related to; because of 380
Guān Hàn-qīng [關 漢 卿]	*author of this play:* Kuan Han-ch'ing 2
guān-qīn [關 親]	concerned 555*
guān [官]	official; magistrate 416; officially 588
guān-bài [官 拜]	is granted an official post 914*
guān-jū [官 居]	to hold the office of 1049
guān-lì [官 吏]	officials 878-9
guān-liào [官 料]	officially sanctioned ingredients 1280
guān-si [官 司]	court; court case 591
guān [冠]	cap 907
guān-cai [棺 材]	coffin 550
guān [鰥]	widower 292
guān guǎ gū dú [鰥寡孤獨]	*see note at* 292
guǎn [管]	to take care of 1352
guàn [灌]	to fill 502

guāng-guāng [光 光]	bright 318–19
guāng-jing [光 景]	time 182
guǎng [廣]	much 38; extensive 402; wide 1215
guī [歸]	to return 91
guǐ [鬼]	ghost 699
guǐ-hún [鬼 魂]	ghost 966
guì [貴]	noble 6
guì [跪]	to kneel 608
gǔn [滾]	to roll 863
Gǔn xiù qiú [滾 繡 球]	*title of a melody:* 'Rolling an Embroidered Ball' 733
gùn-bàng [棍 棒]	rod 667
gùn-zi [棍 子]	stick 665
guǒ [果]	indeed 1183
guǒ-rán [果 然]	indeed 1126
guò [過]	to pass 10, 331*; to exceed 54
guò-mén [過 門]	to marry 297*
guò-shì [過 世]	to die 1089*
hái [還]	still; yet 156; *see also* huán 16
hái [骸]	skeleton 1131
hái-er [孩 兒]	child 9
hǎi [海]	sea 981
hài [害]	to be sick with 124; evil 1343
hài-bìng [害 病]	to be sick 398
hán [寒]	cold; cold weather 291
hán [含]	to hold 1197
hán-hu [含 糊]	ambiguously; in a muddled way 1087
hàn [旱]	drought 1326
Hàn cháo [漢 朝]	Han Dynasty 1193
Hàn-tíng [漢 庭]	Han court 27
hàn-zi [漢 子]	man 388
háng [行]	a group 1363
háng-yè [行 業]	profession 381
hǎo [好]	good; auspicious 21; extremely 187; *an abbreviation of zěn hǎo* 1218*
hǎo-dǎi [好 歹]	for better or worse 400
hǎo-jǐ-ge [好 幾 個]	quite a few 1291
hǎo mǎ... èr fū [好 馬... 二 夫]	*a proverb* 1108–9*
hào-sè [好 色]	to covet women 700
hē [喝]	to call aloud 1259
hē-cuān xiāng [喝 攛 廂]	to call court to order 605*
hē-qian [呵 欠]	to yawn 955
hé [和]	to; and; with 126; even 191; to linger 195; to get along with 1057
hé tiān shòu [和 天 瘦]	even Heaven will grow thin 191*
hé-xié, hé-xiái [和 諧]	harmonious 1248*
hé [何]	what 163

341

hé cháng [何 嘗]   when has it been 369
hé-děng [何 等]   what manner; how 159
hé [合]   to deserve 735; to bend 750; to come together; to close 986; *see also huò* 合 409
hè-shā [嚇 殺]   to frighten to death 573
Hè xīn-láng [賀 新 郎]   *title of a melody:* 'Congratulating the Bridegroom' 515
he, O [呵]   *a particle* 187*
hèn [恨]   grudge 754; to regret 1333
héng [橫]   lying across 197
héng [衡]   scale 1384
hóng-chén [紅 塵]   'red dust', usually implying 'the mundane world' 843-4
hóng-luán [紅 鸞]   red *luán* bird 437*
hŏng [哄]   to cheat 166
hòu [後]   afterward; behind; later; backward 123
hòu-mŭ [後 母]   step-mother 619
Hòu-tíng huā [後 庭 花]   *title of a melody:* 'Back Court Flowers' 271
hū [忽]   suddenly 991
hū-rán [忽 然]   suddenly 643
hū-huàn [呼 喚]   to call 1168
hú [胡]   nonsense 655
hú-luàn [胡 亂]   at random; confused 1028
hú-shuō [胡 說]   to talk nonsense 857
hú-lu-tí [葫 蘆 提]   in confusion 803-4*
hú-tu [糊 突]   to mix up; to confuse 736*; foolish 1188
hŭ [虎]   tiger 1068
hŭ-hè [諕 嚇]   to intimidate 567
hù-wèi [戶 尉]   god of the right door 967*
huā [花]   flowers 4; dim; blurred 1047
huā-hóng [花 紅]   money gifts 544*
huā-hóng cái lĭ [花 紅 財 禮]   betrothal gifts; wedding gifts 544*
huā-yín [花 銀]   pure silver 371*
huā-zhī [花 枝]   flower twigs 197
huà wán-shí [化 頑 石]   to turn into a block of insensitive stone 485*
huà [畫]   painted 288; sign 691
huà táng [畫 堂]   decorated hall 306
huái [懷]   to hold 754
Huái [淮]   *name of a river:* Huai 1333
Huái-nán [淮 南]   area south of the Huai River 931
huài [壞]   to destroy; destroyed 1141
huán [還]   to return 16
huăn [浣]   to wash 483
huàn [喚]   to call 122
huàn-zuo [喚 做]   to be called as 616
huàn [換]   to change 481
huàn-bìng [患 病]   to be sick 638
huāng [慌]   hurriedly 142; panic 417
huāng-zhang [慌 張]   frantic 267

huāng [荒]	deserted 374; wild 865
huāng-pì [荒 僻]	deserted 386–7
huāng-yín [荒 淫]	lecherous 700
huáng [黃]	yellow 354
huáng-huā nǚ-ér [黃花女兒]	young girl; virgin 354–5*
huáng-hūn [黃 昏]	evening 192–3
huáng jīn [黃 金]	yellow gold 523
huáng jīn. . . xī [黃 金 . . . 稀]	a proverb 523–4*
Huáng-tiān [皇 天]	August Heaven 874
Huáng-zhōng-wěi [黃 鐘 尾]	title of melody: 'Yellow-bell Coda' 698
huī [揮]	to sweep 1023
huī-chén [灰 塵]	dust 381
huí [回]	to return 164
huí-de [回 得]	to refuse 298
huí-xīn [回 心]	to change mind 353
huì [會]	while 471
huì-qì [悔 (晦) 氣]	bad luck 422*
hūn [昏]	dark 303
hūn-chén [昏 沉]	dizziness 956
hūn-huā [昏 花]	dim 930
hūn-hūn [昏 昏]	dizziness 529
hūn-mí [昏 迷]	fainted 654
hūn-téng [昏 騰]	unclear 303
hún [魂]	soul 379
hún dàn [魂 旦]	ghost female-role 959*
hún-jiā [渾 家]	wife 32*
Hǔn jiāng lóng [混 江 龍]	title of a melody: 'Roiling River Dragon' 192
huó [活]	life 107; to rescue 345; living 545
huǒ [火]	fire 862
huǒ-sù [火 速]	speedy as fire 1205
huò, huó [合]	to compound 409; see also hé 735
huò [或]	or 538
huò [獲]	to seize 1215
huò [禍]	trouble 1320
huò-yóu [禍 尤]	disaster 219
jī [几]	table 428
jī [饑]	hunger 538
jī [擊]	to strike 1019
jī-guān [機 關]	tricks 471–2
jí [極]	exceedingly 662
jí [疾]	fast 674
jí [急]	quickly 1237
jí-jiān-jiān [急 煎 煎]	anxiously 200*
jí-dì [及 第]	to pass any of the three examinations for jǔ ren 舉 人, jìn shi 進 士, or hàn lin 翰 林 914
jǐ [幾]	several 80
jǐ-shí [幾 時]	what time 194
jì [計]	scheme 88; idea 543

jì [記]	to remember 520
jì-de [記 得]	to remember 816
jì [繼]	to succeed to 1189
jì [祭]	to offer sacrifice 1190
jì [旣]	since 1083
jì-rán [旣 然]	since 687
jì-shì [旣 是]	since 348
Jì-shēng cǎo [寄 生 草]	*title of a melody:* 'Parasite Grass' 299
jiā [家]	family 11
jiā-kè-jì [家 克 計]	household plans 469*
jiā-shǔ [家 屬]	family 8
jiā-táng [家 堂]	ancestral halls 272
jiā-xiǎo [家 小]	family 392
jiā-yuán [家 緣]	property 337-8; household work 806
jiā [加]	to add 499
jiā [枷]	cangue 692*
jiā-shang [枷 上]	to lock up in a cangue 692
jià [嫁]	to give a daughter in marriage 179; to marry a husband 1054
jià-er [架 兒]	rack 481
jiān [間]	midst; within 55
jiān [尖]	tip 202
jiān [瀽]	to pour 798
jiān [堅]	firm 916
jiān-zhí [堅 執]	obstinately; firmly 431
jiān [姦]	to seduce; to rape 1365
jiān zhǎn [監 斬]	to oversee an execution 826
jiān zhǎn guān [監 斬 官]	an official who oversees an execution 719
jiàn [踐]	to step on 91
jiàn [見]	to see, to meet 224, 846; to present oneself 1174
jiàn-shi [見 識]	knowledge 473
jiàn [件]	*a measure word for a thing or event* 550
jiàn [賤]	cheap 664
jiàn [薦]	to offer sacrifice 814*
jiàn [劍]	sword 1023
jiàn [鑑]	a mirror of metal 1384
jiāng [將]	*a pretransitive, same as* 把 *bǎ;* to take hold of 47*; about to 126; to use 166; to take; to bring 260*
jiāng-jiu [將 就]	to be tolerant; to make the best of things 83*
jiāng [漿]	gruel 811
jiāng-shuǐ-fàn [漿 水 飯]	gruel 799
jiàng [降]	to fall 853
jiāo [焦]	worries 201
jiāo [交]	a fall 357
jiāo-huān jiǔ [交 歡 酒]	wedding wine 302
jiāo [椒]	pepper 499
jiāo-kè [嬌 客]	handsome guest; *idiomatically:* son-in-law 320

jiāo-wài [郊 外]	countryside 629*	
jiāo-zī [嬌 姿]	frail manner, frail beauty 1331	
jiǎo [角]	corners 129	
jiǎo [脚]	feet 478	
jiǎo-bù [脚 步]	steps 378	
jiào [教]	to ask; to make 42; to allow 231*	
jiào [叫]	to call, to shout 109	
jiào-zuo [叫 做]	called as 1036	
jiē [接]	to take over 493	
jiē-jiǎo [接 脚]	*see note at* 431	
jiē [jiāi] [街]	street 754, 1323*	
jiē-fang [街 坊]	neighbors 926*	
jiē [嗟]	to sigh 763	
jiē-jiē [嗟 嗟]	to sign 557	
jiē [皆]	all, entirely 846	
jiē [階]	stairs 1270	
jié [潔]	clean 462	
jié [結]	to conclude 952	
jié [節]	section 1231	
jié-cāo [節 操]	moderate and restrained 915–16	
jiè [借]	to borrow 13	
jiè [解]	to forward, to send 1209	
jiè-shěn [解 審]	to bring forward for trial 1205	
jiè-zi [解 子]	guard in charge of a prisoner 1207	
jīn [今]	present 17	
jīn-rì [今 日]	today 21	
jīn-rì-ge [今 日 簡]	today 1142*	
jīn yě-bō shēng [今 也 波 生]	this life 218–19*	
jīn-zhāo [今 朝]	today 1133	
jīn [金]	gold 601	
jīn-pái [金 牌]	golden tally 922*	
jǐn [錦]	brocade, silk 197	
jǐn [緊]	important 836	
jǐn-yào [緊 要]	important 1213	
jìn [盡]	extremely; completely 26; to fulfill 1347	
jìn-tóu [盡 頭]	the end 208	
jìn [儘]	fully; quite 119	
jìn [進]	to enter 228	
jìn [噤]	silence 1045	
jìn-shòu [禁 受]	to suffer 189	
jīng [精]	spirit 379	
jīng [驚]	to alarm 573	
jīng-hài [驚 駭]	fright 1029	
jīng-shī [京 師]	capital 913–14	
jīng-wén [經 文]	scripture 384	
Jīng-zhào [京 兆]	*capital area:* Ching-chao 30*	
jìng [淨]	*ching*-role 105*	
jìng [鏡]	mirror 647	
jíng [競]	to compete 703	

jìng [淨]	clean 829
jìng [敬]	to respect 1057
jìng [竟]	plainly 1380
jìng-ban [靜 辦]	quiet 119*
jiǔ [久]	long time 211
jiǔ [酒]	wine 350
jiǔ-quán [九 泉]	'nine-springs': graveyard 1347–8*
jiù [就]	then 19; just 51;
jiù-shi [就 是]	then is; exactly is 423
jiù-zhōng [就 中]	therein 1329
jiù [救]	to rescue 143
jiù [舊]	old 278
jū [居]	to dwell in 921
jū-zhù [居 住]	to live 37
jū [拘]	to arrest 1203
jú [局]	shop 110
jǔ [舉]	to raise 476; to try 914
jù [句]	sentence 81, M *for words or speech* 751
jù [具]	M *for coffin* 549
jù [俱]	all 652
jù-pà [懼 怕]	afraid 1087
juān [鵑]	cuckoo 847
juàn [卷]	M *for volumes, scrolls, and files* 26
juàn [眷]	family 458
jué [覺]	to feel 379
jùn [郡]	prefecture 1176
kāi [開]	to open 5
kàn [看]	to look; to look upon 74
kàn-chéng [看 承]	to regard, to treat 78
kàn-qǔ [看 取]	to observe 671
kàn-qù [看 覷]	to look after 64
kàn-shang [看 上]	to approve; to take a fancy to 18
kàn [勘]	to examine 744
kàng-hàn [亢 旱]	severe drought 869
kǎo [拷]	to beat 1113
kǎo-dǎ [拷 打]	beating 593
kào [靠]	to depend on 293; to lean on 323
kē [科]	*a technical term in Yüan drama:* gesture; movement 49*
kě [可]	-able; e.g., 可愛 lovable 18; indeed, certainly 181*; *particle for emphasis:* surely 912
kě-ài [可 愛]	lovable 18
kě-bú [可 不]	'isn't it. . . ?' *meaning* 'surely is' 277, 403*
kě-lián [可 憐]	pitiable 27; likable 916
kě-lián jiàn [可 憐 見]	to take pity 1376*
kě-nài [可 奈]	no way to handle 396*
kě-xǐ [可 喜]	likable 17
kě-zhī [可 知]	certainly 575*

kè [刻]	moment 730
kěn [肯]	to be willing 162
kēng-shā [坑 殺]	to trap; to hurt 334*
kōng [空]	empty 214; in vain 534
kǒng-pà [恐 怕]	to fear 1158
kǒu [口]	mouth 222*
kǒu-er [口 兒]	M *for people* 8
kòu [扣]	knot; button 303
kòu-tóu [叩 頭]	kowtow 709*
kū [哭]	to weep 231
kū-kū [哭 哭]	to weep 558
kū dǎo Cháng-chéng [哭 倒 長 城]	to crumble the Great Wall by weeping 483*
kǔ [苦]	bitter 187
kuài [快]	well 445; quickly 746; to hasten 966
Kuài-huó-sān [快 活 三]	*title of a melody:* 'Happy Three' 803
kuài-zi, guì-zi [劊 子]	executioner 723*
kuàng [況]	moreover 45
kuī [虧]	owing to 258; fortunately 1023
kuī-le [虧 了]	fortunately 247
kuī-shā [虧 殺]	fortunately 488
lái [來]	to come 24
lái-shì [來 世]	next life 220
lái-yóu [來 由]	reason 727
lái-zhāo [來 朝]	tomorrow 1155
lài [賴]	to deny 153; to repudiate 1370
lài-gǔ [賴 骨]	bad boned 662-3
lai [來]	*a final particle* 687*; *see p. 17 above*
lán-jié [攔 截]	to intercept 975
lán-shān [闌 刪]	waning 301
làn [濫]	corrupt 919
làn-màn [爛 漫]	shining 197
láng [郎]	man 467
láng [狼]	wolf 1068
làng-dàng [浪 蕩]	vast and open 375
lāo, láo [撈]	to trap 472
lāo lóng [撈 龍]	to trap a dragon; *see note at* 472-3
láo [牢]	prison; prison cell 693
láo-kùn [勞 困]	fatigue 957
láo-yì [勞 役]	hard work 538
lǎo [老]	old 363
lǎo-fū [老 夫]	old man; I 911
lǎo-fù-ren [老 婦 人]	old woman 1305
lǎo-gōng [老 公]	old man 263
lǎo-hàn [老 漢]	old man 429
lǎo-jūn [老 君]	old lord 1237
lǎo-po [老 婆]	wife 162
lǎo-rén-jia [老 人 家]	elderly person 344*

347

lăo-shēn [老身]	old self: I 6*
lăo-shǔ-yào [老鼠藥]	rat poison 1290
lăo-ye [老爺]	old lord; master 710
lăo-zi [老子]	father 171; old fellow 328
lē, lé, lè, lēi [勒]	to strangle 141; to force 1248
lēi-shā-le [勒殺了]	to strangle to death 144
lè [樂]	joy 6
le [了]	*particle; see note at 13 and pp.* 15–16
lèi [淚, 泪]	tears 196
lèi [累]	to involve; to trouble 461
lěng [冷]	cold 883
lí [離]	to separate 178; to leave 912
lí [釐]	a thousandth part of an inch: a particle 1065
lǐ [禮]	to salute 322; gifts 544; propriety 1347; salute 333
Lǐ [李]	*a surname:* Li 467
lǐ [里]	a Chinese mile 527*
lǐ-huì [理會]	to understand 534–5
lǐ-miàn [裏面]	inside 493-4
lì [例]	example 672
lì [立]	to stand 908
lì-diăn [吏典]	clerks and secretaries: government servants 938–9
li [哩]	*a final particle* 140*; *see p.* 19
lián [連]	even 268
lián-lèi [連累]	to involve 392
lián-máng [連忙]	quickly 236
lián [廉]	incorruptible 915
lián-făng shǐ [廉訪使]	surveillance commissioner 968
lián-făng [廉訪]	*abbreviation of lián-făng shǐ:* surveillance commissioner 1384
lián-lì [怜悧]	neat; *see note at* 478
lián-lián [漣漣]	to flow unceasingly 745
liàn [練]	white dressed silk 830*
liáng [良]	good 633
liáng [涼]	cold 811
Liáng-zhōu dì-qī [梁州第七]	*title of a melody:* 'Liang-chou No. Seven' 474
liăng [兩]	two 10; tael: M *for silver* 13*
liăng-bān-er [兩般兒]	both 193
liăng Huái [兩淮]	*see note at* 917
liăo [了]	the end 205; to end 561
liào [料]	spice; ingredients 499
liè [烈]	to burn 812
liè-nǔ [烈女]	a chaste woman 1109
lín [鄰]	a neighbor 570
lín-lǐ jiē-fang [鄰里街坊]	neighbors 926
lín [臨]	on the brink of 781
lín [霖]	long continued rain 876
lín [林]	forest 909

lín-lí [淋 漓]	to drip; dripping wet 680
líng-bī [凌 逼]	punishment 677
líng-chí [凌 遲]	to put to a lingering death by slicing the limbs before beheading 1365*
líng-er [靈 兒]	spirit 1143
líng-shèng [靈 聖]	divine spirit 841
lǐng [領]	to lead 328; M *for mats and coats* 829
lìng [另]	separately 394
lìng [令]	order 1238
lìng-ài [令 愛]	your daughter (a polite usage) 76*
liú [流]	to flow 209; to issue 1101
liú-luò [流 落]	to be stranded 36
liú [留]	to keep 276
liú-xià [留 下]	to leave behind 63
liù [六]	six 255
liù fáng [六 房]	six departments 938
liù-shí [六 十]	sixty 255
liù-xún [六 旬]	sixty years 277
liù-yuè [六 月]	the sixth month 860
lóng [龍]	dragon 473
lòu-miàn [漏 面]	shown on face; discernible 701
lú [鑪]	a place where wine is stored and sold; *in a general sense*, wine jars 28*
Lú [盧]	*a surname:* Lu 108
lǚ [侶]	mate 334
lǚ-lǚ [屢 屢]	frequently 371
lù [路]	road 756
lǜ [律]	law 1238
luàn [亂]	to violate 1147
lún [輪]	to turn 877
lún-huí [輪 廻]	transmigration 535
lùn-yì [論 議]	gossip, criticism 547
luó [鑼]	gong 723
luò [落]	reduced to 92; to lose 379; to fall 832
Luò-yáng [洛 陽]	Lo-yang: *capital of Chou, Han, Chin, Sui, T'ang and Sung dynasties* 91*
luo [嚛]	*a final particle* 85
luo [囉]	*a final particle* 559
mǎ [馬]	horse 583
Mǎ Xiàng-rú [馬 相 如]	*abbreviation of* Ssu-ma Hsiang-ju 27*
mà [罵]	scold 80
Mà yù-láng [罵 玉 郎]	*title of a melody:* 'Scold Jade-man' 667
ma [麽]	*interrogative particle* 56
mái [埋]	to bury 965
mái-yuàn [埋 怨]	harbored resentment; to blame 732
mǎi [買]	to buy 1298
mài [賣]	to sell 51
mài [邁]	old 1352*

mǎn [滿]	whole, fully 188
màn [慢]	slowly 963
màn-màn [慢慢]	slowly 169
màn-màn-li [慢慢裏]	slowly 434*
màn-tēng-tēng [慢騰騰]	slowly 963*
màn-màn [漫漫]	overflowing 233-4
máng [忙]	haste; hastily 434
mào [冒]	falsely 634
mào-er [帽兒]	hat 318
Mào-er...jiāo-kè	
[帽兒...嬌客]	*a jingle* 318-20*
méi [沒]	have not, did not 16
méi [眉]	eyebrow 201
Méi-huā jiǔ [梅花酒]	*title of a melody:* 'Plum Blossom Wine' 1317
měi [每]	*a plural suffix, comparable to men* 們 214*
měi [每]	each 468
měi [美]	delicious 500
mèi-xīn [昧心]	to go against one's conscience 1279
mén [門]	door 110
mén-shén [門神]	door god 967
mén-shén hù-wèi [門神戶尉]	door gods 967*
mén-shǒu [門首]	gate 55
mén-yíng, mén-xíng [門桯]	door frame 976*
mèn-chén-chén [悶沈沈]	deeply depressed 201
méng [蒙]	by; to receive [from a superior] 1145
méng-lóng [朦朧]	dim 304
mèng [夢]	dream 195
mèng-jiàn [夢見]	to dream of 986
Mèng Guāng [孟光]	*name of a person* 476*
Mèng Guāng...méi	
[孟光...眉]	*see note at* 476-7
mián [眠]	sleep 465
mián [綿]	cotton 863
miǎn [免]	to avoid; to do without 863
miàn [面]	face 80; 802*
miàn-shang [面上]	surface 1011
miè [滅]	to rescind 382: to dim 991
míng [名]	given name 29; M *for persons* 1258
míng [明]	clear; bright; to make clear; to brighten 647
míng-bai [明白]	comprehensible 471; clear 1160
míng-mù [瞑目]	*see note at* 1348
mìng [命]	life 539
mò [驀]	to go over; to leap over 128
mò guò [驀過]	to go around 128*
mò [莫]	not 206
mò bú shì, mò bú [莫不是]	isn't it... 206,* 522*
mò [脈]	vein 481
mò qí, mó qí [磨旗]	to wave a flag 723*
mò...qiān [陌...阡]	*see note at* 865-6*

móu [謀]	to plot, plot 414
mǔ-qin [母 親]	mother 35
mù [目]	eyes 402
mù-xià [目 下]	now 62*
mù [暮]	evening 733
mù [睦]	to live in peace 1057
mù [墓]	grave 1200
mù-xuè [墓 穴]	grave 526
mù-lú [木 驢]	'wooden donkey': a wooden stake 1366*
Mù-yáng guān [牧 羊 關]	*title of a melody: 'Pasturing-Sheep Pass'* 649
ná [拿]	to take; to carry 168
nǎ [那]	what; how 146
nà [那]	that 15; *see note at* 787
na, ne [那]	*a final particle* 244*; *see pp.* 18–19
nǎi [乃]	then 1200
nǎi-nai [妳 妳]	nai-nai; mother-in-law 227*
nài [耐]	to endure 1138
nán [南]	south 110
nán [難]	hard 463
nán-dào [難 道]	hard to say; do you mean to say; hardly conceivable 345*
nán [男]	man
nán-ér [男 兒]	man 325
nán-zǐ [男 子]	man 360
Nán-lǚ [南 呂]	*name of a musical mode* 464
nǎo-nǎo [惱 惱]	to fret 819
nǎo-zào [惱 懆]	to be annoyed 344–5
nèi [內]	inside 882
néng [能]	to be able 915
nǐ [你]	you 65; *see note at* 1029
nǐ [擬]	to determine; to sentence 1365
nián [年]	age 9
nián-jì [年 紀]	age 254–5
nián-jié [年 節]	New Year and other festivals 798
nián-lǎo [年 老]	old 1116
nián-tóu [年 頭]	years 125
nián-yòu [年 幼]	young 287
niǎn [撚]	to twist 372
niàn [廿]	twenty 371
niàn [念]	to think 803; to recite 1278
niàn fó chī zhāi [念 佛 吃 齋]	*see note at* 1278–9
niáng [娘]	mother 808
niáng-qīn [娘 親]	mother 500
niǔ [扭]	to twist; to loop 303
niǔ [紐]	to twist 748
nòng [弄]	to handle; to adjust 989
nǚ [女]	female 33
nǚ dà... liú [女 大... 留]	*a proverb* 276*

nǚ-er [女 兒]	daughter 16
nǚ-hái-er [女 孩 兒]	girl 33
nǚ-xu [女 婿]	son-in-law 228; *also used in the sense of* 'husband' *for a young woman* 312*
nù [怒]	anger; angry 1068
ǒu [嘔]	to vomit 508
ǒu-tù [嘔 吐]	to vomit 643
ǒu-rán [偶 然]	by chance 1099
pá [扒]	to strip 1113
pà [怕]	afraid 251
pà-bú-dài [怕 不 待]	perhaps 190–1*
pà zé pà [怕 則 怕]	*see note at* 773
pà [帕]	veil 275
pái [牌]	tally 1021; warrant 1203
pái-huái, pái-huí [徘 徊]	to walk back and forth; to hesitate 241*
pán-chan [盤 纏]	travelling money 39
pàn [拚]	to relinquish 350*
pàn [判]	to sentence; sentence 693
páng [傍]	other 547
páng zhōu lì [傍 州 例]	example 672*
pēi [呸]	*an interjection:* nonsense 1008
pēi-tāi [胚 胎]	embryo 1320–1
péi-dài [陪 待]	to keep company and to serve 364
pèi-he [配 合]	to mate 1073
pèi-ǒu [配 偶]	mates 288
pēn [噴]	to sprinkle 666; to spurt 861
pī, pēi [披]	to wear over the shoulders 777
pí [皮]	skin 678
pǐ-pèi [匹 配]	mated 585
piān [偏]	to incline 749
piān-yí [偏 宜]	to favor 480
pián-yi [便 宜]	benefit; advantageous 596
piàn [片]	slice: *a measure word* 856
piàn-kè [片 刻]	moment 1206
piǎo-xiāng [縹 緗]	blue silk and light yellow silk: valuable books 26*
piē [撇]	to discard 98
piē-xià [撇 下]	to leave 33
pín [貧]	poor 27
pín-nàn [貧 難]	poor and in difficulty 15
pín-qióng [貧 窮]	poor; poverty 738
píng-ān [平 安]	well 503; quiet: *see note at* 1171–2
píng-bái [平 白]	on the basis of nothing; without cause 656
píng-kōng [平 空]	without basis 356
píng-mín [平 民]	common people 377
pō [頗]	fairly 11
pō [潑]	bad 376

pó [婆]	mother-in-law; an old woman 100
pó-po [婆婆]	*an address to mother-in-law or an old woman:* p'o-p'o 7*
pó-zi [婆子]	a woman 159
pò [破]	to split; to break 280
pò [魄]	spirit; soul 674
pò sàn hún fēi [魄 散 魂 飛]	to be frightened out of one's wits 674–5*
pǔ [普]	all 670
pù [舖]	store 1278 ·
qī [七]	seven 17
qī-qiào [七 竅]	seven apertures 1101
qī qiào liú xuě [七 竅 流 血]	seven apertures issuing blood: *a stock phrase* 1101*
Qī dì-xiong [七 弟 兄]	*title of a melody:* 'Seven Brothers' 1294
qī, qí [期]	date 92; to count on 873
qī [妻]	wife 279
qī, qì [戚]	relation by marriage; relatives 520
qī [欺]	to cheat 702; to oppress 740
qí [其]	his; their 10
qí-shí [其 實]	really 554
qí [齊]	up to; to be in line with 477
qí [旗]	flag 723
qí-qiāng [旗 鎗]	flag staff 831
qí-guài [奇 怪]	strange 898
qǐ [豈]	*an interrogative particle which implies a dissenting answer* 20
qǐ-bù [豈 不]	how not; surely 20*
qǐ-bú-shì [豈 不 是]	is it not so? 257
qǐ [起]	to begin to 436; to arise 608
qǐ. . . lai [起. . . 來]	*a split compound complement:* to begin to 436*
qì [氣]	angry; anger 518
qì-xìng [氣 性]	temperament 347
qì [泣]	to weep 1150
qì [器]	utensils 475
qì-ná [緝 拿]	to arrest 1215
qià [恰]	as soon as 675; exactly 986
qiān [千]	thousand 361
qiān [阡]	*see note at* 865–6
qiān [僉]	to sign 1203
qiān [愆]	wrongs 1375
qián [錢]	money 23
qián-cái [錢 財]	money; riches 11
qián-chāo [錢 鈔]	money/cash-notes: money 164
qián [前]	ago 120; previous 217; front 306
qián-hòu [前 後]	front and back 102
qián shì [前 世]	previous life 217–18*
qián-kūn [乾 坤]	Heaven and Earth: the universe 375*
qiǎn [淺]	shallow 840

353

qiàn [欠]	to lack 498
qiāng [腔]	chest 861
qiáng [强]	strongly 1098
qiāo-qiāo [悄悄]	quietly 394
qiáo-cái [喬才]	crooked person 1148
qiáo-jiàn [瞧見]	to see 846
Qiáo pái-er [喬牌兒]	*title of a melody:* 'Lofty Sign' 1027
qiǎo [巧]	skillfully 288
qiě [且]	meanwhile; temporarily; for now 22
qiè-shēn [妾身]	*a humble way for a young woman to refer to herself:* handmaiden 175*
qīn [親]	personally, own 21; relative, relation 458
qīn-juàn [親眷]	family and relatives 758
qīn-shēng [親生]	own born 1052
qīn-shì [親事]	marriage 461
qīn-zì [親自]	personally 186
qìn-jia, qìng-jia [親家]	in-law 65*
qīn chāi [欽差]	imperially sent 1021
qīn [寢]	sleep 194
qīng [輕]	slight 69
qīng [清]	pure, clear 462
qīng [傾]	to pour 497
qīng [青]	green; blue 709
qīng-chūn [青春]	*literally* verdure spring; spring-like; youthful 1157*
Qīng-gē-er [青哥兒]	*title of a melody:* 'Green Parrot' 285
qíng [情]	situation 658; fact 1263
qíng-huái [情懷]	heart; mind 202
qíng-shòu [情受]	to receive; to enjoy 340*
qíng-yì [情意]	affection; feelings 521
qíng-yóu [情由]	a situation and its origin; situation 190
qíng-yuàn [情願]	willing 598
qíng [晴]	clear 903
qǐng [請]	to request: 'please. . .' 57
qǐng [頃]	instant 730
qióng-huā [瓊花]	jade flowers: snow flakes 1131
qiú [裘]	fur garments 291
qiú [囚]	convict 328
qiù [俅]	to look after 216
qū [屈]	injustice; unjustly 699
qū-rèn [屈認]	to confess under pressure when not guilty 1117*; *see note at* 1131
qū-zhāo [屈招]	to confess under torture when not guilty 795; *see note at* 1131
qū-chǔ [區處]	arrangement 353
qǔ [取]	to seek 62
qǔ-yìng [取應]	to take an examination 46
qù [去]	to go 23
qù-chù [去處]	place 152*

qù-lai [去 來]	*comparable to* qù-ba 去 罷 102*; *see pp.* 17–18
qù-nián [去 年]	last year 12
qu [去]	*directional complement:* away, off 49
quán [全]	entirely; complete 258
quán [權]	power 735
quán [泉]	fountain 1379
quán-tái [泉 臺]	spring terrace: *a euphemism for* 'grave' 1331*
quán-jì [痊 濟]	to recover 501
quàn [勸]	to urge; advise 219
quē-shǎo [缺 少]	to lack 46–7
què [卻]	however; yet 431
rǎng [嚷]	to shout 403
rǎng-dào [嚷 道]	to shout 375
ràng-yǔ [讓 與]	to give up to 644
ráo [饒]	to let off; to forgive 420
rě [惹]	to provoke 235
rè [熱]	hot 833
rén [人]	person 5
rén-fàn [人 犯]	criminal 1205
rén-jia [人 家]	other people 235
rén-shì [人 氏]	*an idiom for* 'a native of' *or* 'a resident of' 7*
rén [仁]	kindness 487
rěn [忍]	to bear 339
rěn-nài [忍 耐]	to endure 1137
rěn-qì [忍 氣]	to restrain anger 763
rèn [恁]	this way; such; thus 487
rèn-de [恁 的]	this way; such; thus 1030
rèn [認]	to admit; to claim; to identify 548
rèn-de [認 的]	to recognize 416
rèn-zuò [認 做]	to admit; to confess as 1311
rèn [任]	duty 1186; office 1189
réng-jiù [仍 舊]	still 167
rì [日]	day 5; sun 733
rì-chén [日 辰]	day 21
rì-tou [日 頭]	days 272
róng [容]	to allow 919
rǒng rǒng [冗 冗]	heavy 202–3
ròu [肉]	flesh 101
ròu-shēn [肉 身]	the flesh 364
rú [如]	as; like 36
rú-hé [如 何]	like what; how 444
rú-jīn [如 今]	as of now 13
rú-lǜ lìng [如 律 令]	*see note at* 1237–8
rú-tóng [如 同]	like 545–6
rú-yè [儒 業]	Confucian studies 30
rǔ [辱]	disgrace 1140
rǔ-mò [辱 沒]	disgrace 1061

rù, ròu [褥]	quilt 305*
rù [入]	to enter 982
ruǎn [輭]	soft 393; weak 741
ruì [瑞]	auspicious 853
ruò [若]	if 84
ruò-guǒ [若 果]	if 861
ruò-shì [若 是]	if 190
ruò-xì [若 係]	if 1120
ruò [弱]	weak 592
ruò-zhèng [弱 症]	consumption 124
sā [撒]	to let loose 545
sā-pō [撒 潑]	to behave badly 376
sā shǒu. . . xiū-qì	
[撒 手. . . 休 棄]	*see note at* 544–6
sǎ [灑]	to sprinkle; to shed 844, 1324*
Sài Lú-yī [賽 盧 醫]	*a nickname:* 'Rival Lu-Doctor': the rival of the doctor of Lu 105*
sān [三]	three 8
sān-cóng [三 從]	'Three Obediences' 1055
sān-fú [三 伏]	third *fu*; three *fu* 851*
sān-tòng [三 通]	three times 723*
sān tuī liù wèn [三 推 六 問]	to question repeatedly 591–2*
sān zhāo wǔ xī [三 朝 五 夕]	a few days 542*
sàn [散]	to scatter: 675
sàn-táng-gǔ [散 堂 鼓]	drum to dismiss the court 716
Sēn-luó diàn [森 羅 殿]	the palace of Yama, king in the nether world 730–1*
shā [殺]	extremely 27*; to kill 1342
shā [紗]	silk-yarn 484
Shā-wěi [煞 尾]	coda 885
shān [山]	hill 485
Shān-yáng [山 陽]	*name of a place* 109
shàn [擅]	to follow one's own will 376
shàn [善]	good 737
shàn [膳]	to feed 1307
shāng [傷]	injury 1371
shǎng [賞]	to view; to enjoy 87
Shǎng huā-shí [賞 花 時]	*title of a melody:* 'Enjoying Flowers Season' 87
shàng [上]	to enter 4; at 34; up to 123; top 381; best 391
shàng-cháo [上 朝]	to go up to court 46
shàng-cháo qǔ yìng	
[上 朝 取 應]	to go to the capital to take an examination 46*
shàng-mian [上 面]	top 757–8
shàng. . . míng [上. . . 名]	to go to the capital to seek a higher degree 62–3*
shàng-si [上 司]	a superior 602
shàng-tou [上 頭]	top 999

shāo [燒]	to burn 218
shāo xiāng bú dào tóu [燒 香 不 到 頭]	see note at 218*
shǎo [少]	to owe; to lack 66; little 69
shǎo-bù-dé [少 不 得]	cannot do without 157–8
shǎo-qiàn [少 欠]	to owe 253
shào [少]	young 5
shé [舌]	tongue 402
shě-de [捨 得]	to bear 364
shè [舍]	house 571
shè [赦]	to pardon 951
shè-hún tái [攝 魂 臺]	see note at 1143
shéi [誰]	who 42
shém-me [甚 麼]	what 42
shēn [身]	body 139; life 632
shēn-duàn [身 段]	figure 330
shēn-zi [身 子]	body 592
shén [神]	spirit; god 271
shén-xian [神 仙]	immortals 6
shén-de [甚 的]	same as shém-me 519*
shěn [審]	interrogate 918
shěn-fàn [審 犯]	criminals 1209
shēng [生]	born 17; raw 110; life 219 to grow 1185; to ascend 1338*
shēng-de [生 得]	to grow to be 362
shēng-pà [生 怕]	to fear 547
shēng-shòu [生 受]	to suffer 295
shēng-xiàng [生 相]	natural appearance 1286
shēng-yào [生 藥]	raw medicine 110
shēng [升]	to ascend 604
shēng [聲]	voice 375; M for cry 729
shēng [陞]	to promote 1186
shēng gē [笙 歌]	music and songs 305–6*
shéng-suǒ [繩 索]	rope 377
shéng-zi [繩 子]	rope 139
shěng [省]	secretariat 921
shèng [勝]	better than 501
shèng-ēn [聖 恩]	imperial favor 916
shèng-zhǔ [聖 主]	sage king 1145–6
shī [失]	to miss 379
shī [濕]	wet 538
shī [屍]	corpse 905
shī-hái [屍 骸]	corpse/skeleton 812
shī-shou [屍 首]	corpse 854
shī-yún [詩 云]	the verse says; to say in verse 4*
shí [十]	ten 68
shí-è [十 惡]	see note at 950
shí-fēn [十 分]	very 362
shí-sān [十 三]	thirteen 119

shí [時]	season 87; time; occasion 194; opportunity 821
shí-chen [時 辰]	time 322
shí-jié [時 節]	time; occasion 266; festivals 810
shí-shì [時 勢]	situation 537
shí-yùn [時 運]	time; fate 31
shí [石]	stone 485
shí [食]	food 612
shí [實]	truth; true 614
shǐ [使]	to employ 472; to cause 879; to send 925; to allow 1382
shǐ-xìng [使 性]	to be temperamental; to indulge in 356
shǐ-yòng [使 用]	to use 61
shì [是]	to be 6; *used for emphasis* 285*
shì-fēi [是 非]	right or wrong; gossip 470
shì [侍]	to serve 221
shì [事]	things; affair; incident 278
shì [世]	world 358; generations 1060
shì [識]	to recognize 374
shì [氏]	clan name 475
shì [適]	just 637
shì-cái [適 纔]	just now 770
shì [示]	to show 1326
shì-cáo [市 曹]	market place 694
shì-jiàn jīn-pái [勢 劍 金 牌]	sword and tally given by the emperor as symbols of power 921-2*
shì-yuàn [誓 願]	oath, 886-7
Shōu Jiāng-nán [收 江 南]	*title of a melody:* 'Recovering The South of the River' 1328
shōu-liú [收 留]	to retain 432
shōu-shi [收 拾]	to tidy up; to pack 393; to arrange; to make ready; to mend 551
shōu-yǎng [收 養]	to keep and to provide for 1350
shǒu [守]	to abide; to observe 214; to keep company 542
shǒu-guǎ [守 寡]	to remain a widow; to observe widowhood 125
shǒu [手]	hand 420
shǒu [首]	head 805
shòu [瘦]	thin 191
shòu [受]	to suffer 738; to receive 1031
shòu [壽]	life span 739
shòu-shù [壽 數]	life span 541
shū [書]	book 26
shū àn [書 案]	writing desk 958
shū [舒]	to spread 1353
shū zhe [梳 着]	to have combed in the style of . . . 273
shǔ [暑]	summer 291
shǔ-qì [暑 氣]	summer weather 858

shǔ-shī [暑濕]	rheumatic fever 537–8
shǔ-guān [屬官]	subordinate official 936
shù [數]	several 14
shuā-juàn [刷卷]	an inspector in court cases 602*;
shuā zhào [刷照]	to review court cases 939*
Shuǎ hái-ér [耍孩兒]	*title of a melody:* 'Playing Dolls' 838
shuāi-mài [衰邁]	feeble and old 1352
shuāng [霜]	frost 273
shuāng [雙]	two; pair 1108
Shuāng-diào [雙調]	*name of a musical mode* 960
shuǐ [水]	water 209; river 484
shuǐ-lù-dào-chǎng [水陸道場]	a Buddhist sacrifice service 1338*
shuì [睡]	to sleep 304
shùn [順]	to yield; to obey; to follow 397
shùn shuǐ tuī chuán	
[順水推船]	*see note at* 741–2*
shuō [說]	to say 15
shuō-dào [說道]	to say 259
shuō-huà [說話]	to talk 54–5
sī [廝]	fellow 323*
sī [私]	privately 588
sī [思]	thoughts 908
sī-liàng [思量]	to think of 346; to want 447
sǐ [死]	to die; death 168
sǐ-de [死的]	the dead 106*
sǐ-qiú [死囚]	condemned convict 692
sǐ-shī [死屍]	corpse 1325
sǐ-zuì [死罪]	a capital crime; a capital punishment 899
sì [似]	like 204
sì [四]	four 906
sì bì pín [四壁貧]	poor with only four bare walls 88*
sì-dé [四德]	'Four Virtues' 1054–5
sì lín bá shè [四鄰八舍]	neighbors 570–1*
sì-shí [四十]	forty 19–20
sòng [送]	to send, to hand over 21
sòng-sǐ [送死]	*see note at* 1347
sòng-yǔ [送與]	to give to 48
sòng-tíng [訟庭]	court 655
sū-xǐng [蘇醒]	to awake 675–6
sù [素]	white; plain 845
sù chē bái mǎ [素車白馬]	plain carriage and white horses 864–5*
sù [訴]	to state 1163
sù-bǐng [訴稟]	to report respectfully 1274
sù-zhèng-lián-fǎng shǐ	
[肅政廉訪使]	surveillance commissioner 1022
suàn [算]	to consider 359; to figure out 436
suí [遂]	to attain 32
suí [隨]	to follow 171
suí-chù [隨處]	all places 918

suí-jì [隨 即]	immediately 1101
suí-shēn [隨 身]	to carry on the person 138–9
suí-shùn [隨 順]	to yield; to obey 265
suí-yá [隨 衙]	to be at court *or* close to it 715*
suí-rán [雖 然]	although 285
suì [歲]	year 10
sǔn-tiáo [筍 條]	bamboo shoot 287
suǒ [索]	to collect 22
suǒ-qǔ [索 取]	to demand 15
suǒ [鎖]	lock; to lock 777
suǒ-yǐ [所 以]	therefore 1192
tā [他]	he; she; other person 16
tā shéi [他 誰]	who 669–70*
tā. . . sì-shi liǎng	
[他. . . 四 十 兩]	*see note at* 51–2
tā [闥]	door hanging 197*
tái [擡]	to raise; to carry; to bring 647
tái shěng [臺 省]	*see note at* 921
tài-shàng [太 上]	supreme; high 1237
tài-shàng lǎo-jūn [太 上 老 君]	the Taoist God 1237*
tài-shǒu [太 守]	prefect 603
tài-yáng huī [太 陽 暉]	sunlight 684
tài-yī [太 醫]	doctor 367*
tán-yì [談 議]	to discuss 459
tàn [歎]	to sigh 49
tāng [湯]	soup 447
táng [堂]	hall 908
tǎng [倘]	if 402
tǎng [倘]	surprised 748
Tǎng xiù-cái [倘 秀 才]	*title of a melody:* 'Surprised Scholar' 748
Táo [桃]	*a family name:* T'ao 1186
Táo Wù [桃 杌]	*name of a person* 604
táo [逃]	to flee 1214
tǎo [討]	to ask 85
tǎo de [討 得]	to get 640
tè [特]	especially 510
tī [剔]	to trim 992
tī-tuán-luán [剔 團 圞]	round 198*
tí [提]	to carry; to bring forward 724
tí-xíng [提 刑]	surveillance commissioner 972–3*
tí-xíng-sù-zhèng-lián-fǎng shǐ	
[提 刑 肅 政 廉 訪 使]	surveillance commissioner 917*
tí [啼]	to cry 558
tí-kū [啼 哭]	to cry 101
tí-tí [啼 啼]	to cry 558
tí [題]	theme 887
tí-mu zhèng-míng [題 目 正 名]	*see note at* 1384–5
tǐ [體]	body 444

tǐ-chá [體察]	to uncover 918
tì [替]	for 290; to substitute 540
tiān [天]	Heaven 1
tiān-dào [天道]	season 851*; weather 1123; heaven-decreed 1177–8
tiān-sè [天色]	sky color 882
Tiān xǐ [天喜]	'Heaven's Joy': a certain auspicious day 437*
tiān-xìng [天幸]	heavenly luck 643
tiān-zāi [天災]	natural disaster 1326
Tiān-zhāng [天章]	*name of a person* 29
tiān-zǐ [天子]	the emperor 1343
tiān [添]	to add 499
tián [填]	to fill 1299
tián-chóu [田疇]	arable land 290
tiáo [調]	to engage 472
tiáo-xì [調戲]	to flirt with 1090
tīng [聽]	to hear; to listen 270
tīng-de [聽的]	*comparable to* tīng-jiàn 見 *or* tīng-dao 到 *in modern Mandarin:* to (actually) hear 156
tīng-jiàn [聽見]	to (actually) hear 1168
tīng [廳]	hall 604
tíng [停]	to stop 1068
tíng-zhì [停置]	to prepare 550
tōng [通]	to extend to 1380; cf. *tòng* 723
tóng [同]	together 102; same 303; to share 526
tóng-zhù-rén [同住人]	together-live-man: mate 212
tóng-dǒu-er [銅斗兒]	brass peck 337*
tòng [痛]	pains 696
tòng [通]	M *for drum beating* 723*; cf. *tōng* 1380
tóu [頭]	end; top; head 139; first; first-place 998
tóu [投]	congenial 280; to plunge 484
tú-móu [圖謀]	to make plans 290
tǔ [土]	earth 480
tǔ [吐]	to spit out 1063
tuī [推]	to push 341; to examine 592*; to make excuse 653
tuī-cí [推辭]	to make excuse for 755–6
tuī-wěi [推諉]	to make excuse for 1379
tuì [啐]	*an interjection showing disapproval:* tui! 1169
tūn-shēng [吞聲]	to be silent 763
tūn-shēng rěn-qì [吞聲忍氣]	to endure quietly 763*
tuō [拖]	to drag 414
tuō-lí [脫離]	to redeem from 980
tuō [託]	to entrust 970
tuō yi mèng [託一夢]	to communicate by means of a dream 970*
wāi-la [歪剌]	perverse 354*
wài [外]	outside 127
wài [外]	*a role* 719*

wán [頑]	insensitive 485
wán-lüè [頑 劣]	naughty 84
wán pí [頑 皮]	stubborn skinned: stubborn 663
wán shí [頑 石]	senseless stone 485
wán-quán [完 全]	whole 805
wǎn [晚]	evening; late 291
wǎn [碗]	bowl: M *for rice* 799
wàn [萬]	ten thousand; myriad 26
wáng [亡]	lost 34
wáng-huà [亡 化]	died 32
wáng-shì [亡 逝]	died 8–9*
wáng [王]	imperial 728
wáng-jiā fǎ [王 家 法]	imperial law 1382
wǎng, wàng [往]	to; toward 127
wǎng-lái [往 來]	coming and going 722
wǎng [枉]	to no purpose 280; to cheat 321; in vain 744; useless 978
wàng [望]	to hope; to expect 54; to look about 967
Wàng-dì [望 帝]	*name of a person* 847*
Wàng xiāng tái [望 鄉 臺]	gazing toward native-place terrace 961*
wàng [忘]	to forget 193
wēi [威]	sway; terror 1069
wēi-fēng [威 風]	power 1030-1
wēi-quán [威 權]	power and authority 922
wéi [爲]	to be 179; *cf.* wèi 爲 88 *below*
wéi [危]	danger 781
wéi-cuò [違 錯]	to mismanage; to act contrary 1369
wéi wù [違 悞]	to disobey and to miss 1205–6
wěi [委]	really 686
wěi-shí [委 實]	truly 831–2
wèi [未]	not 32
wèi [爲]	because 88; for 385; *cf.* wéi 179
wèi [畏]	to fear 951
wén [文]	writing 31
wén-cè [文 冊]	documents 1146
wén-juàn [文 卷]	case; file 939
wén-shū [文 書]	documents 67
wén-zhāng [文 章]	learning; writing 31
wén [聞]	to hear 860
wěn [穩]	secure 305
wèn [問]	to require from; from 12; to question 592
wèn-hòu [問 候]	to inquire after 237*
wèn-zhǎn [問 斬]	to be executed 1182
wǒ [我]	me, I 13
wǒ-men [我 們]	we 317
wǒ xiǎng [我 想]	*see note at* 462
wū [屋]	house 129
wū [污]	foul 919
wū-fú [於 伏]	*same as* wū-fú 誣 服: to confess under pressure

wú [無]	what is not true 1356*
	have not; not 5
wú-cí [無 辭]	without words: without argument 1131*
wú-cí . . . qiān [無辭 . . . 愆]	*see note at* 1131
wú jìn-tóu [無 盡 頭]	to have no end 208
wú-qíng [無 情]	to have no feeling 667
wú tóu [無 頭]	irrational 839*
wǔ-di, wǔ-de [兀 的]	*see note at* 66–7
wǔ-di bú tòng shā wǒ yě [兀 的 不 痛 殺 我 也]	*see note at* 696–7
wǔ-nà [兀 那]	*see note at* 139
wǔ-nì [忤 逆]	unfilial; contrary 546–7
wǔ-wèi [五 味]	five flavors 651
wù [物]	things 38
wù [悮]	to miss 746
wù [霧]	fog 965
wù-dé [毋 得]	do not 1205
xī [西]	west 137
xī [稀]	rare 524
xī-huáng [栖 惶]	troubled 555
xí [習]	to learn 30
xí [席]	mat 829
xí [息]	to stop 1068
xí, xì [昔]	formerly 1377
xí-rì [昔 日]	old days 1193
xí-fu [媳 婦]	daughter-in-law; wife 19
xǐ [洗]	scoured 36
xǐ [喜]	joyous 297
xǐ-de [喜 得]	fortunately 391
xì [細]	fine; details 393
xì-xì [細 細]	particularly 300
xì, xī [夕]	evening 542
xì [系]	to be 1191
xiá [霞]	colorful cloud 275
xià [下]	to exit 93; to send down; to pass down 692; M *for beating:* stroke 723
xià-chǎng-tóu [下 場 頭]	outcome 343*
xià-de [下 的]	*same as* shě-de 捨 得: to bear 97*
xià-guān [下 官]	humble official: I 603
xià-shǒu [下 手]	to act 138
xià-yào [下 藥]	to prescribe medicine 106
xià [嚇]	to frighten 377
xiān [先]	formerly 52
xiān zhǎn hòu zòu [先 斬 後 奏]	*see note at* 919–20
xiān [鮮]	fresh 895
Xiān-lǚ [仙 呂]	*name of a musical mode* 87
xián [嫌]	to mind 69

xián-yí [嫌 疑]	suspicion 456–7	
xián [閒]	idle 188	
xián [銜]	to hold 698	
xián [賢]	worthy 744	
xiǎn [顯]	to reveal 891	
xiàn [縣]	district 109	
xiàn [現]	exposed 864	
xiàn-jīn [現 今]	now 1123	
xiāng [香]	incense 218	
xiāng-huǒ [香 火]	incense burning 273	
xiāng [相]	mutually 468	
xiāng-jiàn [相 見]	to see each other 58	
xiāng-lèi [相 類]	similar 1202	
xiāng shǒu [相 守]	to mutually keep company 149	
xiāng [廂]	chambers 1170	
xiáng [詳]	in detail 658	
xiǎng [想]	to think; to expect; to consider 42	
xiǎng [享]	to enjoy 739	
xiàng [向]	toward 450	
xiàng-wài [向 外]	beyond; over 361	
xiàng-gōng [相 公]	sir 609*	
xiàng-kǒu [巷 口]	lane entrance 721	
xiāo [宵]	night 195	
xiāo [消]	to cancel; to wipe out 1375	
xiāo-hún [消 魂]	to lose one's spirit 93*	
xiāo-tíng [消 停]	to calm down; to stop 675	
xiǎo [曉]	to know 478	
xiǎo [小]	young; small 553	
xiǎo-míng [小 名]	humble name 122	
xiǎo-ní-zi [小 妮 子]	little girl 361–2; 1045–6*	
xiǎo-shēng [小 生]	insignificant man: I 29*	
xiǎo-zǐ [小 子]	insignificant man: I 367*	
xiǎo-zì [小 字]	humble name 33–4	
xiào [笑]	to laugh 280	
xiào-hua [笑 話]	laughter 283	
xiào [孝]	filial 1193	
xiào-fù [孝 婦]	woman with great filial piety 877*	
xiào-shùn [孝 順]	filial piety 1319	
xiē [些]	some 11	
xiē-shǎo [些 少]	some 53	
xiē-xi [歇 息]	to rest 943	
xiē-zi [楔 子]	wedge 3*	
xiè [謝]	to thank 70	
xīn [新]	new 279	
xīn-láng [新 郎]	bridegroom 319	
Xīn shuǐ lìng [新 水 令]	*title of a melody*: 'New Water Song' 960	
xīn [心]	heart; intention 303	
xīn-huái [心 懷]	feeling 1319–20	
xīn-tóu [心 頭]	mind 196	

xīn-xù [心 緒]	thoughts 203
xīn-kǔ [辛 苦]	tired 943
xìn [信]	to believe 325
xīng [星]	speck 843
xíng [行]	to act; to commit 105; to walk 128
xíng-dòng [行 動]	to move 725
xíng-li [行 李]	luggage 393
xíng, háng [行]	*see note at 751 for use in a locative expression*
xíng [刑]	to punish 1116
xíng-fǎ [刑 法]	penalty by law 812
xíng-míng [刑 名]	criminal law 921*
xíng-xiàn [刑 憲]	punishment 728–9
xǐng [醒]	to awake 984
xìng [姓]	surname 108
xìng-mìng [性 命]	life 155
xìng [興]	spirit; passion 301
xiōng [兇]	violence 246
xiōng shén [凶 神]	evil spirits 271
xiū [休]	do not 69; is over 278; to end; to settle 588
xiū-qì [休 棄]	to end and give up 546
xiū [羞]	to be embarrassed 239; shame 336
xiū [修]	to cultivate 382
xiū-huò [修 合]	to prepare 1371
xiù [繡]	to embroider 197
xiù-cai [秀 才]	scholar 12*
xiù-er [袖 兒]	sleeve 319
xū [須]	need; should 5; truly 286
xū [虛]	false; devoid of content 651
xū-xià [虛 下]	to indicate exit by turning one's back toward the audience 984*
xū-xiāo [虛 囂]	falsehood 472
xū-fǎ [鬚 髮]	beard and hair 930
xǔ [許]	to promise; to consent 267
xǔ-duō [許 多]	much 71
xù [續]	to continue 1258
xù [恤]	compassion 1346
xù-yòng [敍 用]	to employ 1369
xuān [喧]	warm 858
xuán [懸]	to hang 734
xuán [旋]	whirls 886
xuán-fēng [旋 風]	whirlwind 964
xuǎn [選]	to select 331
xuǎn-chǎng [選 場]	examination place 45
xuě [雪]	snow 273
xuě, xiě [血]	blood 678
xún [旬]	a period of ten days or ten years 277
xún-de, xín-de [尋 得]	to have found 1255
xún-sī, xín-sī [尋 思]	to think 169

365

yā [押]	to send under guard 707
yā-fù [押 付]	to send under guard to 694
yā [壓]	to press 954
yá [衙]	courthouse 604
yá-men [衙 門]	courthouse 1300
yá-men. . . zāi [衙 門 … 哉]	*see note at* 1328–30
ya, yā [呀]	*particle for expression of surprise* 414
yān [煙]	mist 909; vaporous 1372
yán [鹽]	salt 496
yán [延]	extensive 739
yán-cí [言 詞]	words 222
yán-yǔ [言 語]	speech 163–4
yǎn [眼]	eye, vision 302
yǎn-mù [眼 目]	eye 929–30
yǎn [掩]	to cover 1132
yàn [嚥]	to swallow 301
yàn [燕]	swallow 334
yàn lǚ yīng chóu [燕侶鶯儔]	swallows and orioles in pairs 334–5*
yàn [偃]	to incline 750
Yàn-ér luò [雁 兒 落]	*title of a melody:* 'A Wild Goose Descends' 1135
yáng [羊]	sheep 543
yáng [揚]	raised; loud 674
yǎng [養]	to care for 221
yǎng-shàn [養 膳]	to provide for 632
yǎng shēng [養 生]	to take care of someone while he is alive 1347*
yāo-he [么 喝]	to call 605
yāo-guài [妖 怪]	evil spirit 974
yǎo [杳]	obscure 767
yào [要]	to want 43; must 271; to get 359
yào [藥]	drug 399
yào-pù [藥 舖]	medicine shop 116
yào-shā [藥 殺]	to kill with poison 704
yé [爺]	father 83
yě [也]	also 54, 87*, 1354*; *an intensifier:* even, indeed 355, 359, 596
yě [也]	*a particle* 7*; *a vocative* 187*
yě mo-ge [也 麼 哥]	*see note at* 779*
ye-bo [也 波]	*a compound particle* 219*
yè [夜]	night 378
yī, yí, yì [一]	one 9
Yí-bàn-er [一 半 兒]	*title of a melody:* 'One Half' 233
yí-dìng [一 定]	certainly 1287
yí-gè-gè [一 個 個]	one by one 383
yí-jìng-de [一 徑 的]	straight 59*
yí-miàn [一 面]	once 759*
Yí-shà [一 煞]	*title of a melody:* 'Penultimate Coda' 872
yí shì [一 世]	a lifetime 207

yí-xiàng [一 向]	for some time 118*; up to the present 432
yì diǎn [一 點]	a drop; a little 1319
yì huǐ-er [一 會 兒]	one moment 882
yì jiā yí jì [一 家 一 計]	one family one plan: harmonious family 542-3*
yì kǒu-er [一 口 兒]	one mouthful 512
yì mǎ... bèi [一 馬 … 韝]	*see note at* 583
yì pín rú xǐ [一 貧 如 洗]	completely poor as if scoured: destitute 36*
yì-qǐ [一 起]	one group 947*
yì shēng [一 生]	whole life 465
yì-shí [一 時]	one moment 373
yì shǒu hǎo yī [一 手 好 醫]	*see note at* 108
yì-yīng [一 應]	all 936
Yì zhī huā [一 枝 花]	*title of a melody:* 'One Twig of Blossoms' 464
yī [醫]	medicine 105; to doctor 107
yī pù [醫 舖]	doctor's shop; apothecary shop 1224
yī [依]	according to 106; to agree to 172
yī-jiù [依 舊]	still 266
yī [衣]	clothing 253
yí [移]	to change 490
yí [疑]	to doubt 996
yí-xīn [疑 心]	doubtful 1027
yí-liú [遺 留]	to leave 289
yǐ-guò [已 過]	already; passed 9
yǐ-hòu [以 後]	afterward 425, 868
yǐ-qián [以 前]	formerly 382
yǐ-wài [以 外]	outside of; beyond 255*
yǐ-wǎng [已 往]	in the past 806
yì [異]	other 73; strange 894
yì [意]	mind; feelings; intention 200
yì-xià [意 下]	your idea 163
yì [義]	fidelity 487
yì [亦]	also 608
yì [縊]	to hang 1194
yīn [因]	because 38; cause; factor 382*
yīn-cǐ shàng [因 此 上]	because of this 89*
yīn-wei [因 爲]	because 150
yīn [陰]	darkened 882
yīn-yuán [姻 緣]	causes; fate 307*
yīn-xìn [音 信]	news 767*
yín [銀]	silver 601
yín-zi [銀 子]	silver 13
yín-bēn [淫 奔]	wanton 487
yǐn [引]	to lead 25
yǐn [飲]	to drink 501
yīng [鶯]	oriole 335
yíng-jiē [迎 接]	to greet 236-7
yíng-jiù [營 救]	to rescue 286
yíng-shēng [營 生]	to make a living 88

yǐng [影]	shadow 762
yìng [應]	to respond 904
yìng-jǔ [應 舉]	to take a state examination 54*
yìng-kǒu [應 口]	to fulfill what has been said 222*
yìng-yàn [應 驗]	to come true 900
yìng [硬]	strong 740
yǒng [永]	permanently 1369
yǒng-shì [永 世]	permanently 1066
yǒng-yuǎn [永 遠]	permanently 1372
yōu [憂]	sorrow 207; to worry 1343
yōu-chóu [憂 愁]	sorrow 204; to worry 930
yōu-yōu [悠 悠]	anxious and long 203
yóu [猶]	still 481
yóu [由]	to follow; according to 674
yóu [遊]	drift 730
Yóu hú-lu [油 葫 蘆]	*title of a melody:* 'Oil Gourd' 206*
yǒu [有]	to have 4; there is 139
yǒu guǐ . . . chì [有 鬼 . . . 勑]	*see note at* 1236–8
yǒu lèi nǐ [有 累 你]	*an idiomatic phrase:* to have troubled you: thanks for the trouble you took 507–8
yǒu-xīn [有 心]	to have the intention 18
yòu [幼]	childhood 30
yòu [又]	again 46; moreover 392
yòu [右]	right 749
yú [愚]	fool 744
Yú gōng [于 公]	Lord Yü 1197–8
yú-tóu [隅 頭]	corner of a wall 128–9
yǔ [與]	for; to; with 18; to give 383
yǔ [雨]	rain 932
yù [遇]	to encounter 153
yù-jian [遇 見]	to encounter 388
yuān [冤]	injustice; grievance 1
yuān-chóu [冤 讎]	grievances 1149
yuān-qì [冤 氣]	grievance 820
yuān-qíng [冤 情]	grievance 840
yuān-wang [冤 枉]	grievance 680; wronged 832
yuān-zhuàng [冤 狀]	grievance 1167–8
yuān-yang [鴛 鴦]	Mandarin ducks 1340*
Yuān-yang shā-wěi [鴛 鴦 煞 尾]	*title of a melody:* 'Mandarin-Ducks Coda' 1340
yuān zhàng [鴛 帳]	Mandarin-duck nets 465*
yuán [緣]	cause 265
yuán-yóu [緣 由]	reason 238
yuán [元]	originally 636
yuán-lái [元 來]	after all 741
yuán [原]	original 1336
yuán-gào [原 告]	plaintiff 615
yuǎn [遠]	distant 90
yuàn [願]	to wish 500; wishes 839

yuàn [怨]	to blame 669; grievance; grievous 763
yuàn-yuàn [怨 怨]	to grieve 557–8
yuè [月]	month 11; moon 733
yuè-sè [月 色]	moon 199
yuè [越]	more 202
yuè-yuè [越 越]	more 425–6
yún [雲]	cloud 274
yún-xiá-bān [雲 霞 般]	colorful 274–5*
yùn [運]	luck 821
zá-jù [雜 劇]	*see note at* 1
zá, zán [咱]	I, we 519
za [咱]	*particle for a mild imperative* 75*; *particle for a tentative statement:* I suppose 251*; *see pp.* 16
zāi [災]	disaster 1295
zài-zhe [載 着]	to carry 207
zài [再]	again; moreover 5; *an intensifier before a negative* 309*
zài-yě [再 也]	*an intensifier before a negative* 818*
zài [在]	at; to rest on 23; to exist 584
zài yá. . . shū-àn [在 衙. . . 書 案]	*see note at* 1171–2
zán [喒]	I 1314
zāo [遭]	to suffer 728
zǎo [早, 蚤]	early, soon 55; already 181; morning 291*
zǎo-wǎn [早 晚]	*idiom for* time 23–4*; day and night 61
zào [造]	to do 738
zé [則]	only 80*; just 192
zé [擇]	to select 271
zé-ge [則 個]	*a final particle* 64*; *see p.* 17
zè-zè [窄 窄]	*literally* 'narrow', *here a sound indicating approval* 319–20*
zéi [賊]	thief 701
zěn [怎]	how 60
zěn-d; [怎 地]	how; why 413
zěn gē-shě-de bù kěn [怎 割 捨 得 不 肯]	*see note at* 363–4
zěn-hǎo [怎 好]	how 349
zěn-shēng [怎 生]	how 223*
zhá-zhēng [扎 挣]	to struggle 531
zhái [宅]	residence 717
zhài [債]	debt 235
zhān [沾]	to stain 833
zhǎn [展]	to spread 201
zhǎn [斬]	to decapitate 693
zhàn [站]	to stand 836
zhàn-lì [站 立]	to stand on 830
zhàn [暫]	temporarily 1068
zhàn [佔]	to take by force 1365

zhàn-zhàn [湛 湛]	deep and clear 842
Zhāng [張]	a surname 467
Zhāng lǎo [張 老]	Chang elder 247
Zhāng Lǘ-er [張 驢 兒]	Donkey Chang 142
Zhāng Qiān [張 千]	Chang Ch'ien 907*
zhǎng [長]	to grow 10
zhǎng [掌]	to administer 921
zhǎng-shàng [掌 上]	to light 942
zhǎng-zhu [掌 著]	to control 734
zhàng [杖]	rod; blow 677; to beat with a stick 1369
zhàng [丈]	a unit of measurement: ten Chinese feet 830
zhàng [障 (瘴)]	malarial 1372
zhàng-fu [丈 夫]	husband 161
zhāo [招]	to call for 219; see note at 313; to confess 664
zhāo-rèn [招 認]	to confess 593
zhāo zhàng-fu [招 丈 夫]	to take a husband into a wife's family 249*
zhāo-zhuàng [招 狀]	confession paper 1318
zhāo-zuì [招 罪]	confession affidavit 705*
zhāo [朝]	day 542; morning 733
zhāo [召]	to summon 856
zháo [著]	to have; to make; to send 43*; to let 147
zhào [照]	to shine on; to reflect 650
zhē-yǎn [遮 掩]	to cover 853
zhé [折]	a unit in a Yüan play, usually translated as Act 104*
zhé-biàn [折 辯]	to argue 1232
zhé-duì [折 對]	to argue face to face 1256*
zhè [這]	this 19
Zhè… bú qì: [這… 不 氣]	see note at 516–18
zhè-li [這 裏]	here 11–12
zhè yí… àn [這 一… 案]	see note at 1231
zhe [著]	particle indicating present tense and continued action 110; a final particle 665*; see p. 17–18
zhe [者]	a final particle 1206*; see pp. 17–18
zhēn-ge [眞 個]	really 411*
zhēn-xīn-ér [貞 心 兒]	a chaste mind 326
zhēn-zhuo [斟 酌]	care 106
zhèn [陣]	M for dizziness: spell 955
zhēng [爭]	to struggle 702
zhēng-dòu [爭 鬬]	to fight 236
zhēng [睜]	to open (eyes) 1281
zhēng-nài [爭 奈]	what to do 31
zhēng-xie [爭 些]	nearly 144*
zhēng-zhái [爭 閣]	to work hard 337*
zhèng [正]	just; exactly 45; to uphold 879; to correct 1160
zhèng dàn [正 旦]	principal female-role 25*
Zhèng-gōng [正 宮]	name of a musical mode 727
zhèng-hǎo [正 好]	just right 405

zhèng-míng [正 名]	proper title 1385*
zhèng-hòu [證 候]	symptom 539*
zhī [之]	*particle indicating modification in classical Chinese* 54
zhī [知]	to know; to realize 91
zhī-dao [知 道]	to know 610–11
zhī-qì [知 契]	intimate friend 525
zhī [隻]	M *for an animal or thing* 762
zhī-duì [支 對]	to answer 655
zhī-zhuǎn [支 轉]	to send away 641
zhí [直]	really 97*; simply 486
zhí [值]	to encounter 536; to happen 637
zhí [職]	post 918
zhí-liào [執 料]	to attend to things 102
zhǐ [止]	only 9
zhǐ [只]	just; only 15
zhǐ-guǎn [只 管]	just; merely 78
zhǐ [指]	to point 1272
zhǐ-jiǎo de fū-qī [指 脚 的 夫 妻]	*see note at* 554
zhǐ-wàng [指 望]	to expect 792
zhǐ-cóng [祗 從]	attendant 907–8*
zhǐ-hòu [祗 候]	attendant 600*
zhǐ-qián [紙 錢]	paper money 800
zhì [至]	to reach 180
zhì [智]	senses 373
zhì [致]	to result in 947
zhì [治]	to govern 1052
zhì yù [治 獄]	to examine prisoners and make decisions 1198
zhì-jiù [置 就]	to secure; to amass 339
zhì-lìng [致 令]	to cause 1197
zhì-qì [志 氣]	purpose 488
zhì-xià [置 下]	to secure 290
zhōng [中]	in, within 11
zhōng-jiān [中 間]	in the midst of 1162
zhōng-nián [中 年]	middle age 278
zhōng [中]	to fit 251
zhōng [終]	finally 379; entire 632
zhǒng [種]	kinds 677
zhōu-gūan [州 官]	prefect 1114
zhōu-shǒu [州 守]	governor 1186
zhōu-tīng [州 廳]	an official hall in a sub-prefecture 933
zhòu [皺]	frown 202
zhú-li, zhóu-li [妯 娌]	sister-in-law 1057
zhú-yi [主 意]	idea 115
zhǔ-fu [囑 咐]	to enjoin 76
zhù [住]	to stop 401
zhuān [專]	solely 23
zhuǎn-yì [轉 意]	change of mind 353

zhuàn, zuàn [賺]	to trick; to lure 152
Zhuàn-shā, Zuàn-shā [賺 煞]	*title of a melody:* 'Coda' 324
zhuāng [庄]	village 134
zhuāng [椿]	M *for an affair or an oath* 1012
zhuāng-lóu [妝 樓]	lady's chamber 199
zhǔn [准]	to let go; to settle 19*; true 901
zhuō [桌]	desk 1019
Zhuō-zhōu [涿 州]	*name of a place* 427
Zhuó [卓]	*a surname* 475*
zhuó [濁]	foul 736
zī wèi [滋 味]	flavor 499
Zǐ-xū [子 虛]	*title of a literary composition by Ssu-ma Hsiang-ju* 28–9*
zì [自]	oneself 115; since 122
zì-jǐ [自 己]	oneself 267
zì-jiā [自 家]	own; oneself 100
zì shì. . . bù mián [自 是. . . 不 眠]	*see note at* 910–11
zì [字]	word 693
zōng [宗]	M *for documents* 946*
zòng, [縱]	indulgence 521
Zōu Yǎn [鄒 衍]	*name of a person* 860*
zǒu [走]	to walk; to travel 142
zòu [奏]	to report to the throne 920
zú-lü-lü [足 律 律]	quickly 963–4*
zǔ-guàn [祖 貫]	ancestral domicile 29*
zǔ-jū [祖 居]	ancestral home 176
zǔ-shàng [祖 上]	ancestor 1140
zǔ-zong [祖 宗]	ancestor 1062
zuàn [賺]	*see* zhuàn
zuǐ [嘴]	mouth 870
zuì [最]	most; utmost 346
zuì [罪]	sin; crime 382
zuì-fàn [罪 犯]	crime 594
zuì-míng [罪 名]	criminal charge 950
zuì-qiān [罪 愆]	sin; crime 804
zuì-zé, zuì-zái [罪 責]	sin; crime 1250*
zuì [醉]	drunk 556
zuó [昨]	yesterday 195
zuó-rì [昨 日]	yesterday 1162
zuó-xiāo [昨 宵]	last night 195
zuǒ [左]	left 749
zuǒ-yòu [左 右]	left/right: about 277*; attendants 605*
zuò [做]	to be 19; to do 49
zuò-chū [做 出]	to (actually) perform 479
zuò-gōng-de [做 公 的]	officers 721*
zuò shém-me [做 甚 麼]	'to do what', *meaning* 'why' 661
zuò-zhǔ [做 主]	to make decision 620
zuò zuǐ-liǎn [做 嘴 臉]	to make grimace 329
zuò [坐]	to sit 57
zuò yá [坐 衙]	to hold court 604

SELECTED BIBLIOGRAPHY ON
OLD MANDARIN AND THE LANGUAGE OF
YÜAN DRAMA AND WORKS CITED

This list includes books and articles useful in the study of both the language of Yüan drama and Old Mandarin, the northern dialect of the Yüan times. It consists of two major parts. Part One, consisting of source material for the study of Yüan colloquial language, is divided into two sections: the first section includes the Yüan plays themselves, and the second selected vernacular and semi-vernacular non-dramatic writings of the Yüan as well as the Sung and Ming dynasties. Part Two, consisting of critical and scholarly works, is divided into four sections: general studies, phonology, vocabulary, and grammar.

Daggers (†) indicate cited works not specifically related to the subject of Old Mandarin; those pertaining to vocabulary are in the 'Vocabulary' section; others are in 'General Studies'.

A few brief notes on some of the works, especially those in Chinese and Japanese, are included in the hope that they may be of use to readers not familiar with the subject.

PART ONE: SOURCE MATERIAL

I. YÜAN PLAYS

A. *Yüan edition*

Yüan k'an tsa-chü san-shih chung 元刊雜劇三十種.
  A wood-block edition, this is the oldest extant text of Yüan drama. The thirty plays in the collection consist mainly of song-sequences and very scanty prose dialogue. Modern editions include the following: (1) a wood-block, tidied-up facsimile, published by Kyoto University in 1914; (2) a photo-reprint edition of the original Yüan copy, in the *Ku pen hsi-ch'ü ts'ung-k'an ssu chi*, Shanghai, 1958 (hereafter referred to as *KPHCTK*, 4th series).

B. *Ming editions*

Ku ming-chia pen 古名家本, or *Ku ming-chia tsa-chü* 古名家雜劇, compiled by Ch'en Yü-chiao 陳與郊, 1588 *(KMCP)*.
  A Mr Hsü 徐 of Lung-feng 龍峯 is thought to be the engraver of this edition (see *Kuan Han-ch'ing hsi-ch'ü chi* 關漢卿戲曲集, ed. Wu Hsiao-ling 吳曉鈴, *et al.*, Peking, 1958, pp. 1056-7). It consists of at least 78 Yüan and Ming plays: 55 of these are included in the *Mo-wang kuan ch'ao-chiao pen ku chin tsa-chü*; 13 are not extant; and 10 are included in the photo-reprint edition of *KPHCTK*, 4th series, vols. 93-5 (see note to the table of contents, vol. 93, pp. 1*a–b*).

Tsa-chü hsüan 雜劇選 (also known as *Yüan jen tsa-chü hsüan* 元人雜劇選 or *Ku chin tsa-chü hsüan* 古今雜劇選), compiled by Hsi Chi-tzu 息機子, with a preface dated 1598 (Wan-li wu-hsü 萬曆戊戌).

It consists of 30 plays; 15 of these are in *Mo-wang kuan ch'ao-chiao pen ku chin tsa-chü*, 4 are not extant, and 11 are included in a photo-reprint edition of *KPHCTK*, 4th series, vols. 96–8.

Mo-wang kuan ch'ao-chiao pen ku chin tsa-chü 脈望館鈔校本古今雜劇, compiled by Chao Ch'i-mei 趙琦美 (1563–1624).

The collection consists of 242 Yüan and Ming plays (some of which are only fragments); of these, 55 are from *Ku ming-chia tsa-chü (Ku ming-chia pen)*; 15 from Hsi Chi-tzu's *Tsa-chü hsüan*; and the remaining 172 plays exist as hand-written copies. *Mo-wang kuan* was the name of the library of the compiler (see Sun K'ai-ti 孫楷第 *Yeh-shih-yüan ku chin tsa-chü k'ao* 也是園古今雜劇考 Shanghai, 1953). A photo-reprint edition is included in *KPHCTK*, 4th series, vols. 9–92.

Some of the plays in this collection contain more information on costumes, properties, and stage directions than is customarily available in other editions.

Yang-ch'un tsou 陽春奏, compiled by Huang Cheng-wei 黃正位, with a preface dated 1609.

A Ming dynasty wood-block edition, it consists of 39 Yüan and Ming plays. Three of the Yüan plays are included in a photo-reprint edition of the *KPHCTK*, 4th series, vol. 99 (see note to the table of contents, vol. 99, p. 1*a*).

Yüan ch'ü hsüan 元曲選, edited by Tsang Mou-hsün 臧懋循 (styled Chin-shu 晉叔), 1616. A wood-block edition.

This edition is used as the basic text in my translation and study of *Tou O Yüan* (see p. xv above). This collection of 100 plays has enjoyed great popularity. Modern editions include the following: a photo-reprint edition, Shanghai: The Commercial Press, 1918, and a block-print edition, Chung-hua Book Co., Shanghai, 1936. This collection, originally known as *Yüan-jen pai chung ch'ü* 元人百種曲, was given its present title in 1918.

Ku chin ming chü he-hsüan 古今名劇合選, edited by Meng Ch'eng-shun 孟稱舜, 1633. A wood-block edition.

This collection of 56 Yüan plays originally existed in two separate editions: *Liu-chih chi* 柳枝集, of 26 plays, and *Luo-chiang chi* 酹江集 of 30 plays, both dated 1633. Included in the *KPHCTK*, vols. 101–20.

c. *Modern editions*

Ku-pen Yüan Ming tsa-chü 孤本元明雜劇. Chang-sha: The Commercial Press, 1941. A typeset edition with an introduction by Wang Chi-lieh. 王季烈.

The 144 plays of this collection are all from *Mo-wang kuan ch'ao-chiao pen ku chin tsa-chü*. 36 of these plays have been placed in the Yüan dynasty, and 17 others are possibly of the same period. A number of these plays had never appeared in print before.

Ku-pen hsi-ch'ü ts'ung-k'an ssu-chi 古本戲曲叢刊四集 compiled by Ku-pen hsi-ch'ü ts'ung-kan pien-chi wei-yüan-hui. Shanghai: Commercial Press, 1958; 120 vols.

This is a photocopy reprint of rare Yüan and Ming dramatic texts, some in hand-written and some in printed versions. The collection is in 120 volumes as follows: *Yüan k'an tsa-chü san-shih chung* 元 刊 雜 劇 三 十 種 (vols. 1-3); *Ku tsa-chü* 古 雜 劇, compiled by Wang Chi-te 王 驥 德 (vols. 4-8); *Mo-wang kuan ch'ao-chiao pen ku-chin tsa-chü* 脈 望 館 鈔 校 本 古 今 雜 劇, compiled by Chao Ch'i-mei 趙 琦 美 (vols. 9-92); *Ku-ming-chia tsa-chü* 古 名 家 雜 劇, compiled by Ch'en Yü-chiao 陳 與 郊 (vols. 93-5); *Tsa-chü hsüan* 雜 劇 選, compiled by Hsi Chi-tzu 息 機 子 (vols. 96-8); *Yang-ch'un tsou* 陽 春 奏, compiled by Huang Cheng-wei 黃 正 位 (vol. 99); *Yüan Ming tsa-chü ssu chung* 元 明 雜 劇 四 種 (vol. 100); *Ku-chin ming-chü he-hsüan* 古 今 名 劇 合 選, consisting of *Liu-chih chi* 柳 枝 集 and *Luo-chiang chi* 酹 江 集 compiled by Meng Ch'eng-shun 孟 稱 舜 (vols. 101-20).

Yüan ch'ü hsüan wai pien 元 曲 選 外 編, compiled by Sui Shu-sen 隨 樹 森 Peking: Chung-hua Book Co., 1959-61. A typeset edition, 3 vols.

A collection of 62 plays, these volumes include the best available texts of all the extant Yüan plays not found in *Yüan ch'ü hsüan*. The plays are grouped by authors, who are listed chronologically as well as can be determined. The source of each text is noted in the table of contents. As many of these plays were discovered in this century and are scattered in various collections, this compact edition, as a supplement to *Yüan chü hsüan,* is a great convenience for students in the field.

II. NON-DRAMATIC WRITINGS IN THE VERNACULAR OR SEMI-VERNACULAR LANGUAGE IN THE SUNG, YÜAN, AND MING DYNASTIES

A. *Works of the Sung-Yüan Period*

Chu, Hsi 朱 熹. *Chu-tzu yü-lei* 朱 子 語 類.
Originally lecture notes taken by the disciples of the great Sung philosopher Chu Hsi (1130-1200), they represent a language which was verbally transmitted. Compiled by Li Ching-te 黎 靖 德, 1270. A photo-reprint edition of a Ming edition (1473) is by Cheng-chung Book Co., Taipei, 1962.

Ta Sung Hsüan-ho yi-shih 大 宋 宣 和 遺 事. Shanghai: Commercial Press, 1925.
An account of the Hsüan-ho reign, written in a mixture of classical and colloquial language, it dates around the last years of the Southern Sung Dynasty and the early Yüan dynasty.

Ta T'ang San-tsang ch'ü-ching shih-hua 大 唐 三 藏 取 經 詩 話. Shanghai: Chung-kuo ku-tien wen-hsüeh ch'u-pan she, 1954.
A short, fragmentary promptbook of seventeen chapters dating from the Southern Sung period and written in the colloquial prose interspersed with verses, it tells the story of Tripitaka of the Great T'ang in search of scriptures. (Chapter 1 is missing.)

Tung, Chieh-yüan 董 解 元, *Hsi hsiang chi chu-kung-tiao* 西 廂 記 諸 宮 調. Peking: Wen-hsüeh ku-chi k'an-hsing-she, 1955.
Tung is believed to have lived in the twelfth century during Chang Tsung's 章 宗 reign (*ca.* 1190-1208) in the Chin dynasty. His *Western Chamber Medley,* a narrative consisting of prose and verse, is the most significant among the forerunners of Yüan drama and the immediate source of the Yüan play *The Romance of The Western Chamber.*

Ch'üan-hsiang p'ing-hua wu-chung 全相平話五種 (five fully illustrated *p'ing-hua*). Peking: Wen-hsüeh ku-chi k'an-hsing-she, 1956. A photo-reprint edition of the 1321–4 Yüan edition.

The five historical romances are *Ch'üan-hsiang Wu wang fa Chou p'ing-hua* 全相武王伐紂平話, *Yüeh-yi t'u Ch'i ch'i kuo ch'un-ch'iu* 樂毅圖齊七國春秋, *Ch'üan-hsiang hsü Ch'ien Han shu p'ing-hua* 全相續前漢書平話, *Ch'üan-hsiang Ch'in ping liu kuo p'ing-hua* 全相秦併六國平話, *Hsin ch'üan-hsiang san-kuo chih p'ing-hua* 新全相三國志平話. Given on the title-page of this last work is the time of publication: (Yüan) Chih-chih 至治 (1321–4); given also in four of the five works are the place of publication and the name of the publisher: Chien-an Yü-shih 建安虞氏 (Fukien province). An original copy is in the Imperial Cabinet Library, Japan.

Hsin-k'an ch'üan-hsiang Ch'eng-chai Hsiao-ching chih-chieh 新刊全相成齋孝經直解. Peking: Lai Hsün-ke 來薰閣, 1938. A photocopy edition of a Yüan edition.

The *Classic of Filial Piety* paraphrased in the vernacular language.

Hsü, Heng 許衡 (1209–81). *Hsü Wen-cheng-kung i-shu* 許文正公遺書, 1887.

Chüan 3: *Ta-hsüeh yao-lüeh* 大學要略; *chüan* 4: *Ta-hsüeh chih-chieh* 大學直解; *chüan* 5: *Chung-yung chih-chieh* 中庸直解. These three paraphrased versions of the Confucian classic in the vernacular language are scripts of lectures (*chin chiang* 進講) for the benefit of Emperor Shih-tsu 世祖 (reign 1260–94). (See Yoshikawa, p. 243, listed in Part II, Section A here.)

Lo, Ch'ang-p'ei 羅常培 and Ts'ai, Mei-piao 蔡美彪. *Pa-ssu-pa tzu yü Yüan-tai Han-yü* 八思巴字與元代漢語. Peking: Chung-kuo k'o-hsüeh yü-yen yen-chiu so, 1959.

A collection of source material: several of the Yüan stone inscriptions which are discussed by F.W. Cleaves in his articles in the *HJAS*; a copy of the British Museum manuscript of the *Meng-ku tzu-yün*.

Mōko Ji-in 蒙古字韻. Kansai Daigaku Tōzai gakujitsu kenkyū-jo kan 關西大學東西學術研究所刊, 1956.

A Chinese dictionary in *h*Phags-pa script of the early fourteenth century.

Nogŏldae ŏnhae 老乞大諺解. Seoul: Keijō Teikoku Daigaku Hōbun Gakubu 京城帝國大學法文學部, 1944.

This is a textbook of spoken Chinese used in Korea during the Yüan dynasty. The content indicates that it was intended to give the Koreans an adequate knowledge of the spoken language for visits to China. Choe Se-jin 崔世珍 (1506–44) is known to have edited the work. The extant edition is based on a 1670 version (with Korean explanations, *ŏnhae* 諺解, which is most likely a revised edition of the original. *Lao ch'i-ta* 老乞大 probably came from the term 'Lao Ch'i-tan' 老契丹, a reference to China because of the association with Khitan.

P'ak T'ongsa ŏnhae 朴通事諺解. Seoul: Keijō Teikoku Daigaku Hōbun Gakubu, 1943.

This is a textbook of spoken Chinese used in Korea during the Yüan dynasty. Choe Se-jin 崔世珍 is known to have edited the work. The extant edition is based on a 1677 version, which is most likely a revised edition of the original. *P'ak* 朴 is a family name, and *t'ung-shih* 通事 means 'interpreter'.

Ta Yüan sheng cheng kuo-ch'ao tien-chang 大元聖政國朝典章 (generally referred to as *Yüan tien-chang* 元典章). Editor unknown. *Chien-yang shu-fang* 建陽書坊, 1322. 60 *chüan*. An original copy is at the National Palace Museum of Art, Taipei.

   Yüan code. Contains many vernacular expressions.

Ts'ai, Mei-piao 蔡美彪. *Yüan-tai pai-hua pei chi lu* 元代白話碑集錄 Peking: Chung-kuo k'o-hsüeh yü-yen yen-chiu so, 1955.

   A collection of 94 stone inscriptions (dated A.D. 1223–1366) in the colloquial language of the Yüan dynasty. Arranged chronologically.

T'ung-chih t'iao-ke 通制條格. Peking: National Peiping Library, 1930. A photocopy edition of the Yüan version.

   A body of Yüan official documents consisting of laws and regulations, written partly in the vernacular language.

Wu, Ch'eng 吳澄. 'Ching-yen chin-chiang' 經筵進講 in *Wu Wen-chen-kung chi* 吳文正公集. 1838.

   Chüan 44, pp. 15*b*–17*b* contains a script of Wu Ch'eng's lecture (*chin chiang* 進講) for the benefit of Emperor T'ai-ting 泰定 (reign 1324–8); it is a paraphrased version in the vernacular of passages from *Ti fan* 帝範 and *T'ung chien* 通鑑.

Yüan-ch'ao pi-shih 元朝秘史. Shanghai: Commercial Press *(SPTK san pien)*, 1935–6.

   Secret history of the Yüan dynasty. A Mongolian text transcribed in Chinese characters, with word-for-word translation in Chinese, and a straight translation in vernacular Chinese.

c. *Yüan-Ming works*

Ch'ing-p'ing-shan-t'ang hua-pen 清平山堂話本. Peking: Wen-hsüeh ku-chi k'an-hsing she, 1955.

   The extant fragmentary collection contains 27 stories, of which twenty some are in colloquial language and two are in the classical style. Originally in six sets of ten stories each, printed by Hung P'ien 洪楩 of the Chia-ching period (1522–66).

Feng, Meng-lung 馮夢龍, compiler. *Ku-chin hsiao-shuo* 古今小說 (also known as *Yü-shih ming-yen* 喻世明言). 1620–1. 40 *chüan*. Shanghai: Commercial Press, 1947.

   The name of the printing house T'ien-hsü-chai 天許齋 appears on the title page. With a preface by Lu t'ien-kuan chu-jen 綠天館主人 Contains 40 stories.

—— *Ching-shih t'ung-yen* 警世通言. 1625. 40 *chüan*.

   With a preface by 'Wu ai chü-shih' 無礙居士. Contains 40 stories.

—— *Hsing-shih heng-yen* 醒世恆言. 1627. 40 *chüan*.

   With a preface by 'K'o-yi chü-shih' 可一居士. Contains 40 stories.

Kao, Ming 高明. *P'i-pa chi* 琵琶記. Shanghai: Chung-hua Book Co., 1960.

Lo, Kuan-chung 羅貫中. *San kuo chih t'ung-su yen-i* 三國誌通俗演義. 24 vols. Shanghai: Commercial Press, 1929.

   An elaborated popular version of *San-kuo chih*.

Shih, Nai-an 施耐菴 and Lo, Kuan-chung 羅貫中. *Shui-hu ch'üan chuan* 水滸全傳 (the complete *Shui-hu chuan*). Peking: Jen-min-wen-hsüeh ch'u-pan she, 1954. 4 vols.

377

A variorum edition prepared by Cheng Chen-to, Wang Li-ch'i, *et al.*

Wu, Ch'eng-en 吳承恩. *Hsi yu chi* 西遊記. Peking: Tso-chia ch'u pan-she, 1954. 2 vols.

PART TWO: CRITICAL AND SCHOLARLY WORKS

I. GENERAL STUDIES

Chao, Yuen Ren. *A Grammar of Spoken Chinese*. Berkeley and Los Angeles: University of California Press, 1968.

†—— *Mandarin Primer: An Intensive Course in Spoken Chinese*. Cambridge, Mass.: Harvard University Press, 1948.

Chu, Ch'üan 朱權. *T'ai-ho cheng-yin p'u* 太和正音譜. *Chung-kuo ku-tien hsi-ch'ü lun-chu chi-ch'eng* 中國古典戲曲論著集成 edition. Peking, 1959. Vol. III.

Chung, Ssu-ch'eng 鍾嗣成. *Lu kuei pu* 錄鬼簿. First edition: 1330. References are made to *Chung-kuo ku-tien hsi-ch'ü lun-chu chi-ch'eng* 中國古典戲曲論著集成 edition. Peking, 1959. Vol. II.

†Fu, Hsi-hua 傅希華. *Ku-tien hsi-ch'ü sheng yüeh lun-chu ts'ung-pien*. 古典戲曲聲樂論著叢編. Peking, 1957.

Halliday, M. A. K. *The Language of the Chinese Secret History of the Mongols*. Oxford: B. Blackwell, 1959.

†Hawkes, David. *A Little Primer of Tu Fu*. Oxford University Press, 1967.

Ho, Ch'ang-ch'ün 賀昌羣. 'Yüan-ch'ü te yüan-yüan chi ch'i yü Meng-ku yü te kuan-hsi' 元曲的淵源及其與蒙古語的關係, in *Yüan-ch'ü kai-lun* 元曲概論 Shanghai: Commercial Press, 1930. Chapter 4.

Hsieh, Wan-ying 謝婉瑩. 'Yüan-tai te hsi-ch'ü' 元代的戲曲. *Yenching hsüeh-pao* 燕京學報, I (June, 1927), 15–52.

The author quotes many passages from the Yüan plays to illustrate the excellence of the language, without, however, giving a critical analysis.

Johnson, Dale. 'The Prosody of Yüan Drama'. *T'oung Pao*, LVI (1970), pp. 96–146.

Kallgren, Gerty. *Studies in Sung Time Colloquial Chinese as Revealed in Chu Hi's Ts'üanshu*. Reprinted from *The Museum of Far Eastern Antiquities*, Bulletin No. 30, Stockholm, 1958.

An investigation of the many colloquial expressions in the sayings of the famous Sung philosopher Chu Hsi (1130–1200) as found in *Yü-ts'un Chu-tzu ch'üan-shu* 御存朱子全書.

†Kan, Pao 干寶 (Fourth century). *Sou shen chi* 搜神記. References are made to Shih-chieh Book Co., 1959 edition.

Ku-tien wen-hsüeh ch'u-pan she 古典文學出版社, ed. *Kuan Han-ch'ing yen-chiu lun-wen chi* 關漢卿研究論文集. Shanghai, 1958.

†Liu, An 劉安 ed. *Huai-nan tzu* 淮南子. In *T'ai-p'ing yü lan* 太平御覽 (*SPTK san-pien*), chüan 14.

Liu, James [劉若愚]. *Elizabethan and Yüan: A Brief Comparison of Some Conventions in Poetic Drama*. London: The China Society (Occasional Papers, no. 8), 1955, pp. 1–12.

This paper contains a few remarks on the poetic languages of Yüan drama and Elizabethan drama.

—— *The Art of Chinese Poetry*. Chicago: The University of Chicago Press, 1962.
Contains a perceptive analysis of many passages from Yüan plays.

Maspero, H. 'Sur Quelques Textes Anciens de Chinois Parlé'. *Bulletin de l'École Française d'Extrême-Orient*, XIV (1914), 36.

Ōta, Tatsuo 太 田 辰 夫. *Chūgokugo rekishi bumpō* 中 國 語 歷 史 文 法. Tokyo: Kōnan shoin, 1958.

Schlepp, Wayne. *San ch'ü: Its Technique and Imagery*. Madison: Wisconsin University Press, 1970.

Seaton, Jr., Jerome Potter. A Critical Study of Kuan Han-ch'ing: The Man and His Works. Bloomington: Indiana University, 1969. An unpublished Ph.D. dissertation.

Shafer, Robert. *Bibliography of Sino-Tibetan Languages*. 2 vols. Weisbaden: Harrassowitz, 1957 (vol. I); 1963 (vol II).
It contains bibliographical information on Chinese linguistics in general.

†Stimson, Hugh. 'Song Arrangements in Shianleu Acts of Yuan Tzarjiuh'. *Tsing Hua Journal of Chinese Studies*, New Series V, no. 1 (July 1965), 86–106.

Sun K'ai-ti 孫 楷 第. *Ts'ang-chou chi* 滄 州 集. Peking: Chung-hua Book Co., 1965.
This contains several essays pertaining to Yüan drama, including discussions of many obscure expressions.

†T'an Cheng-pi 譚 正 璧. *Yüan ch'ü liu ta-chia lüeh chuan* 元 曲 六 大 家 略 傳. Shanghai, 1955.

Tōdō, Akiyasu 藤 堂 明 保. 'Development of Mandarin from 14c. to 19c.'. *Acta Asiatica*, VI (1964), 31–40.

—— 'Kanwa no seiritsu katei kara mita *Seiju jimoku shi*' 官 話 の 成 立 過 程 か ら 見 た 西 儒 耳 目 資. *Tōhōgakuhō* 東 方 學 報, V (1952), 99–112.
A study of the development of Mandarin as seen in *Hsi-ju erh-mu tzu*. (See under 'Trigault' on p. 382.)

—— 'Mindai gengo no ichi sokumen' 明 代 言 語 の 一 側 面. *Nihon chūgoku-gakkaihō* 日 本 中 國 學 會 報, XVI (1964), 177–87.

†Ts'ai, Ying, 蔡 瑩. *Yüan chü lien-t'ao shu-li* 元 劇 聯 套 述 例. Shanghai, 1933.

Wang, Kuo-wei 王 國 維. *Sung Yüan hsi-ch'ü shih* 宋 元 戲 曲 史. Shanghai: Commercial Press, 1915.
Chapter 12 comments on the excellence of the Yüan drama language.

Wang, Li 王 力. *Han yü shih kao* 漢 語 史 稿. Peking, 1950. 3 vols.
These three volumes, dealing with the phonology, syntax, and vocabulary of the Chinese language, were originally lectures.

†Wang, Yü-chang 王 玉 璋. *Yüan tz'u chiao lü* 元 詞 斠 律. Shanghai Commercial Press, 1936.

†Wu, Hsiao-ling 吳 曉 鈴. 'Shih-lun Kuan Han-ch'ing te yü-yen' 試 論 關 漢 卿 的 語 言. *Chung-kuo yü-wen*, VI (1958), 264–7.

Yang, Paul Fu-mien 楊 福 綿 'Chinese Linguistics: A Selected and Classified Bibliography' 中 國 語 言 學 參 考 書 目. Washington: Dept. of Far Eastern Languages, Georgetown University, 1970. Mimeographed edition.

†Yen-nan Chih-an 燕 南 芝 菴 (Yüan Dynasty; also referred to as Chih An). *Ch'ang lun* 唱 論. References are to *Chung-kuo ku-tien hsi-ch'ü lun-chu chi-ch'eng* edition. Peking, 1959. Vol. I.

Yoshikawa, Kōjiro 吉 川 幸 次 郎. *Gen zatsugeki kenkyū* 元 雜 劇 研 究. Tokyo: Iwanami shoten, 1948. Translated from the Japanese by Cheng Ch'ing-mao 鄭清茂. Taipei: I-wen, 1960.

Chapters 3 and 4 of Part II give a perceptive discussion of the language of Yüan drama. The material appeared originally in article form: 'Gen zatsugeki no bunshō 元雜劇研の文章, *Tōhōgakuhō*, xv (1945), 35–82; 'Gen zatsugeki no yōgo' 元雜劇の用語, *ibid.* xv, no. 3 (Nov. 1946), 283–313.

II. PHONOLOGY

Chao, Hsia-ch'iu 趙遐秋 and Tseng, Ch'ing-jui 曾慶瑞. 'Chung-yüan yin-yün yin-hsi te chi-ch'u he "ju p'ai san sheng" te hsing-chih' 中原音韻音系的基礎和入派三聲'的性質. *Chung-kuo yü-wen* 中國語文, VII (1962),312–24.

Chao, Yin-t'ang 趙蔭棠. *Chung-yüan yin-yün yen-chiu* 中原音韻研究. Shanghai: Commercial Press, 1936.

A reprint of the T'ieh ch'in t'ung chien lou edition of *CYYY* in a new format with phonetic transcriptions. Contains many mistakes. Second printing has added preface and appendix, Shanghai, 1956.

—— 'Yüan Ming hsi yün-shu k'ao-lun mu-lu' 元明系韻書考論目錄. *Kuo-yü chou k'an* 國語週刊 (Peking), CCXXXIX (2 May 1936).

A list of rhyme books of the Yüan and Ming dynasties.

Chao, Yuen Ren 趙元任, Li Fang-kuei 李方桂, and Lo Ch'ang-p'ei 羅常培 (trans.). *Chung-kuo yin-yün-hsüeh yen-chiu* 中國音韻學研究. Ch'ang-sha: Commercial Press, 1940; Taipei: Commercial Press, 1962 (reprinted).

Translation of Karlgren's *Études sur la phonologie chinoise* with much revision (listed below).

Chi Fu 忌浮. 'Chung-yüan yin-yün erh-shih-wu sheng-mu chi-shuo' 中原音韻二十五聲母集說. *Chung-kuo yü-wen* 中國語文, V (1964), 337–59.

Chou, Te-ch'ing 周德清. *Chung-yüan yin-yün (CYYY)* 中原音韻. Edited by Chung-kuo hsi-ch'ü yen-chiu yüan 中國戲曲研究院. Peking, 1959. Vol. I in the series of *Chung-kuo ku-tien hsi-ch'ü lun-chu chi-ch'eng* 中國古典戲曲論著集成.

Contains textual notes (pp. 257–85).

—— *Yüan-pen chung-yüan yin-yün* 元本中原音韻. 1922. T'ieh ch'in t'ung chien lou 鐵琴銅劍樓 edition.

A photo-reprint of a Yüan dynasty block-print edition, which is the oldest extant edition, formerly in the collection of Ch'ü Shao-chi 瞿紹基 of the Ch'ing dynasty. (T'ieh ch'in t'ung chien lou is the name of Ch'ü's library.)

Demiéville, P. 'Archaismes de prononciation en chinois vulgaire'. *T'oung Pao* XL (1951), pp. 1–59.

Denlinger, Paul B. 'Studies in Middle Chinese.' Seattle: University of Washington, 1962. An unpublished Ph. D. dissertation.

Discusses mainly the pronunciation of Old Mandarin.

—— 'Chinese in hPhags-pa script'. *Monumenta Serica*, XXII (1963), 407–33.

Dragunov, A. A. 龍果夫. *Pa-szu-pa-tzu yü ku Han-yü* 八思巴字與古漢語. Trans. by T'ang Yü 唐虞 and revised by Lo Ch'ang-p'ei 羅常培. Peking: K'o-hsüeh, 1959.

—— 'The hPhags-pa script and Ancient Mandarin'. *Izvestiya Akademii Nauk SSSR, 7th series, Otdelenie Gumanitarnyx Nauk*, IX (1930), 627–47; X (1930), 775–97.

A significant study on Chinese hPhags-pa, which includes tables of hPhags-pa readings for Chinese characters.

Hashimoto, Mantaro J. 橋本萬太郎 'Phonology of Ancient Chinese'. An unpublished dissertation, Ohio State University, 1965. 2 vols.

Hattori, Shiro 服部四郎 and Tōdō, Akiyasu 藤堂明保. *Chugen on'in no kenkyū* 中原音韻の研究. Tokyo: Kōnan shoin, 1958.

A variorum edition of the *Chung-yüan yin-yün*. The authors use the T'ieh ch'in t'ung chien lou 鐵琴銅劍樓 edition as a basis for textual comparison with seven other versions.

Hsüeh, Feng-sheng. 'Phonology of Old Mandarin: A Structural Approach'. An unpublished dissertation, Indiana University, 1968.

Hu, Ming-yang 胡明陽. '*Lao Ch'i-ta yen-chieh* ho *Pu T'ung-shih yen-chieh* chung so chien te Han yü Ch'ao-hsien yü tui-yin' 老乞大諺解和朴通事諺解中所見的漢語朝鮮語對音. *Chung-kuo yü-wen* 中國語文, III (1963), 185–92.

Phonetic correspondence of Chinese and Korean transcriptions found in the *Lao Ch'i-ta yen-chieh* and the *Pu T'ung-shih yen-chieh*.

Jen, Na 任訥. '*Chung-yüan yin-yün* tso-tz'u shih fa shu-cheng' 中原音韻作詞十法疏證. *San ch'ü ts'ung-k'an* 散曲叢刊, vol XXII. Shanghai, 1931 (preface dated 1924).

This is an expanded and annotated version of 'tso-tz'u shih fa', a section of *Chung-yüan yin-yün*.

Karlgren, Bernhard. *Études sur la phonologie chinoise*. Leyden and Stockholm, 1915–26.

This work, applying the scientific linguistic method to the study of Chinese historical phonology, contains a wealth of information, especially on ancient Chinese.

Keiya, Toshinobu 慶谷壽信. 'Nisshō inbi shōshitsu no kateini tsuite no ichi kasetsu: *Mōko jiin* kara no apurōchi' 入聲韻尾消失の過程についての一假說一蒙古字韻からのアプローチ. *Nagoya daigaku bungakubu kenkyū ronsō* 名古屋大學文學部研究論叢, XXXVII (1965), 149–86.

Based on the knowledge of *Meng-ku tzu-yün*, a hypothesis is made concerning a development which ends in the disappearance of the entering-tone finals (-p, -t, -k).

Li, Hsin-k'uei 李新魁. 'Kuan-yü *Chung-yüan yin-yün* yin-hsi te chi-ch'u ho "ju p'ai san sheng" te hsing-chih' 關於中原音韻音系的基礎和 '入派三聲' 的性質. *Chung-kuo yü-wen* 中國語文, IV (1963), 275–81.

This is a study of the basis of the phonological system of the *Chung-yüan yin-yün* and the nature of the 'distribution of the entering-tone into the other three tones'.

Liao, Hsün-ying 廖珣英. 'Kuan Han-ch'ing hsi-ch'ü te yung-yün' 關漢卿戲曲的用韻. *Chung-kuo yü-wen* 中國語文, IV (1963), 267–74.

Ligeti, L. 'Le *Po kia sing* en écriture "phags-pa"'. *Acta Orientalia* [Hungaria], VI (1956), 1–52.

In his study of the *Pai chia hsing* 百家姓 in hPhags-pa script, Ligeti compares a Japanese edition with a copy from the National Library (Peking). Besides the Chinese text and corresponding *h*Phags-pa version, it contains an introduction and notes.

Lo, Ch'ang-p'ei 羅常培. 'Chiu chü chung te chi-ko yin-yün wen-t'i' 舊劇中的幾個音韻問題. *Tung-fang tsa-chih* 東方雜誌, XXXIII, no. 1 (1936), 393–410.

    In the discussion of some phonological problems in classical drama (*ching hsi*), many references are made to *CYYY*.

—— 'Chung-yüan yin-yün sheng-lei k'ao' 中原音韻聲類考. *Bulletin of the Institute of History and Philology* (Academia Sinica), II (1932), 423–40.

    An important study of the initials of *Chung-yüan yin-yün*.

—— 'Lun Lung Kuo-fu te *Pa-szu-pa-tzu ho ku kuan-hua*' 論龍國夫的八思巴字和古官話. *Chung-kuo yü-wen* 中國語文 XII (1959), 575–81.

—— and Ts'ai Mei-piao 蔡美彪. *Pa-szu-pa-tzu yü Yüan-tai Han-yü: Tzu-liao hui-pien* 八思巴字與元代漢語資料彙編. Peking: K'o-hsüeh ch'u-pan she, 1959.

Lo, Shao-feng 樂韶鳳 et al. *Hung-Wu cheng yün* 洪武正韻 16 vols. Issued under imperial auspices, Peking, 1375.

    This is a rhyme book and a dictionary from early Ming. Entries are classified according to *p'ing, shang, ch'ü, ju* tones.

Lu, Chih-wei 陸志韋. 'Shih *Chung-yüan yin-yün*' 釋中原音韻 *Yenching hsüeh-pao* 燕京學報, XXXI (1946), 35–70.

    This is a study of the phonology of the *Chung-yüan yin-yün*.

Pai, Ti-chou 白滌州. 'Pei-yin ju-sheng yen-pien k'ao' 北音入聲演變考. *Nü-shih-ta hsüeh-shu chi-k'an* 女師大學術季刊, II, no. 2 (1931).

    On the development of *ju-sheng* in the Northern Mandarin.

Stimson, Hugh M. 'Ancient Chinese -p, -t, -k Endings in the Peking Dialect'. *Language*, XXXVIII (1962), 376–84.

—— *The Jongyuan in yunn: A Guide to Old Mandarin Pronunciation*. New Haven: Far Eastern Publications, Yale University, 1966.

    In the author's words: 'This book is essentially a list of all the graphs in the *Jongyuan in yunn*, an Old Mandarin rime book.' He has kept the nineteen original groups, but has rearranged them, and the graphs within them, to conform to an order based on phonological principles. Middle Chinese, Old Mandarin, and modern Peking readings are given.

—— 'Phonology of the *Chung-yüan yin-yün*' *Tsing Hua Journal of Chinese Studies, New Series*, III (1962), 114–59.

Tanaka, Kazunari 田中一成. 'Genkyoku no seichō ni tsuite' 元曲の聲調について. *Chūgoku gogaku* 中國語學, III and IV (1967), 12–29.

Trigault, Nicholas, S. J. (Chin, Ni-ko 金尼閣). *Hsi-ju erh-mu tzu* 西儒耳目資. First published in 1626. Reprinted by Peking University, Peking, in 1933 and 1957.

    An early romanization of Chinese dictionaries used by the Jesuit missionaries in the late Ming period, it provides information on the pronunciation of contemporary spoken Chinese.

Tung, T'ung-ho 董同龢. *Chung-kuo yü-yin shih* 中國語音史. Taipei, 1954.

    A remarkable and concise text on Chinese historical phonology, it contains comments on Northern *ch'ü;* tone, initials, and finals as described in *CYYY*; and on other studies of Old Mandarin.

—— *Han-yü yin-yün hsüeh* 漢語音韻學. Taipei, 1968.

A revised and much enlarged version of *Chung-kuo yü-yin shih*; published posthumously.

Wang, Ching-ch'ang 王經昌. *Chung-yüan yin-yün chiang shu* 中原音韻講疏. Taipei: Kuang-wen, 1961. Commentaries on the *Chung-yüan yin-yün*.

Wang, Li 王力. *Han-yü shih-lü hsüeh*. 漢語詩律學. Shanghai: Chiao-yü ch'u-pan she, 1962.

A study of the prosodic rules of Chinese poetry, containing an extensive section on the tones and rhymes of Yüan *ch'ü*.

—— *Han-yü yin-yün hsüeh* 漢語音韻學. Peking: Chung-hua Book Co., 1956. Originally *Chung-kuo yin-yün hsüeh* 中國音韻學. Changsha: Commercial Press, 1937.

A basic text in Chinese historical phonology.

III. VOCABULARY

A. *General works*

†Chao, Yuen Ren and Yang, Lien-sheng. *Concise Dictionary of Spoken Chinese.* Cambridge, Mass.: Harvard University Press, 1947.

Chang, Hsiang 張相. *Shih tz'u ch'ü yü tz'u-tien* 詩詞曲語辭典. Taipei: I-wen Book Co., 1957. References are made to this edition because of its availability to me.

The original version is entitled *Shih tz'u ch'ü yü tz'u hui-shih* 詩詞曲語辭滙釋. Shanghai: Chung-hua Book Co., 1953. 2 vols. Reviewed by Yang Lien-sheng in *Tsing Hua Journal of Chinese Studies, New Series*, 1, no. 2 (1957, 225–8). A very useful book.

†Ch'en, Yao-wen 陳耀文, ed. *Hua ts'ao ts'ui pien* 花草粹編. First ed. in Ming Wan-li period.

†Ch'in ching 禽經 in *Han Wei ts'ung-shu* 漢魏叢書, ed. Ch'eng Yung 程榮. Ming dynasty, Wan-li edition.

Chu, Chü-i 朱居易. *Yüan-chü su-yü fang-yen li-shih* 元劇俗語方言例釋. Shanghai: Commercial Press, 1956.

†Chou Mi 周密. *Kuei-hsin tsa-chih pieh-chi* 癸辛雜識別集, in *Hsüeh-chin t'ao yüan* 學津討原. 1805, Ser. 19, vol. 6.

†*Chung-kuo wen hsüeh shih* 中國文學史. Peking: Jen-min wen-hsüeh ch'u-pan-she, 1963. 3 vols.

†Doré, Henri. *Recherches sur les Superstitions en Chine.* Shanghai, 1911.

†*Erh-shih-ssu shih* 二十四史. Shanghai: Commercial Press, 1930–7. *SPTK Po-na* 百衲 edition.

Feng, Yüan-chün 馮沅君. *Ku-chü shuo-hui* 古劇說彙. Peking: Tso-chia ch'u-pan-she, 1956.

Contains lists of references and discussions of certain terms in Yüan drama.

Gekigo shinyaku 劇語審譯. Kyōtō: Tōhō Bunka Kenkyūjo, Kyoto University, 1940.

A glossary of Yüan drama with explanations given in classical Japanese. Author and date unknown. This Toho Bunka Kenkyujo version is hand-copied and mimeographed.

†*Han shu* 漢書. See *Erh-shih-ssu shih* above.

Hatano, Tarō 波多野太郎. 'Chūgoku shōsetsu gikyoku no yōgo kenkyū nōto: kazō hakuwa kenkyū bunken teiyō' 中國小說劇曲の用語研究ノート—家藏白話研究文獻提要. 11 parts. Part 1 in *Nihon daigaku bungakubu kenkyū nempō* 日本大學文學研究年報, 4 (1954); Part 2, *ibid.* 5 (1955). Part 3 in *Yokohama shiritsu daigaku ronsō* 横濱市立大學論叢, VIII, no. 3, (1957); Part 4, *ibid.* IX, no. 2 (1958); Part 5, *ibid.* XI, no. 1 (1959); Part 6, *ibid.* XI. no. 3 (1960); Part 8, *ibid.* XIII, no. 1 (1962); Part 9, *ibid.* XVI, nos. 2–3 (1965); Part 10, *ibid.* XVII, no. 1 (1966); Part 11 *ibid.* XIX, no. 1 (1968). Part 7 in *Tōyō shisō ronshū* 東洋思想論集, Waseda daigaku, 1960.

—— *Chūgoku shōsetsu gikyoku shii kenkyū jiten: sōgō sakuin hen* 中國小說戲曲詞彙研究辭典—綜合索引篇. *Yokohama shiritsu daigaku kiyō* 横濱市立大學紀要, Series A–9, no. 44 (March, 1956); A–10, no. 45 (March, 1956); A–14, no. 66 (March, 1957); A–16, no. 75 (Jan., 1958); A–20, no. 90 (Sept., 1958); A–23, no. 102 (July, 1959); A–25, no. 115 (March, 1960); A–27, no. 131 (Nov. 1961); A–30, no. 135 (March, 1963).

Each of the seven volumes is an index to entries in Chinese and Japanese glossaries, lexical works, commentaries, etc. on the vocabulary of Chinese fiction and drama. Vol. I is an index of entries in 7 such works; vol. II, 2 works; vol. III, 2 works; vol. IV, 15 works; vol. V, 1 work; vol. VI, 18 works; vol. VII, 19 works. Index is by pronunciation and/or by the number of strokes.

†*Hou Han shu* 後漢書. See *Erh-shih-ssu shih*, p. 383 above.

†Hsiao T'ung 蕭統 (501–531) ed. *Wen Hsüan* 文選. *SPTK* edition.

Hsü, Chia-jui 徐嘉瑞. *Chin Yüan hsi-ch'ü fang-yen k'ao* 金元戲曲方言考. Shanghai: Commercial Press, 1948; revised in 1956.

Entries are arranged by number of strokes. Brief meanings are given and often followed by citations from Yüan plays as well as from other vernacular literature of the Yüan-Ming period. A slim volume.

†Hu, Chi 胡忌. *Sung Chin tsa-chü k'ao* 宋金雜劇考. Shanghai, 1957.

Huang, Li-chen 黃麗貞. *Chin Yüan pei-ch'ü yü-hui chih yen-chiu* 金元北曲語彙之研究. Taipei: Commercial Press, 1968.

Consisting of eight sections and an index, it deals with colloquial expressions, onomatopoeia, foreign words, implied partial quotations, particles, extra-metrical words (*ch'en-tzu*), words of unusual meaning, and words with extended meaning in the Northern *ch'ü*.

Huo, Yüan-chieh 火原潔 and Ma-ch'ih-i-hei 馬赤懿黑. *Hua-i i-yü* 華夷譯語. Shanghai, 1918. First ed., 1389.

A reprint in two parts: Part 1, on popularly used vocabulary, is divided into 17 sections under the headings of seasons, flowers, trees, etc. The text is in Chinese with corresponding Mongolian pronunciations given in Chinese characters; e.g., under the Chinese entry 皇帝 (*huang-ti*, emperor) is given 合罕 (*huo-han*). A total of 844 terms are given. Helpful in the understanding of the scattered Mongolian words found in Yüan drama. Part II consists of a number of documents.

Inada, Osamu 稻田尹. 'Sō Gen wahon ruikei kō' 宋元話本類型考. *Kagoshima daigaku bungakubu hōkoku* 鹿兒島大學文學部報告, VII (1958), 73–94.

In the discussion of the types of *hua-pen* in the Sung-Yüan period, reference is also made to the vocabulary in the vernacular literature of the time.

Kōsaka, Jun'ichi 香坂順一. 'Kinsei kindai kango no gohō to goi' 近世近代漢語の語法と語彙. *Gengo*, CXIV, 296–356.

A study of the grammar and the vocabulary of Middle and modern Chinese.

†Kracke Jr., Edward A. *Civil Service in Early Sung China (960–1067)*. Cambridge, Mass.: Harvard University Press, 1953.

Lewicki, Marian. *La Langue Mongole des Transcriptions Chinoises de XIVe siècle. Le Houa-yi yi-yu de 1389*. Poland, 1949.

Contains a photo-reprint of *Hua-i i-yü* of 1389, pp. 149–225.

Liu, Fu 劉復 and Li, Chia-jui 李家瑞. *Sung-Yüan i-lai su-tzu p'u* 宋元以來俗字譜. Peking: Academia Sinica, 1930.

A compendium of the popular form of characters since Sung.

Lu, Tan-an 陸澹安. *Hsiao-shuo tz'u-yü hui-shih* 小說詞語匯釋. Peking: Chung-hua Book Co., 1964.

This collection of vocabulary in Chinese vernacular fiction contains many entries that are useful in the study of Yüan plays.

†Morohashi, Tetsuji 諸橋轍次. *Dai Kanwa Jiten* 大漢和辭典. Tokyo: Taishūkan, 1955–60; repr. in 1968, 13 vols.

†*San kuo chih* 三國志. See *Erh-shih-ssu shih*, p. 383 above.

†*Shih chi* 史記. See *Erh-shih-ssu shih*, p. 383 above.

Shōsetsu jii 小說字彙. Compiled by Shūsuien shujin 秋水園主人 (pseudonym). Osaka, 1791.

A glossary of 4600 entries from Chinese fiction.

†*Ssu pu pei yao* 四部備要. Shanghai: Chung-hua Book Co., 1927–35.

†*Ssu pu ts'ung k'an* 四部叢刊 Shanghai: Commercial Press, 1929–36 edition.

†*Sung shih* 宋史 See *Erh-shih-ssu shih*, p. 383 above.

Tai, Wang-shu 戴望舒. 'T'an Yüan ch'ü te Meng-ku fang-yen' 談元曲的蒙古方言, *Hsiao-shuo hsi-ch'ü lun-chi* 小說戲曲論集, edited by Wu Hsiao-ling. (See Wu, Hsiao-ling).

Ts'ai, Mei-piao 蔡美彪. 'Yüan-tai tsa-chü chung te jo-kan i-yü' 元代雜劇中的若干譯語. *Chung-kuo yü-wen* 中國語文, I (1957), 34–6.

On some Mongolian and Persian expressions found in Yüan drama.

†Ts'ao, Hsüeh-ch'in 曹雪芹. *Hung lou meng* 紅樓夢 *Dream of the Red Chamber*. Peking: Jen-min wen-hsüeh ch'u-pan-she, 1964.

†Ts'ui, Pao 崔豹. *Ku chin chu* 古今注. First ed. Chin dynasty. In *SPTK*, san-pien.

Wang, Chi-szu 王季思. 'Yüan-chü chung hsieh-yin shuang-kuan-yü' 元劇中諧音雙關語. *Kuo-wen yüeh-k'an* 國文月刊 LXVII (May 1948), 15–19.

†Wang Chia 王嘉 (Chin 晉). *Shih yi chi* 拾遺記 (in *Pi shu nien-yi chung* 秘書廿一種,ed., Wang Shih-han 王士漢, 1668).

†Wang Kuo-wei 王國維. *Hai-ning Wang Ching-an hsien-sheng i shu* 海寧王靜安先生遺書. Ch'ang-sha, 1940.

Wu, Hsiao-ling 吳曉鈴, ed. *Hsiao-shuo hsi-ch'ü lun-chi* 小說戲曲論集 Peking: Tso-chia ch'u-pan-she, 1958.

Contains several short essays by Tai Wang-shu dealing with the language of Yüan drama; comments on Yoshikawa's *Genkyoku kinsenki* 元曲金錢記 (pp. 71–5); notes on '*p'en tiao* 盆弔' (p. 78), '*peng p'a* 棚扒' (pp. 79–80), '*tiao-yen-tzu* 掉罨子', '*t'o shao-er* 脫稍兒' (p. 83), '*hu-lu-t'i* 葫蘆提', '*ming-*

tzu li 酪 子 里' (pp. 84–6); and on the use of Mongolian dialect in Yüan *ch'ü* (pp. 87–90). (See entry Tai, Wang-shu).

†Yang, Lien-sheng. *Money and Credit in China. A Short History.* Cambridge Mass.: Harvard University Press, 1952.

†Yang, Lien-sheng. 'Notes on Maspero's *Les Documents chinois de la troisième expédition de Sir Aurel Stein en Asie centrale*'. *H JAS*, XVIII (1955), 142–58.

†Yang, Yu 楊 瑀. *Shan chü hsin hua* 山 居 新 話 (in *Chih-pu-tsu-chai ts'ung-shu* 知 不 足 齋 叢 書, vol. 12).

†*Yüan shih* 元 史. See *Erh-shih-ssu shih*, p. 383 above.

B.   *Annotated texts (arranged by title)*

The following works provide useful annotations for the study of individual plays. A comprehensive glossary of Yüan drama is presently being compiled by a group of noted scholars at Tōhō Bunka Kenkyūjo, Kyoto University, Kyoto, Japan.

1.   *Chinese*

Genkyokusen shaku 元 曲 選 釋. Edited by Aoki Masaru 青 木 正 兒, Yoshikawa Kōjirō 吉 川 幸 次 郎, Iriya Yoshitaka 入 矢 義 高, and Tanaka Kenji 田 中 謙 二. Kyoto: Kyoto University, 1952.

The annotations all in Chinese are copious, including citations from other plays, poems, and notes by Chinese commentators. Vol. I contains three plays: *Han Kung ch'iu* 漢 宮 秋, *Chin ch'ien chi* 金 錢 記, and *Sha kou ch'üan fu* 殺 狗 勸 夫 (*Yüan ch'ü hsüan* nos. 1, 2, and 7). Vol II contains: *Hsiao Hsiang yü* 瀟 湘 雨, *Hu t'ou p'ai* 虎 頭 牌, and *Chin hsien ch'ih* 金 線 池 (*Yüan ch'ü hsüan* nos. 15, 24, and 72).

Hsi-hsiang-chi 西 廂 記. Edited by Wang Chi-ssu 王 季 思. Shanghai: Hsin-wen-i ch'u-pan-she, 1954.

Contains extensive annotation.

Hsi-hsiang-chi 西 廂 記. Edited by Wu Hsiao-ling 吳 曉 鈴. Peking: Tso-chia ch'u-pan-she, 1954.

The volume contains notes and commentary, and a discussion of the history of this play and its many different versions.

Hsi-hsiang-chi chu 西 廂 記 注. Edited by Wang Yü-chün 王 毓 駿. Peiping: Wen-hua hsüeh-she, 1938.

Extensive annotation dealing with linguistic and lexical matters.

Kuan Han-ch'ing hsi-ch'ü chi 關 漢 卿 戲 曲 集. Edited by Wu Hsiao-ling 吳 曉 鈴, *et al.* 2 vols. Peking: Chung-kuo hsi-chü ch'u-pan-she, 1958.

A collection of eighteen plays attributed to Kuan Han-ch'ing, the volume is based on the wood-block edition of *Ku tsa-chü* and the *Mo-Wang-kuan* manuscript. Copious annotation and commentary.

Kuan Han-ch'ing hsi-ch'ü hsüan 關 漢 卿 戲 曲 選. Peking: Jen-min wen-hsüeh ch'u-pan-she, 1958.

A collection of eight plays by Kuan. Good annotation and notes.

Kuan Han-ch'ing tsa-chü hsüan 關 漢 卿 雜 劇 選. Hong Kong: Commercial Press, 1961.

This volume consists of two plays, *Chiu feng-ch'en* and *Tou O Yüan*, with brief annotations.

'Notes on the *Yüan ch'ü hsüan*', *Tōhōgakuhō* 東方學報 (Tōhō Bunka Kenkyūjo, Kyoto University). *Ch'en T'uan kao wo* 陳摶高臥, XI (1940), 111–22; *Jen feng tzu* 任風子, XI (1940), 408–17; *Yü-hu ch'un* 玉壺春, XI (1940), 417–27; *Yü ch'iao chi* 漁樵記, XI (1940), 427–39; *Mo-ho-lo* 魔合羅, XII (1941), 140–56; *Yen-ch'ing po yü* 燕青博漁, XII (1941), 156–68; *Chiu feng-ch'en* 救風塵, XII (1941), 297–308; *T'ao-hua nü* 桃花女, XII (1941), 437–49; *Hsieh T'ien-hsiang* 謝天香, XII (1941), 581–92.

Notes are on selected lines of the plays.

Ta hsi-chü chia Kuan Han-ch'ing chieh-tso chi 大戲劇家關漢卿傑作集 Edited by Wu Hsiao-ling 吳曉鈴, *et al.* Peking: Chung-kuo hsi-chü chu-pan-she, 1958.

A collection of six plays by Kuan. A glossary is appended, with the entries transcribed in the *Pin-yin* system, and arranged in alphabetical order. The vocabulary list is long and the explanations are detailed and helpful (pp. 133–260). An index of Chinese characters, arranged by the number of strokes, is also appended (pp. 261–71).

Tou O Yüan 竇娥冤. Peking: Jen-min wen-hsüeh ch'u-pan-she, 1959.

A slim annotated edition.

Yüan ch'ü 元曲. Edited by T'ung Fei 童斐. Shanghai: Commercial Press, 1931.

The collection includes four plays with brief lexical notes.

Yüan jen tsa-chü hsüan 元人雜劇選. Edited by Ku Chao-ts'ang 顧肇倉 Peking: Chung-kuo hsi-chü ch'u-pan-she, 1956; reprinted in 1959.

Contains fifteen Yüan plays with copious and excellent annotations.

2. *Japanese*

Genjin zatsugeki 元人雜劇. Translated and annotated by Aoki Masaru 青木正兒. Tokyo: Shunjū sha, 1957.

A Japanese translation of three plays: *Wu-t'ung yü*, *Huo lang tan*, and *Mo-ho-lo* (*YCH*, nos. 21, 94, 79). The volume includes a glossary (pp. 234–94) with words listed in the order in which they appear.

Genkyoku kinsenki 元曲金錢記. Translated by Yoshikawa Kōjirō 吉川幸次郎. Tokyo: Chikuma shobō, 1943.

This work, a Japanese translation, also includes notes and a commentary dealing with many lexical and grammatical problems of the language of the play.

Genkyoku kokukan tei 元曲酷寒亭. Translated by Yoshikawa Kōjirō. Tokyo: Chikuma shobō, 1948.

This work, a Japanese translation, also includes notes, commentaries, and a study of Yüan dynasty colloquial language.

Genkyoku sen 元曲選. Translated by Shiyonoya On 鹽谷温. Tokyo: Meguro shoten, 1910.

Gikyoku shū 戲曲集. Compiled by Aoki Masaru. Tokyo: Heibon sha, 1959.

This collection, volume 33 of the *Chūgoku koten bungaku zenshū* 中國古典文學全集, contains a Japanese translation of six Yüan and Ming plays, the four Yüan plays being *Chiu feng-ch'en*, *T'ieh-kuai Li*, *Mo-ho-lo*, and *Ho han-shan*.

Li K'uei Carries Thorns. Translated by J. I. Crump. *Occasional Papers*, no. 1, Ann Arbor: University of Michigan, 1962, pp. 38–61.

With annotation. (The annotation was later deleted in the version in *Anthology of Chinese Literature*, ed. Cyril Birch, New York, 1965.)

Selected Plays of Kuan Han-ch'ing. Translated by Hsien-yi Yang and Gladys Yang. Peking: Foreign Language Press, 1958.

Contains eight plays as follows: *Snow in Mid-summer (Tou O yüan)*; *The Wife-snatcher (Lu chai lang)*; *The Butterfly Dream (Hu-tieh meng)*; *Rescued by a Coquette (Chiu feng-ch'en)*; *The River-side Pavillion (Wang-chiang t'ing)*; *The Jade Mirror-stand (Yü ching t'ai)*; *Lord Kuan Goes to the Feast (Tan tao hui)*; *Death of the Winged-tiger General (K'u Ts'un-hsiao)*. Annotations sparse.

IV. GRAMMAR

Aiura, Takashi 相 浦 杲. '*Suikoden* no gengo' 水 滸 傳 の 言 語, *Chugoku no hachidai shōsetsu* 中 國 の 八 大 小 說. Edited by Osaka shiritsu daigaku Chūgoku bungaku ken-kyūshitsu. Tokyo: Heibon sha, 1965.

Chi, Po-yung 紀 伯 庸. 'Yüan-ch'ü chu tzu tsa-k'ao' 元 曲 助 字 雜 考. *Kuo-wen yüeh-k'an* 國 文 月 刊, LXX (August 1948), 5–11.

A free adaptation of Iriya's article on the same subject (see Iriya below).

Crump, James. 'On Chinese Medieval Language'. *Wennti*, V (November 1953), 65–74.

—— 'Some Problems in the Language of the *Shin-bian-wuu-day-shyy pyng-huah*' (新編五代史平話). 2 vols. Unpublished Ph.D. dissertation, Yale University, 1949.

Analysis and translation.

Forke, A. 'Die Chinesische Umgangssprache im XIII Jahrhundert'. *Actes du Douzième Congrès International des Orientalistes*, Rome 1899, II, 49–67.

Based upon three Yüan plays: *K'an-ch'ien-nu* 看 錢 奴, *Wu-t'ung yü* 梧 桐 雨, and *Huo-lang-tan* 貨 郎 旦, this is an early Western study of grammar and vocabulary of Chinese colloquial language.

Haenisch, von E. 'Beiträge zur Geschichte der Chinesische Umgangssprache'. *Mitteilungen des Seminars für Orientalische Sprachen (Ostasiatische Studien)*, Jahrgang XXXV, Berlin, 1932, pp. 106–35.

This study on the early Chinese colloquial language is based on the *Yüan-ch'ao pi-shih (Secret History of the Yüan Dynasty)*.

Hu, Chu-an 胡 竹 安 'Sung Yüan pai-hua tso-p'in chung te yü-ch'i chu-tz'u' 宋 元 白 話 作 品 中 的 語 氣 助 詞. *Chung kuo yü-wen* 中 國 語 文, VI (1958), 270–4.

Intonational particles in the colloquial writings of the Sung and Yüan dynasties.

Huang, Yüeh-chou 黃 岳 州. '*Shui-hu* chung "tan" tzu te yung-fa' 水 滸 中 但 字 的 用 法. *Yü-wen hsüeh-hsi* 語 文 學 習, IX (1955), 37–8.

Ikeda, Takeo 池 田 武 雄. 'Gen jidai kōgo no kaishi ni tsuite' 元 時 代 口 語 の 介 詞 に つ い て. *Ritsu-meikan bungaku* 立 命 館 文 學, CLXXX (1960), 170–9.

Iriya, Yoshitaka 入 矢 義 高. 'Genkyoku joji zakkō' 元 曲 助 字 雜 考

Tōhōgakuhō 東方學報, XIV (1943), 70–97.

A study of auxiliary particles in Yüan drama.

Kao, Ming-k'ai 高明凱. 'Han-yü kuei-ting tz'u "ti"' 漢語規定詞 [的]. *Han-hiue* 漢學 (Peking), I (1944), 27–81.

Labeling *ti* as a determinative, Kao describes synthetically the function of *ti* and its development, from the point of view of a historical phonologist.

—— 'T'ang-tai ch'an-chia yü-lu so chien te yü-fa ch'eng-fen' 唐代禪家語錄所見的語法成分. *Yenching hsüeh-pao* 燕京學報, no. 34 (1948), 49–84.

The author claims that his article is a continuation of Maspero's article on ancient spoken Chinese.

Lü, Shu-hsiang 呂叔湘. *Han-yü yü-fa lun-wen-chi* 漢語語法論文集. Peking: K'o-hsüeh ch'u-pan she, 1955.

Lü, (Shu-) hsiang 呂 (叔) 湘. '"Pa" tzu yung-fa yen-chiu' [把] 字用法研究. *Chung-kuo wen-hua yen-chiu hui-k'an* 中國文化會研究彙刊, VIII (1948), 111–30 and 148–9.

A study of the use of *ba*.

Miller, Robert P. 'The Particles in the Dialogues of Yüan Drama. A Descriptive Analysis.' Unpublished Ph.D. dissertation, Yale University, 1952.

Osada, Natsuki 長田夏樹. 'Tōseishō bumpō hikki (jō)' 董西廂文法筆記 (上). *Kōbe gaidai ronsō* 神戶外大論叢, XI (1960), 113–31.

Notes on the grammar of the language in Tung's *Western Chamber*.

Ōta, Tatsuo 太田辰夫. 'Chūgokugo kushūshi no rekishiteki kenkyū' 中國語句終詞の歷史的研究. *Kōbe gaidai ronsō* 神戶外大論叢, II, no. 4 (1951), 15–39.

A historical study of the final particle in the Chinese language.

—— 'Rōkitsudai no gengo ni tsuite' 老乞大の言語について. *Chūgoku gogaku kenkyūkai ronshū* 中國語學研究會論集, I (1953), 1–14.

—— 'Sōdai gohō shitan' 宋代語法試探. *Kobe gaidai ronso* 神戶外大論叢, IV, no. 2 (1953), 78–90.

Průšek, J. 'La Fonction de la Particule *ti* dans le Chinois Médiéval'. *Archiv Orientální*, XV, nos. 3–4 (June 1946), 303–40.

Sofronov, M.V. 'Suiko no gengo ni okeru dōshi no shi kōsei no gensoku' 水滸の言語における動詞の詞構成の原則. *Chūgoku gogaku* 中國語學, II (1958), 13–16, and I (1959), 18–22. Translation by Kawakami Hisatoshi 川上久壽.

Tanaka, Kenji 田中謙二. 'Tōseishō ni mieru zokugo no jo ji' 董西廂見える俗語の助字. *Tōhōgaku* 東方學報 (Kyoto), XVIII (1950), 55–77.

Auxiliary words in the colloquial language found in Tung's *Western Chamber*.

Wang, Ching-ju 王靜如. 'Chiu *Yüan-mi-shih* i-wen so-chien chih Chung-kuo jen-ch'eng tai-ming tz'u' 就 [元秘史] 譯文所見之中國人稱代名詞. *Bulletin of the Institute of History and Philology* (Academia Sinica), V (1935), 545–9.

Yang, Lien-sheng 楊聯陞. 'Lao Ch'i-ta, P'u T'ung-shih li te yü-fa yü-hui' [老乞大] [朴通事] 裏的語法語彙. *Bulletin of the Institute of History and Philology* (Academia Sinica), XXIX (1957), 197–208.

Vocabulary and syntax in *Lao Ch'i-ta* and *P'u T'ung shih*.

Yoshikawa, Kojirō, *see* 'General Works' in Part II.
Yün Pan 運班. 'Tsao-ch'i pai-hua "hsü" tzu li-shih' 早期白話 [須] 字例釋.
  Chung-kuo yü-wen 中國語文, XI (1956), 31-2.